Business Intelligence Cookbook: A Project Lifecycle Approach Using Oracle Technology

Over 80 quick and advanced recipes that focus on real-world techniques and solutions to manage, design, and build data warehouse and business intelligence projects

John Heaton

[PACKT] enterprise 88
PUBLISHING
professional expertise distilled

BIRMINGHAM - MUMBAI

Business Intelligence Cookbook: A Project Lifecycle Approach Using Oracle Technology

First published: July 2012

Production Reference: 1050712

Published by Packt Publishing Ltd.
Livery Place
35 Livery Street
Birmingham B3 2PB, UK.

ISBN 978-1-84968-548-1

www.packtpub.com

Cover Image by Artie Ng (artherng@yahoo.com.au)

Credits

Author
John Heaton

Reviewers
Chandan Banerjee
Ajay Kalia
Toon Loonen
Clive Seymour
Michael Verzijl

Acquisition Editor
Rukshana Khambatta

Lead Technical Editor
Arun Nadar

Technical Editors
Merin Jose
Ameya Sawant

Copy Editor
Insiya Morbiwala

Project Coordinator
Joel Goveya

Proofreader
Aaron Nash

Indexer
Rekha Nair

Graphics
Valentina D'silva
Manu Joseph

Production Coordinator
Shantanu Zagade

Cover Work
Shantanu Zagade

About the Author

John Heaton graduated top of his class with a Diploma in Information Technology from Technikon Witwatersrand in South Africa (equivalent to a Bachelors degree in Computer Science), and worked for more than 10 years with Oracle Corporation, including as a Practice Manager. John had been co-running the North Business Intelligence and Warehouse Consulting practice, delivering business intelligence solutions to Fortune 500 clients. During this time, he steadily added business skills and business training to his technical background.

In 2005, John decided to leave Oracle and become a founding member in a small business, iSeerix. This allowed John to focus on strategic partnerships with clients to design and build business intelligence and data warehouse solutions.

John's strengths include the ability to communicate the benefits of introducing a business intelligence solution into a client's architecture. He has consistently become a trusted advisor to his clients. John's philosophy is based on responsibility and mutual respect. He relies on the unique abilities of individuals to ensure success in different areas, and strives to foster a teamed environment of creativity and achievement.

Today, John specializes as a Solution/Technical Architect, assisting customers in designing large, complex data warehouses. Through his years, John has worked in numerous industries with differing technologies. This broad experience base allows John to bring a unique perspective and understanding when designing and developing a data warehouse. His strong business background, coupled with technical expertise, and his certification in Project Management, make John a valued asset to any data warehouse project.

Acknowledgement

John would like to thank the following people who helped to contribute:

- Leanne, my wife, for giving me the support, confidence, and valuable hours necessary to dedicate to writing this book.
- Ajay Kalia for being a trusted business partner and close friend for many years. Without your continued support and tireless editing efforts, this book would not be nearly as polished.
- The iSeerix Development team, thank you for the code snippets, and for highlighting some of the real issues we face day in and day out.
- Clive Seymour, for reading many hours of technical pages and providing valuable feedback.

About the Reviewers

Chandan Banerjee is the Director and Principal Consultant at BA IT Consulting Pvt. Ltd. (www.baconsultinggroup.com), and also a Partner and Principal Consultant at Beetra Consulting (www.beetraconsultancy.com).

He has more than 20 years of experience in leading and deploying IT solutions, out of which he has spent 18 years in the field of Business Intelligence (BI). He provides consulting services in BI Education, Data Integration, and Solution Architecture design. Managing deployments of common BI tools and applications is his forte. He is an expert in all the phases of lifecycle development for business intelligence projects. He has also been the architect of two BI-based, pre-built application products.

He has been one of the reviewers of "Oracle BI Publisher 11g: A Practical Guide to Enterprise Reporting".

Ajay Kalia, P.M.P., Director at iSeerix, is one of the co-founders of iSeerix, a software development company based in Pittsford, New York. Ajay has a BSc degree in Computer Science from the University of Toronto. He has 26 years of experience in the IT industry, focusing primarily on software development and on-site client consulting services. During his years in the industry, Ajay has established a successful track record delivering high-quality projects to numerous satisfied customers. This is indicative of his understanding of client IT requirements, and his ability to adapt, understand, and efficiently utilize the fast-changing technologies involved.

Toon Loonen, has specialized in Data Modeling (logical and physical) for OLTP and OLAP/ DW/BI systems, Database Design, and Data Warehousing. He has broad experience with several databases, of which over 10 years is with Sybase, 10 years with Oracle/Oracle Spatial, and a few years with other relational databases (Informix, Mimer, MS SQL Server, and others).

An important part of Mr. Loonen's work is coaching junior colleagues, so they can take over his task on the projects, and he can move on to a new challenge.

After his study in Physics, Mr. Loonen joined Capgemini in 1975. He followed a technical path, from a programmer, tester, technical and functional designer, to data modeling and database designing. As an employee of Capgemini, he worked on projects for many organizations, both public and private, such as DHL, Philips, KPN, AHOLD, and many departments of the Dutch Government.

In the period between 1982-1985, he worked in Montreal, Canada, as a Manager of Software Quality Assurance for Philips, and as a Consultant for Coopers and Lybrand.

Mr. Loonen wrote a book on Data Modeling and Database Design, which covered the very start of this process (selection of the data domain), through conceptual, logical, and physical data modeling, up to the implementation in a database management product such as Oracle.

Mr. Loonen gave presentations on these topics, both within Capgemini as well as at international conferences. He has written many articles that are published on the Capgemini intranet, and 25 articles that are published in a Dutch magazine for DBAs—Database Magazine.

Clive Seymour has been implementing and using data warehouses for business intelligence and organisational performance management for more than 15 years. He advises organisations on business intelligence and information management strategies, governance, cultural change, solution and technical architecture, tool selections, and implementation options.

Clive has advised and worked for organisations in the financial services, mining, utilities, media, consumer goods, and manufacturing industries. He has led teams from small domestic to large multi-country international implementations, using Oracle's BI and IM capabilities and other leading vendor's solutions.

Michael Verzijl is a Business Intelligence Consultant, specialized in Oracle Business Intelligence, Oracle Data Warehousing, and Oracle GoldenGate.

Michael has a wide experience in the financial, utilities, and government industries, which include BI technologies such as Oracle, IBM Cognos, and SAP Business Objects.

Currently he is employed as a BI Consultant for Aorta Business Intelligence in the Netherlands, specializing in Business Intelligence and Data Warehousing.

www.PacktPub.com

Support files, eBooks, discount offers and more

You might want to visit www.PacktPub.com for support files and downloads related to your book.

Did you know that Packt offers eBook versions of every book published, with PDF and ePub files available? You can upgrade to the eBook version at www.PacktPub.com and as a print book customer, you are entitled to a discount on the eBook copy. Get in touch with us at service@packtpub.com for more details.

At www.PacktPub.com, you can also read a collection of free technical articles, sign up for a range of free newsletters and receive exclusive discounts and offers on Packt books and eBooks.

PACKTLiB®

http://PacktLib.PacktPub.com

Do you need instant solutions to your IT questions? PacktLib is Packt's online digital book library. Here, you can access, read and search across Packt's entire library of books.

Why Subscribe?

- ▶ Fully searchable across every book published by Packt
- ▶ Copy and paste, print and bookmark content
- ▶ On demand and accessible via web browser

Free Access for Packt account holders

If you have an account with Packt at www.PacktPub.com, you can use this to access PacktLib today and view nine entirely free books. Simply use your login credentials for immediate access.

Instant Updates on New Packt Books

Get notified! Find out when new books are published by following @PacktEnterprise on Twitter, or the *Packt Enterprise* Facebook page.

Table of Contents

Preface   **1**

Chapter 1: Defining a Program   **7**
Introduction   7
Program or a project   8
Mapping your business culture   11
Adapting your project delivery methodology   15
Assessing your project team   17
Organizing your project team   20

Chapter 2: Establishing the Project   **23**
Introduction   24
Creating Definition work practice   24
Creating Data Discovery work practice   26
Creating Development work practice   28
Creating Testing work practice   30
Creating Promote work practice   32
Creating Production work practice   34
Building a standard work breakdown structure   36
Identifying and quantifying the effort drivers   38
Creating your estimation tool   40

Chapter 3: Controlling the Project   **43**
Introduction   43
Requirements Traceability Matrix   44
Creating an effective risk register   50
Creating an effective issue management register   53
Creating a defect and enhancement register   55
Creating a cyclical build and test process   58
Setting up a collaborative environment   60
Installing client tools for a collaborative environment   65

Chapter 4: Wrapping Up the Project   71

Introduction   71

Creating OWB code artifacts   72

Creating OBIEE code artifacts   75

Creating APEX code artifacts   77

Creating ODI code artifacts   79

Creating script artifacts   80

Building a continuous development capability for enhancements   81

Creating a constant feedback and communications loop   84

Chapter 5: The Blueprint   87

Introduction   87

Outlining your business processes   88

Categorizing your metrics, analysis, and reports within
the business process   92

Decomposing your analysis and reports to define business entities   97

Developing your semantic data model   100

Identifying your source of record for your business entities   106

Building the blueprint   111

Chapter 6: Analyzing the Requirements   115

Introduction   115

Decomposing the reports and requirements   116

Defining the business rules   119

Categorizing the business requirements by business drivers   120

Prioritizing the business requirements   122

Adding hierarchies to your semantic data model   124

Adding metrics to your semantic data model   128

Defining your data dictionary   129

Defining your security requirements   132

Defining your data retention requirements   134

Chapter 7: Architecture and Design   137

Introduction   137

Choosing your database type   137

Defining your database layout   140

Selecting the Third Normal Form or a Dimensional model   145

Chapter 8: Analyzing the Sources   147

Introduction   147

Validating and enhancing a conceptual data model   148

Creating a business process matrix   150

Creating a report requirements matrix   152
Creating a source matrix   153
Developing the data lineage   155
Defining the detailed transformations   157

Chapter 9: Analyzing the Data   **159**
Introduction   159
Building high and low data profiling scripts   160
Building domain/distinct values profiling   162
Building record count profiling scripts   163
Building density data profiling scripts   164
Building hierarchy data profiling scripts   166
Building data lengths data profiling scripts   168
Building significant columns data profiling scripts   169
Building changing information data profiling scripts   170
Building automated data profiling with Oracle Warehouse Builder   172

Chapter 10: Constructing the Data Model   **189**
Introduction   190
Connecting Oracle SQL Data Modeler to Subversion   190
Importing data models into Subversion   194
Checkout data models from Subversion   199
Synchronizing data model changes with Subversion   200
How to import data models   207
How to reverse engineer your relational data model to
a logical data model   213
Creating your domains   216
Creating your glossary   220
Adding Standard columns to your data model   224
How to forward engineer your logical data model to a
relational data model   226
Creating your enterprise data models   230

Chapter 11: Defining the ETL/ELT   **237**
Introduction   237
Abstracting your source system   238
Separating your extraction from your loading and transforming routines   240
Adding additional columns to facilitate error trapping and correction   245
Designing ETL error trapping and detection routines   246
Designing ETL data reconciliation routines   251
Designing a notification routine   255

Chapter 12: Enhancing the Data — 261

Introduction — 261
Creating your application schema — 262
Creating your application tables — 263
Developing the journal tables to track changes — 264
Defining the audit triggers — 265
Defining the APEX Upload application — 270
Creating the Upload interface — 274

Chapter 13: Optimizing the Access — 281

Introduction — 281
Developing your standards and guidelines — 282
Abstracting your tables using aliases — 283
Developing level-based hierarchies — 284
Creating multi-table hierarchies — 286
Consolidating reports using the column selector — 288
Enabling dynamic column headings — 292
Enabling dynamic descriptions — 298
Enabling multi-language for the shared captions — 302

Chapter 14: Security — 305

Introduction — 305
Creating an APEX custom authentication procedure — 306
Creating a row-level Virtual Private Database (VPD) — 311
Creating a column-level Virtual Private Database — 315
Creating Virtual Private application context — 317
Configuring OBIEE for multiple security providers — 320
Integrating Microsoft Active Directory into OBIEE — 323
Creating and configuring OBIEE roles — 328
Configuring OBIEE privileges — 331
Configuring OBIEE catalog security — 332
Enabling Virtual Private Database in OBIEE — 336

Index — 343

Preface

Business intelligence and data warehousing projects can be challenging and complex. Dealing with new technologies, processes, and different stakeholders presents an array of potential problems. To aid the project manager, there are recipes about project definition, scope, control, and risk management. Requirements, design, data analysis, security, and data enhancing will help in guiding the technical project member.

The *Business Intelligence Cookbook: A Project Lifecycle Approach Using Oracle Technology* book offers insight and real-world experience to assist you through the business intelligence and data warehouse lifecycle. Recipes from the first six chapters of this book, focus more on processes and practices to aid with the definition and management of the project. From *Chapter 7, Architecture and Design* onwards, this book provides more technical recipes for the business intelligence and data warehousing project.

What this book covers

Chapter 1, Defining a Program, assesses your current project delivery methodology to identify areas that may need enhancing to support your business intelligence initiative.

Chapter 2, Establishing the Project, reviews and enhances the project delivery phases in order to define a consistent set of work practices for the delivery of a successful project.

Chapter 3, Controlling the Project, focuses on communication and control, essential to a business intelligence project. Developing efficient and effective ways to do this is the key aim of this chapter.

Chapter 4, Wrapping Up the Project, focuses on business intelligence projects that continue for numerous iterations, understanding the information that needs to flow from project to project. Setting up ways to hand over that information is key to the long term success of the solution.

Chapter 5, The Blueprint, journeys a roadmap needed to guide one from the start to the destination, for a business intelligence and data warehouse solution.

Chapter 6, Analyzing the Requirements, talks of succinctly capturing and understanding the requirements of a project. Keeping requirements simple and providing transparency is key to demystifying the project for stakeholders.

Chapter 7, Architecture and Design, focuses on creating a successful foundation to interactively build your solution, which can save large amounts of time and money. Getting the basics right is the topic of this chapter.

Chapter 8, Analyzing the Sources, talks about identifying the right source with the most correct information, which is essential to the success of the project. Gaining a deeper understanding of your source systems will enable you to make intelligent decisions in determining which system contains the most accurate information for the subject area.

Chapter 9, Analyzing the Data, talks about how data profiling or data discovery can uncover a wealth of information. Identifying efficient ways and methods to interrogate information will unlock some of this wealth.

Chapter 10, Constructing the Data Model, talks about the Data Model, which is the key asset of the project. Understanding how to effectively design and develop this model enables organizations to reuse this asset many times.

Chapter 11, Defining the ETL/ELT, focuses on building an efficient framework and extraction, transformation, and loading routines, which leads to a simpler and easier-to-manage solution.

Chapter 12, Enhancing the Data, provides information about the data gaps normally existing within organizations. Once identified, effective means to capture and contribute information into the solution are required.

Chapter 13, Optimizing the Access, gives an insight into understanding the key technological capabilities within your reporting tool, allowing you to deliver information to your stakeholders in a meaningful and accurate way.

Chapter 14, Security, provides information on business intelligence and data warehouse solution security. This chapter focuses on showing you how to integrate common industrial security technology and requirements into your solution.

What you need for this book

This book covers the product suite from Oracle, to design and build a data warehouse. The softwares that are needed to support the recipes are as follows:

- Oracle 11gR2 Enterprise Edition 11.2.0.2 or higher
- Oracle Business Intelligence Enterprise Edition 11.1.1.5
- Oracle Application Express 4.0.0 or higher
- Oracle SQL Developer 3.0 or higher
- Oracle Data Modeler 3.0 or higher
- Oracle Warehouse Builder 11GR2 11.2.0.2 Mega Patch 3

Additional products to support the project are as follows:

- ▸ Visual SVN
- ▸ Tortoise
- ▸ Office Suite

Who this book is for

If you are a project manager or IT professional looking to manage, design, and develop a data warehouse and business intelligence solution, then this is the best guide for you.

Conventions

In this book, you will find a number of styles of text that distinguish between different kinds of information. Here are some examples of these styles, and an explanation of their meaning.

Code words in text are shown as follows: "The table `hier_balanced` is a balanced hierarchy and the table `hier_ragged` is a ragged hierarchy".

A block of code is set as follows:

```
select hier, count(*) from (
SELECT LPAD(' ', level*2, ' ') || col2 as hier
FROM hier_ragged
START WITH col1 = 'Root'
CONNECT BY PRIOR col2 = col1)
group by hier
having count(*) > 1;
```

New terms and **important words** are shown in bold. Words that you see on the screen, in menus or dialog boxes for example, appear in the text like this: "View **Connection Information**, and click on **Edit** to update it".

Warnings or important notes appear in a box like this.

Tips and tricks appear like this.

Reader feedback

Feedback from our readers is always welcome. Let us know what you think about this book—what you liked or may have disliked. Reader feedback is important for us to develop titles that you really get the most out of.

To send us general feedback, simply send an e-mail to feedback@packtpub.com, and mention the book title via the subject of your message.

If there is a book that you need and would like to see us publish, please send us a note in the **SUGGEST A TITLE** form on www.packtpub.com or e-mail suggest@packtpub.com.

If there is a topic that you have expertise in and you are interested in either writing or contributing to a book, see our author guide on www.packtpub.com/authors.

Customer support

Now that you are the proud owner of a Packt book, we have a number of things to help you to get the most from your purchase.

Downloading the example code

You can download the example code files for all Packt books you have purchased from your account at http://www.PacktPub.com. If you purchased this book elsewhere, you can visit http://www.PacktPub.com/support and register to have the files e-mailed directly to you.

Errata

Although we have taken every care to ensure the accuracy of our content, mistakes do happen. If you find a mistake in one of our books—maybe a mistake in the text or the code—we would be grateful if you would report this to us. By doing so, you can save other readers from frustration and help us improve subsequent versions of this book. If you find any errata, please report them by visiting http://www.packtpub.com/support, selecting your book, clicking on the **errata submission form** link, and entering the details of your errata. Once your errata are verified, your submission will be accepted and the errata will be uploaded on our website, or added to any list of existing errata, under the Errata section of that title. Any existing errata can be viewed by selecting your title from http://www.packtpub.com/support.

Piracy

Piracy of copyright material on the Internet is an ongoing problem across all media. At Packt, we take the protection of our copyright and licenses very seriously. If you come across any illegal copies of our works, in any form, on the Internet, please provide us with the location address or website name immediately so that we can pursue a remedy.

Please contact us at copyright@packtpub.com with a link to the suspected pirated material.

We appreciate your help in protecting our authors, and our ability to bring you valuable content.

Questions

You can contact us at questions@packtpub.com if you are having a problem with any aspect of the book, and we will do our best to address it.

1

Defining a Program

The chapters in this book are intended to give you recipes aiding you in defining, starting, controlling, and wrapping up your **Business Intelligence Initiative** (BI Initiatives).

This chapter assesses your current project delivery methodology, and highlights areas which may need to be modified or enhanced to support your business intelligence program. In order to do this, you will be using the **Project Readiness Worksheet**, which is split into the following recipes:

- ▶ Program or a project
- ▶ Mapping your business culture
- ▶ Adapting your project delivery methodology
- ▶ Assessing your project team
- ▶ Organizing your project team

Introduction

This chapter explores recipes designed to give you an insight into your BI Initiative.

BI Initiatives can be daunting, and seem complex to project managers or team members who have never been part of a Business Intelligence project before.

By analyzing a few key processes, understanding your organization and culture, adapting your methodology, and determining your project team, you can kick your BI Initiative off with the right start.

In order to facilitate this assessment, the project readiness worksheet will be used. The worksheet will ask a series of questions which you can complete, and at the end of each recipe give recommendations based on your responses. This worksheet will provide valuable insight into your organization.

Program or a project

Determining whether the BI Initiative is a program or a project can be very subjective. Labeling the initiative is not important, but rather understanding its characteristics better to structure your initiative.

Getting ready

Before starting the assessment, it is important to have some general information regarding your initiative, namely:

▶ Intended scope of the BI Initiative

▶ Targeted consumers

▶ Planned deadline dates

▶ Understanding of the type of software and hardware which will be utilized

▶ Resources which may be assigned to the project, both internal and external

How to do it...

The most efficient way to understand your initiative and gather information, is to develop a questionnaire or survey. To do this, you could use any of the standard web tools available to build a survey or a simple spreadsheet.

1. Open a spreadsheet application and create a worksheet called **Definition**:

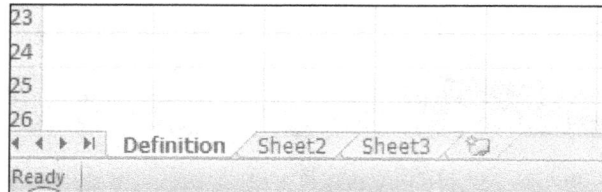

2. Create a series of questions which focus on determining if your initiative is a project or a program. Questions should focus on Initiative type, Scope, Support, Integration, and Costing. Some sample questions are as follows:

Question #	Category	Question	Answer
1	Initiative Type	Does the initiative have a set duration?	Y/N
2		Is the initiative unique?	Y/N
3	Support	Does the initiative support higher level of goals and visions?	Y/N
4	Scope	Does the initiative have multiple intended subject areas?	Y/N
5		Is the initiative a Global rollout to multiple locations?	Y/N
6		Do you have multi language requirements?	Y/N
7	Integration	Do you need to integrate into existing architectural components (for example LDAP, Server Farms etc)	Y/N
8		Is this the first implementation of the intended technology ?	Y/N
9	Costing	Do you need to track cost and benefit by subject area or rollouts?	Y/N

3. Ensure that your questions only allow a Yes or No answer. This solicits direct answers and starts people thinking about the answers.

4. Save the spreadsheet as Readiness Assessment.

5. Email the questionnaire to the key supporters of the Business Initiative.

How it works...

Based on the answers from the survey, you can determine whether you have a potential program or a project. A set of general definitions for a program and project are as follows:

► **A program** – This is defined as several interrelated projects that have a goal of improving an organization's performance

► **A project** – This is defined as a unique and temporary construct with a defined beginning and end, to meet a set of goals or objectives

BI Initiatives are normally focused on organizational improvements, or initiatives (regulatory and so on) of some description. These initiatives do not have a set duration, but rather are implemented using a system of measurement and feedback. As long as they attain the objectives (set measurements), they are normally continued.

> Determining whether a BI Initiative is a program or a project is an important part of the BI Initiative, because a key success factor is the way it influences the organization, and how the initiative morphs as the environment changes, ensuring long term benefits.

Each project within the BI Initiative should be focused on delivering unique benefits to the organization. These deliverables should be identified and sequenced to ensure that multiple projects or phases can run simultaneously. BI Initiatives are normally mapped to organizational or departmental goals, objectives, and metrics. These metrics are normally evolving and perpetual. The BI Initiative should include continued feedback and improvement to ensure that the program or project remains aligned with the business.

Multiple work packages, subject areas, or rollouts need to be analyzed before development, to understand how the deliverables of one project or phase have an impact on and contribute to subsequent projects or phases.

BI Initiatives rely on a good technical architecture, infrastructure, and integration to be successful. The integration points can easily become projects of their own, given the complexity and the deliverables. It is key to identify these projects early in the process and begin the key foundation infrastructure and integration early in the BI Initiative.

Subject areas can be prioritized and delivered based on costs. Tracking costs and estimates by subject area delivers valuable information to the project. It is important to agree upon and build a standard estimation model to cost a subject area; use a similar means to track expenditure and completion. It is best to start this from the beginning, else trying to manage and reconcile this information after the fact can be cumbersome and time consuming.

Global or multi-site rollouts require you to understand the type of architecture you are putting in place, and the support mechanism for this. Deploying development tools across large networks or geographic locations will have an impact on schedules as you cannot be as efficient. Additional techniques such as remote desktops or access are required for remote locations. Additional support teams or shifts may be necessary to support multi-site implementations. Both of these will affect cost and schedule, and are commonly forgotten within BI Initiatives.

Multi-language requirements not only affect the technical solution but also the business solution. Translating information is costly and time consuming. These factors need to be incorporated into the overall program.

There's more...

Whether you classify your initiative as a program or a multi-phase large project, it is important to realize that you will have multiple streams, and should structure the program or project into smaller modules.

By doing so you have the opportunity for running these smaller modules simultaneously.

Deliverables, templates, and work practices should be efficiently and effectively planned to facilitate reuse, and minimize overhead. By understanding and communicating this early in the lifecycle, you will gain the correct support and awareness.

With the Readiness Assessment you can schedule additional meeting sessions with the necessary stakeholders. The additional sessions include the following:

- ▶ Overview
- ▶ Data Source Review
- ▶ Business Process Review
- ▶ System Architecture
- ▶ ETL/ELT Overview
- ▶ Database Standards

These sessions will give you valuable information to gain insight into your Business Intelligence Initiative, outlining high-level information or gaps. If you are implementing BI applications, you will want to alter the questions to focus more on the pre-defined requirements for the application, and how they will integrate into your environment.

Mapping your business culture

The business culture of the organization will greatly influence the way in which you will structure and gather requirements for your BI Initiative. It is important to understand your business community so that you can tailor the communications and information to be effective and relevant. By asking a few simple questions, it is possible to determine the type of business community.

Getting ready

Before starting the exercise, you need to identify a few key resources to gather some information. The resources you will need to identify are as follows:

- ▶ A **C-Level** or upper management executive sponsor of the BI Initiative
- ▶ A **line manager** who will utilize the solution
- ▶ An **IT manager** who will be responsible for maintaining the solution

How to do it...

To understand your business culture you will need to enhance the Readiness Assessment. The assessment will be enhanced by more open-ended questions which enable insight into the businesses growth strategy, and how the information is managed and consumed.

1. Open your Readiness Assessment Worksheet and add a new worksheet called **Business Culture**:

8	What information a
9	Which systems prov
10	Do you need to enha you can report it?
11	What tools are avai

| Definition | Business Culture |

2. Create questions in the worksheet which focus on the way the organization has grown, the phase in which the organization is, information accessibility, tools availability, and so on. See the Readiness Assessment for more sample questions.
3. This time distribute the worksheet to a selective people within the organization at first to gain an understanding.
4. Collect responses to the questions and collate the information.
5. Set up follow-up meetings with the survey participants to review their answers.

How it works...

By understanding the business culture of your organization, you can approach BI Initiative effectively.

Review the information returned from the Readiness Assessment. Should your results indicate that your organization manages by using multiple reports from one or more systems, then you should focus on using the reports as a basis for your analysis. By following a bottom-up approach to analyze these reports, you can understand the key information required by the business. You can use the **Report Register** to identify and register all the different reports you uncover.

If however your organization has a good understanding of the metrics, they will be used to monitor the business processes across one or more systems by following a top-down approach to analyzing your requirements. With this approach, you need to understand the metrics used by the organization and how they identify and correct an issue. You can use the **Metric Register** to identify and register all the different metrics you uncover.

There's more...

By understanding your organization you will be more equipped to tailor your BI Initiative to your audience and organization's culture. Understanding the basics of the organization can facilitate more effective communication, and hopefully a greater adoption rate for the initiative. Now we'll look at some key examples of different organizational cultures and the insights they can provide.

Organizations that have grown through acquisition

In these organizations, there could be a lot of different business processes and systems storing for key information. If this is so, then there could be a master data management concern to the real source of information, for key business information. It is best to include additional time for data discovery within the project plan, as a real understanding is required to understand the different sources of information and the nuances based on the source system.

> Be aware of any standardization projects or system migration projects which may be active as these are a good source of information for the BI Initiative.

Expect to see an increase in systems and differences in business processes as the new organizations are folded into your organization. For your BI Initiative to consume information from these new sources, a flexible architecture and methodology will need to be developed and adopted. The BI Initiative can provide a vital role in this strategy, by having a standard integration model enabling the business to integrate new organizations quicker and more efficiently.

Organizations that have grown organically

This organization normally limits the number of systems and variations in business processes. These main systems, similar to an ERP system, are good sources of information for business processes and key information.

A standardization of business processes and consolidation of systems are the normal progression of an organization growing organically. Be aware of upgrade projects or a project that will replace existing systems; these will normally introduce enhancement for business processes and key functionality in core systems. Again, a flexible architecture and methodology are key to ensuring that the BI Initiative is capable of embracing this change.

Organizations and growth phases

For an organization in a **growth phase**, typically information requested will be to do with expansion metrics, sales, volumes, and so on. The focus of the organization will be external, and to the markets. This enables the BI Initiative to focus efforts on delivering information which can increase these metrics, or provide insight into increasing the revenue, market share, and so forth.

If the organization however is in a **contraction phase**, the metrics and focus are normally on cost reduction and containment. For this, the BI Initiative should focus effort on optimizing existing business processes, and look for ways to reduce cost. Finding relationships between metrics is essential in this phase of an organization. Thus, correlations between spend and efficiency are invaluable at this stage.

Metric driven organizations

These organizations normally use management by exception. They use metrics to identify problem areas, and then drill into the problem areas to understand issues. If your organization has adopted such practices, then they are an advanced organization and the BI Initiative should assist by automating and distributing these metrics. Organizations like these normally have a single version or very few variations of the same information, making it easier to find the trusted source of the information. BI Initiatives in these environments are normally very rare.

Report managed organizations

Organizations that manage by means of reports or details are normally very early in their BI Initiative. Organizations at this point require a gradual approach to adopting Business Intelligence. For these organizations, it is essential to invest a lot of time in education and communication around the BI Initiative, to outline the benefits and approach. It will be key to prove to business users that the BI Initiative can produce reports of equal or better quality, in a more efficient manner than the current manual processes. In an organization you will normally find multiple reports that represent the same information in a slightly different manner. This will be evident if you analyze a business process and gather all the reports and information used during the business process. Reducing the number of reports, gaining consensus, and providing automated information are paramount to success in these situations. BI Initiatives in these environments are normally very common.

Once this is done, taking the organization to the next step of common business metrics and enabling them to manage by exception is possible.

Understanding if a line manager has the necessary information, and the amount of effort needed to obtain this information, is a great way to determine whether the area of responsibility requires immediate attention. This helps set priorities for the BI Initiative.

Utilizing existing reports as a basis for requirements gathering helps the project to contain scope, and business users to understand the charter of the initiative. It is not recommended to ask a business user what they want as it is a very ambiguous question.

Identify the key information that is required to operationally manage a department, or report information to higher levels of management. Try and identify which systems provide key pieces of information. This helps not only to identify this information, but gives you insight into which systems the business determines as the source of record for the information.

Information is normally extracted from systems and then manually manipulated in spreadsheets. The spreadsheets inherently contain a lot of business rules in the form of the following:

- ► Calculations
- ► Data standardizations
- ► Groupings
- ► Filters
- ► Key attributes
- ► Visualization cues

It is important not only to look at the spreadsheets as example reports, but also to capture these business rules and standardize across the organization.

See also

For information about **Blueprint**, look at *Chapter 5, The Blueprint*. For more information about using this information, look at *Chapter 2, Establishing the Project*.

Adapting your project delivery methodology

This recipe focuses on how to adapt your current project delivery methodology to cater for a BI Initiative. For BI Initiatives there is no correct or incorrect methodology. So if you follow Mike 2.0, Scrum, Prince2, DSDM Atern, Waterfall, Prototyping, Spiral, or some other methodology, it does not really matter. These are personal preferences and standards set by your organization. It is important to understand a few characteristics of a BI Initiative, and how to adapt your methodology to cater for these characteristics.

Getting ready

Contact your project management office if one has been created, or look for projects which have successfully been completed within your organization. From these projects, gather the project methodology.

To use this recipe, you need to be familiar with your project delivery methodology.

How to do it...

From the artifacts gathered, create a simple process flow for your methodology outlining your phases.

1. Review the typical project delivery methodology phases:

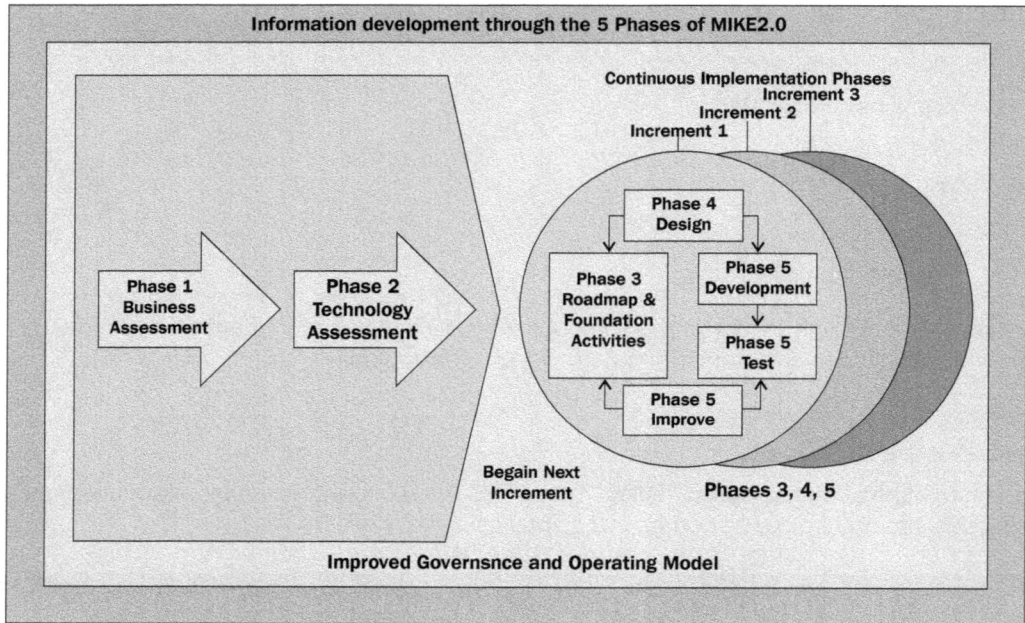

2. Create a lightweight methodology which is easy to understand with a few phases, by defining the phases that make sense within your organization. For example, Definition, Data Discovery, Development, Testing, Promote, and Production:

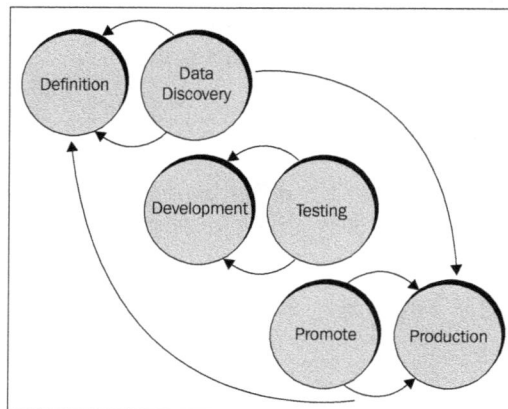

How it works...

By understanding some of the more prevalent characteristics of a BI Initiative, you have the opportunity to adapt your project delivery methodology to cater for these characteristics.

The methodology should be clear and easy to understand. The phases should be encapsulated enough to be self-contained, but have sufficient inputs and outputs to allow for interaction with other phases while running in parallel. All phases should be broken into defined time spans. The key to the methodology is to make it efficient and repeatable. If it does not make sense, it is probably too complicated.

There's more...

The key to adapting your project delivery methodology is to deliver results in a short amount of time, while providing visibility into the process by the business user. Delivering the benefit quickly, consistently, and efficiently is essential for a BI Initiative to be deemed as a success whilst maintaining constant communication, feedback, and improvement.

See also

For more information on how to structure the different work practices, refer to the recipes in *Chapter 2, Establishing the Project*.

Assessing your project team

In a BI Initiative it is important to have a mix of skills within the team. These skills range from presentation and information gathering, to technical development and implementation. With the right mix of skills, your project can be very successful, as a BI Initiative is not all about the technology.

How to do it...

In order to assess your project team, it is important to first understand the skills which you will require from your team to complete the project:

1. Categorize your team members into two different buckets:
    a. Members with good communication skills, and more business acumen and knowledge.

  b. Members with good technical skills.

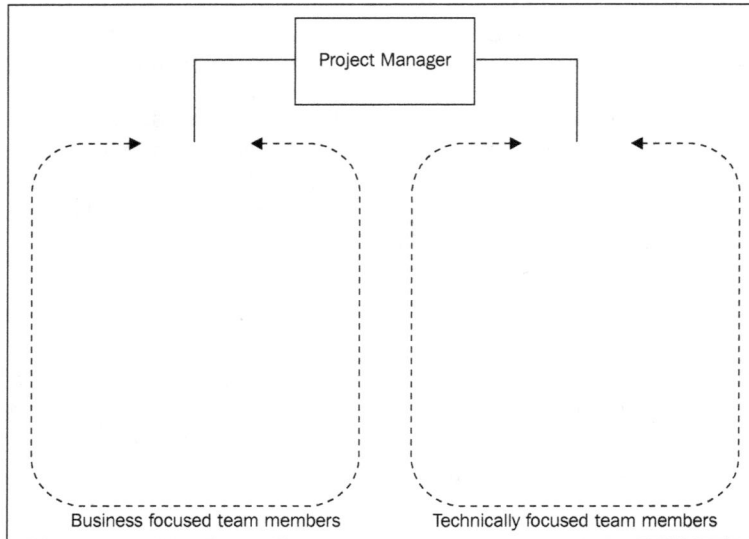

Business focused team members   Technically focused team members

2. Create technical and business placeholders for roles required, and assign team members to the different roles:

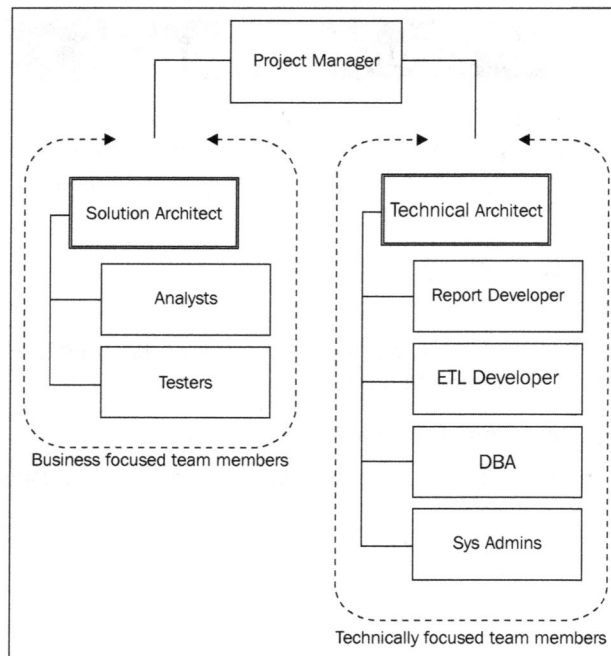

3. Identify supporting and contributing roles for your initiative:

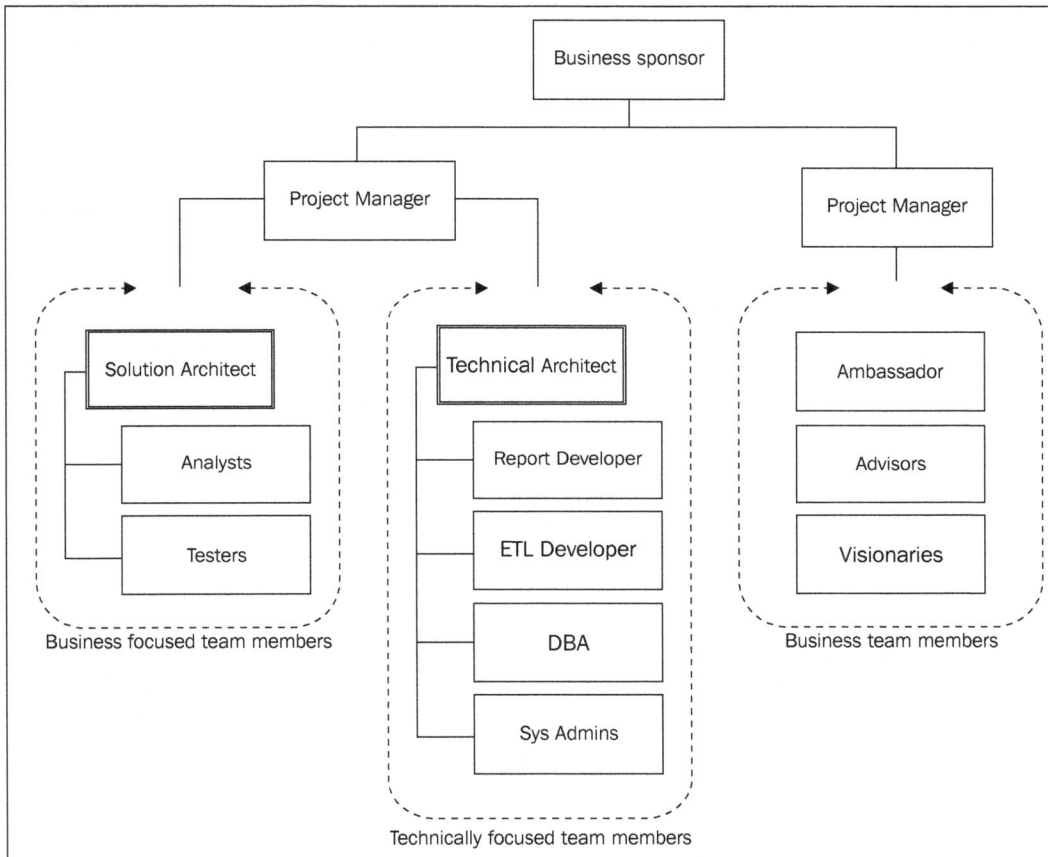

How it works...

By understanding the roles required for the project, you can effectively recruit your team and identify any gaps in your resource pool.

See also

For more information on the different responsibilities by the roles, refer to the work practices recipes, in _Chapter 2, Establishing the Project_.

Organizing your project team

Once you have identified your project team, it is important to organize your team efficiently. There are two major models to organize your team.

How to do it...

Depending on how you plan to run your project, you could choose one of the following models for your team:

Option 1: Model based on subject areas with multi-skilled resources.

1. Separate your team into **business initiative** and **subject area** resources:

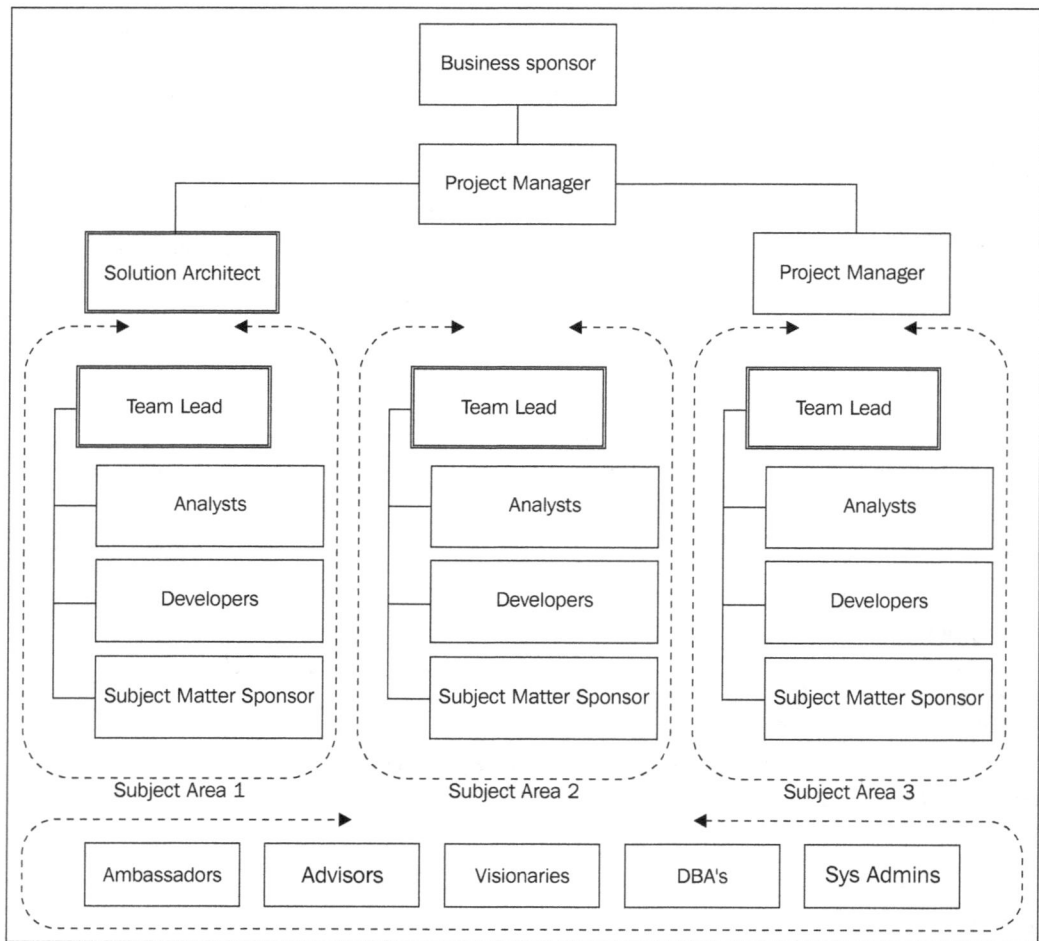

Option 2: Model based on resource specialized skills.

1. Separate your teams based on **technology** and **business** skills:

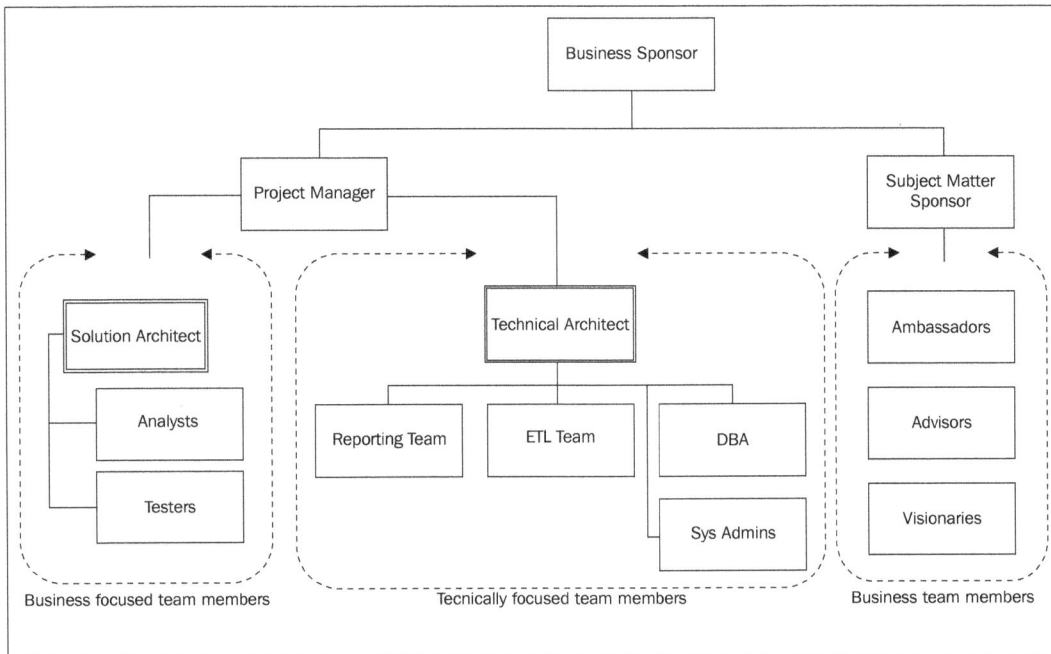

There's more...

Option 2 is the more advanced model for an initiative which will run multiple subject areas concurrently. This model is effective if you have a good grasp of the methodology, and some experience.

> Option 1 is normally the best model to start your initiative with and then migrate to Option 2 at a later date.

See also

For more information on the different deliverables by the roles, refer to the work practices recipes, in *Chapter 2, Establishing the Project*.

2
Establishing the Project

Successful projects are like good directions—they have step-by-step instructions on how to get from your origin to the destination. A good foundation with an efficient, lightweight, set standard work practice, aids greatly in the success of a project and establishes an effective project delivery methodology. This chapter has recipes to set up the project delivery phases for a consistent way to deliver, manage, and estimate the efforts for a project. Recipes include:

- ▶ Creating Definition work practice
- ▶ Creating Data Discovery work practice
- ▶ Creating Development work practice
- ▶ Creating Testing work practice
- ▶ Creating Promote work practice
- ▶ Creating Production work practice
- ▶ Building a standard work breakdown structure
- ▶ Identifying and quantifying the effort drivers
- ▶ Creating your estimation tool

Introduction

This chapter explores the recipes designed to show you how to build repeatable phases for your project with standard tasks. Once you have the standard tasks, you are in a position to determine effort drivers and build an estimation tool.

Creating Definition work practice

The definition work practice outlines the **definition phase** of the project. The purpose of this work practice is to highlight the major deliverables/products and processes. The definition phase defines the project and captures the requirements.

Getting ready

Before starting, it is important to have an understanding of your project methodology and determine:

- The existing work practices
- The key roles which will be involved in the work practice

How to do it...

Work practices are best created as a visual tool. To do this, start up a diagramming tool such as Microsoft Visio or Microsoft PowerPoint.

1. In the diagramming application, create a new diagram called **Work Practices**.
2. Create a tab or a slide called **Definition**.
3. On the diagram, create swimlanes. In each swimlane, add the key role.
4. Step through this phase of the project logically, and add the key products/ deliverables and processes.
5. A sample definition work practice is shown here:

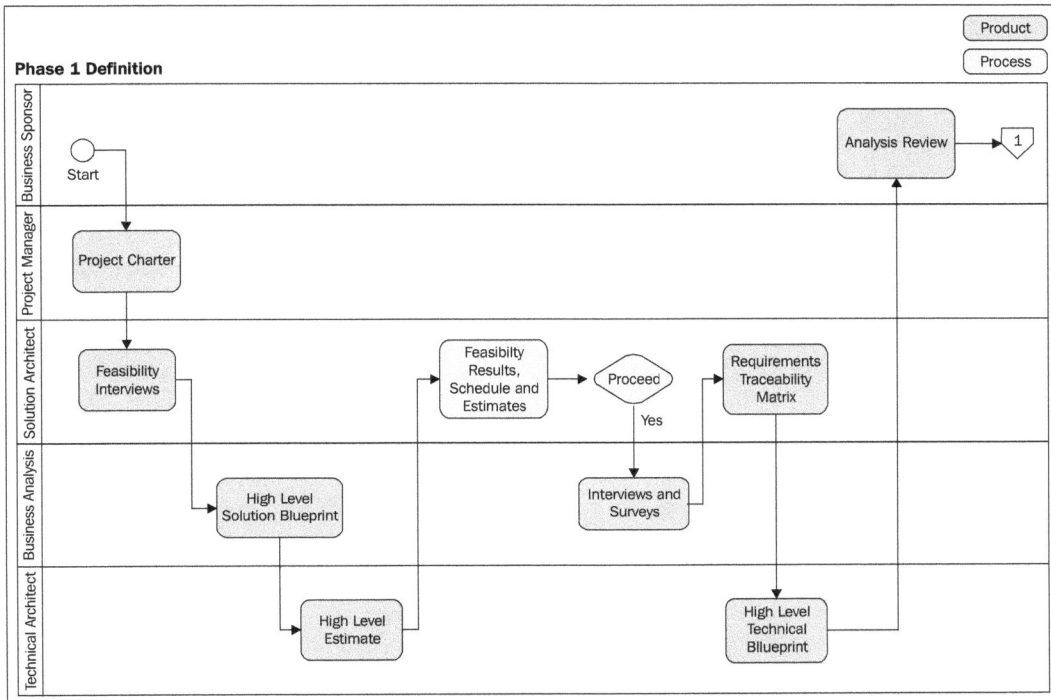

Phase 1 Definition

6. Once you have created your products and processes, you will need to describe each of them.

   For example, **Project Charter** outlines the scope, objectives, benefits and participants for the project.

7. Once all the products and processes are described, you can determine the deliverables for each product and the role responsible for delivering it, based on the swimlane.

   For example, the deliverable for **Project Charter** is the Project Charter Document created by the Project Manager.

How it works...

Work practices give members of the project a quick and easy way to understand the flow of activities within the phase, and all the deliverables required with the phase.

There's more...

Creating templates for deliverables can be a large undertaking. Two good sources of templates include:

- ▶ Project in a box
- ▶ Mike 2.0

Both can be found with a simple Internet search. Templates included in these sources are comprehensive, and contain most deliverables required within a project. The key templates to develop are:

- ▶ Project Charter
- ▶ Requirements
- ▶ Solution Design
- ▶ Data Lineage and Mapping
- ▶ Requirements Traceability Matrix
- ▶ Data Dictionary and Conceptual Data Model

Depending on your project requirements, you may need to utilize templates from different sources to obtain the content you feel is comfortable for your deliverables within the project.

Creating Data Discovery work practice

The data discovery work practice outlines the **data discovery phase** of the project. The purpose of this work practice is to highlight the major deliverables/products and processes. The data discovery phase analyzes the sources of information in detail, to determine patterns, and also to determine the similarities and differences of the source systems. This is a very interactive and exploratory phase.

Getting ready

Before starting, it is important to have an understanding of your project methodology and determine the key roles that will be involved in the work practice.

How to do it...

Work practices are best created as a visual tool. To do this, start up a diagramming tool such as Microsoft Visio or Microsoft PowerPoint:

1. In the diagramming application, create a new tab or slide called **Data Discovery**.
2. On the diagram, create swimlanes. In each swimlane, add the key role.

3. Step through this phase of the project logically, and add the key products/deliverables and processes.

4. A sample data discovery work practice is shown in the following screenshot:

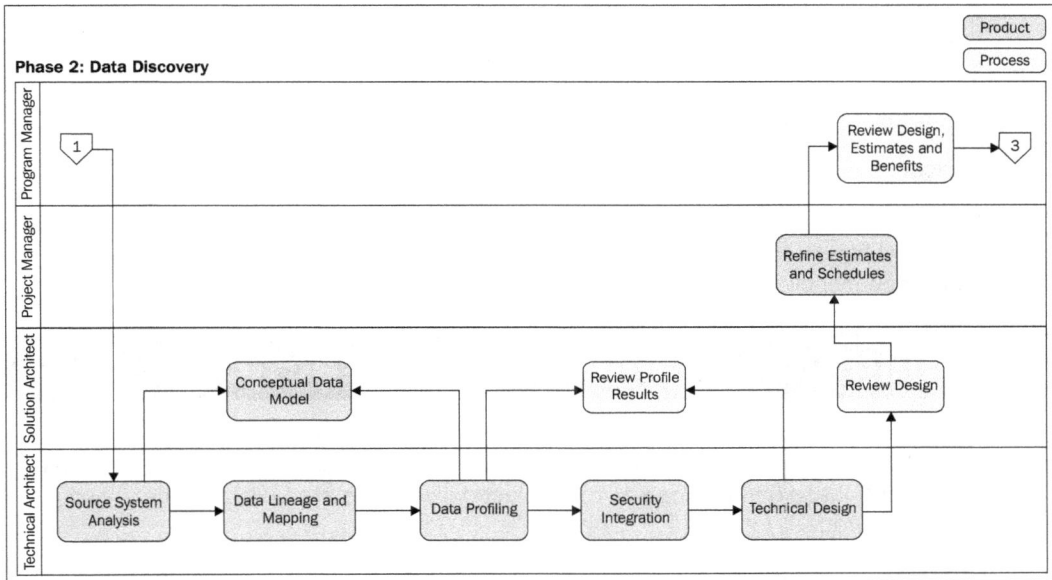

5. Once you have created your products and processes, you will need to describe each of them.

    For example, **Source System Analysis** identifies the key systems for the information, which are relevant to the project as well as the major information contained within each system.

6. Once all the products and processes are described, you can determine the deliverables for each product and the role responsible for delivering it, based on the swimlane.

    For example, the deliverable for **Source System Analysis** is the document outlining key source system information prepared by the Technical Architect.

How it works...

Work practices give members of the project a quick and easy way to understand the flow of activities within the phase, and all the deliverables required with the phase.

There's more...

Gathering information can become tedious and time-consuming. Consider using a survey tool to gather and consolidate information, for example:

- ▸ Survey Monkey
- ▸ Survey Gizmo
- ▸ SharePoint
- ▸ Excel

These tools are generally inexpensive, already available within the environment, and provide an effective, unobtrusive way to gather initial information. Be familiar with your company's information security policy before using external applications.

Creating Development work practice

The development work practice outlines the **development phase** of the project. The purpose of this work practice is to highlight the major deliverables/products and processes. The development phase defines the way the project deliverables are built, and the major components required.

Getting ready

Before starting, it is important to have an understanding of your project methodology and determine:

- ▸ The existing work practices
- ▸ The key roles which will be involved in the work practice

How to do it...

Work practices are best created as a visual tool. To do this, start up a diagramming tool such as Microsoft Visio or Microsoft PowerPoint:

1. In the diagramming application, create a new tab or slide called **Development**.
2. On the diagram, create swimlanes. In each swimlane, add the key role.
3. Step through this phase of the project logically, and add the key products/ deliverables and processes.
4. A sample development work practice is shown here:

Phase 3 : Development

Product

Process

| | | | |

3 · 4

Program Manager

Project Manager

Solution Architect — Solution Reviews

Technical Architect — Code Reviews

Report Developers — Reporting

4

ETL Developers — ETL Mappings, Summary Mangement, Job Process Flows

DBA — Physical Data Model, Performance Management, Archive and Purge, Backup and Recovery

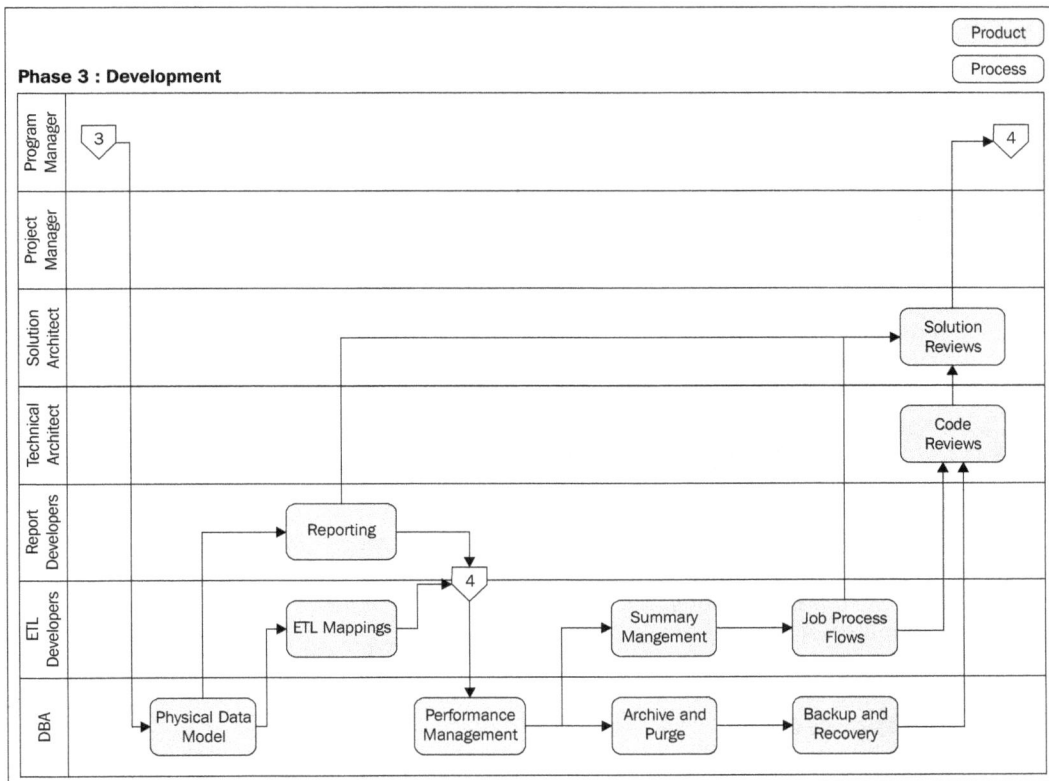

5. Once you have created your products and processes, you will need to describe each of them:

   For example, **Physical Data Model** is the actual scripts required to build the objects for the project data model

6. Once all the products and processes are described, you can determine the deliverables for each product and the role responsible for delivering it, based on the swimlane.

   For example, the deliverable for **Physical Data Model** is the single script per object within the data model, outlining all the characteristics and definitions for the object developed by the DBA.

How it works...

Work practices give members of the project a quick and easy way to understand the flow of activities within the phase, and all the deliverables required with the phase.

There's more...

In the development phase, it is easy to overdo a documentation. In order to avoid this, divide your documentation into two parts:

1. **Project document**: This is required by the project, to deliver.
2. **Production documentation**: This is required by the users and maintainers of the project to understand and work with the application.

Try and reduce the number of documents in the first category and replace them with documents from the second category, which will live on and become useful user guides or working documents.

Creating Testing work practice

The testing work practice outlines the **testing phase** of the project. The purpose of this work practice is to highlight the major deliverables/products and processes. The testing phase defines how deliverables will be assessed, and defects corrected. This work practice does not cater to all the different testing that can be performed on a project, but rather for testing specific components of the project.

Getting ready

Before starting, it is important to have an understanding of your project methodology and determine:

▸ The existing work practices
▸ The key roles which will be involved in the work practice
▸ If testing is executed within your projects

How to do it...

Work practices are best created as a visual tool. To do this, start up a diagramming tool such as Microsoft Visio or Microsoft PowerPoint.

1. In the diagramming application, create a new tab or slide called **Testing**.
2. On the diagram, create swimlanes. In each swimlane, add the key role.
3. Step through this phase of the project logically, and add the key products/ deliverables and processes.

4. A sample testing work practice is shown here:

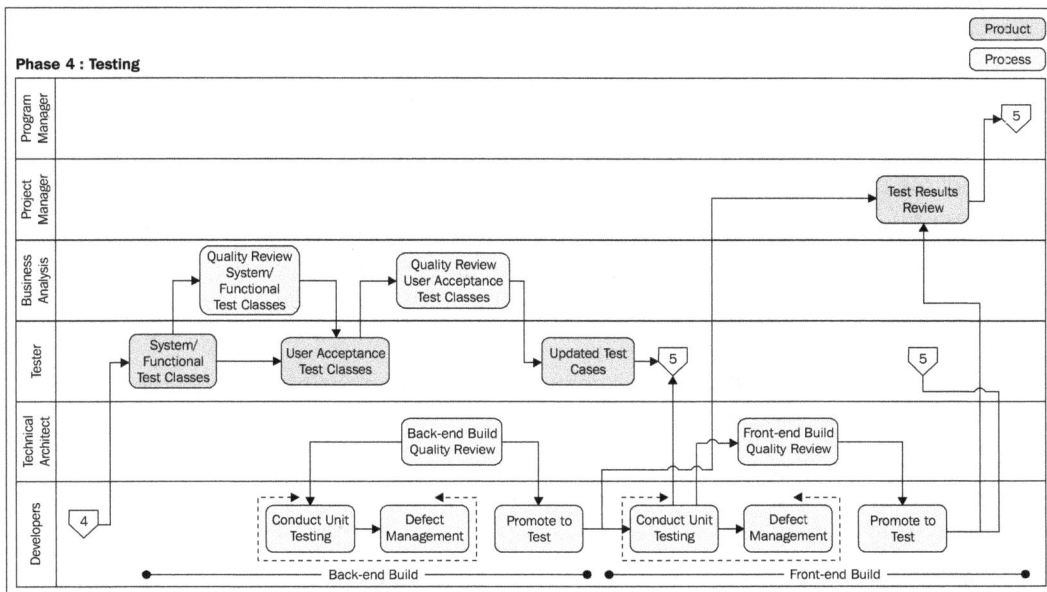

5. Once you have created your products and processes, you will need to describe each of them.

    For example, **System/Functional Test Cases** are test scripts outlining the ways to test a component.

6. Once all the products and processes are described, you can determine the deliverables for each product and the role responsible for delivering it, based on the swimlane.

    For example, the deliverable for **System/Functional Test Cases** is a set of instructions on how to test a component, and the expected outcome created by Testers.

How it works...

Work practices give members of the project a quick and easy way to understand the flow of activities within the phase, and all the deliverables required with the phase.

There's more...

The testing phase may not be a defined phase in your project but may be spread among the other phases. This phase is generally broken down to account for effort and to aid in estimation. Additional testing on the project will be required, such as:

- **Integration Testing** – also known as **black box testing**, focuses on the outcomes of the process
- **Performance Testing** – focuses on the capabilities and thresholds of a solution
- **Unit Testing** – also known as **white box testing**, focuses on tracing the inputs and outputs as they are processed by a unit, to validate whether the information outcomes are correct

As the data in business intelligence and data warehouse solutions can utilize large data sets, it is important to spend some time to prepare the positive and negative data sets.

Positive data sets are based on production quality data, which can be placed through the solution to determine outcomes. This may not be actual production data as it may be stripped off of the sensitive information.

Negative data sets are based on production quality data, the same as the positive data set. The difference is that this data set is intentionally altered to included errors and anomalies, to force errors and warnings within the solution.

It is important to understand that due to the vast quantities of data in the solution, it may not be feasible to test all scenarios.

Creating Promote work practice

The promote work practice outlines the **promote phase** of the project. The purpose of this work practice is to highlight the major deliverables/products and processes. The promote phase defines how the deliverables migrated from the development to the production environment.

Getting ready

Before starting, it is important to have an understanding of your project methodology and determine:

- Existing work practices
- The key roles which will be involved in the work practice

How to do it...

Work practices are best created as a visual tool. To do this, start up a diagramming tool such as Microsoft Visio or Microsoft PowerPoint:

1. In the diagramming application, create a new tab or slide called **Promote**.

2. On the diagram, create swimlanes. In each swimlane, add the key role.

3. Step through this phase of the project logically, and add the key products/ deliverables and processes.

4. A sample promote work practice is shown here:

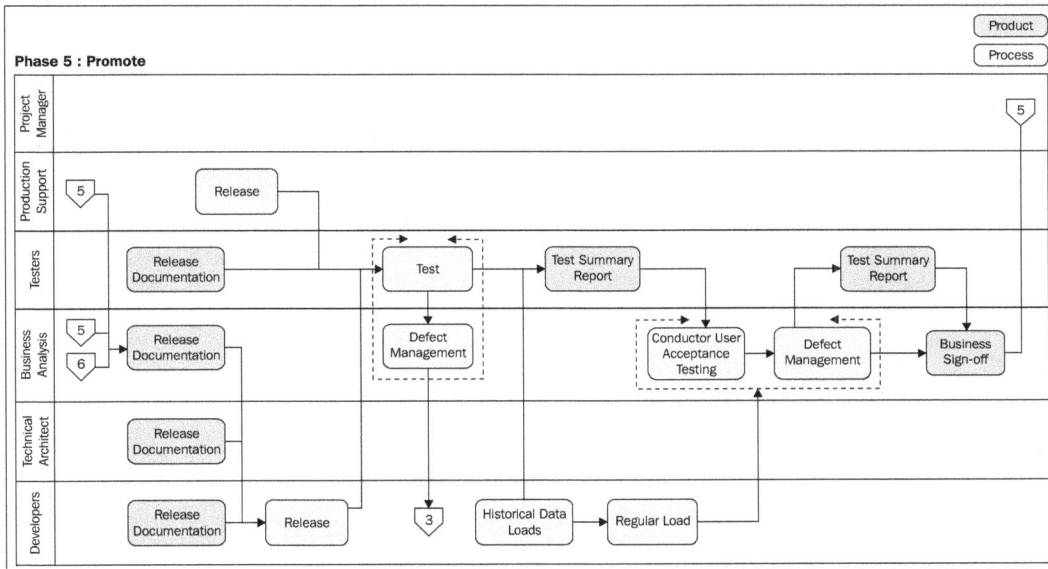

5. Once you have created your products and processes, you will need to describe each of them.

   For example, the **Release** process is used to promote code from one technical environment to another in order to validate or make the application available to additional users.

6. Once all the products and processes are described, you can determine the deliverables for each product and the role responsible for delivering it, based on the swimlane.

   For example, the deliverable for **Release** is a set of components, which are assembled to deliver the application of the project performed by the Production Support aided by the Developers.

How it works...

Work practices give members of the project a quick and easy way to understand the flow of activities within the phase, and all the deliverables required with the phase.

There's more...

It is important to capture and store all the development artifacts for the project. A release management with version control could aid you in managing and storing these artifacts. See the *Setting up a Collaborative environment* recipe, in *Chapter 3, Controlling the Project*.

> Subversion can be used to store and share artifacts in a multi-user environment.

Creating Production work practice

The production work practice outlines the **production phase** of the project. The purpose of this work practice is to highlight the major deliverables/products and processes. The production phase defines how the application will transition from a project to a production system.

Getting ready

Before starting, it is important to have an understanding of your project methodology and determine:

▶ The existing work practices

▶ The key roles which will be involved in the work practice

▶ How production support is delivered within your organization

How to do it...

Work practices are best created as a visual tool. To do this, start up a diagramming tool such as Microsoft Visio or Microsoft PowerPoint:

1. In the diagramming application, create a new tab or slide called **Production**.
2. On the diagram, create swimlanes. In each swimlane, add the key role.
3. Step through this phase of the project logically, and add the key products/ deliverables and processes.

4. A sample production work practice is shown here:

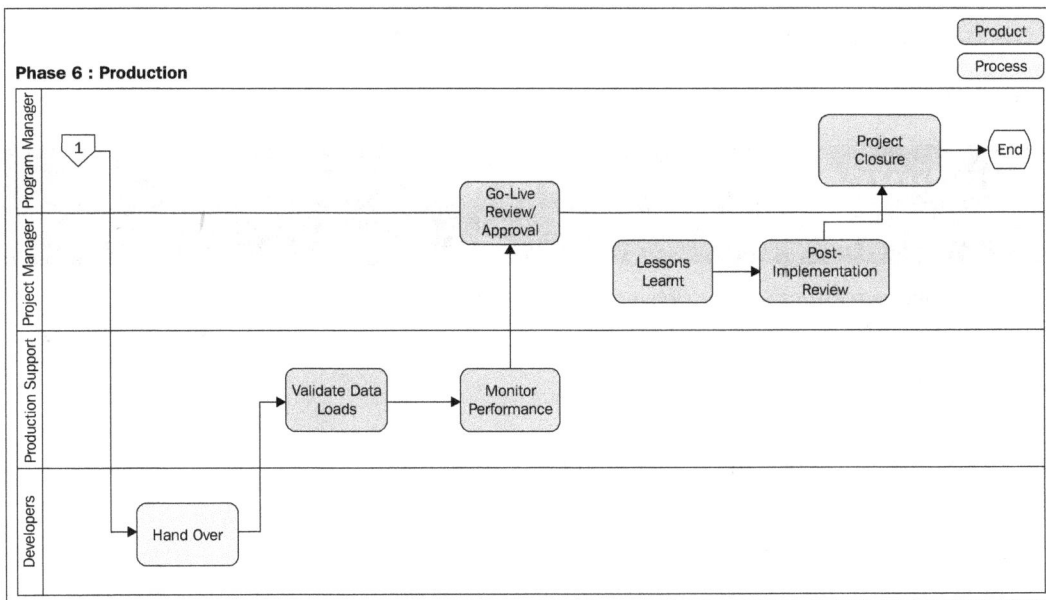

5. Once you have created your products and processes, you will need to describe each of them.

   For example, the **Hand Over** process is used to transition the application from development into production support.

6. Once all the products and processes are described, you can now determine the deliverables (information relating to the definition of the product) for each product (component you are building) and the role responsible for delivering it, based on the swimlane.

7. For example, the deliverable for **Hand Over** is a set of steps that are discussed and documented. These steps outline how to manage and maintain the application, developed by the developers during the software development lifecycle.

How it works...

Work practices give members of the project a quick and easy way to understand the flow of activities within the phase, and all the deliverables required with the phase.

There's more...

It is important to understand your organization's production support capabilities and processes. These will determine which artifacts are required to execute this work practice and can drive project timelines.

Building a standard work breakdown structure

A work breakdown structure is a deliverable that decomposes the project into smaller components.

Getting ready

Before starting, it is important to have an understanding of your project methodology and determine:

- ▶ Your new work practices

How to do it...

Your work practices have new productions and processes outlined. Start up a tool such as Microsoft Excel or Microsoft Project, and begin recording these work practices and their associated products and processes:

1. Open a spreadsheet application.
2. Create a tab called **DW WBS**:

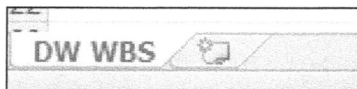

3. Start by entering your work practice names or project phases:

Data Warehouse
Phase 1 - Definition
Phase 2 - Data Discovery
Phase 3 - Development
Phase 4 - Testing
Phase 5 - Promote
Phase 6 - Production

4. Start to decompose the phases with the major products and processes from your work practices:

Data Warehouse
Phase 1 - Definition
WP 110 - Feasibility
WP 120 - Analysis
Phase 2 - Data Discovery
WP 210 - Source System Analysis
WP 220 - Data Lineage and Mapping
WP 230 - Conceptual Data Model
WP 240 - Logical Data Model
WP 250 - Data Profiling
WP 260 - Security
WP 270 - Technical Design
WP 280 - Review Design
Phase 3 - Development
WP 310 - Physical Data Model
WP 320 - ETL Mappings
WP 330 - Performance Management
WP 340 - Summary Management
WP 350 - Archive and Purge
WP 360 - Backup and Recovery
WP 370 - Job Process Flow
WP 390 - Reporting

5. Assign a number to each major product or process identified within your work practices.

6. Further decompose these products and processes to the major deliverable components or work tasks required by the project:

Phase 3 - Development
WP 310 - Physical Data Model
CDC
Staging Tables
Base Data Model
Lookup Tables
Application / Reference Tables
Dimensions
Facts

How it works...

By decomposing your work practices to products and processes, and then to tasks and components, you get a comprehensive view of the activities for the project.

There's more...

Try not to decompose the deliverables and tasks beyond a manageable level. A good rule of thumb—the detail is sufficient if you can record the time and cost to it, without creating a burden on the project. For example, staging tables is a sufficient level of detail, and it is not required to list each individual staging table.

Identifying and quantifying the effort drivers

Effort or task drivers are those components which increase the time taken to complete a task.

Getting ready

Before starting, it is important to have an understanding of the size of the project and, if possible, some historical data from past projects.

How to do it...

Once you have created the work breakdown structure, reopen this spreadsheet:

1. Create a column called **Effort Drivers**:

Task	Effort Drivers
Data Warehouse	
Phase 1 - Definition	
WP 110 - Feasibility	

2. For each task, identify what will drive an increase or decrease in the amount of effort required to complete the task:

Task	Effort Drivers
Data Warehouse	
Phase 1 - Definition	
WP 110 - Feasibility	
Project Charter	Single
Fesability Interviews	Number of Interviews
High Level Solution Blueprint	Integrate Project Blueprint into Program
High Level Estimate	Single
Prepare Feasibility Results, Schedule and Estimates	
WP 120 - Analysis	
Interviews and Surveys	Number of Interviews
Develop Business Process and Requiremen	Single
High Level Technical Blueprint	
Review Analysis	
Phase 2 - Data Discovery	
WP 210 - Source System Analysis	Number of Components
WP 220 - Data Lineage and Mapping	Number of Components
WP 230 - Conceptual Data Model	Number of Components
WP 240 - Logical Data Model	Number of Components
WP 250 - Data Profiling	Number of Components
WP 260 - Security	Number of Security Models
WP 270 - Technical Design	Single
WP 280 - Review Design	Number of Review Sessions

3. Complete step 2 for all the tasks identified at the lowest level.

4. Add an additional column for the number of effort drivers, for example, **Number of Interviews** – 5:

Data Warehouse		
Phase 1 - Definition		
WP 110 - Feasibility		
Project Charter	Single	1
Fesability Interviews	Number of Interviews	5
High Level Solution Blueprint	Integrate Project Blueprint into Program	1
High Level Estimate	Single	
Prepare Feasibility Results, Schedule and Estimates		1
WP 120 - Analysis		
Interviews and Surveys	Number of Interviews	10
Develop Business Process and Requiremen	Single	1
High Level Technical Blueprint		1
Review Analysis		1

How it works...

By identifying the task drivers, you are getting an understanding of the number of components or variables within your project, which can drive the scope and duration.

There's more...

Lessons learned, or historical data from past projects, is a great asset to be used. If this is your first project, complete it to the best of your understanding at this stage. Later in the project, you should reuse this spreadsheet to refine your estimates.

Creating your estimation tool

An estimation tool is a great asset to a project as it defines a standard way to deliver and size a project.

Getting ready

Before starting, it is important to have an understanding of how long standard tasks take within your organization and which algorithms are used for estimation.

How to do it...

Once you have created the work breakdown structure, reopen this spreadsheet:

1. Decide on an estimation algorithm, for example, three point estimation with a weighted average and standard deviation:

Data Warehouse Tasks and Effort Projection								
			Base		Effort hrs			
Task	Effort Drivers	#	Hrs	Optimistic	Most Likely	Pessimistic	Weighted	Standard Deviation
Data Warehouse								
Phase 1 - Definition								
WP 110 - Feasibility								
Project Charter	Single	1	40	40	46	58	47	3
Fesability Interviews	Number of Interviews	5	1.25	6	7	9	7	0
High Level Solution Blueprint	Single	1	16	16	18	23	19	1
High Level Estimate	Single	1						
Prepare Feasibility Results, Schedule and Estimates		1	24	24	28	35	28	2
WP 120 - Analysis								
Interviews and Surveys	Number of Interviews	10	1	10	12	14	12	1

2. For each task, identify how many hours you estimate a single task or component will take.

3. Apply your formula across each task.

4. Sum the tasks at the end to get a grand total of effort:

		Base	Effort hrs				
2							
3	Data Warehouse Tasks and Effort Projection						
4		Base		Effort hrs			
5	Task	Hrs	Optimistic	Most Likely	Pessimistic	Weighted	Standard Deviation
110	Total Effort Hours		2890	3518	4398	3560	251

How it works...

Identifying the task drivers, base hours, and a standard estimating tool makes it easier to get a realistic effort for your project. This is, however, only an effort for one resource, and not duration. For an extra step, you will need to add dependencies and resources to a calendar of working days and additional project management time.

There's more...

Many project estimation algorithms are used. The sample spreadsheet uses the following:

- **Three point estimation**:
    - Optimistic = base hoursx#
    - Most likely = (base hoursx#)+15%
    - Pessimistic = (base hoursx#)+25%
- **Weighted Average with Estimate** E = (optimistic+4 most likely+pessimistic)/6
- **Standard Deviation** = (pessimistic-optimistic)/6
- Confidence levels based on **Weighted Average** (E):
    - E value is approximately 50%
    - E value+SD is approximately 85%
    - E value+1.645×SD is approximately 95%
    - E value+2×SD is approximately 98%
    - E value+3×SD is approximately 99.9%

Weighted Average with Estimate (E) takes into account the optimistic, pessimistic, and most likely estimates for each task.

Standard Deviation determines variation from the average. The Confidence levels shown in the preceding bullet list indicate how likely you are to achieve your goals within your estimate, if you combine the different values.

Therefore, if you need an estimate with about 50% probability achievability to actual, then using the Weighted Average (E) value would suffice. If you required an 85% probability of being able to deliver within your estimate, then Weighted Average+Standard Deviation should be used. For information systems, normally 95% is the standard to utilize.

		Base	Effort hrs				
				Most			Standard
	Task	Hrs	Optimistic	Likely	Pessimistic	Weighted	Deviation
2							
3	Data Warehouse Tasks and Effort Projection						
4							
5							
6							
7	Data Warehouse						
8	Phase 1 - Definition						
9	WP 110 - Feasibility						
10	Project Charter	40	40	46	58	47	3
11	Fesability Interviews	1.25	6	7	9	7	0
12	High Level Solution Blueprint	16	16	18	23	19	1
13	High Level Estimate						
14	Prepare Feasibility Results, Schedule and Estimates	24	24	28	35	28	2
15	WP 120 - Analysis						
16	Interviews and Surveys	1	10	12	14	12	1
17	Develop Business Process and Requirements Traceability Ma	16	16	18	23	19	1
18	High Level Technical Blueprint	24	24	28	35	28	2
19	Review Analysis	24	24	28	35	28	2
20	Phase 2 - Data Discovery						
31	Phase 3 - Development						
65	Phase 4 - Testing						
96	Phase 5 - Promote						
102	Phase 6 - Production						
107			2477	3016	3769	3051	215
108	Technical Project Management 50% Calendar Duration		413	503	628	509	36
109							
110	Total Effort Hours		2890	3518	4398	3560	251
111							
112							
113	Confidence Value						
114	Weighted Value	50%	3560				
115	Weighted Value + Standard Deviation	85%	3811				
116	Weighted Value + 1.645 x Standard Deviation	95%	3973				
117	Weighted Value + 2 x Standard Deviation	98%	4063				
118	Weighted Value + 3 x Standard Deviation	99.90%	4314				

Over a period of time, you can refine these calculations to reflect your environment more accurately once you have the actual values, which can replace the effort drivers and quantity.

Additional information for this topic can be found at:

http://en.wikipedia.org/wiki/Three-point_estimation.

3

Controlling the Project

Business Intelligence and Data Warehouse projects require a lot of communication and can unearth numerous issues. Effective methods to control and manage the scope of the project are essential to success, while keeping stakeholders engaged and enlightened. Efficient and effective methods of collaboration can assist in the communication of information to the various team members. This chapter covers how to control scope, collaborate, and educate stakeholders along the way. Recipes include:

- ▶ Requirements Traceability Matrix
- ▶ Creating an effective risk register
- ▶ Creating an effective issue management register
- ▶ Creating a defect and enhancement register
- ▶ Creating your cyclical build and test process
- ▶ Setting up an effective collaboration mechanism
- ▶ Installing client tools for a collaborative environment

Introduction

Business Intelligence and Data Warehouse projects always unearth additional requirements and features as the project progresses. It is important to be able to capture these requirements efficiently and to uniquely identify them. Once uniquely identified, they can be tracked through the development lifecycle. As the defects, issues, risks, and enhancements are identified within the project development lifecycle, you can then associate these with the unique requirements they are related to. This chapter outlines how to track and trace the requirements and their associated risk, issues, enhancements, and defects.

Requirements Traceability Matrix

The Requirements Traceability Matrix is an important cross reference document. It traces the progress of a requirement from inception to delivery. The document is crucial to understanding how the solution will meet the requirements, or where you have issues within your project. This document can have the tendency to become very large and overwhelming. So it is important to find the right level of detail to manage the project, but not so much detail that this document becomes impossible to maintain.

The Requirements Traceability Matrix should be focused on the components the project will create in order to support the requirements.

Getting ready

Before starting, it is important to have an understanding of the scope of the project and its high-level requirements. It is best to start the Requirements Traceability Matrix before you have detailed the requirements, so that you can arrange your requirements in the same structure as your traceability matrix. The Requirements Traceability Matrix does not contain the actual requirements, but merely a link to the requirement or detailed requirement via the unique number.

How to do it...

Creating the Requirements Traceability Matrix has several steps involved. The traceability matrix should be created for each project/work package:

1. Create your numbering system: The numbering system should be hierarchical so that it is easy to understand and simple to follow. For example:

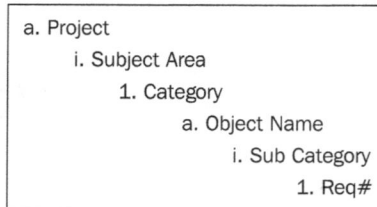

> a. Project
> > i. Subject Area
> > > 1. Category
> > > > a. Object Name
> > > > > i. Sub Category
> > > > > > 1. Req#

A typical hierarchical number system is as follows:

1. The object name will be derived from the component that needs to be developed to support the requirements, and the sub-category is all the sub components which need to be developed for the component.

2. The listed sub-categories under the object name should be limited to the actual sub-components, whose information needs to be gathered, documented, and agreed upon via stakeholders. This hierarchical numbering should be closely correlated information collected during detail requirements.

3. The sub-category will be specific to each type of object needed to be developed. Different object types (**Reports**, **Data**, and so on) will have different sub categories:

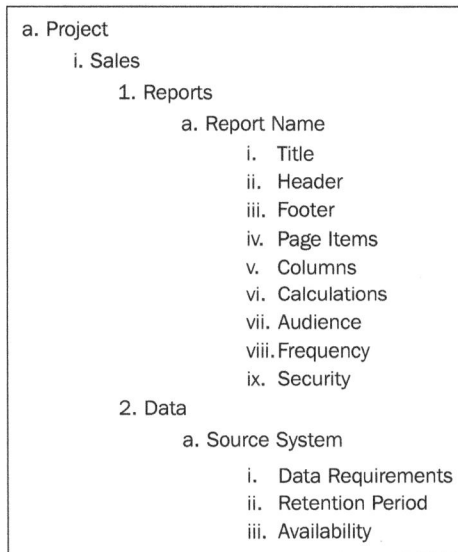

```
a. Project
    i. Sales
        1. Reports
            a. Report Name
                    i.   Title
                    ii.  Header
                    iii. Footer
                    iv.  Page Items
                    v.   Columns
                    vi.  Calculations
                    vii. Audience
                    viii.Frequency
                    ix.  Security
        2. Data
            a. Source System
                    i.   Data Requirements
                    ii.  Retention Period
                    iii. Availability
```

4. Open a spreadsheet application and create a tab for your project:

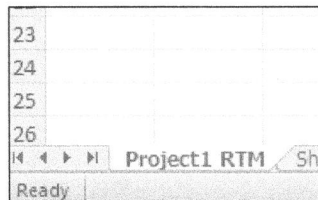

23	
24	
25	
26	

Project1 RTM / Sh

Ready

5. In your spreadsheet create vertical swim lanes that correspond to your project methodology:

	A	B	C	D	E	F	G	H	I	J	K
1	Requirements		Data Discovery		Development		Testing		Promote		Production

6. Start with your **Requirements** column (**Column A** in the figure above) and include your hierarchical numbering scheme. It is important to update this document at the end of each phase. For example, when you have gathered requirements, you would include all the requirements in this matrix.

	A	B	C	D	E	F	G
				Requirements			
	Row #	Project Name	Subject Area	Category	Object Name	Sub Category	Req #
	1	Project 1	Sales	Reports	Sales Volume	Title	1
	2	Project 1	Sales	Reports	Sales Volume	Header	2
	3	Project 1	Sales	Reports	Sales Volume	Footer	3
	4	Project 1	Sales	Reports	Sales Volume	Page Items	4
	5	Project 1	Sales	Reports	Sales Volume	Page Items	5
	6	Project 1	Sales	Reports	Sales Volume	Page Items	6
	7	Project 1	Sales	Reports	Sales Volume	Calculations	7
	8	Project 1	Sales	Reports	Sales Volume	Audience	8
	9	Project 1	Sales	Reports	Sales Volume	Audience	9
	10	Project 1	Sales	Reports	Sales Volume	Audience	10
	11	Project 1	Sales	Reports	Sales Volume	Audience	11
	12	Project 1	Sales	Reports	Sales Volume	Frequency	12
	13	Project 1	Sales	Reports	Sales Volume	Security	13
	14	Project 1	Sales	Reports	Sales Volume	Security	14
	15	Project 1	Sales	Reports	Sales Volume	Security	15
	16	Project 1	Sales	Reports	Sales by Region	Title	16
	17	Project 1	Sales	Reports	Sales by Region	Header	17
	18	Project 1	Sales	Reports	Sales by Region	Footer	18
	19	Project 1	Sales	Reports	Sales by Region	Page Items	19
	20	Project 1	Sales	Reports	Sales by Region	Page Items	20
	21	Project 1	Sales	Reports	Sales by Region	Page Items	21
	22	Project 1	Sales	Reports	Sales by Region	Calculations	22
	23	Project 1	Sales	Reports	Sales by Region	Audience	23

7. The matrix can be completed as you progress through the project lifecycle:

			Requirements				Data Discovery		Development		
Row #	Project Name	Subject Area	Category	Object Name	Sub Category	Req #	Artifact	Section	Component Type	Component Name	Status
1	Project 1	Sales	Reports	Sales Volume	Title	1	Technical Solution Design	1.1.5	OBIEE Report	Sales Volume	Unit Tested
2	Project 1	Sales	Reports	Sales Volume	Header	2	Technical Solution Design	1.1.5	OBIEE Report	Sales Volume	Unit Tested
3	Project 1	Sales	Reports	Sales Volume	Footer	3	Technical Solution Design	1.1.5	OBIEE Report	Sales Volume	Unit Tested
4	Project 1	Sales	Reports	Sales Volume	Page Items	4	Technical Solution Design	1.1.5	OBIEE Report	Sales Volume	Unit Tested
5	Project 1	Sales	Reports	Sales Volume	Page Items	5	Technical Solution Design	1.1.5	OBIEE Report	Sales Volume	Unit Tested
6	Project 1	Sales	Reports	Sales Volume	Page Items	6	Technical Solution Design	1.1.5	OBIEE Report	Sales Volume	Unit Tested
7	Project 1	Sales	Reports	Sales Volume	Calculations	7	Technical Solution Design	1.1.5	OBIEE Report	Sales Volume	Unit Tested
8	Project 1	Sales	Reports	Sales Volume	Audience	8	Technical Solution Design	2.1	OBIEE Security	Sales Role	Unit Tested

How it works...

The Requirements Traceability Matrix primarily maps requirements to components which are required to be developed. The matrix also tracks the progress of these components through the project development lifecycle. It helps to ensure the requirements are included into components, developed, tested, and released. It becomes the heart of the project as it tracks each individual component of the project.

There's more...

All your requirements may not have the entire hierarchy with all columns completed. This is acceptable, but each requirement must have a unique number. Therefore, a requirement may be at the project-level or the subject area-level, and will have a unique requirement number. This is important to note for the subsequent recipes.

Looking at the Requirements Traceability Matrix can seem overwhelming. It is important to establish this document early in the project and to make it a living document, which is managed and maintained real time within your project by key team members. Team members who should be responsible for updating the document are as follows:

- **Solution Architect/Business Analyst** – This role contributes the requirements and completes the initial part of the matrix.
- **Technical Architect** – This role adds the cross relationship from the requirements to the solution design. They can also be responsible for dividing the components into releases, and scheduling the releases.
- **Business Analyst/Tester** – This role is responsible for cross referencing the requirements with use cases and test scripts. Once the component is tested within an environment, the status is updated.
- **Project Manager** – This role can fill in the final step to indicate that the information is successfully promoted and closed within the release.

Not all projects will be large enough to have dedicated team members in these positions. Multiple roles will be assigned to individuals who will be required to update the Requirements Traceability Matrix.

Oracle Application Express and a Requirements Traceability Matrix

Oracle Application Express is an application development environment, which is available as part of your Oracle database. This will need to be installed and configured. In Oracle Application Express (APEX), there is an application called **Team Development**.

This is a potential alternative to using a spreadsheet as a Requirements Traceability Matrix. This module within APEX can be used to manage the relationship between features (requirements), To Dos (project tasks), releases, and bugs.

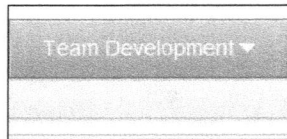

This module has basic project management, feature management, and bug tracking capabilities.

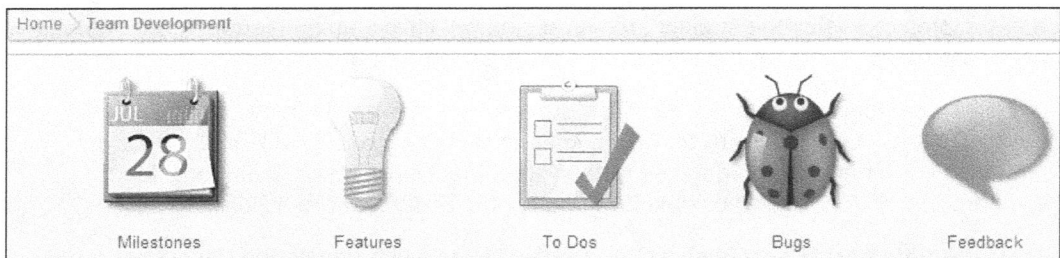

1. Click on the **Features** tab option:

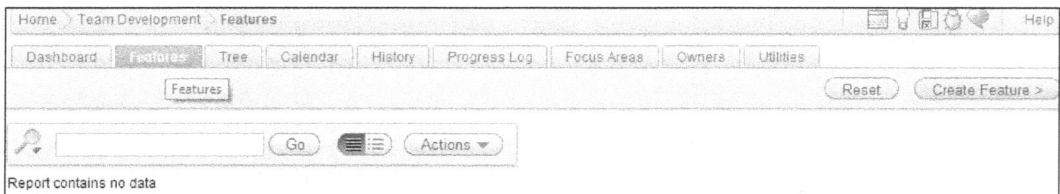

2. Click on the **Create Feature** button. From here you can enter the feature information. The following fields are similar to the columns and information in the Requirements Traceability Matrix:

   ❑ Feature is a requirement

   ❑ Focus Area is the same as the Subject Area

   ❑ Parent Feature is the main requirement

3. Features can be linked in a hierarchical relationship. So the hierarchical naming and numbering system you created will still be valid. In order to relate features together, you have to assign the features to the same release. To view the relationship, click on the **Tree** tab:

The limitation that features belong to a release, makes it a little more challenging; features can be copied if you require, keeping the same structure. A feature may need to be released numerous times through the lifecycle. Due to this limitation of the software, you would require additional features, one for each release.

4. Features also have the ability to have To Dos (tasks) associated with them. These to-dos would be all the tasks required to complete the feature.

Creating an effective risk register

Project risks are a fact of life on any software development project. The key is to identify and quantify the risks in a way that is easy to understand and communicate. A method to achieve this is FMEA—Failure Mode and Effect Analysis. A derivative of this is RFMEA—Risk Failure Mode and Effect Analysis.

Getting ready

Before starting, it is important to have a list of all the potential risks related to your project. An easy way to do this is to solicit information from all the team members and stakeholders. Do not try and categorize or justify the risk; purely collect the information and record the risk.

How to do it...

The risk register is key to the project. It is important to keep this a living document.

1. Open your Project Control Register and create a new tab called **RFMEA**:

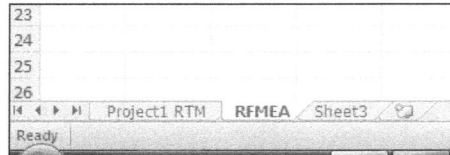

23
24
25
26

    Project1 RTM | **RFMEA** | Sheet3

    Ready

2. Create your basic headings for your **RFMEA** or Risk Log:
    a. **Risk ID** is a unique number assigned to each risk.
    b. **Risk event** is a description of the risk.
    c. **Likelihood** is the probability that the risk event will occur.
    d. **Risk score** is the calculated and determined score of the risk event.
    e. **Detection** outlines the ability to detect a particular risk event.
    f. **Risk Priority Number** (**RPN**) calculates the priority of the risk event.
    g. **Requirements #** is the unique requirement ID that the risk is related to. The Requirements # is from the Requirements Traceability Matrix.

A	B	C	D	E	F	G	H
Risk ID	Risk Event	Likelihood	Impact	Risk Score	Detection	RPN	Requirements #

3. Set up your calculations:

   a. Risk Score = `Likelihood*Impact`

   b. Risk Priority Number (RPN) = `Likelihood*Impact*Detection`

A	B	C	D	E	F	G	H
Risk ID	Risk Event	Likelihood	Impact	Risk Score	Detection	RPN	Requirements #
		10	10	100	5	500	

4. Enter your risks; the typical guidelines for values include:

   a. Likelihood:

      i. 9 or 10 – Very likely to occur

      ii. 7 or 8 – Will probably occur

      iii. 5 or 6 – Equal chance of occurring or not occurring

      iv. 3 or 4 – Probably will not occur

      v. 1 or 2 – Very unlikely

   b. Impact – if one of the below is true then the impact is:

      vi. 9 or 10

         1. Schedule – impacts delivery of related component by > 25% OR

         2. Cost – impacts cost of related component by > 25% OR

         3. Solution – renders related component unusable

      vii. 7 or 8

         1. Schedule – impacts delivery of related component between 10% and 25% OR

         2. Cost – impacts cost of related component between 10% and 25% OR

         3. Solution – changes the specification of the component which may only deliver partial requirements and may not obtain client approval

      viii. 5 or 6

         1. Schedule – impacts delivery of related component between 5% and 10% OR

         2. Cost – impacts cost of related component between 5% and 10% OR

         3. Solution – changes the specification of the component which may only deliver partial/all requirements but will meet with client approval

ix. 3 or 4

1. Schedule – impacts delivery of related component by < 5% OR

2. Cost – impacts cost of related component by < 5% OR

3. Solution – changes the specification of the component and the original scope of work and may require internal or client approval

x. 1 or 2 - Very unlikely

1. Schedule – impact insignificant and can be absorbed OR

2. Cost – cost increase inconsequential or can be contained within current budget OR

3. Solution – changes are not noticeable

c. Detection

xi. 9 or 10 –Cannot be detected or forewarned, therefore no contingency can be included

xii. 7 or 8 – Detection method is available but not proven very difficult to identify and react within sufficient time

xiii. 5 or 6 - Detection method is identified and has been used in the past with mixed success

xiv. 3 or 4 - Detection method is well known and a moderate degree of effectiveness

xv. 1 or 2 - Detection method is well known and has been very successful in the past

5. Enhance you risk register to include your strategy to deal with risk. Some common strategies include:

- ❑ **Avoidance**: eliminate, withdraw from, or not become involved with

- ❑ **Reduction**: optimize, mitigate

- ❑ **Sharing**: transfer, outsource, or insure

- ❑ **Retention**: accept and budget

A	B	C	D	E	F	G	H	I	J	K
Risk ID	Risk Event	Likelihood	Impact	Risk Score	Detection	RPN	Requirements #	Strategy	Outline	Issue ID
						0				

6. Monitor your risks frequently and assign an issue ID should a risk be realized. Additional columns which are useful to include to effectively manage the risk are as follows:

- ❑ **Risk Owner**: The person who owns the risk.

- ❏ **Mitigation actions**: Actions that can be taken to reduce the risk.
- ❏ **Date actions due**: When the actions are due by.
- ❏ **Date risk was last reviewed**.
- ❏ **Risk status**: The status of the risk. (New, Escalated to Issue, In Progress, Closed).

How it works...

The risk register exists to give you a forewarning of the events that can affect your project and strategy, should they occur. If a risk is realized, then this should be opened as an issue and managed accordingly.

There's more...

This book does not go into detail about RFMEA; there is a good white paper from the *Engineering Management Journal* namely:

Page 28 – 35, Engineering Management Journal Vol. 16 No. 4 December 2004 Project Risk Management Using the Project Risk FMEA, by Thomas A. Carbone, Fairchild Semiconductor Corporation and Donald D. Tippett, The University of Alabama in Huntsville.

Creating an effective issue management register

The issue register is an effective tool within a project, if your issues can be identified and quantified. Issues should, in an ideal world, only come from your risk register; however, this is not always true. Therefore, it is important to review and record issues as they arise.

Getting ready

Before starting, it is important to understand that issues can occur anywhere within the project. Therefore, it is important to allow all the team members to raise issues within the project and provide periodic feedback.

How to do it...

Open the Project Control Register:

1. Open your Requirements Traceability Matrix and create a new tab called **Issues**:

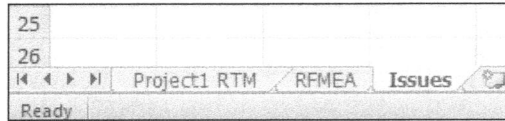

25			
26			

⏮ ◀ ▶ ⏭ | Project1 RTM / RFMEA | **Issues**

Ready

2. Identify the key information to record for all issues:

   ❑ **Issue ID**: A unique ID assigned to the issue

   ❑ **Risk ID**: The associated Risk ID the issue is related to

   ❑ **Requirements #**: The associated requirement # for the issue

   ❑ **Decision/Action/Note**: The decisions, actions, or notes for the issue

   ❑ **Status**: The status of the issue

   ❑ **Description**: The description of the issue

   ❑ **Assigned To**: The individual that the issue is assigned to

   ❑ **Start Date**: The date the issue was raised

   ❑ **Planned End Date**: The date the issue is expected to be resolved

   ❑ **Comments**: Any additional information for the issue

A	B	C	D	E	F	G	H	I	J	K
			Decision /Action / Note	Status: Open Closed Pending	Priority (High, Medium, Low)	Description	Assigned To	Start Date	Planned End Date	Comments
Issue ID	Risk ID	Requirement #								

3. For issues, it is important to have a very simple priority mechanism. Typical values for this include:

   ❑ Priority:

      i. Critical – should only be used when this causes a stoppage to activities on the project.

      ii. High – realized risk or new issue that will have significant impact on the project if not solved.

      iii. Medium – realized risk or new issue that will have moderate impact on the project if not solved.

      iv. Low – realized risk or new issue that will have low impact on the project if not solved.

How it works...

Issues on a project are events which are required to be scheduled and actioned for work. If an issue does not directly affect the schedule in the short or medium term, cost, or solution, then it is not an issue and needs to be migrated to the risk register.

There's more...

Projects often confuse issues and risks. This causes projects to focus a lot of time and energy trying to resolve issues, which do not exist or have not been realized. Therefore, you need to immediately differentiate between issues and risks. Risks are events which may occur and affect your project; issues are risks which have occurred, or other events, which have taken place in your project. Issues impact the project; risks may impact the project.

Creating a defect and enhancement register

During testing, you will uncover defects and enhancements. These need to be recorded and prioritized so that they can be included into the work schedule and fixed.

Getting ready

Identify the defects which have been uncovered, and to which requirements they relate.

How to do it...

A Project Control Register enables you to track all your issues, defects, and enhancements in one location. This creates a centralized location for this information, reducing the risk of missing or forgetting issues.

1. Open the **Project Control Register**.
2. Create a new tab called **Defect & Enhancement**:

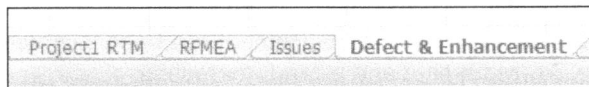

| Project1 RTM | RFMEA | Issues | Defect & Enhancement |

3. Identify the key information to record for all defects or enhancements:
    - ❑ **#**: This is the defect or enhancement number
    - ❑ **Type**: This determines whether this is a defect or enhancement
    - ❑ **Test Script**: This contains the test script which uncovered the issue
    - ❑ **Requirement #** : This is the associated requirement

- **Date**: This contains the date when the defect or enhancement was raised
- **Priority**: This is the priority for the defect or enhancement
- **Status**: This is the status of the defect or enhancement
- **Description**: This is an outline of the defect or enhancement
- **Test Release**: This is the release in which the defect or enhancement was found
- **Schedule Date**: This is the date the defect or enhancement is scheduled to be completed
- **Prod Release**: This is the production release the defect or enhancement will be included into

A	B	C	D	E	F	G	H	I	J	K
#	Type	Test Script	Requirement #	Date	Priority	Status	Description	Test Release	Schedule Date	Prod Release

4. Define your domains for **Priority** and **Status**. Typical values for this include:

- **Priority**
  - **Critical**: Should only be used when this causes a stoppage to activities on the project
  - **High**: Realized risk or new issue that will have significant impact on the project if not solved
  - **Medium**: Realized risk or new issue that will have moderate impact on the project if not solved
  - **Low**: Realized risk or new issue that will have low impact on the project if not solved

- **Status**
  - **New**: New defect or enhancement. No action taken
  - **Open**: Defect or enhancement is being worked on
  - **Test Migrate**: Defect or enhancement is completed and ready for migration to test environment
  - **Test**: Defect or enhancement has been migrated to a test environment and is ready for testing
  - **Prod Migrate**: Defect or enhancement has passed testing and is ready for migration to production
  - **Prod Sign Off**: Defect or enhancement passed testing in production and is ready to be closed
  - **Closed**: Defect or enhancement is resolved
  - **Re-Open**: Defect or enhancement does not pass testing and requires additional work

How it works...

Defects should be estimated within a project and prioritized as a team. Once prioritized, these can be scheduled and assigned to be completed. Having an understanding of the defects and enhancements will give the project an insight into the amount of additional work that is necessary to complete the project.

There's more...

Enhancements are a little different from defects. While defects are against existing requirements, enhancements can be entirely new requirements. For enhancements or changes to existing requirements, it is recommended that additional information is gathered. Additional information would outline how to reproduce defects, and the desired outcome. Enhancements should include sufficient information to be able to understand the requirement and the impact to the project. The Requirements Traceability Matrix should be updated, and the new requirements should be included to facilitate tracking and identify any other artifacts/ documents that require updating.

Oracle Application Express and bug tracking

In team development, there is a bug tracking module:

1. Click on the **Bugs** option.

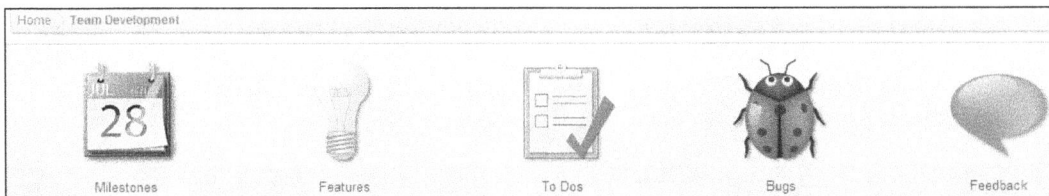

2. This is a bug dashboard that shows **Percent Closed**, **Assigned Developers**, **Severity**, and **Status**:

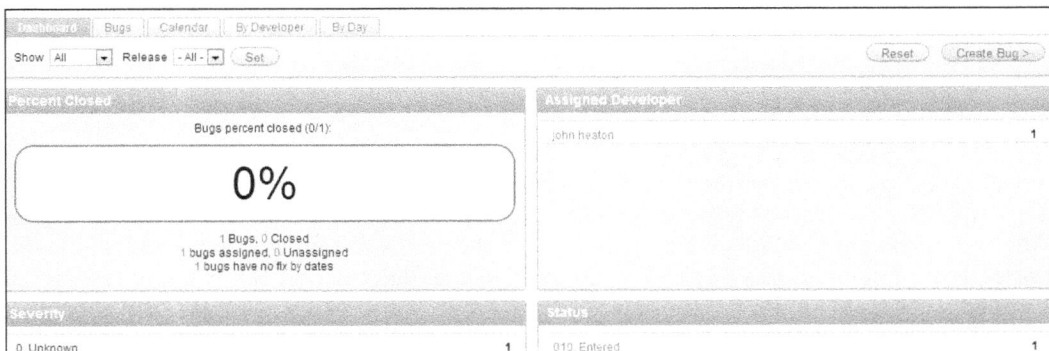

3. Click on the **Create Bug** button:

| Show All | Bug | Resolution | Description | Application Context | Context | Impact | Customer |

Bug

# Bug	
Status	10. Entered ▾
Severity	0. Unknown ▾
Priority	4. Not prioritized ▾

Resolution

Assigned To	- Select Assignee - ▾	New Assignee	
Fix By Release	- Select Release - ▾	New Release	
Target Milestone	- Select Milestone - ▾		
Estimated Fix Date			
Actual Fix Date			
Duplicate of Bug			

Description

Bug Description

You can add information to the bug, and assign the bug to a feature. You can assign this to a release. **Status**, **Severity**, and **Priority** are all pre-defined by the application.

Creating a cyclical build and test process

Defects and enhancements are required to be placed into releases and environments. To enable this, a cyclical build and test process is required.

Getting ready

Before starting, it is important to determine how often you require builds. The builds should be frequent enough to show progress, but not so frequent that they add unnecessary overhead to the project. To start with, a frequency of once a week should be sufficient. You can increase or decrease your build cycle as required. It is important to get into the build cycle directly from the start of the project. Releases into the test environment can be more frequent than releases into production. This enables components, defects, and enhancements to be reviewed more regularly. Production releases are a culmination of test releases, and should be on a scheduled basis so that stakeholders are aware and expecting releases.

How to do it...

1. Open the Project Control Register.

2. Go to the **RTM** tab and ensure all the requirements are allocated to a release and a release date.

Development			Promote				Testing			Production		
Component Type	Component Name	Status	Environment	Release Number	Status	Date	Use Case	Test Script	Status	Release Number	Status	Date
OBIEE Report	Sales Volume	Unit Tested	Test	1.0.1	Complete	14/10/2011	1.0	1	Passed	1.0	Scheduled	28/10/2011
OBIEE Report	Sales Volume	Unit Tested	Test	1.0.1	Complete	14/10/2011	1.0	1	Passed	1.0	Scheduled	28/10/2011
OBIEE Report	Sales Volume	Unit Tested	Test	1.0.1	Complete	14/10/2011	1.0	1	Passed	1.0	Scheduled	28/10/2011
OBIEE Report	Sales Volume	Unit Tested	Test	1.0.1	Complete	14/10/2011	1.0	1	Passed	1.0	Scheduled	28/10/2011
OBIEE Report	Sales Volume	Unit Tested	Test	1.0.1	Complete	14/10/2011	1.0	1	Passed	1.0	Scheduled	28/10/2011
OBIEE Report	Sales Volume	Unit Tested	Test	1.0.1	Complete	14/10/2011	1.0	1	Failed	1.0	Scheduled	28/10/2011

3. Open the **Defect & Enhancement** tab. Ensure all the defects have a release date.

4. Group the requirements and defects and enhancements into a release package.

5. Prepare a release note for the release. In the release note you should have the following:

   ❑ Environment

   ❑ Release Number

   ❑ Requirements included in the release

   ❑ Defects included in the release

   ❑ Enhancements included in the release

   ❑ Requirements which did not make the release

   ❑ Defects which did not make the release

   ❑ Enhancements which did not make the release

6. Remember to update the status of the requirements and defects/enhancements to the appropriate statuses, before and after the release.

How it works...

By creating a cyclical release pattern, you enable the project team to validate requirements as you move through the lifecycle of the project. This allows for a defined rhythm when new information and fixed defects are available. Understanding how to maintain and manage business intelligence and data warehouse solution is as important as creating the application.

There's more...

Each product has the capability to migrate code from one environment to another. Some of these utilities can be very rudimentary. It is important to understand the capabilities of each product, so that you can build an effective release management process.

Setting up a collaborative environment

A business intelligence and data warehouse project has multiple software products. None of these products operates or produces the same collateral. In order to do this, you need to create an environment where you can check code in and out, as information is updated. Version control tools can be used to track changes to code, or to enable collaboration. A lot of information is contained on individual workstations. By setting up a version control environment, information can be shared and stored centrally, and versioned.

Getting ready

Choosing a version control tool is not easy. Some of the main contenders are:

- Subversion
    - VisualSVN Server Standard Edition is available at low cost or no cost
    - Collabnet
    - Subversion Edge is another server product available at low or no cost

- Perforce

Both of these are viable as there is some level of integration into Oracle toolsets. Subversion is the general tool of choice. These tools require a server version installed, so that developers can connect and check their code in and out. For this recipe, we will use VisualSVN Server Standard Edition to set up a collaborative environment.

How to do it...

The standard edition of VisualSVN can be downloaded from: `http://www.visualsvn.com/server/download/`.

1. Download the software from the website and start the installation by double-clicking on the `MSI` package; the installation wizard will start.

2. Click on the **Next** button:

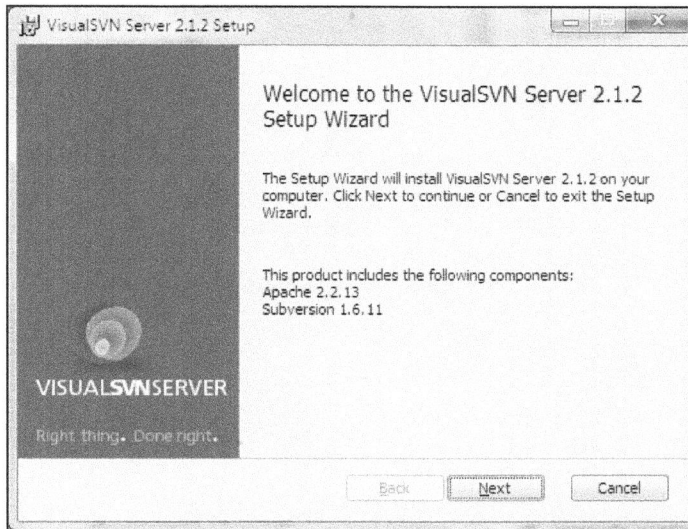

3. Accept the software license, and click on the **Next** button:

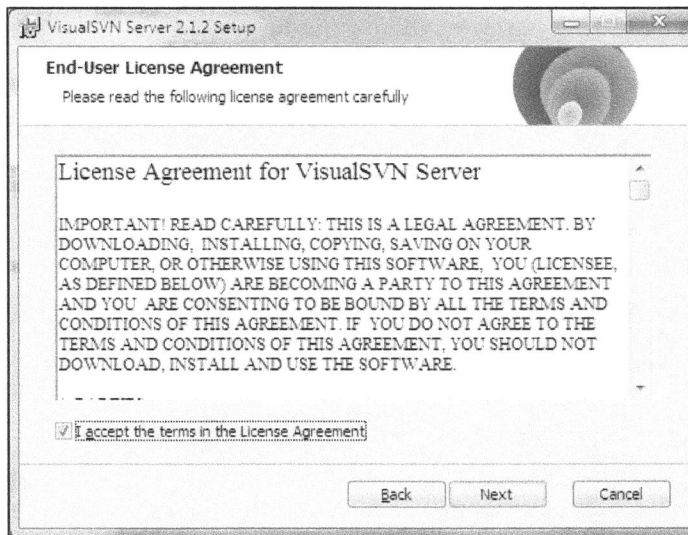

4. Select **VisualSVN Server and Management Console**, and click on the **Next** button:

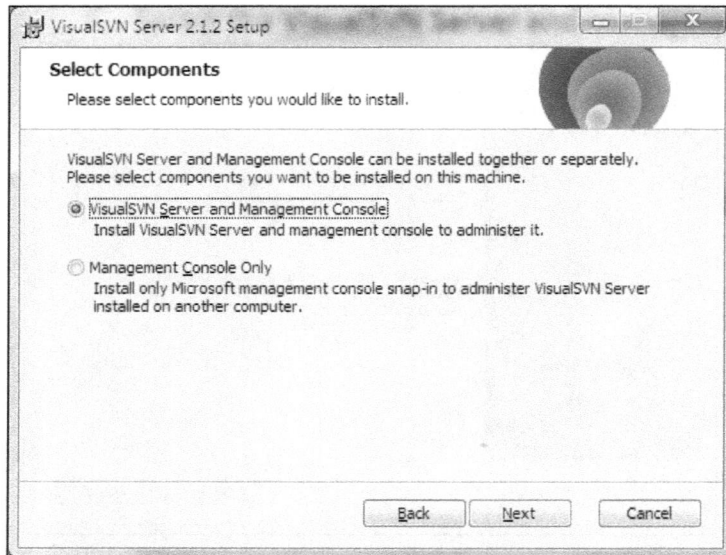

5. Select the default location for the installation file and SVN Repository.

6. Select **Use Windows authentication** for **Authentication**, and click on the **Next** button:

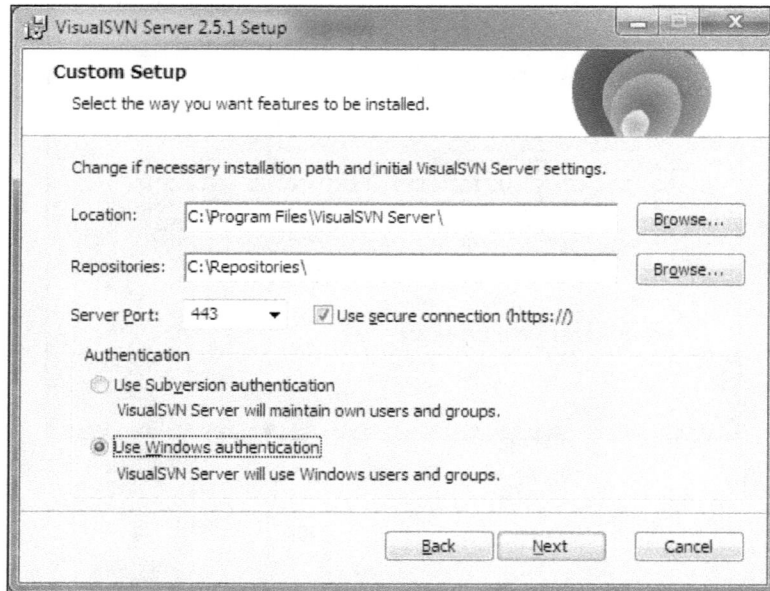

7. Select **Install** to start the installation:

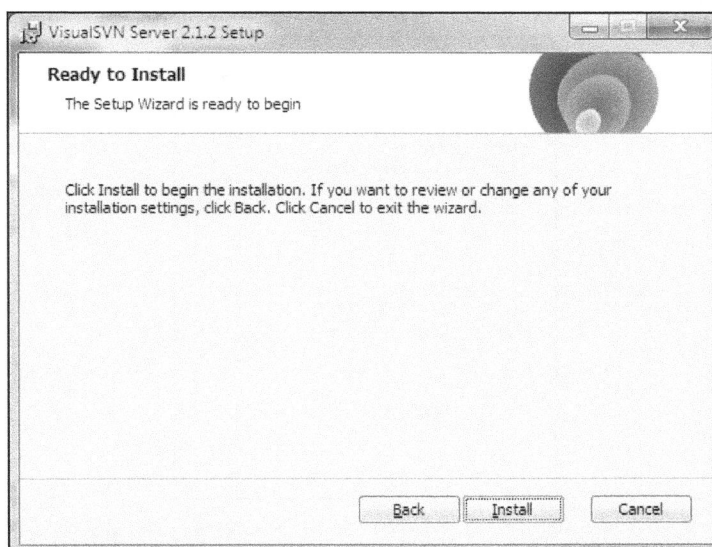

8. Upon completion, select the **Start VisualSVN Server Manager** option, and click on the **Finish** button:

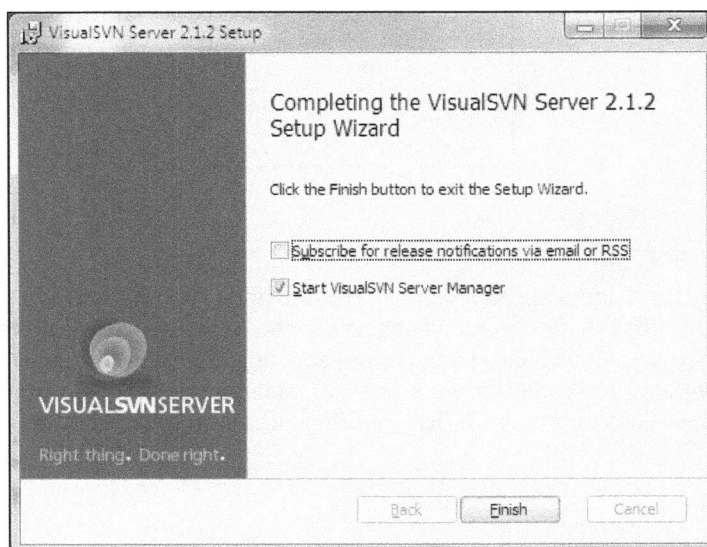

9. Start the VisualSVN Server Manager from the Start menu—**Start** | **Programs** | **VisualSVN** | **VisualSVN Server Manager**.

10. Create a new repository. Right-click and select **Create New Repository**, and enter the `Repository` name. For example: `Code Repository`.

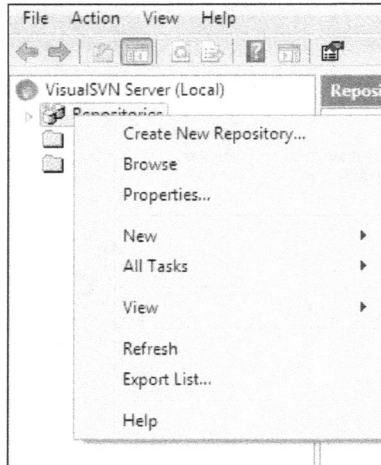

11. Create the target folders for code. For example, **Development**, **Test**, and **Production**. Right-click on the repository and select **New | Folder**.

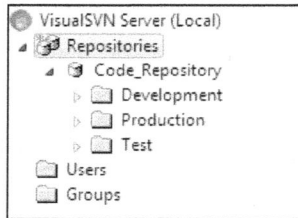

How it works...

By installing a Version Control server, you have created an environment where you can share code and information. Information such as scripts, code snippets, exports from tools, and documentation can all be shared and controlled using a Version Control environment. Using this environment, you would create additional folders under each environment that corresponds to the release numbers within your Requirements Traceability Matrix.

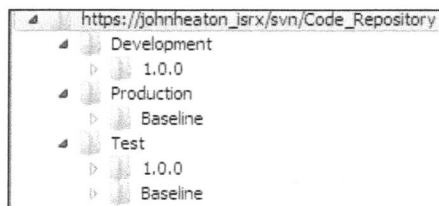

Installing client tools for a collaborative environment

To collaborate within a development environment, a Version Control server and client tools are required. The **server** stores all the code, and allows developers to check a code in and out. The **client tools** enable the developers to interact with the server from their workstations.

Getting ready

In order to upload information into the environment, you will need a client tool. For this, Tortoise is the most well-known. A download is available from the website in either 32-bit or 64-bit—http://www.tortoisesvn.net.

How to do it...

The download will create an MSI file. This is a Microsoft package file, which when executed will install the software. Once Tortoise has been installed, it will require a reboot.

1. Double-click on the MSI package to start the installation.

2. Accept the license agreement to continue:

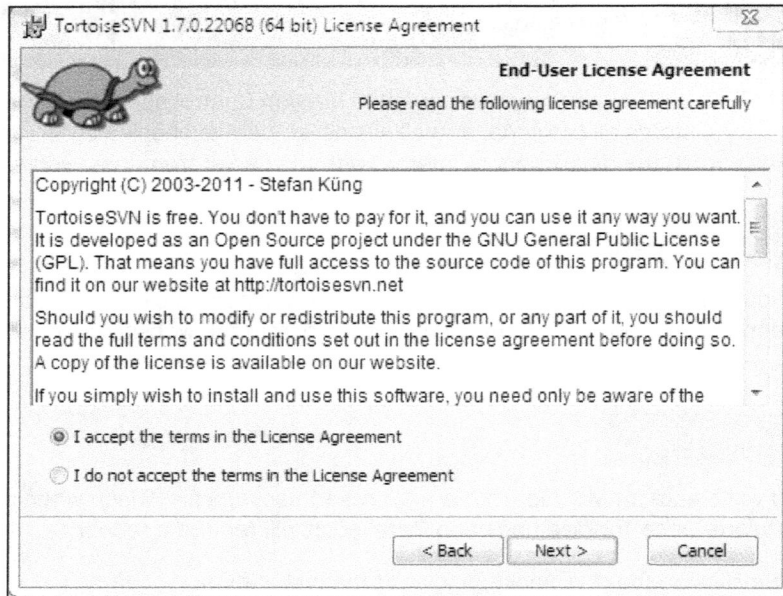

3. Select the default configuration to install:

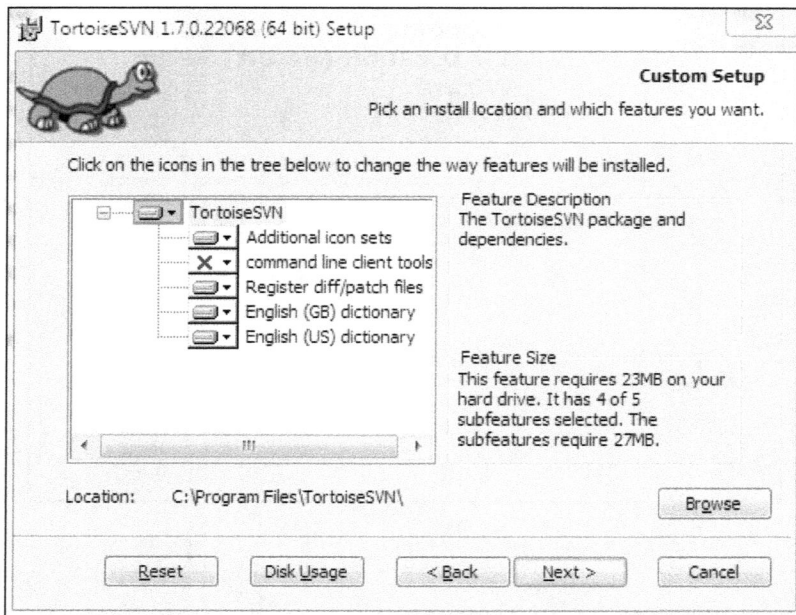

4. Click on the **Install** button to begin the installation:

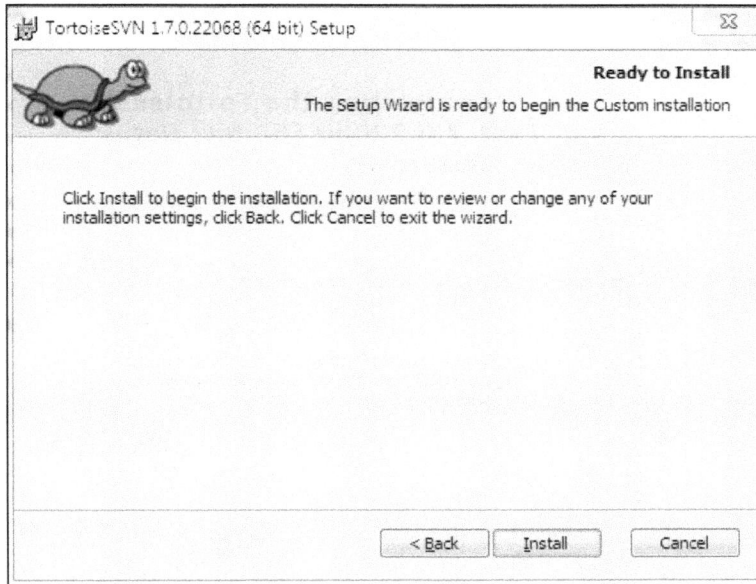

5. The installation begins as shown in the following screenshot. This process may take several minutes.

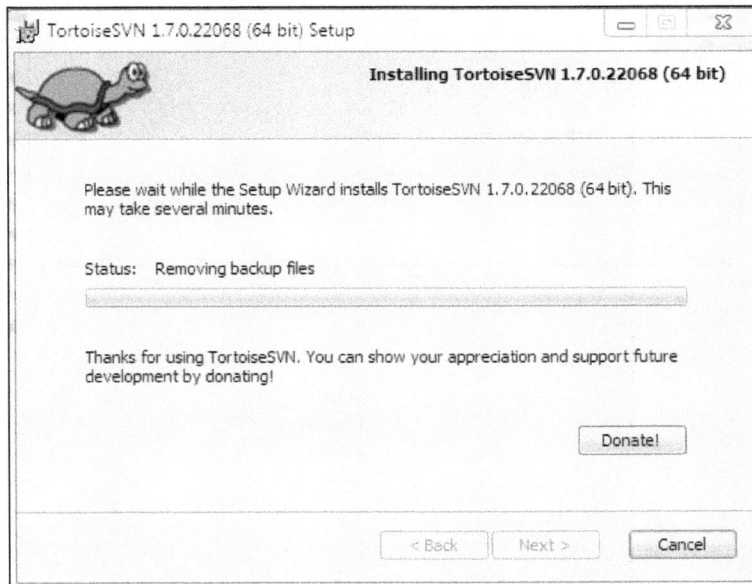

6. Once complete, click on the **Finish** button:

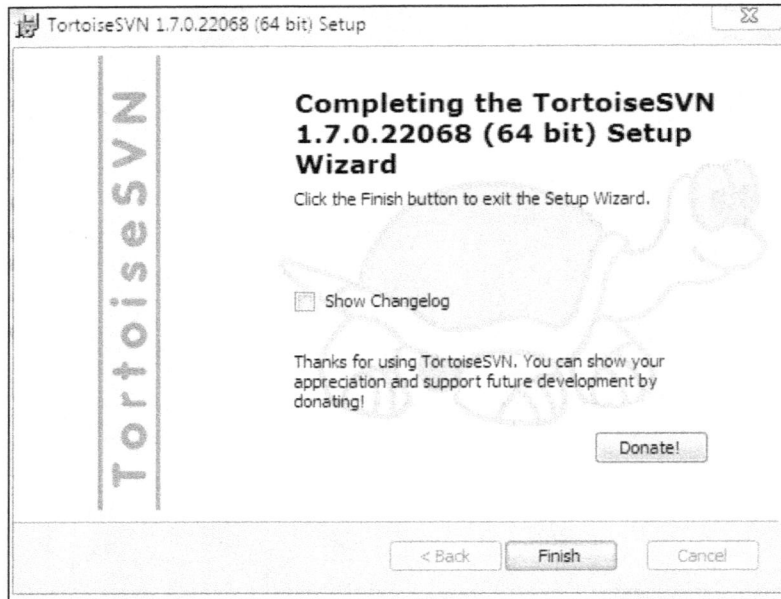

7. In **Windows Explorer**, if you right-click within your folders, you will get your Subversion menu. Select **Repo-browser** to connect to your SVN Repository.

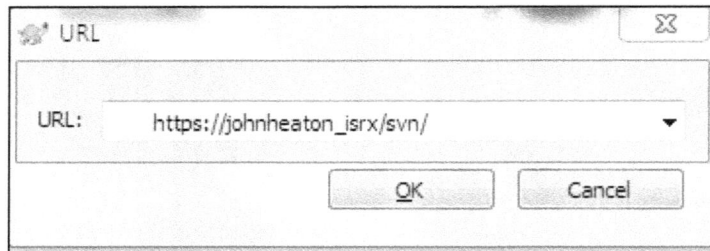

How it works...

Storing code and information within Subversion allows developers to share information and version code, to maintain the most up-to-date information.

The following are a few Subversion tips:

- ▸ **Check out**: This creates a local version of the information on your hard drive
- ▸ **Add**: This adds a file or folder
- ▸ **Update**: This resyncs your copy of information with the server copy of information
- ▸ **Commit**: This saves your copy of information to the server

As a best practice, since multiple developers will be using the repository simultaneously, it is always recommended to update your copy before you continue to work.

Business intelligence and data warehouse projects involve a lot of artifacts. Understanding these artifacts you are creating using the RTM, and having a collaborative environment to work in, makes managing the project a lot easier.

4
Wrapping Up the Project

Upon completion of the business intelligence and data warehouse project, it is important to realize that these projects will continually grow and be enhanced. For this reason, it is essential that key information is handed over, so that it can be effectively maintained during the lifecycle. Understanding this early in the project will allow you to identify the required information and ensure it is ready upon hand over. The recipes include:

- Creating OWB code artifacts
- Creating OBIEE code artifacts
- Creating APEX code artifacts
- Creating ODI code artifacts
- Creating Script artifacts
- Building a continuous development capability for enhancements
- Creating a constant feedback and communications loop

Introduction

Business intelligence and data warehouse projects have a lot of information and artifacts, once the project wraps up. It is important to identify which of these need to be transferred to production support and which can be archived. Most of the documentation that was used and useful during the project should not be transferred. The key documents and information that should be transferred are as follows:

1. Business information, such as:
   - Project Charter
   - Metadata and Conceptual Data Model
   - Frequently asked questions (derived from defect and enhancement register)

2. Technical information, such as:

   ❑ Technical architecture overview and design

   ❑ Design standards

   ❑ Security overview

   ❑ Runbook for ETL

   ❑ Data lineage from report to source data

   ❑ Software support manual

   ❑ Code repository

Creating OWB code artifacts

Code artifacts are normally time consuming and difficult to obtain. Oracle Warehouse Builder is no exception to this rule.

Getting ready

Subversion is an ideal place to store this kind of information. It is important to have a standard naming convention for where and how the code resides within Subversion. All incremental releases within the development environment and test environments are no longer important, when you hand over the code. It is important to have a single baseline of the code, in order to effectively hand over the environment.

How to do it...

Subversion is ideal to track code and changes to code. In order to do this effectively, code should be checked in at a level of granularity that will allow you to manage individual objects as follows:

1. Create a folder that relates to the target environment, say **Production**, as shown in the following screenshot:

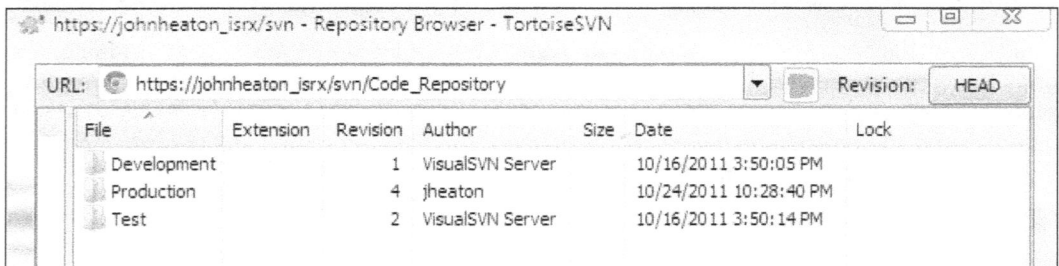

File	Extension	Revision	Author	Size	Date	Lock
Development		1	VisualSVN Server		10/16/2011 3:50:05 PM	
Production		4	jheaton		10/24/2011 10:28:40 PM	
Test		2	VisualSVN Server		10/16/2011 3:50:14 PM	

2. Create a subfolder named **OWB** for the technology component under **Baseline** within the **Production** folder, as shown in the following screenshot:

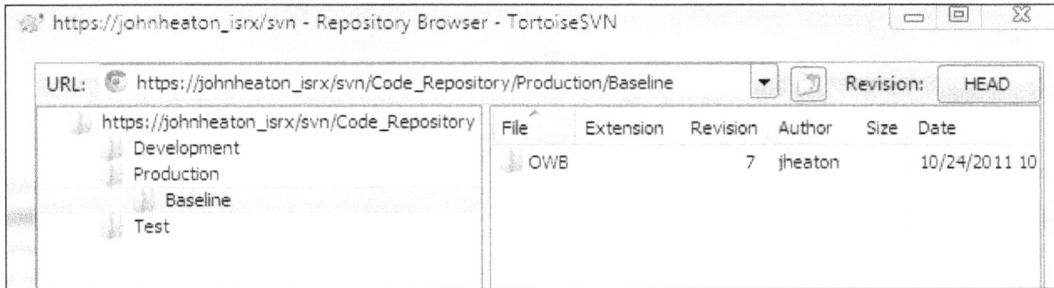

3. Export the OWB code using OWB Design Center, OMBPlus Scripts, or another tool. Each object should be an individual export file. Refer to Oracle documentation for OMBPlus or OWB Design Center to achieve this, should you not be familiar with the steps available at `http://docs.oracle.com`.

4. Place the exports into separate subfolders depending on the object type. Add the file and folder artifacts to Subversion by right-clicking and selecting **Add File** or **Add Folder**. Browse and select the relevant files or folders. OWB can export into a text or binary (zipped) format. Depending on the export method, you can chose whichever is more appropriate for your environment, as shown in the following screenshot:

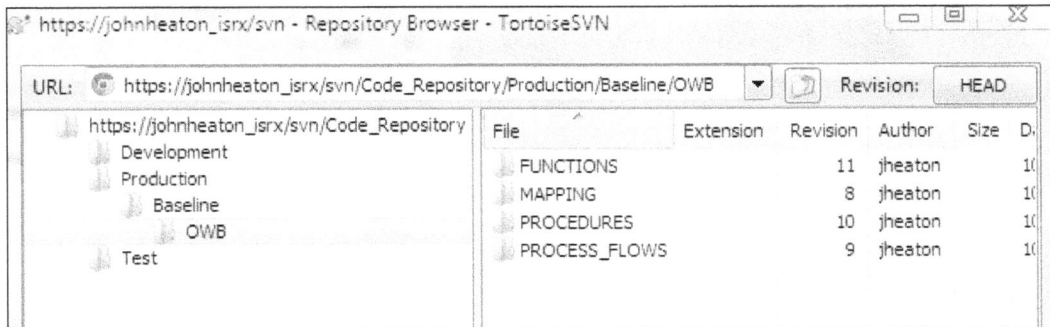

5. Export the location information by logging into SQL Developer as OWBSYS and executing the following SQL statement. Once executed, export the information and save as an Excel file or into a password program, for example, KeePass. Complete the information with all the connection information and passwords, as follows:

```
Worksheet     Query Builder
select WORKSPACE_NAME, WORKSPACE_OWNER  from ALL_IV_WORKSPACES
/

begin
  -- Use WORKSPACE_NAME, WORKSPACE_OWNER FROM Query Above
  WB_WORKSPACE_MANAGEMENT.SET_WORKSPACE('p_workspace_name', 'p_workspace_owner');
end;
/

select LOCATION_NAME, LOCATION_TYPE, LOCATION_TYPE_VERSION from ALL_RT_LOCATIONS
/
```

How it works...

Once you have set up your structure in Subversion, you can export the code within OWB. Once exported, you can check the code into Subversion under the relevant folders.

By creating a baseline of code when you hand over the project, it simplifies the questions about the code repository. Baseline is a culmination of all releases that were used to build the production environment. It is recommended that code from OWB be exported at an object level. This makes it easier to manage changes in the future.

There's more...

Multiple OMBPlus scripts or tools, for example, iSeerix Release Manager and AntHill Pro, exist to help in release management for OWB. These tools can be invaluable and time saving.

The baseline should be maintained with the latest code from the initial release and then all subsequent releases. By exporting information at the object level, you have the ability to replace individual components over time.

Creating OBIEE code artifacts

Oracle Business Intelligence Enterprise Edition currently has minimal support for lifecycle or release management. This limited support makes moving code from environment to environment challenging.

Getting ready

OBIEE is easier to migrate and manage as an entire code base. There are several files that you need, depending on your implementation. Before you start, you will need to know the answers to a few questions, as follows:

1. Have we used or are we planning to use the multi-language capabilities of OBIEE?
2. Do we require column headings to change depending on certain criteria or language?
3. Are we planning to externalise the column names and store them in the database?
4. Have we configured security to integrate into a provider other than the default?

How to do it...

OBIEE is mainly file-based. It is important to check the files you require in Subversion. The folder structure of OBIEE is very deep. A configuration file is a good idea to identify where files should be located within the target system, instead of mirroring the deep folder structure.

1. Open your Subversion code repository, and under the **Baseline** folder, create a folder named **OBIEE**, as shown in the following screenshot:

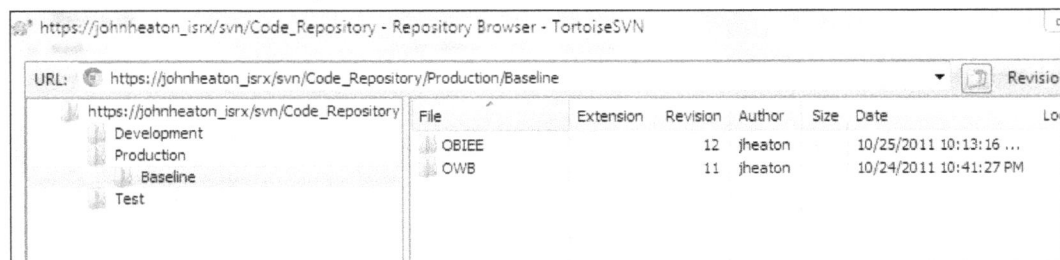

2. Under **OBIEE**, create relevant folders to store different artifacts, as shown in the following screenshot:

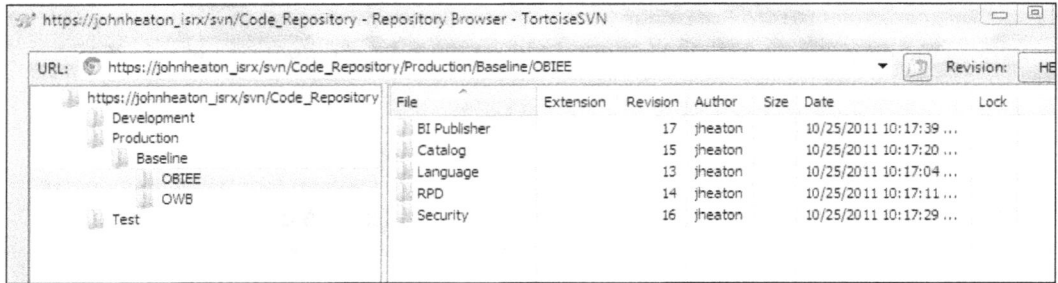

3. Copy the code artifacts from the server, and check them in Subversion. Add the file and folder artifacts to Subversion by right-clicking and selecting **Add File** or **Add Folder**. Browse and select the relevant files or folders. Some common artifacts are as follows:

- Language files and folders
- Catalog
- RPD
- Security
- Instance settings
- Images
- Skins
- BI Publisher

How it works...

OBIEE is a manual process to collect and check code into a version control repository such as Subversion. OBIEE has a few command-line capabilities to support release management. It is important to place this code into such a repository that it can be useful for restoring an environment or creating a new environment. Note that if you are copying your RPD from environment to environment, it is important to remember that the password will be the same across environments.

Creating APEX code artifacts

Oracle Application Express is a good product to develop quick interfaces. In a business intelligence and data warehousing solution, this can be valuable to capture missing information or enhance business processes.

Getting ready

Oracle Application Express provides an export utility through the frontend, which creates an SQL script file. This script file can be used to install an APEX application within a new environment.

How to do it...

Open Oracle Application Express and perform the following steps:

1. Navigate to Oracle Application Express Application Builder, normally at `http://machine_name:port/apex`, and log in using an administrator account, as shown in the following screenshot:

2. Export the application by choosing the necessary options. Note the DOS or UNIX file format. Use the appropriate file format for the environment. When saving the file, use the name for the application without spaces, as follows:

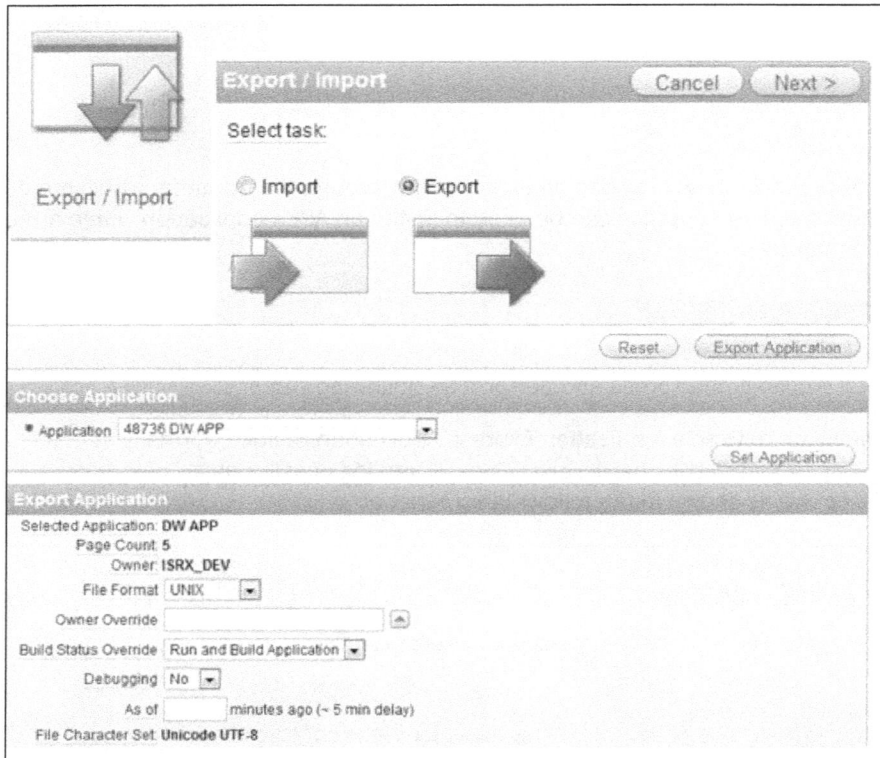

3. In Subversion, create a folder under **Baseline**, named **APEX**, as shown in the following screenshot:

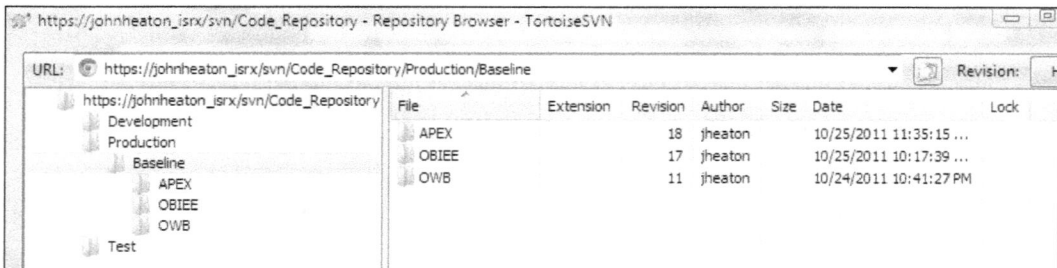

4. Add the file to the **APEX** folder by right-clicking and selecting **Add File** to the folder.

How it works...

APEX applications, when exported, are a single SQL script file. This file contains the complete GUI required for the application. Dependant objects can also be included in the script. However, for tables, views, sequences, and other database objects, you may wish to maintain these separately.

There's more...

Importing APEX SQL scripts can be done in the following ways:

- ▶ Using the Web Application Builder
- ▶ Using the SQL Developer APEX Import function
- ▶ Using SQL Developer, perform the following steps:
  - ❏ Log on as the schema owner of the objects for the application.
  - ❏ Execute the following syntax:

    ```
    ALTER SESSION SET CURRENT_SCHEMA = APEX_040000;
    ```

  - ❏ Right-click on the **Application Express** option in the navigation panel, and follow the export wizard. Release Management tools integrated into APEX.

Creating ODI code artifacts

Oracle Data Integrator is very complicated, when it comes to exporting and importing code. Suffice it to say that there is much collateral on how to export and import master and work repositories.

Getting ready

Before starting, it is important to understand ODI issues with exporting and importing objects. The typical files to be exported and imported are as follows:

- ▶ Topology
- ▶ Logical topology
- ▶ Context
- ▶ Agent
- ▶ Scenario

How to do it...

Open Oracle Data Integrator and perform the following steps:

1. Select **Export** or **Export Multiple**, from the **Designer, Topology, Security,** or **Operator Navigator** toolbar menus.

2. Once the files have been exported, use Subversion to create an ODI folder and check the code in ZIP or XML files into the relevant folder.

How it works...

Defects should be estimated within a project and prioritized as a team. Once prioritized, these can be scheduled and assigned to be completed. Having an understanding of the defects and enhancements will give the project an insight into the amount of additional work that is necessary to complete the project.

There's more...

Oracle Data Integrator Export and Import is further explained in *Chapter 20, Exporting/ Importing,* in section 20.2.7 of *Oracle® Fusion Middleware Developer's Guide for Oracle Data Integrator 11g Release 1 (11.1.1).*

In the latest release of ODI, it does include Smart Import and Export to help with object dependencies.

Creating script artifacts

Scripts are common within business intelligence and data warehouse projects. Script files are used for tables, functions, procedures, packages, sequences, grants, views, data, and much more.

Getting ready

Gather the scripts into a central location to begin sorting.

How to do it...

1. Sort the scripts. The ones that have been used once and are not needed again, and the ones that are required to rebuild the environment. One-off scripts should be included into the release but not necessarily into the baseline.

2. Ensure the scripts are named correctly and checked into Subversion under the relevant folder.

How it works...

Scripts are the final set of objects required for your environment. By identifying all the objects, you should have a complete baseline to recreate your environment.

Building a continuous development capability for enhancements

Once all your code is checked into a single environment in a single location, it becomes more manageable to maintain. Each release from this point onwards should be created in a separate folder uniquely named for the release. Once the release has been successful, it should be merged into the baseline.

Getting ready

Understand the export and import capabilities of the products that are present within your business intelligence and data warehouse environments. By identifying the objects that are required to be handed over at the end of the project, it is an easier target to work towards, during the project.

How to do it...

In order to develop a continuous development capability, it is important to define the process:

1. For all changes raised on the project (by an enhancement, bug, or change request), you need to identify the impact on the artifacts in the Requirements Traceability Matrix. Under the **Development** branch of your code, create a new **Release** folder. The folder will become the centralized source for the code release, as follows:

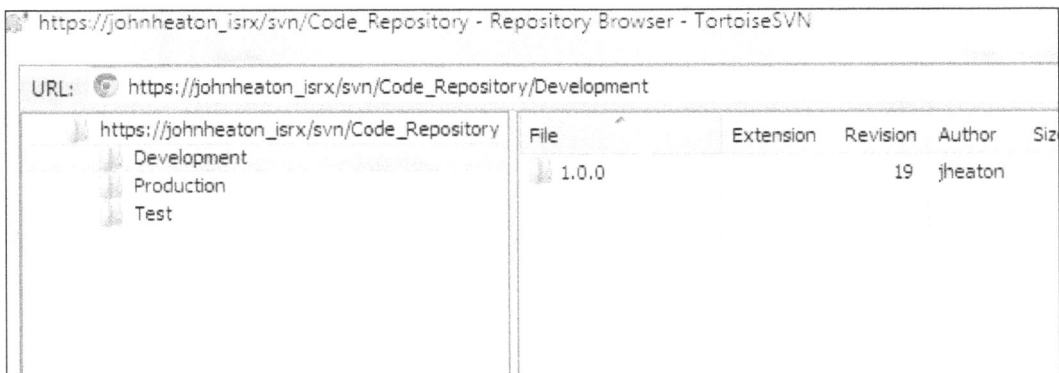

2. Identify all the changes for **Release**, and add the technology component folders under **Release**, as shown in the following screenshot:

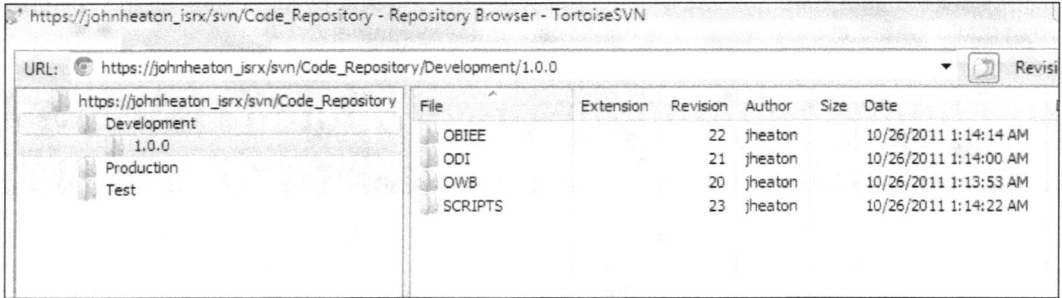

3. Build your code release by exporting the code. This creates a copy of the code, and then development work can continue if necessary.

4. Version the code by checking the code into Subversion, as follows:

5. Once the code is imported into Subversion, it is important to create a RunBook for the code. The RunBook outlines the code and how to install the code into the new environment, in the sequence required, as follows:

Seq	Name	Execute	Credentials	Status
1	external_dir.sql	sqlplus	User – staging	Built
			Database – Test	
2	user_roles.sql	sqlplus	User – staging	Built
			Database – Test	
3	fine_grain_sec.sql	sqlplus	User – staging	Built
			Database – Test	

6. Deploy the code into the target environment by following the RunBook. Once completed, update the RunBook if successful. Upon success, copy the code release into the target environment, as follows:

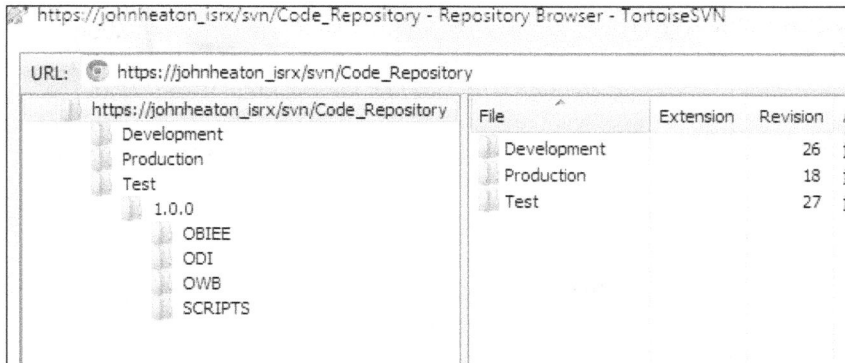

7. Upon successful deployment, merge the code into the baseline. The code is exported at the object level. The baseline should be a merger of all the releases. The baseline contains the most recent versions of all the objects. Subversion enables you to see the history and different versions of the components that you need to rollback to a previous version, as follows:

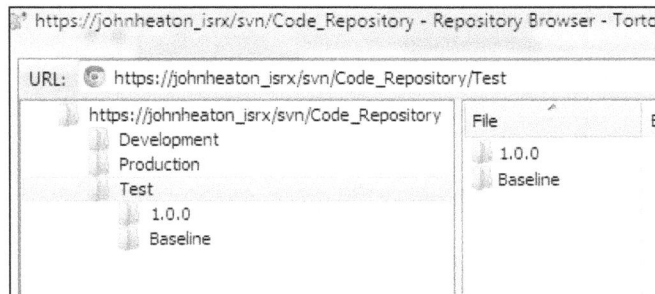

How it works...

Creating a continuous development process allows one to continuously develop and deploy code into different environments. The identify, build, version, and deploy process is an effective lifecycle management process for Oracle technology. Oracle does not have a comprehensive solution for lifecycle management across the tool range. Therefore, an effective process will add some discipline and enable you to have a repeatable process.

Creating a constant feedback and communications loop

In a business intelligence and data warehouse project, there is much information that is lost in an e-mail. A more appropriate mechanism for sharing information is required. Wikis such as XWiki can sometimes be a good solution. The overhead to maintain these should be reviewed and understood, to ensure these solutions are efficient and effective. Corporate portal solutions to share information may just be as appropriate, for example, Microsoft Sharepoint.

Getting ready

Review your project requirements for information sharing. Wiki could be a short-term or long-term solution. The document sharing solutions still do not effectively share information but rather documents.

How to do it...

1. Download a Wiki at `http://www.xwiki.org`.

2. Copy the expanded Tomcat to the following directory in the Middleware Windows Server:

   `C:\Apache\apache-tomcat-7.0.6`

3. Copy the expanded WAR file to:

   `C:\Apache\apache-tomcat-6.0.29\webapps\xwiki`

4. Modify the `hibernate.cfg.xml` file in `xwiki\web-infdirectoy` to use the Oracle database with the correct JDBC driver, as follows:

Downloading the example code

You can download the example code files for all Packt books you have purchased from your account at `http://www.PacktPub.com`. If you purchased this book elsewhere, you can visit `http://www.PacktPub.com/support` and register to have the files e-mailed directly to you.

```
-->
 <property
name="connection.url">jdbc:oracle:thin:@machine:1521:DWH</property
>
 <property name="connection.username">xwiki</property>
 <property name="connection.password">xwiki</property>
 <property
name="connection.driver_class">oracle.jdbc.driver.OracleDriver</pr
operty>
```

```
<property
name="dialect">org.hibernate.dialect.Oracle10gDialect</property>
 <property
name="connection.provider_class">com.xpn.xwiki.store.DBCPConnectio
nProvider</property>
 <property name="connection.pool_size">2</property>
 <property name="statement_cache.size">2</property>
- <!--
 Tell Oracle to allow CLOBs larger than 32K
 -->
 <property
name="hibernate.connection.SetBigStringTryClob">true</property>
 <property name="hibernate.jdbc.batch_size">0</property>
 <mappingresource="xwiki.oracle.hbm.xml" />
<mappingresource="feeds.oracle.hbm.xml" />
 -<!—
```

5. Navigate to the Apache home directory and run the `services.bat` file located at `C:\Apache\apache-tomcat-7.0.6\bin\services.bat install`.

How it works...

XWiki allows the sharing of information and experiences. Wikis, blogs, and forums create an environment where information can be communally updated and shared more collaboratively than with standard documents. Users can subscribe to sections of Wiki to be informed when updates are made. The communal collaboration and notifications for updates create your constant feedback and communication loop, as follows:

During the project, information or decisions can be captured. Towards the end of the project, these can be turned into FAQs for the project. The informal information (not contained in documents) for the project is often invaluable at the end of the project.

5
The Blueprint

Before beginning your business intelligence and data warehousing build, it is important to have a high-level plan. The blueprint outlines the journey and the destination of the solution. The blueprint is essential to communicate the clear vision of the solution. The following recipes will assist to define this clear vision:

- ▶ Outlining your business processes
- ▶ Categorizing your metrics, analyses, and reports within the business process
- ▶ Decomposing your analysis and reports to define business entities
- ▶ Developing your semantic data model
- ▶ Identifying the source of record for your business entities
- ▶ Building the blueprint

Introduction

To build a blueprint effectively, it is important to gather sufficient information to gain an understanding of the requirements and the scope of the required solution, but not so much information that you end up in detailed requirements gathering. A good rule at this stage is to limit the requirements to single lines that outline the intent and the benefit of the requirement. A business intelligence and data warehousing solution can be complex, so having a map that outlines the journey is vital. The journey for a business intelligence and data warehousing solution is as important as the destination.

The solution should take into account that requirements will evolve through the project lifecycle and the solution will need to be flexible enough to accommodate these changes. It is very likely that through the iterative process of designing, developing the solution requirements will not only change, but be invalidated during the lifecycle.

Outlining your business processes

Business processes for the business intelligence and data warehousing solution do not need to be documented or outlined as exhaustively as would be used in other non BI or DW projects, or for the business. The business process outline for the solution needs to contain sufficient information to highlight major processes and process steps. This will represent the flow of information and the areas which are required to be measured.

Getting ready

In order to outline the business process, it would be ideal if you have some business documentation outlining the processes, or knowledgeable people who understand the business process you are dealing with.

How to do it...

This recipe focuses on creating a simplified graphical representation of the business process that the business intelligence and data warehouse project will be developing a solution for. The purpose of this is to gain and communicate an understanding of the business process by all stakeholders.

1. Create a new diagram in your drawing software such as Microsoft Visio:

    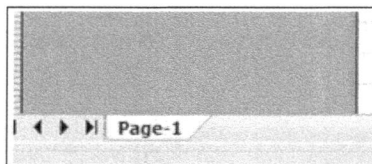

2. Rename the page to the name of the process:

    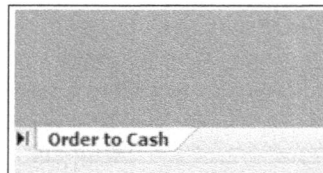

3. To start the business process documentation, determine the major steps within the business process. For example, number, name, and a brief description of the task:

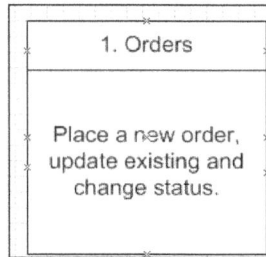

```
┌─────────────────────────┐
│         1. Orders        │
├─────────────────────────┤
│                          │
│      Place a new order,  │
│      update existing and │
│       change status.     │
│                          │
└─────────────────────────┘
```

4. Continue to identify the major steps within the business process:

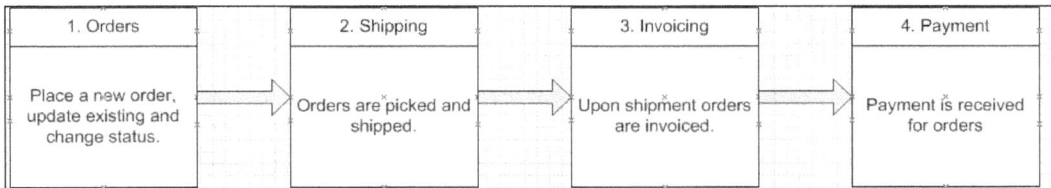

1. Orders	2. Shipping	3. Invoicing	4. Payment
Place a new order, update existing and change status.	Orders are picked and shipped.	Upon shipment orders are invoiced.	Payment is received for orders

How it works...

Identifying the business processes and the major steps involved focuses on the solution of the area processes within the business on which it will have the most impact. By doing this, it clearly outlines the content the business intelligence and data warehouse will contain. Key business definitions are socialized and agreed upon immediately.

There's more...

Oracle SQL Developer Data Modeler has the ability to depict data flow diagrams that can be used for the same purpose. Oracle SQL Developer Data Modeler is available from Oracle Technology Network for free, as a download. The product is available within Oracle SQL Developer or from a standalone Oracle SQL Developer Data Modeler. The following information is based on the standalone version of Oracle SQL Developer Data Modeler:

1. Open **Oracle SQL Developer Data Modeler**.
2. Create a new data flow diagram.

3. Right-click on **Data Flow Diagrams** and select **New Data Flow Diagram**:

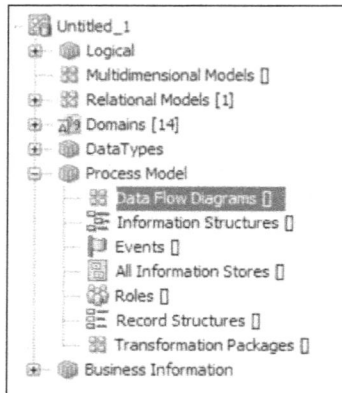

4. Right-click on the default name for the new data flow diagram. Select **Properties**. Rename the diagram to your process name. For example, Order to Cash.

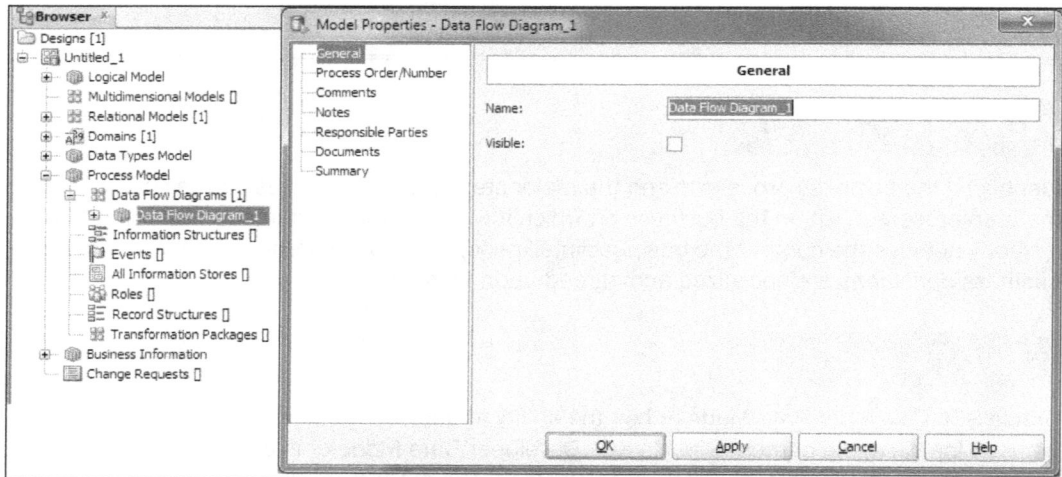

5. Click on the **new process** icon in the top-left corner of the screen under **File**:

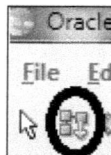

6. Click on the canvas and rename the process. Also, enter a short definition of the process.

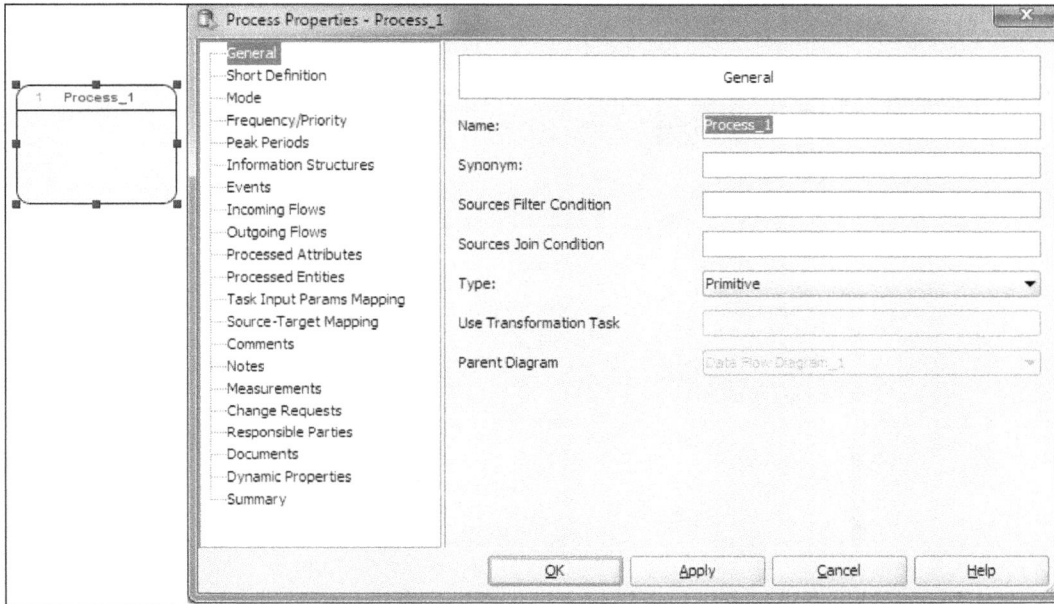

7. Continue to create the processes in order until you have covered all the steps:

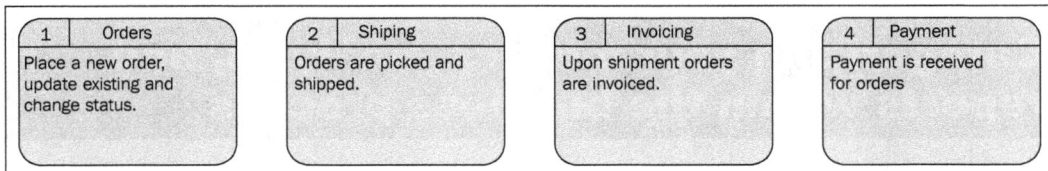

1	Orders	2	Shiping	3	Invoicing	4	Payment
Place a new order, update existing and change status.		Orders are picked and shipped.		Upon shipment orders are invoiced.		Payment is received for orders	

8. Click on the **flow** icon in the top-left corner of the screen:

9. Link all your processes with the flows. Double-click on a flow to rename it:

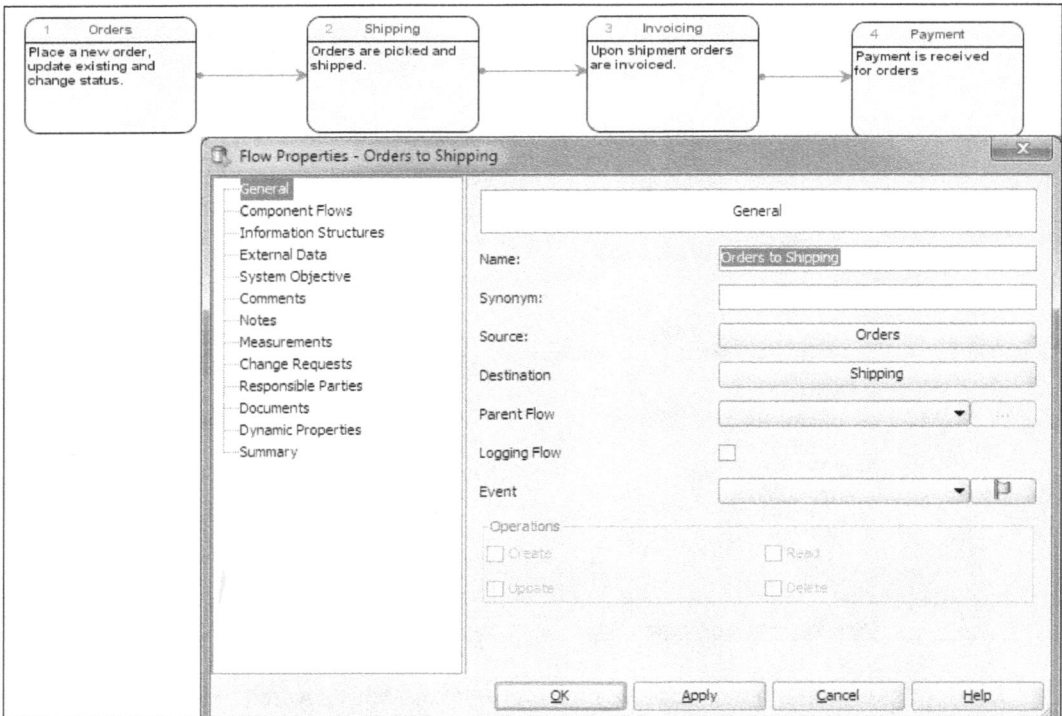

Categorizing your metrics, analysis, and reports within the business process

Identifying the key information used within the business can be tricky. To start this process, you can use your newly defined business process to identify which areas of the business process to investigate. Make sure not to get wrapped up in requirements gathering at this stage. All that is required is to gather the information for an understanding of the information within the business process.

Getting ready

To start with, you need to identify key contact people within the organization for each of the processes and process steps. Business Process Owners may be identified within the organization; if not, it may become a little more challenging to gather the information. In this case, look for people in the organization who are responsible for compiling or reporting information on a periodic basis for the business process. These people will become the subject matter experts for the process steps.

How to do it...

After completing your business process outline in your diagramming tool, you will need to enhance the process by documenting the metrics, reports, analysis, and key source information for each step.

1. In your process diagram, add a triangle for each of the process steps:

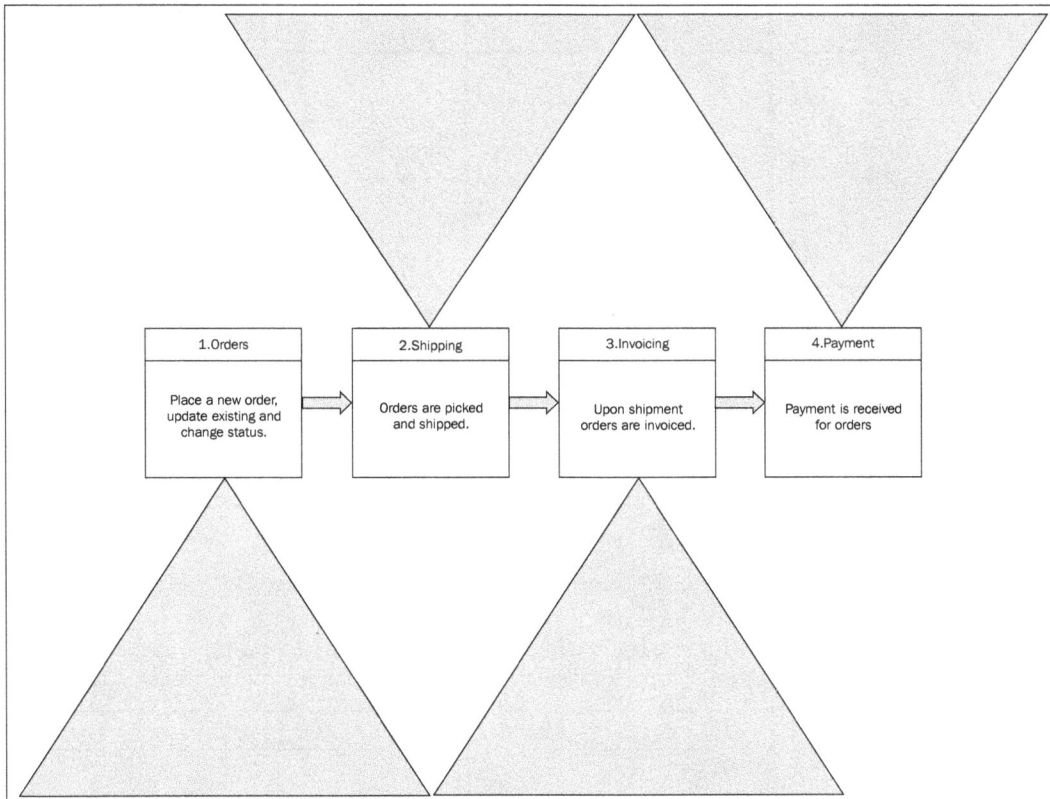

1.Orders	2.Shipping	3.Invoicing	4.Payment
Place a new order, update existing and change status.	Orders are picked and shipped.	Upon shipment orders are invoiced.	Payment is received for orders

2. Split your triangles into three swimlanes and label them **Metrics**, **Analysis**, and **Reports**:

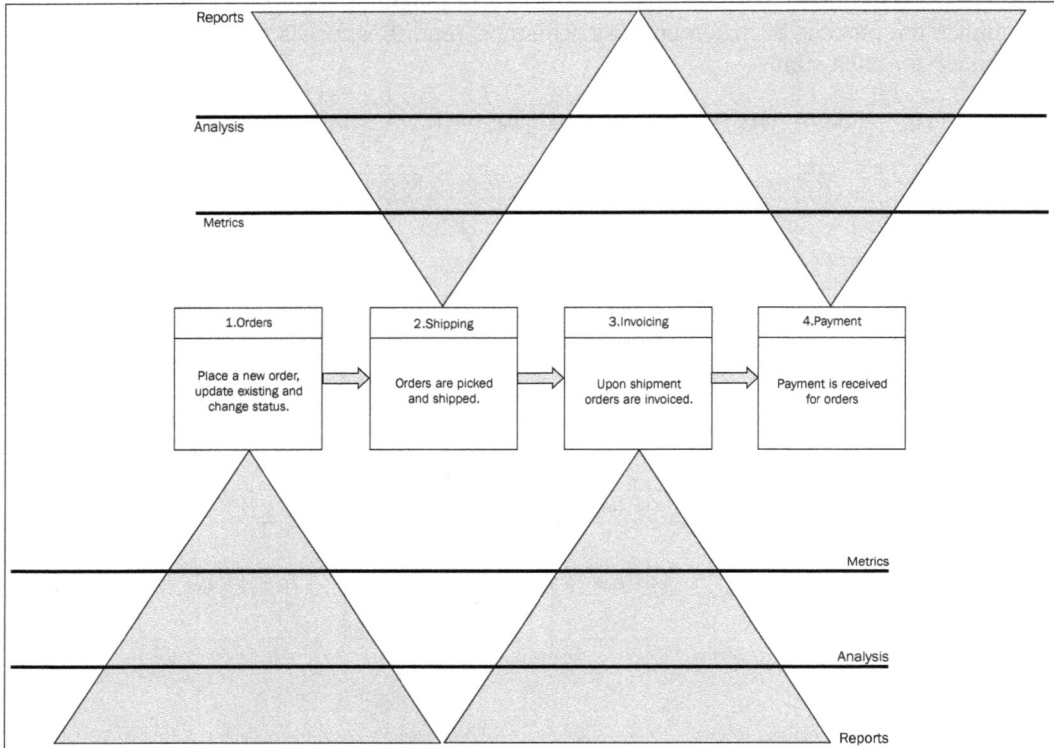

1.Orders	**2.Shipping**	**3.Invoicing**	**4.Payment**
Place a new order, update existing and change status.	Orders are picked and shipped.	Upon shipment orders are invoiced.	Payment is received for orders

3. For each process step, create a basic table and collect the following information. For example, for Process 1, Step 1 of the Order to Cash process:

Process #	1	Step #	1
Definition	Orders		
Objectives	Collect information in batches for switches		
Inputs	Customer places an order.		
Outputs	Order record		
Business Rules			
Flow Narrative	Customer or Sales person places an order either via the online website or internal order management application.		
Actors / Stakeholders	• Customer • Sales people		

Process #	1	Step #	1
Metrics	• Number of orders per period • Value of orders per period		
Analysis	1. Orders by geographical region within a time period 2. Orders by sales people within a time period 3. Orders by product within a time period 4. Backlog orders		
Reports	Order Receipt		
Info Source	To be determined		
Notes			
Entities	To be determined		
Questions			

4. Pick the highest priority metrics, analysis, and reports and include them in your diagram:

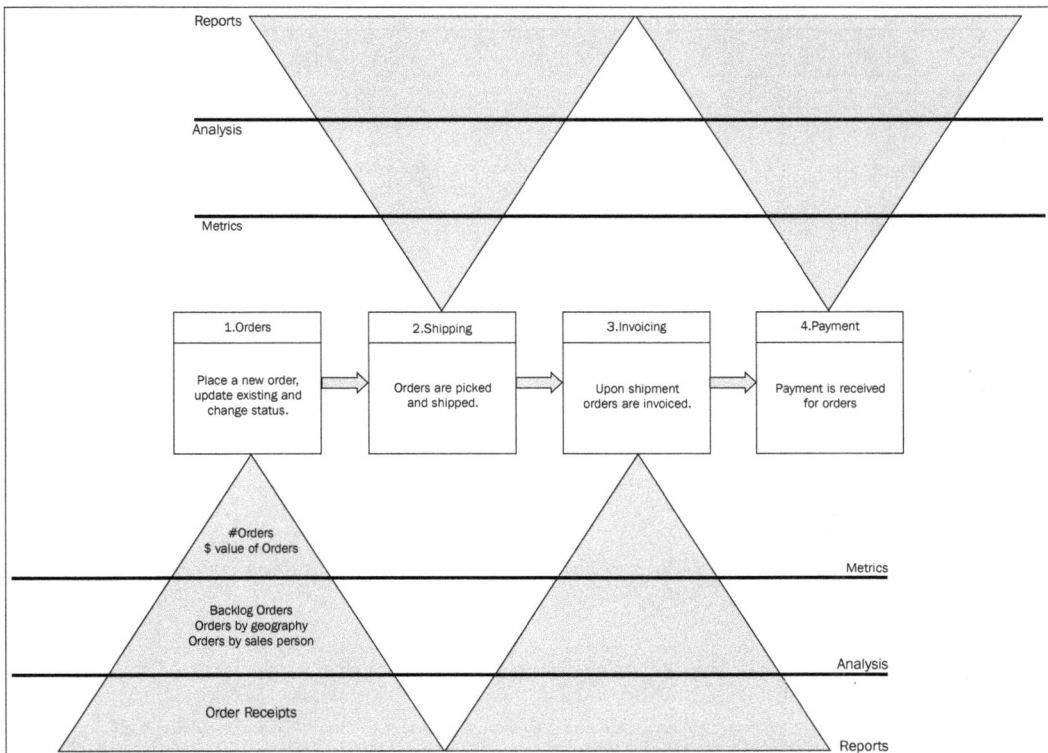

How it works...

This is a very rapid way to gain an understanding of the information available and being requested within the business processes. The visual representation of the information serves as a common communications mechanism for people to understand what information is present and being requested within a business process. This also directly ties the business intelligence and data warehouse solution to a legitimate business process and makes it easier to understand how the solution can add value to the organization. It is important to gather samples of the metrics, reports, and analyses to support the enhancement of the business process in later recipes.

There's more...

Oracle SQL Developer Data Modeler has similar abilities to capture the information.

1. Double-click on your process within Oracle SQL Developer Data Modeler. Navigate to the necessary properties to complete the information. Typical properties that need to be completed are **Responsible Parties**, **Measurements**, and **Documents**:

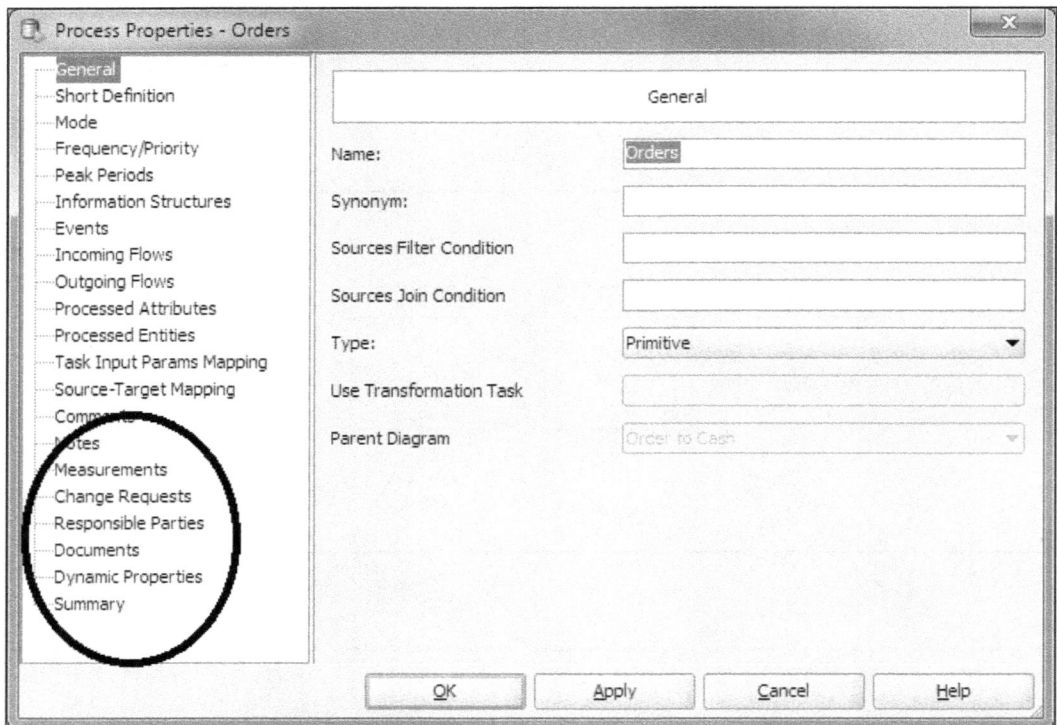

2. Add information within the process properties:

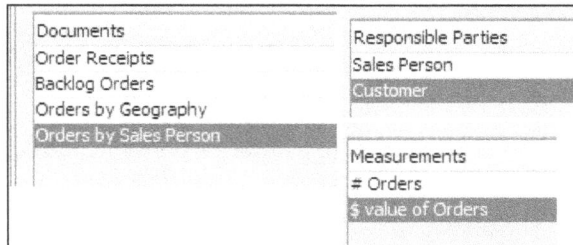

Documents	Responsible Parties
Order Receipts	Sales Person
Backlog Orders	Customer
Orders by Geography	
Orders by Sales Person	
	Measurements
	# Orders
	$ value of Orders

3. Navigate through all the processes and complete the same information.

Decomposing your analysis and reports to define business entities

Starting to define your business entities is a key step in understanding the information in which the business intelligence and data warehouse solution is interested. In this step you will not only identify the key business information for a process, but also give each business entity and attribute a business definition.

Getting ready

To complete this step, you will need samples of the analysis and reports you identified in the previous steps. If these are new analysis or reports which do not currently exist, then endeavor to create a simple mock-up of each of the reports. A few simple definitions will also help you understand what you are looking for:

▶ **Entity** – Entity is something that exists as an independent, self-contained, discrete unit. This can be living or non-living. For example, sales person, product, geography, orders, invoices, and so on.

▶ **Attribute** – Attribute is a characteristic or a piece of data relating to an entity. For example, name, product type, geographical region, and so on.

How to do it...

After identifying the major reports, metrics, and analyses for each process, it is key to identify the major entities. This outlines the main business information, which is a required support for each business process.

1. Within your drawing software, create a new tab/page and label it **Entities**:

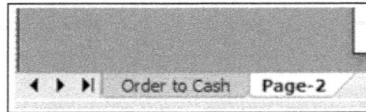

2. Identify and list all the entities:

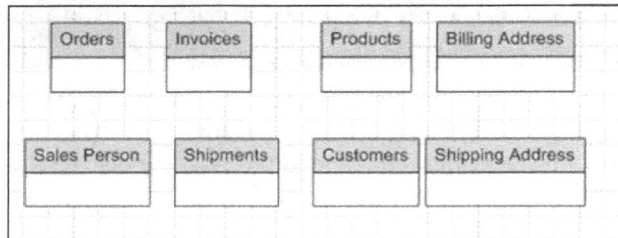

3. Give a description for each entity.

How it works...

Identifying your entities and supplying each with a description becomes the basis for the data dictionary or your semantic model. This will be used later in the project to represent information to the users within the metrics, analyses, and reports. It is important to gain an understanding and consensus on the names and meanings of the entities at an early stage in the project, so as not to have confusion and disagreements later in the project.

There's more...

Oracle SQL Developer Data Modeler allows one to capture entities within the tool. Under the Logical branch in the tree you will see **Entities**.

1. Open the **Logical** diagram and navigate to the **Entities** branch in the tree:

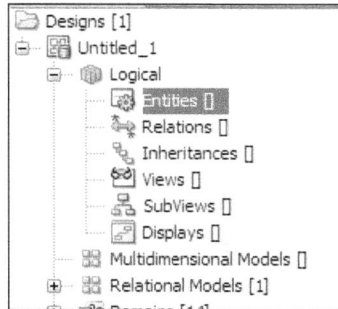

2. Navigate to the top-left corner of the screen and select **New Entity**:

3. Click on the canvas to create a new entity:

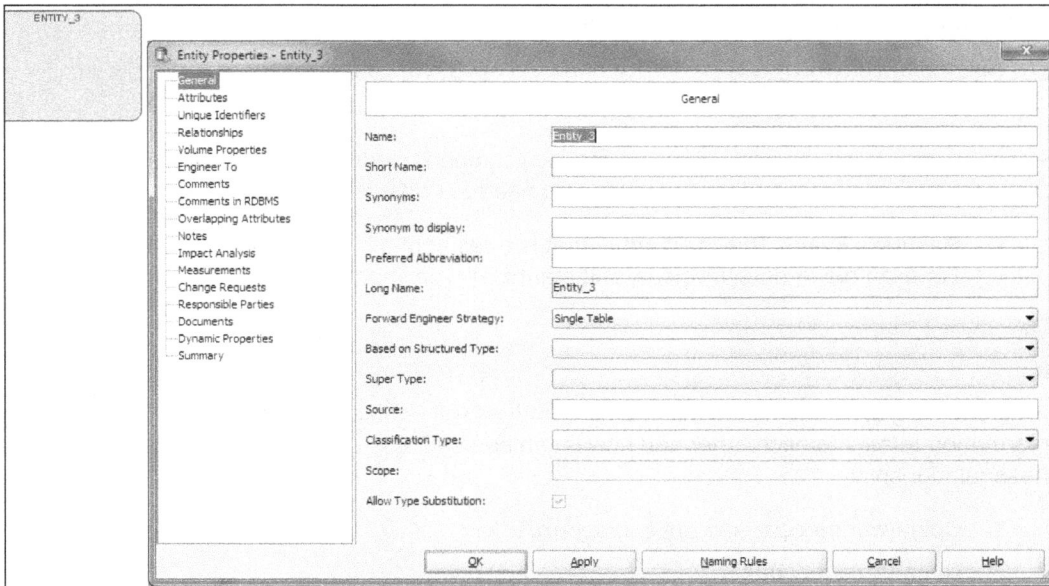

4. Name the entity:

	General
Name:	Orders

5. Add a description under the **Comments** property:

Comments
Orders are requests by customers to purchase products. Orders ares split into two different levels of information. The first is the header and the second is the line item.

Developing your semantic data model

The semantic data model is a business model that outlines the relationships between entities. The semantic data model is the model that the business users will use to interact and retrieve information from the Business Intelligence and Data Warehouse solution.

Getting ready

Before you can build the semantic data model, you need to ensure you have a good sampling of the metrics, analysis, and reports. Also, you need to understand another key definition:

▶ **Business Event**: This is an entity that is a result of a business operation or event. For example, orders, invoices, shipments, and payments.

How to do it...

Understanding the relationship between the entities will enable you to determine how the information relates to each other and how it can be used. It is the key to depict and define these relationships.

1. Open your process and entity diagram.
2. Open the entity page.

3. Arrange the business events in the same sequence as the business process flow:

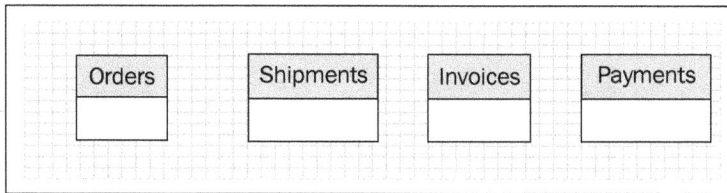

Orders	Shipments	Invoices	Payments

4. Arrange the entities around the business event entities, which are related:

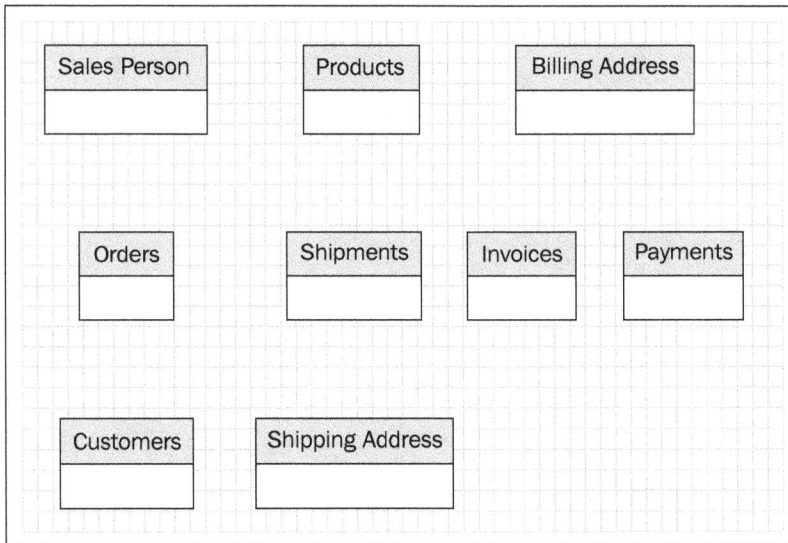

Sales Person	Products	Billing Address

Orders	Shipments	Invoices	Payments

Customers	Shipping Address

5. Connect the related entities. Connecting the entities gives you the basis for your semantic model.

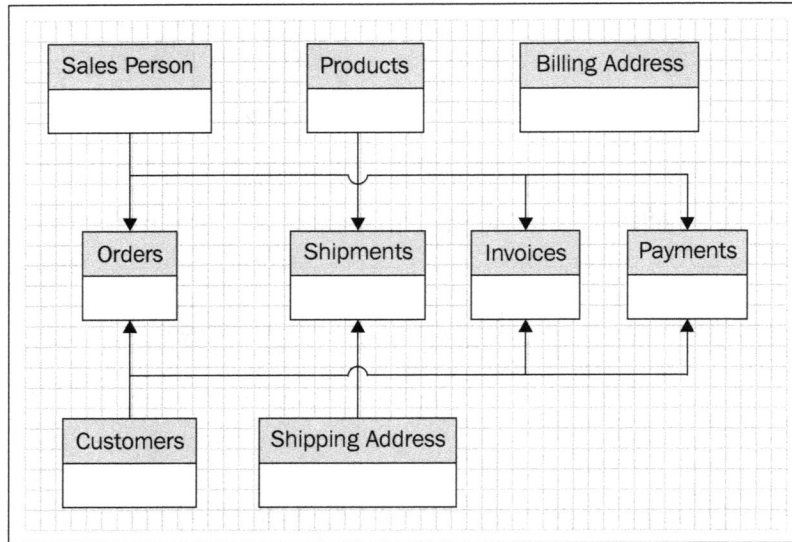

6. Review the sample reports you have collected and associate the attributes with the appropriate entities:

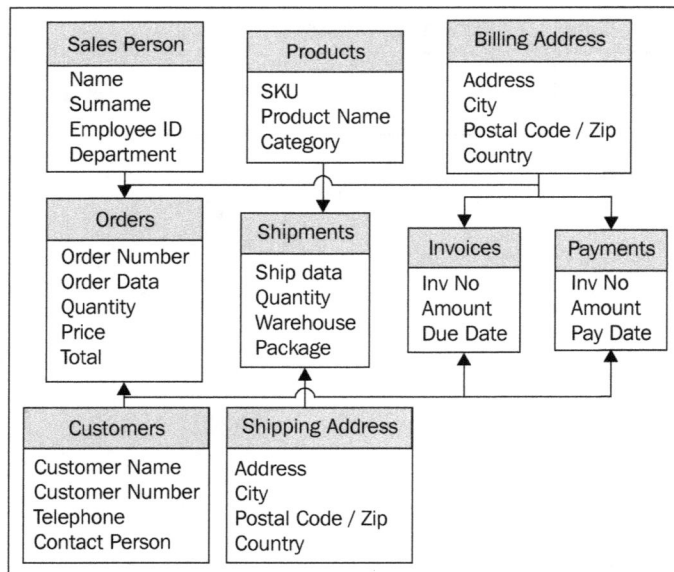

How it works...

By socializing the semantic model earlier in the project, you accomplish two key objectives:

- ▸ User agreement to the definitions of the entities and attributes
- ▸ User familiarity with the information that will be available

This model can be used to validate and verify business requirements.

There's more...

Oracle SQL Developer Data Model can be used to define your semantic data model:

1. Arrange the business events in the same sequence as the business process flow:

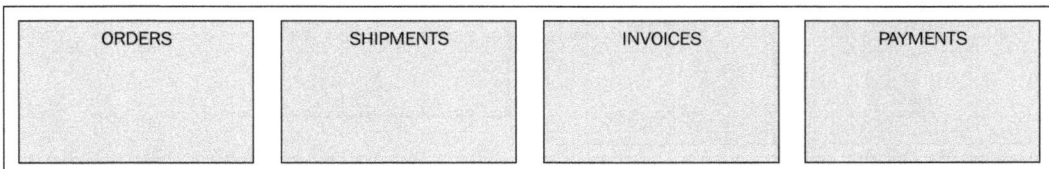

ORDERS	SHIPMENTS	INVOICES	PAYMENTS

2. Double-click on the business event entities and change the **Classification Type** to **Fact**. Click on **Apply**:

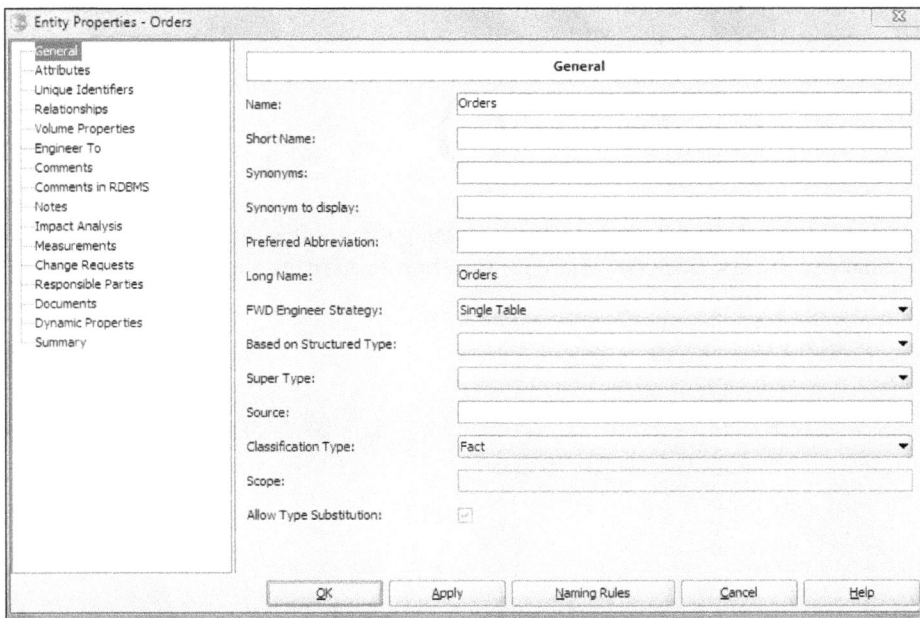

3. You will notice the color of the entity changes once the classification is changed. All the business event entities are now classified as `Fact`.

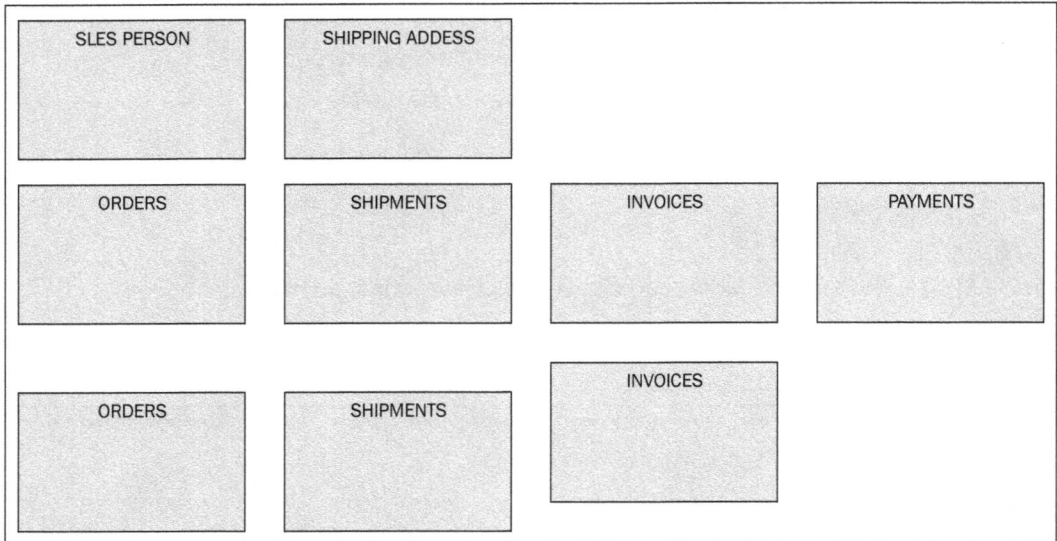

SLES PERSON	SHIPPING ADDESS		
ORDERS	SHIPMENTS	INVOICES	PAYMENTS
		INVOICES	
ORDERS	SHIPMENTS		

4. Click on the **New 1:N Relation** icon in the top-left corner of the screen. The 1:N relation is a notation used to identify how entities relate. The **1:N** icon specifies that each entity can be related to other multiple entities. For example, a customer (1) may have multiple orders (N).

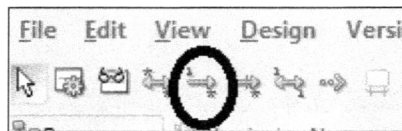

5. Connect the related entities by first selecting the entities on the outside of the business events. Click **OK** when the **Relation Properties** window appears:

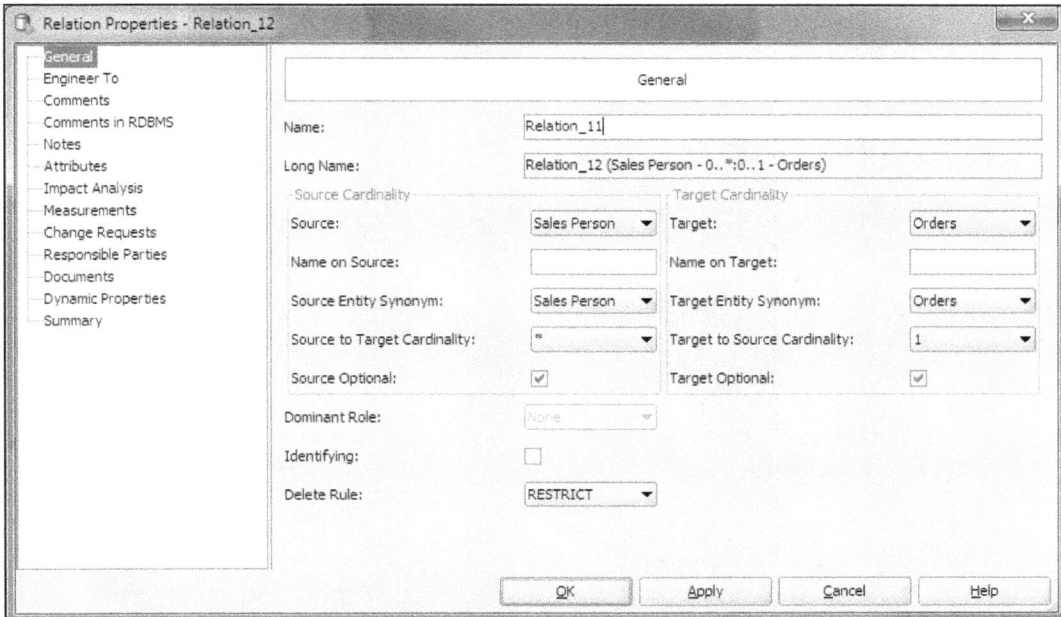

6. Connect all the related entities.

7. Double-click on the entities and enter the attributes. Clicking on the **+** icon adds new attributes. Do not worry about defining the datatype or type.

8. In the **Comments** section, enter the definition for each of the attributes:

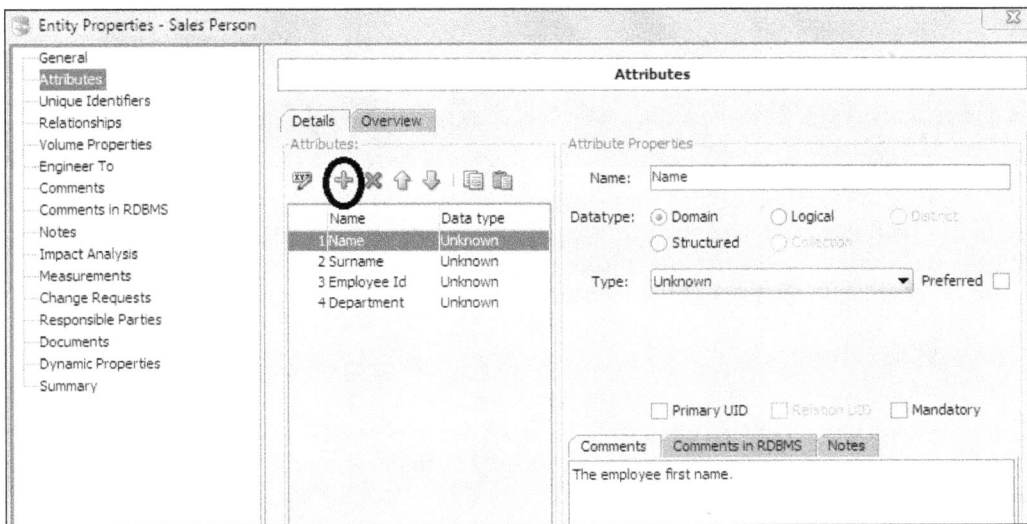

9. Once completed, the semantic data model should include all the attributes and comments:

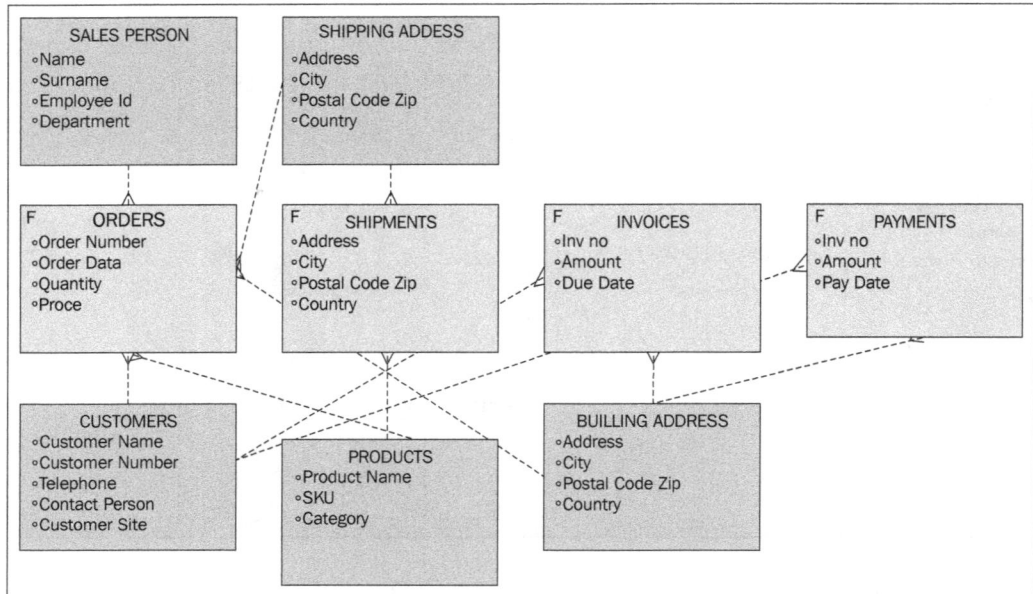

It is important to understand that this is not the logical or physical model for the business intelligence solution. The model here is for the semantic model. This model is meant to be a simplistic model, which can be used to communicate with stakeholders, the information that has been identified to be included into the solution.

Identifying your source of record for your business entities

Once you have a skeleton semantic data model, the next step is to identify where the information comes from. It is important to try and identify all the potential sources for the entity, and equally important to identify the authoritative source of record. The authoritative source of record is the master of the information.

Getting ready

To identify the source of information, ask the business users where they source information for the reports. If these are new reports, look to key business systems for information, as a starting point.

How to do it...

It is important for the business to tell you what information it requires to support each business process, and the source that it considers to be the truth. Often we go to the technical people to understand where the information is coming from only to find out the business relies on different systems/processes to gather information.

1. For each process and step, identify which entities support the information requirements. This is derived from the semantic model and the relationship between the entities:

Process #	1	Step #	1

Definition	Orders
Objectives	Collect information in batches for switches
Inputs	Customer places an order
Outputs	Order record
Business Rules	
Flow Narrative	Customer or sales person places an order either via the online website, or through an internal order management application
Actors/Stakeholders	• Customer • Sales people
Metrics	• Number of orders per period • Value of orders per period
Analysis	1. Orders by geographical region within a time period 2. Orders by sales people within a time period 3. Orders by product within a time period 4. Backlog orders
Reports	Order Receipt
Info Source	
Notes	
Entities	1. Sales Person 2. Product 3. Customer 4. Orders
Questions	

2. For each process and step, identify which information sources are the authoritative sources for the entities:

Process #	1	Step #	1
Definition	Orders		
Objectives	Collect information in batches for switches		
Inputs	Customer places an order		
Outputs	Order record		
Business Rules			
Flow Narrative	Customer or sales person places an order either through the online website or internal order management application		
Actors / Stakeholders	- Customer		
	- Sales people		
Metrics	- Number of orders per period		
	- Value of orders per period		
	1. Orders by geographical region within a time period		
Analysis	2. Orders by sales people within a time period		
	3. Orders by product within a time period		
	4. Backlog orders		
Reports	1. Order Receipt		
Info Source	- Oracle E-Business Suite		
	- WebStore Application		
Notes			
	- Sales Person		
Entities	- Product		
	- Customer		
	- Orders		
Questions			

How it works...

Identifying the sources of information and the entities provide you with the last pieces of information necessary to understand the scope and high-level requirements of the business intelligence and data warehouse solution. By identifying the entities and information sources that the business considers relevant, you can potentially uncover discrepancies within business processes.

There's more...

Oracle SQL Developer Data Modeler allows you to identify and document your data sources:

1. Double-click on your **Order to Cash** under **Data Flow Diagram**:

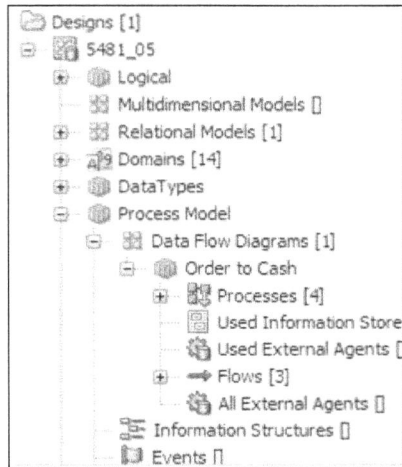

2. Double-click on the flow between your two processes:

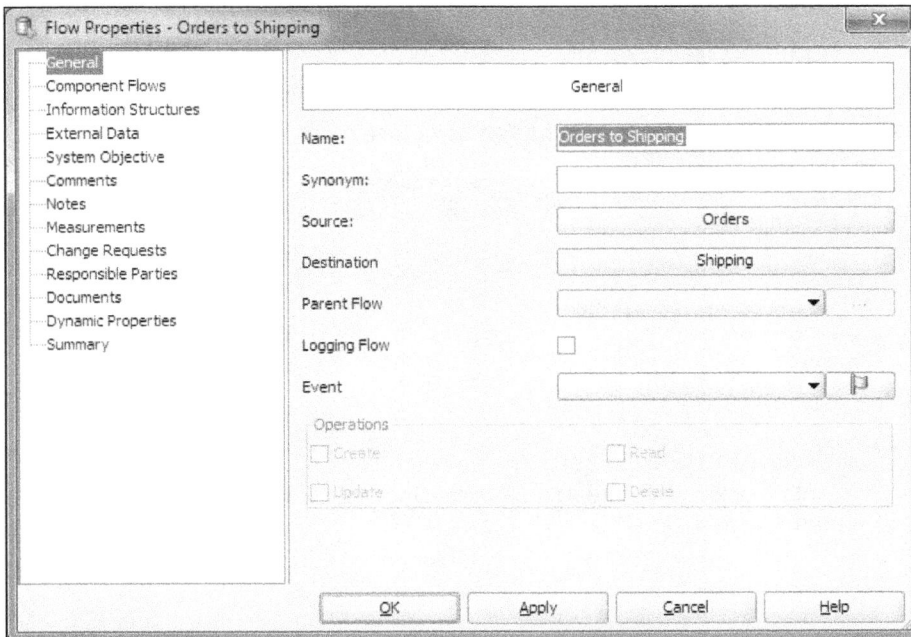

3. Click on the **Information Structures** property. Then, click on the **+** icon and select **New Information Structure**. Click **OK**:

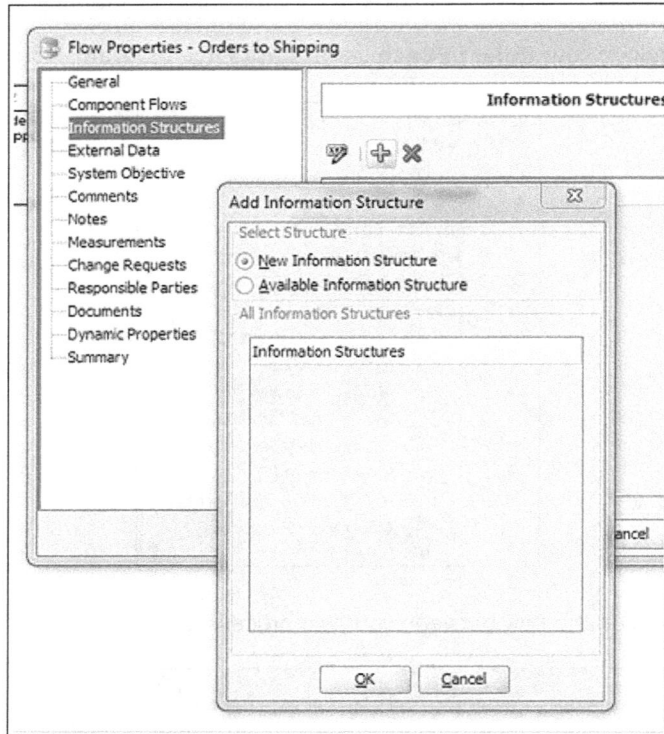

4. Double-click on the **New Information Structure** option and rename:

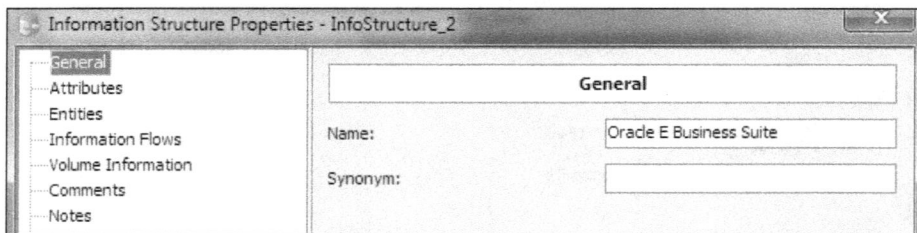

5. Click on the **Attributes** property and select the attributes that are relevant to the information structure and process. Once selected, the entities are automatically associated.

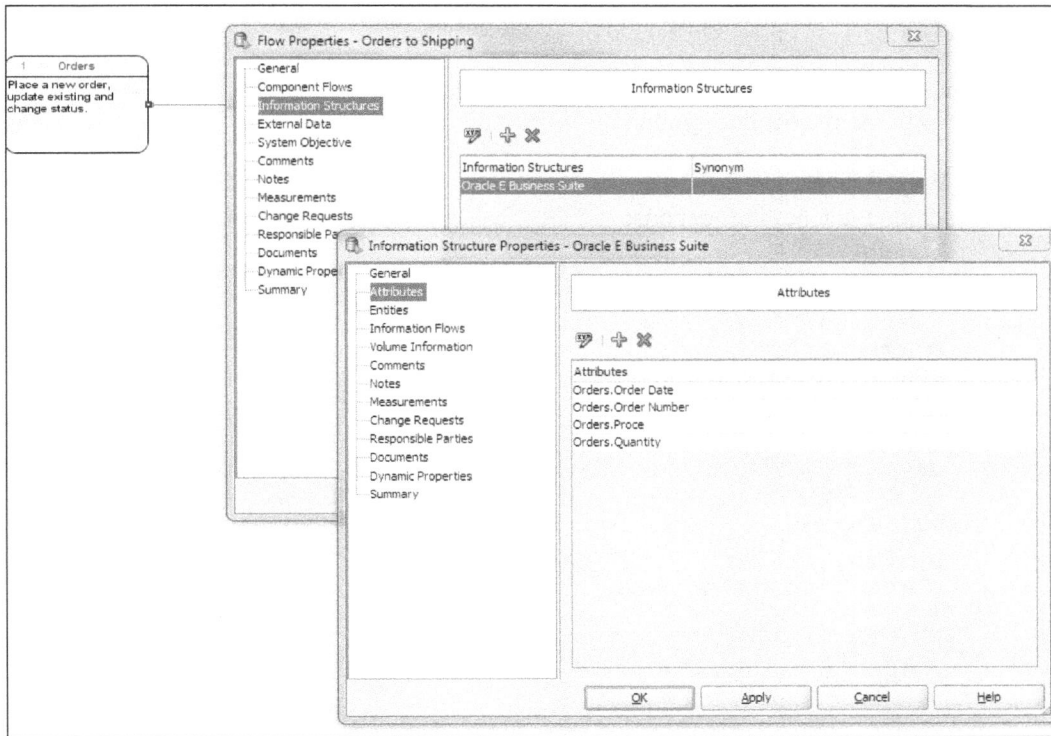

Building the blueprint

The blueprint is very similar to a project charter; however, it has a few more technical details included. This is the main document that outlines the scope and direction of the business intelligence and data warehouse solution.

Getting ready

To build the blueprint, you need to consolidate the information contained in this chapter and include some additional information:

- ▶ Background of the solution
- ▶ Objectives of the solution

How to do it...

The blueprint is a consolidation of the information collected throughout this chapter, integrated with the project background:

1. Create a document.

2. Include the following sections:

1	OVERVIEW	4
1.1	BACKGROUND	4
1.2	PROJECT OBJECTIVES	4
1.3	PROJECT APPROACH	4
1.4	PROJECT ASSUMPTIONS	4
1.5	DOCUMENT OVERVIEW	4
1.6	DOCUMENT PURPOSE	5
1.7	DOCUMENT AUDIENCE	5
1.8	RELATED DOCUMENTS	6
2	BUSINESS PROCESS	7
2.1	OVERVIEW	7
2.2	BUSINESS PROCESS – ORDER TO CASH	7
2.2.1	*Orders*	*8*
2.2.2	*Shipping*	*8*
2.2.3	*Invoicing*	*8*
2.2.4	*Payments*	*9*
3	ROADMAP	10

3. Integrate the previous business process information into section 2, BUSINESS PROCESS.

4. Section 3, ROADMAP, involves prioritizing and building. For this, arrange the process and steps in the order of implementation.

How it works...

By identifying the business processes and the information contained within each business process, it is easy to understand the content of the solution that will be provided, should the Business Intelligence and Data Warehouse project focus on a particular business process or step within a business process. From this information, the business can prioritize which business process or steps will provide the greatest benefit to begin the project.

From the prioritization of the business processes and steps, it gives business users, stakeholders, and project management a clear roadmap of the solution. This information can also be used to estimate and determine the effort required for each phase.

Major gaps and risks will also be uncovered during this process, allowing for the prioritization of processes and steps which are feasible to implement. For example, identifying business processes that are not supported by key information systems but rely on manual processes, or areas that require information for decisions, which is not available within the organization.

There's more...

Oracle SQL Developer Data Modeler can add the logical and physical model information to the document in the form of additional information. As you have started to capture information within the tool, this starts to become the foundation for the data model design of the business intelligence and data warehouse solution. To retrieve information you can:

1. Click on **File | Reports** and select the entities for available reports:

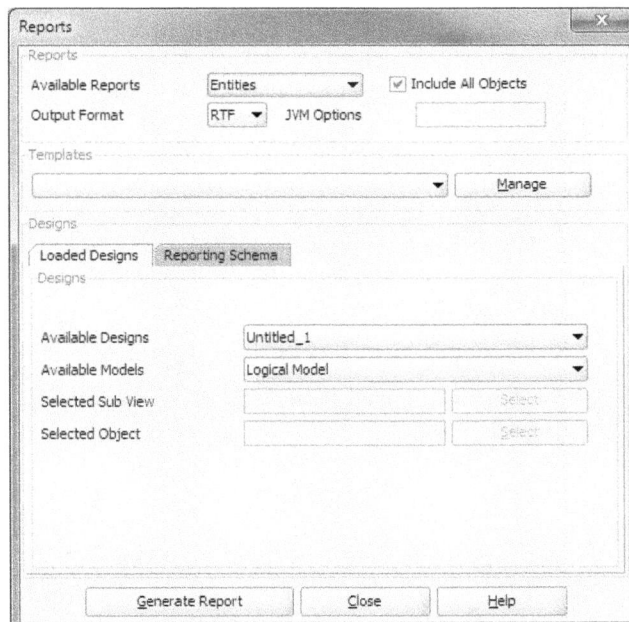

2. Click on **Generate Report**:

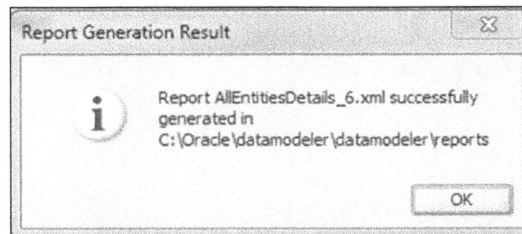

The report can be opened, and the relevant information can be copied into the document or added as an appendix.

Oracle SQL Developer Data Modeler enables you to start your business intelligence and data warehousing solution, and then reuse this information later in the project to produce logical and ultimately physical data models.

The tool is a little limited and does not allow for all the information that will be required to be presented to the stakeholders, for example, roadmaps and prioritizations. For this reason if you choose to use Oracle SQL Developer Data Modeler, then you must be aware that the information will need to be supplemented.

It is recommended, however, to keep as much in Oracle SQL Developer Data Modeler as possible, since the environment is a lot more flexible to incorporate changes as your solution evolves over time.

6
Analyzing the Requirements

Business requirements in a business intelligence and data warehouse project can be very high level and vague. Gaining an understanding of the business processes and persistence of data can help considerably in obtaining and decomposing valued business requirements. The following recipes help in obtaining, categorizing, and prioritizing requirements:

- ▶ Decomposing the reports and requirements
- ▶ Defining the business rules
- ▶ Categorizing the requirements by business drivers
- ▶ Prioritizing the requirements
- ▶ Adding hierarchies to your semantic data model
- ▶ Adding metrics to your semantic data model
- ▶ Defining your data dictionary
- ▶ Defining your security requirements
- ▶ Defining your data retention requirements

Introduction

Once the blueprint is complete and prioritized, it is time to start the detailed requirement gathering. Requirements can be vague and limited in a business intelligence and data warehousing project. It is important to align the information collected during requirement gathering closely to the information required to enable the construction of the solution. The easiest way to do this is to build templates to gather information. Starting with a high-level requirement, you can decompose, categorize, prioritize, and enhance the semantic data model to wrap up the requirement gathering. Adding security and data retention requirements rounds off the information required to build a business intelligence and data warehouse solution.

Decomposing the reports and requirements

Epics, stories, or requirements need to be easy to read, understandable, and concise.

Epics are generally large stories which are too vague to implement for reasons such as complexity, having many unknowns, and high levels of risk or size. You will need to decompose epics or requirements into actionable and implementable stories and requirements.

Getting ready

Go back to your Requirements Traceability Matrix, and extract your numbering scheme. This is a good template to start gathering requirements, and ensuring that you are capturing the correct information.

How to do it...

The standard numbering scheme and standard business requirement format ensures that information is collected consistently and concisely within the organization. By enabling this, there is a clear understanding of the components required to be developed to support the business requirement. The numbering scheme is constructed with a focus on the objects which need to be developed as they are the deliverables of the project:

1. Identify the different categories of requirements which are relevant for your business intelligence and data warehouse project. For example:

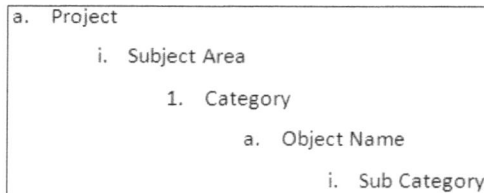

   ```
   a.  Project
         i.  Subject Area
               1.  Category
                     a.  Object Name
                           i.  Sub Category
   ```

2. Define the requirements. For example, as an order clerk, I require an orders report to track open orders to be fulfilled, enabling procurement to invoice the customer for goods.

3. Always try and ensure that business requirements are broken into a standard format, for example, *as a (Role) wants or requires (something) so that a benefit can be realized.*

4. Decompose the requirement (linked requirements) into a greater level of detail, based on the standard numbering scheme from your Requirements Traceability Matrix. For example:

```
Project 1
    b.  Orders
            i.  Reports
                    1.  Open Order Report
                                a.  Tooltip – Open Orders
                                b.  Title – Open Orders
                                c.  Header - None
                                d.  Footer - Filters
                                e.  Page Item – Region
                                f.  Columns – Customer Name, Item Name, Item
                                    Quantity, Item Price, Total
                                g.  Calculations – Total = Item Quantity x Item Price
                                h.  Filters – Calendar Period
                                i.  Audience – Sales, Indirect Sales
                                j.  Frequency - Daily
                                k.  Security – Sales
                                l.  Drill Paths
                                        i.  Customer Name -> Customer Site
                                m.  Navigation Paths
                                        i.  Open Orders Report – Total column
                                            hyperlink to Customer Invoice Report
```

The sub categories in the preceding example are based on each of the features which are required to be built. These will be driven by requirements by the user. These are normally taken from existing report standards or driven by the capabilities of the tool which has been selected.

5. It is important to capture these requirements in an easy manner to understand the format. Open a spreadsheet application, and create a tab for your project **Requirements** as follows:

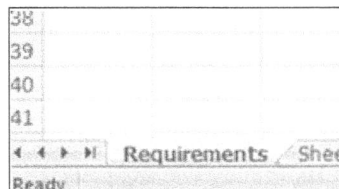

6. Create columns in the spreadsheet to capture **Requirement** (step 2) and **Linked Requirement** (step 4), as shown in the following screenshot:

Req#	Requirement	Linked Requirement	
1	As an order clerk I require an orders report to track open orders.	Report Name	Open Orders Report
2		Tooltip	Open Orders
3		Title	Open Orders
4		Header	None
5		Footer	Filter values
6		Page Item	Region
7		Columns	Customer Name
			Item Name
			Item Quantity
			Item Price
			Total
8		Calculations	Total = Item Quantity x Item Price
9		Filters	Calendar Period
10		Audience	Sales, Indirect Sales
11		Frequency	Daily
12		Security	Sales
13		Drill Paths	Customer Name -> Customer Site
14		Navigation Paths	Total column hyperlink to Customer Invoice Report

7. Determine the implied requirements. From the above requirements, there may be additional non-business requirements needed to support the solution; these need to be recorded and tracked as well. Examples of these additional requirements are multilanguage, multicurrency, security model, visualizations, and so on.

How it works...

Capturing the requirements in a concise fashion reduces the ambiguity, and enables one to design and build an efficient and effective solution. It is important to understand the technology the project has chosen to implement so that the requirement gathering exercise can capture any specific information required for the technical implementation.

Requirements directly drive the effort for the project; therefore, it is of utmost importance to socialize, review, and obtain approval. In addition to gaining formal approval, it is also important to recognize that there are additional requirements which are not directly gathered from a user. These are implied requirements or standards to which the project must adhere. The implied requirements could be system, language requirements, currency, or any standard operating procedure which requires work to be presented in a specific way. The standards are a form of these implied requirements which must be added to all components. The implied requirements should also be documented in a general standards document which also is required to be agreed upon and signed off by the business.

A business intelligence and data warehouse solution will uncover and refine requirements through the project lifecycle. This approach does not preclude, but does recommend that requirements are approved and then amended, should changes be uncovered at a later stage.

There's more...

For information about how to enter requirements using Oracle Application Express Team development, see the *Requirements Traceability Matrix* recipe in *Chapter 3, Controlling the Project*.

Defining the business rules

Whenever you derive or determine a calculation or some other rule, it is important to capture them separately. The reason for this is that calculations and business rules are normally reused multiple times within the business. It is important to ensure a consistent definition of the rules and information across all business requirements.

Getting ready

To start, look at all your requirements where there may be, business rules or calculations.

How to do it...

Business rules are ways in which the business calculates, manipulates, or categorizes information. There are normally many of these within an organization with many differing definitions. It is important to identify and define these so that the business can agree upon which version of the business rule is correct:

1. Open your requirements spreadsheet, and create an additional tab called **Business Rules**, as shown in the following screenshot:

   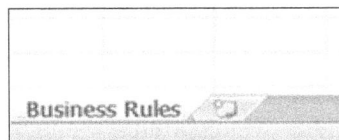

2. Set up the columns to capture the necessary information:

A	B	C	D
Rule #	Rule Name	Rule Description	Rule Logic

3. Extract the rules from the business requirements as follows:

Rule #	Rule Name	Rule Description	Rule Logic
1	Order Line Total	Total value of the Order Line	Total = Item Quantity x Item Price
2	Order Total	Total value of the Order Line	(Sum of Order Line Total + Freight + Insurance - Discounts) + Tax

4. Cross-link the business requirements with the business rules:

Req#	Requirement	Linked Requirement		Rule#
1	As an order clerk I require an orders report to track open orders.	Report Name	Open Orders Report	
2		Tooltip	Open Orders	
3		Title	Open Orders	
4		Header	None	
5		Footer	Filter values	
6		Page Item	Region	
7		Columns	Customer Name	
			Item Name	
			Item Quantity	
			Item Price	
			Total	
8		Calculations	Total = Item Quantity x Item Price	1
9		Filters	Calendar Period	
10		Audience	Sales, Indirect Sales	
11		Frequency	Daily	
12		Security	Sales	
13		Drill Paths	Customer Name -> Customer Site	
14		Navigation Paths	Total column hyperlink to Customer Invoice Report	

How it works...

Business rules can be basic as outlined above by **Calculations** or could be very complex such as **Security** logic and who is allowed to view certain information. Each is required to be documented in business terms so as to capture the intent and requirement. Business rules form part of business requirements and as such should be socialized, reviewed, and approved.

Capturing them individually highlights the importance of the business rules, and enables easy visibility into complex areas of the project. Additional tasks such as testing give the opportunity to review these rules, and create specific test scripts to validate these business rules.

Categorizing the business requirements by business drivers

Business drivers are internal or external influences which cause a business to act. Business drivers are normally linked to a company's goals and objectives. Linking business drivers to a requirement enables the stakeholders to understand the impact of each requirement.

Getting ready

The business intelligence and data warehouse project should have a **business case** or **project charter** defined that outlines the reasons for the project and how the project can contribute to the business goals and objectives.

How to do it...

Gather the business drivers from the business case for the project or from your company's objectives and goals:

1. Define or enhance your list of business drivers, for example:

    ❏   Reduce cost – the requirement will result in a cost reduction

    ❏   Increase revenue – the requirement will result in an increase in revenue

    ❏   Data standardization – the requirement will result in the standardization of information within the organization

    ❏   Business process gap – the requirement will fill a business process gap

    ❏   Regulatory – the requirement is to comply with a regulatory requirement

2. Add a column to your **Requirement** for the **Business Driver** as shown in the following screenshot:

Req#	Requirement	Business Driver
1	As an order clerk I require an orders report to track open orders.	Reduce Cost

3. Try and quantify the **Business Driver** as follows:

Req#	Requirement	Business Driver	Amount
1	As an order clerk I require an orders report to track open orders.	Reduce Cost	4hrs per week per sales person to 10 minutes per week

How it works...

These business drivers also allow the business to understand the impact of the requirements, and how they will contribute to the business goals and objectives.

By identifying the business driver, you are specifying how you think the business requirement will impact the business. Once identified, the size of the impact should be quantified. This may be difficult to quantify the impact of the requirement, but can be beneficial as it clearly articulates the need for the requirement and the impact.

It is important to always return and validate these business drivers and actual impact once the project has been delivered. Only the parent requirement and not the linked requirements should be assigned business drivers.

There's more...

The amount of impact a requirement has on the business can be a very subjective issue. It is important to be able to justify the benefit the requirement will have on the business. Solicit this information from the business wherever possible or insert evidence of how long or how much a certain requirement is taking today.

Prioritizing the business requirements

Business intelligence and data warehouse projects have a tendency to go for longer periods of time without delivering to the business. It is important to understand how your project is perceived by the business and what your key success factors are.

Getting ready

Understand the key success factors for the project and how the business will determine if you are a success. These key success factors should have been outlined within your business strategy and again in the business case.

How to do it...

Review your business strategy and business case. Understand the key success factors for your project to enable you to successfully prioritize the business requirements:

1. Create an additional column within the business requirements named **Priority** as shown in the following screenshot:

Req# Requirement	Business Driver	Amount	Priority

2. Decide on a scale to prioritize the requirements. There are many different ways to do this. There are a few examples as follows:

   ❑ Must have, Should have, Could have, Won't have (MoSCoW)

   ❑ High, Medium, Low

Req#	Requirement	Business Driver	Amount	Priority
			4hrs per week per sales person to 10	
1	As an order clerk I require an orders report to track open orders.	Reduce Cost	minutes per week	Must
15	As a report user I require access to information which pertains to my roles within the organisation			Must
16	As a report user I require to see information in my local language			Should
17	As a report user I require to see information in my local currency			Must

> Note you should only prioritize the requirement and not the linked (decomposed) requirement.

3. Once you have assigned the priority, it is important to assign an initial **Release**. See the recipe *Creating a cyclical build and test process* in *Chapter 3, Controlling the Project*, for assigning a **Release**.

Req#	Requirement	Business Driver	Amount	Priority	Release
			4hrs per week per sales person to 10		
1	As an order clerk I require an orders report to track open orders.	Reduce Cost	minutes per week	Must	1
15	As a report user I require access to information which pertains to my roles within the organisation			Must	1
16	As a report user I require to see information in my local language			Should	2
17	As a report user I require to see information in my local currency			Must	1

How it works...

By soliciting information from business with regards to priority and release, you are setting the expectation and conveying the understanding of the importance of the specific business requirement. It is important that the step of prioritization and release assignment is done by a stakeholder (a subject matter expert on behalf of the business or steering committee). This ensures visibility in the process and an understanding by the business about the information that will be delivered by the project. Business needs to approve the requirements which are bundled into specific prioritized releases. The implied requirements should also be prioritized and added to the releases. This ensures an understanding between the project team members and the stakeholders of what is required for each release.

Any changes to this should be conveyed to the stakeholders and the reasons for the changes. It is common to rearrange some requirements based on delivery, timeframes or foundation technology which is required to be delivered in a specific release.

Adding hierarchies to your semantic data model

During your requirement gathering, you have collected your hierarchies, groups, and drill paths. This needs to be added to your semantic data model.

Getting ready

Review your requirements and find all the columns which are included in groupings, drill paths, or hierarchies.

How to do it...

Hierarchies, **drills**, and **groupings** are ways in which people consolidate information. The examples can include the following:

- ▶ **Hierarchy**: As a user, I expand country to see invoices by city
- ▶ **Groupings**: Show me all the invoice dollars by product
- ▶ **Drill**: From product category, I want to drill down to and see all the dollars via SKU

These are different ways in which business can articulate the need to group attributes at higher levels, and then navigate to lower levels to see the detail. From a technical perspective, there are different ways to solve these problems. From a semantic model, we are interested in the perceived relationship between the attributes and recording that relationship as follows:

1. Open the Process Flow diagram which you created in *Chapter 5, The Blueprint,* for your blueprint and navigate to the semantic data model:

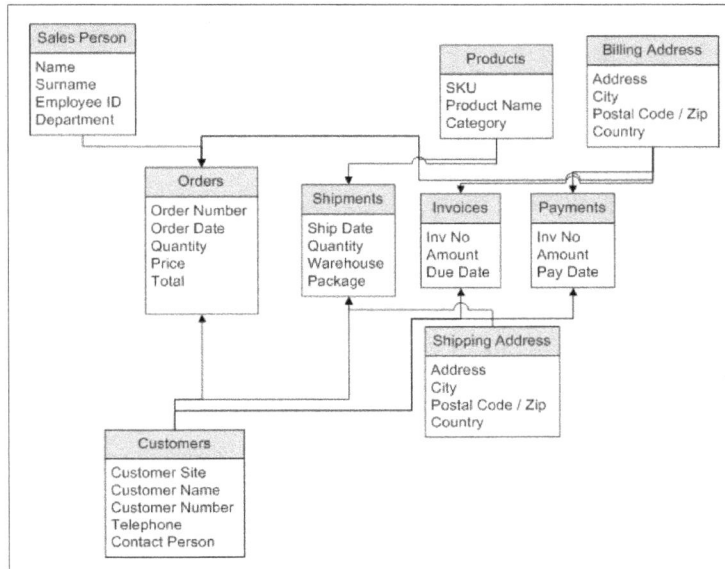

2. Identify the entities where you have groupings, hierarchies, or drill paths. Add the attributes to the entity if they do not exist. For example, from the Open Order Report, we have a drill path of **Customer Name | Customer Site**:

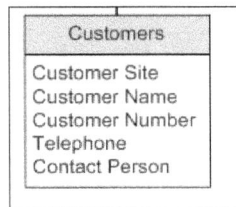

3. Create a name for **Hierarchy**, and add the levels with the associated attributes, for example, **Customer** as follows:

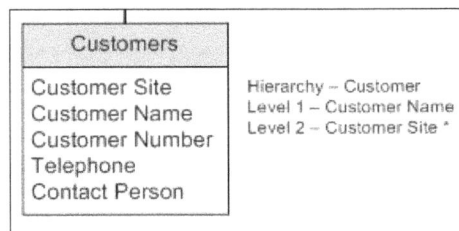

4. Identify the lowest level in the hierarchy. Note: if you have more than one hierarchy on the entity, it is important that the lowest level is the same.

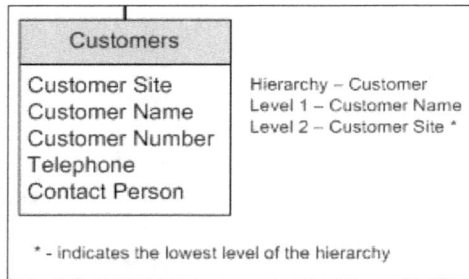

```
┌─────────────────────────────┐
│        Customers            │       Hierarchy – Customer
├─────────────────────────────┤       Level 1 – Customer Name
│  Customer Site              │       Level 2 – Customer Site *
│  Customer Name             │
│  Customer Number           │
│  Telephone                 │
│  Contact Person            │
└─────────────────────────────┘

   * - indicates the lowest level of the hierarchy
```

5. Review the semantic data model, and try and identify natural hierarchies which may exist between the attributes which will be of value to the business.

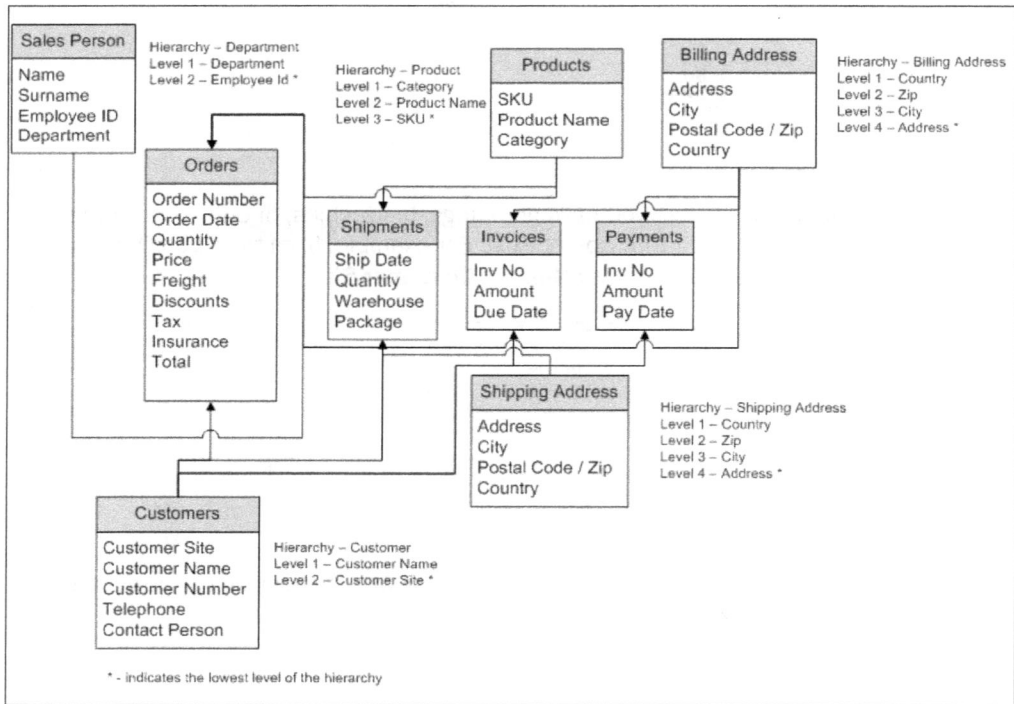

How it works...

Identifying hierarchies, groupings, and drill paths enables you to define the ways in which information is aggregated and analyzed within the organization. This identifies how the business will be able to aggregate data as well as drill to the detailed information. By identifying the lowest level of the hierarchies, you are demonstrating to the business at what grain or level of granularity the information will be stored, that is, the lowest level of detail available to report on. This is important for the business to understand as they often request or require information at certain levels to validate issues or make business decisions.

There's more...

Oracle SQL Data Modeler does not provide native support to annotate your hierarchies. If you wish to include hierarchies into your semantic data model in Oracle SQL Developer, there are two options:

1. Open you data model from *Chapter 5*, *The Blueprint*, and double-click on **Customer**. Add the additional **Customer Site** attribute:

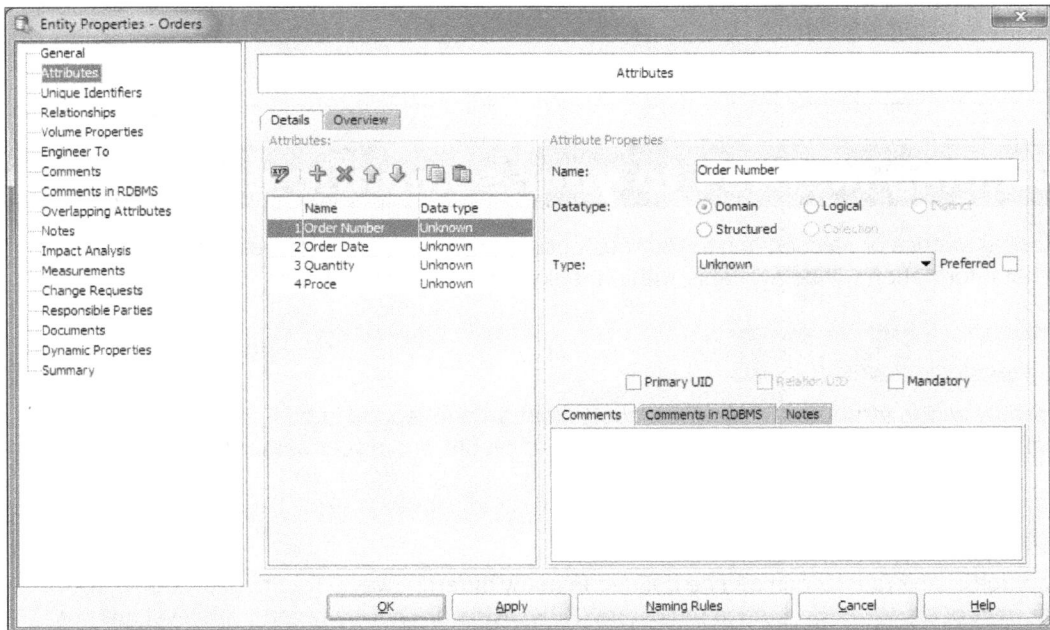

2. In the **Notes** section, annotate **Hierarchy** and **Level**, as shown in the following screenshot:

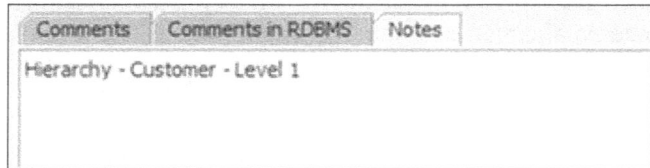

Comments	Comments in RDBMS	Notes

Hierarchy - Customer - Level 1

3. Alternatively, select **Dynamic Properties** and add the hierarchies under the **Dynamic Properties**. Additional **Dynamic Properties** can be added to record additional information such as Data Retention and Security, outlined in the following recipes:

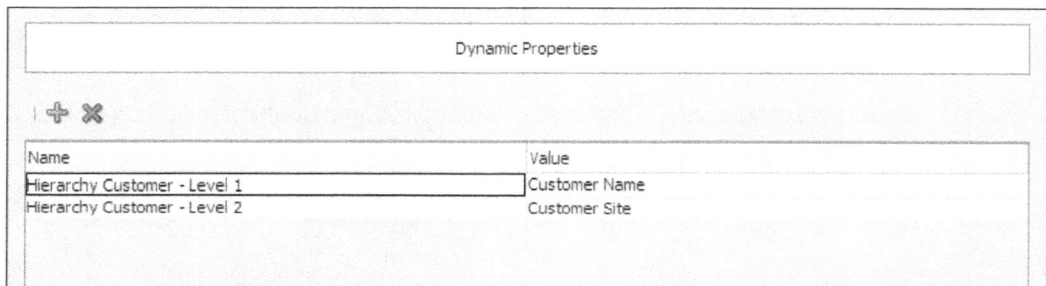

Dynamic Properties

Name	Value
Hierarchy Customer - Level 1	Customer Name
Hierarchy Customer - Level 2	Customer Site

Adding metrics to your semantic data model

Adding metrics or calculations to your business events allows the business to start seeing what information will be available within the semantic data model.

Getting ready

Identify all the attributes within your reports that are embedded in business rules, calculations, or those belonging to the business events within your semantic data model.

How to do it...

Metrics in an organization can be defined in many different ways. Traditionally, these are thought of as Key Performance Indicators (KPIs). **KPIs** are normally very high-level metrics with distinct meanings which are derived from multiple metrics. It is important to understand the metrics which make up these KPIs, and record them within your semantic model. The KPIs should be driven from your business rules as defined in the *Defining the business rules* recipe of this chapter.

Metrics can be additive (used in a calculation) or non-additive (textual or statistical), for example, Total Invoice Amount is a KPI derived by multiplying quantity by price and deducting Discounts, Tax, and Freight. Total Invoice Amount, Price, Quantity, Discounts, and Freight are all metrics.

1. Open the Process Flow diagram which you updated earlier, and navigate to the semantic data model.

2. Include the metric and calculation attributes into the semantic data model if not already captured.

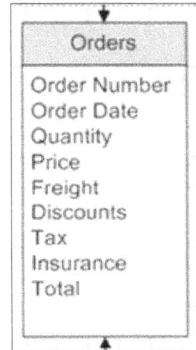

```
                    Orders

            Order Number
            Order Date
            Quantity
            Price
            Freight
            Discounts
            Tax
            Insurance
            Total
```

How it works...

Adding your metrics to your semantic data model ensures you understand the business rules which previously have been captured and the necessary metrics required to support those business rules.

Defining your data dictionary

The **data dictionary** captures all the metadata for your project, and defines the information which will be presented to the business.

Getting ready

Review your semantic data model for all the attributes which lie below the dimensions and business entities (facts).

How to do it...

Creating your data dictionary early in the project allows you to socialize the project, understanding the information required by the business. This relays not only the understanding of the requirements but also the definition of the information gathered from the business. The data dictionary is a key as it will be used as an asset to define and describe information contained within the solution. This will not only be used for the project but will also be used throughout the existence of the solution:

1. Open your **Business Requirement** document, and create a new sheet called **Data Dictionary**, as shown in the following screenshot:

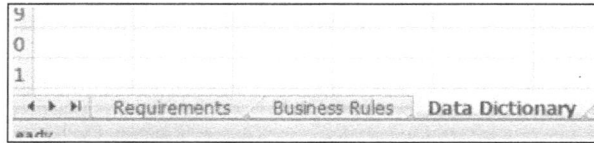

9	
0	
1	

◄ ► ►│ Requirements   Business Rules   **Data Dictionary**

2. Create column headings to record the information within the data dictionary for dimensions:

A	B	C	D	E	F
Entity Type	Entity Name	Attribute Name	Description	Hierachy Name	Hierarchy Level

3. Complete the information for each attribute belonging to a dimension:

A	B	C	D	E	F
Entity Type	Entity Name	Attribute Name	Description	Hierachy Name	Hierarchy Level
Dimension	Customer	Customer Name	The legal trading name for the customer.	Customer	Level 1
		Customer Site	The Physical Location Name for the customer.		Level 2
		Customer Number	The unique number assigned to the customer by Sales.		
		Telephone	The main contact number of the customer at the site location.		
		Contact Person	The main contact person from the customer at the site location		

4. Create column headings to record the information within the data dictionary for **Fact** (this can either be on a separate tab or in the same tab) as follows:

Entity Type	Entity Name	Attribute Name	Description	Aggregation Type	Calculation
Fact	Orders	Order Number	Unique order number for each order line	Non Additive	
		Order Date	Date on which the order was placed	Non Additive	
		Quantity	The quantity of the item requested	Additive - Sum	
		Price	The price of an individual item pre discount	Additive - Sum	
		Freight	The cost associated with shipping the item	Additive - Sum	
		Discounts	The percentage discount applied to the item	Additive - Sum	
		Tax	The amount of tax for each item	Additive - Sum	
		Insurance	The amount of insurance for the item	Additive - Sum	
		Total	Total cost of the item to the customer	Additive - Sum	Rule 2

How it works...

By enhancing your semantic data model, you are capturing the definitions and meanings of the information within the business. Identifying this early in the project allows you to socialize this information with all the stakeholders so that there is chance to review and change definitions if necessary. By socializing the information with all the stakeholders, a common understanding and definition of the information is communicated. This keeps the stakeholders informed and abreast of the progress of the project.

The earlier the semantic data model can be socialized, the quicker errors will be found, and the sooner a common understanding of information can be achieved within the business. In business, information is the asset. It is therefore important to get the definitions of the attributes and entities correctly. Over time, there may be many reporting and business intelligence tools to visualize the same information.

There's more...

Oracle SQL Developer Data Modeler allows one to capture descriptive information within the tool. This eliminates the need for a separate document to capture this information. This is important as eventually the semantic data model will be converted into a logical and physical data model. These descriptions and definitions will be carried forward to the data model on the database:

1. Open **Entity Properties** within Oracle SQL Developer Data Modeler by double-clicking on the entity:

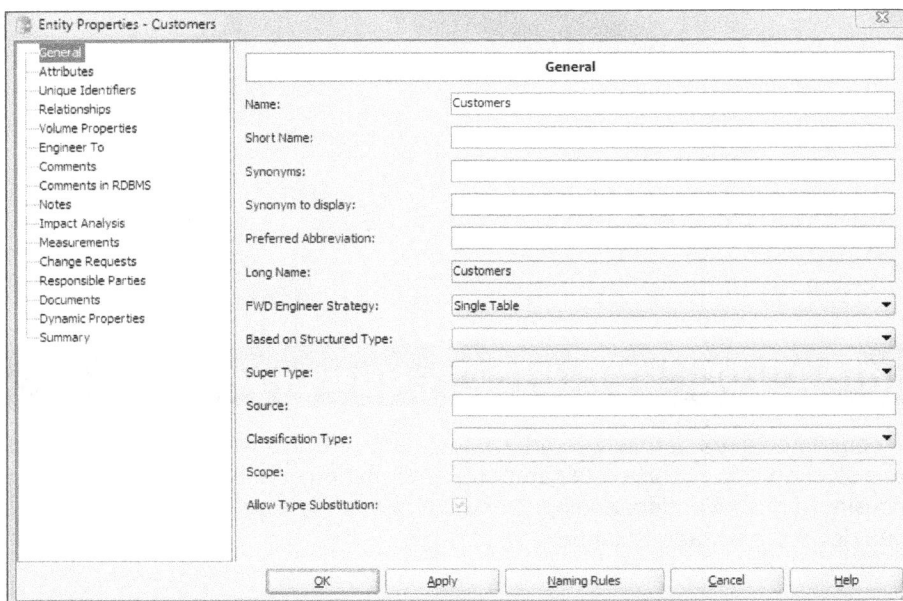

2. Navigate to the property **Comments in RDBMS**, and enter a description for the entity, as shown in the following screenshot:

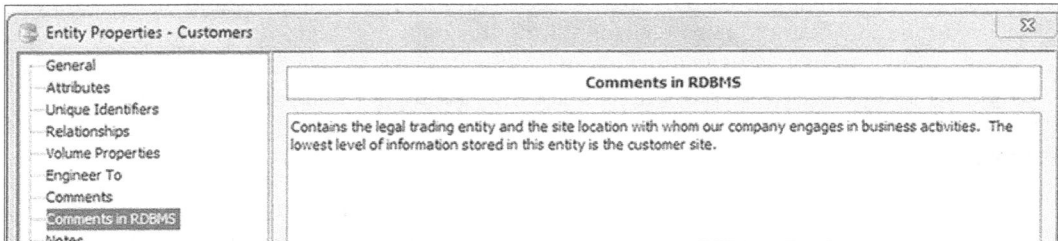

3. Navigate to the property **Attributes**, select **Comments in RDBMS**, and enter a description for **Attributes**, as shown in the following screenshot:

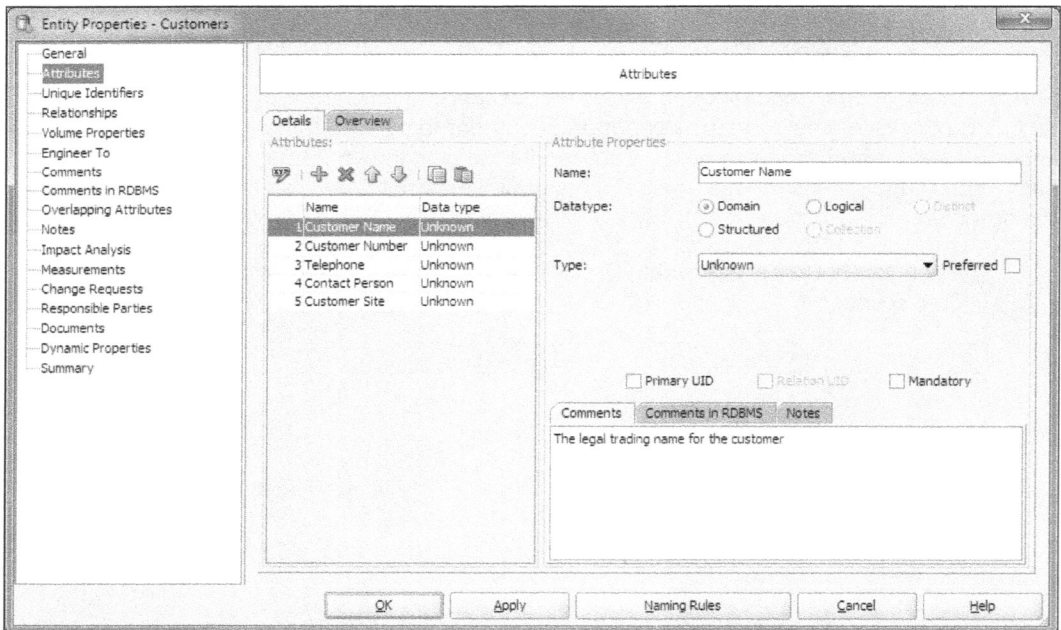

Defining your security requirements

Security requirements are normally an afterthought within a business intelligence and data warehouse solution. It is important to gather this information during requirement gathering so that the business has an understanding of how information is required to be secured, and the project can develop a suitable solution.

Getting ready

Identify any security or governance information within the business which can guide the requirements for security. There are normally three levels of security:

1. **Authentication**: Validate whether the user is who they say they are, and have a valid password.

2. **Authorization**: Identify the role of the user, and map the role to content which the user has access.

3. **Data**: Interpret the role and the data (either attributes or rows), and allow or disallow the user to access sensitive information based on the security profile.

How to do it...

Security is very important within a business intelligence and data warehouse solution. You are normally consolidating information from many aspects of the business which could have been segmented by different systems. For this reason, security was adequate from an operational perspective but may not be for this solution.

1. Open your **Requirement**, and identify your security requirements. Decide how you wish to authenticate the user.

Req#	Requirement
18	As a user I require to be authenticate by the solution using my network username and password to minimize the number of username and password I need to remember.

2. Understand the way you wish to secure reports or content from the users, and record this as a requirement:

Req#	Requirement
15	As a report user I require access to information which pertains to my roles within the organisation

Determine if you have any sensitive information within the organization, or if you require hiding certain information from different users:

Req#	Requirement
19	As a sales user I can only access sales information from my customers to maintain customer confidentiality.
20	As a region manager I require access to all customers within my region to enable me to determine the performance of my region
21	As an region manager I have access to all sales peoples commision information within my region so I can effectively allocate bonuses
22	As a sales person I only have access to my commission information to ensure confidentiality

How it works...

By identifying security requirements early in the project, it allows you to build a comprehensive security model which protects access to content and information. The aim of the security model is to integrate into existing models, and not be too overwhelming to maintain and manage. It requires enough flexibility to allow users to perform their job functions, but enough governance to protect sensitive content and information.

There's more...

For additional information about security review, refer to the recipes in *Chapter 14, Security*.

Defining your data retention requirements

Data retention, or how long information is accessible within the business intelligence and data warehouse solution, is a key requirement. It affects the way information is sourced and the capacity of the hardware required for the project.

Getting ready

Understand any regulatory requirements around the information you are planning to load into the solution and the business requirements to retain information. Data retention is not limited to the length of time information is kept or accessible, but also covers how changes to the information over time are recorded. For this, you will want to understand the level of information you require to store for each business entity.

How to do it...

Data retention not only affects the way information is stored and retained, but also the necessary resources required to keep the information. Not gathering this requirement can have disastrous effects on the success of your project.

1. Open your requirements, and enter a parent requirement for the data retention citing the reasons for data retention:

> For the solution the business requirements information to be
> retained to maintain business continuity and regulatory reporting
> 21 requirements.

2. As part of **Linked Requirement**, list all the entities which are in the semantic data model as follows:

Req#	Requirement	Source	Date	Linked Requirement	
	For the solution the business requirements information to be retained to maintain business continuity and regulatory reporting 21 requirements.				
				Customer	Retain all customers and track changes when Customer name changes
				Sales Person	Retain all sales people, do not track changes only reflect the most recent information for each sales person
				Products	Retain all products which have been order, track changes if the sku and product name combination change
				Billing Address	Retain all billing addresses for orders
				Shipping Address	Retain all shipping addresses for orders
				Orders	Retain a rolling 5 years of information based on calendar year
				Shipments	Retain a rolling 5 years of information based on calendar year
				Invoices	Retain a rolling 7 years of information based of fiscal year
				Payments	Retain a rolling 7 years of information based of fiscal year

3. Data retention may differ by entity. For business entities, you need to specify what data is to be retained and when to track the changes. For business events, you normally specify a period of time for which you require to retain the information.

Customer	Retain all customers and track changes when Customer name changes
Sales Person	Retain all sales people, do not track changes only reflect the most recent information for each sales person
Products	Retain all products which have been order, track changes if the sku and product name combination change
Billing Address	Retain all billing addresses for orders
Shipping Address	Retain all shipping addresses for orders
Orders	Retain a rolling 5 years of information based on calendar year
Shipments	Retain a rolling 5 years of information based on calendar year
Invoices	Retain a rolling 7 years of information based of fiscal year
Payments	Retain a rolling 7 years of information based of fiscal year

How it works...

Data retention is important in a business intelligence and data warehouse solution as it determines how much information is available for reporting and the types of analysis which can be performed.

7
Architecture and Design

Setting the foundation of your business intelligence and data warehouse solution is key to the project. By making specific architecture and design decisions, you will be required to build the solution in a particular way. It is essential to understand some of the different architectural options and how they will affect your design, before you begin the development effort. The following recipes will review some of the key architecture and design issues that should be addressed by the project:

- ▶ Choosing your database type
- ▶ Defining your database layout
- ▶ Selecting the Third Normal Form or a Dimensional model

Introduction

Making a mistake at the architecture and design stage of the project will have many ramifications in the form of rework and additional time, cost, and expense. Business intelligence and data warehouse projects have been around for many years, and there is a wealth of best practice information available, which is a great place to begin your project.

Choosing your database type

There are three broad categories for setting up a database when you install Oracle database using the installation wizard:

- ▶ **Transaction Processing**: Online transaction processing is typically for applications with multiple users inserting and updating low volumes per transaction

▶ **General Purpose**: A batch application that loads large volumes of data during specific windows

▶ **Data Warehouse**: An application that can have multiple users (transactions) requesting large volumes of data for read-only

Getting ready

Identify the key stakeholders, business process owners, and system owners within the identified process flows.

How to do it...

To determine the initial configuration of the database, it is important to get an understanding of the number of users and the expected volumes you will be processing:

1. Schedule meetings with the stakeholders.

2. Ask key questions to understand the nature of the solution:

    a. How many anticipated users do you expect for the solution?

    b. What time of the month/day do you expect the highest number of users utilizing the information?

    c. Does the information need to be updated real time, and why?

3. Schedule meetings with the business process owners.

4. Ask key questions to understand the nature of the business process:

    a. Is the business process updated real time by users, or is information entered and then processed within a batch?

    b. How many business users are involved with the business process?

5. Schedule meetings with the system owners.

6. Ask key questions to understand the source system:

    a. What is the database upon which the system resides?

    b. How large is the current database?

    c. Where is the system located?

    d. How is the system connected to the network?

    e. Does the system do a lot of batch processing?

    f. Can we connect to the system directly?

    g. What is the preferred method to connect to the system to extract information?

    h. What is the process to request access to extract information?

How it works...

There are many other questions that can and should be asked. The aforementioned questions are focused on gathering information to determine how many databases should be created, and the general configuration for each database.

Generally, a business intelligence solution is logically structured in the following way:

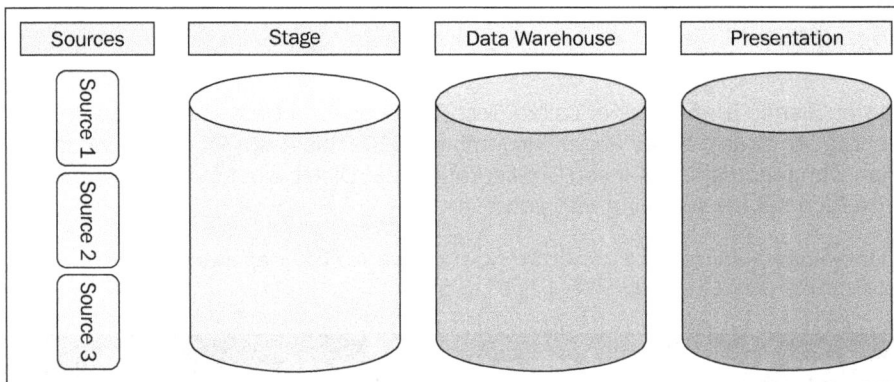

Sources	Stage	Data Warehouse	Presentation
Source 1			
Source 2			
Source 3			

Information comes from multiple sources, and is loaded into a staging area. From the staging area, the information is transformed and loaded into the data warehouse. In the data warehouse, this information can be summarized or enhanced (additional calculations), ready to be consumed from the presentation area.

For the information sessions, if you have determined that you will be continuously extracting large volumes of data from multiple sources, which are geographically dispersed, then you will probably require a separate staging database to collect and consolidate the information. It is advantageous to select a separate database, so that as your information grows over a period of time, you can tune the stage environment to suit the requirements. When you perform the installation for Oracle, you can select a General Purpose template as the initial configuration for the stage database.

For the data warehouse, if you have a large number of users who access information 24 hours per day, 7 days per week, then it is recommended that the data warehouse again be a separate database. This will allow you to prepare the information within the staging database and load the results into the data warehouse. You can minimize the impact of the data transformation and loading on the users, and only require a smaller window to load information. The Data Warehouse template should be used when creating this database.

For the presentation area, if you are using a relational tool to publish information, then this should be located within the same database as the data warehouse. The main reason for this is the ease of administration and the ability to utilize the Oracle technology (summary management, query optimization, and so on), and minimize the amount of data movement.

For most projects, if you have a handful of sources with data loads happening during a preset window and reasonable user counts, a single General Purpose database will be the correct place to start. Data Marts would also be classified under this definition.

There's more...

Oracle has published a white paper called *Best Practices for a Data Warehouse on Oracle Database 11g, An Oracle White Paper,* November 2010. This has a lot of very valuable information with regards to Balanced Configuration and Disk Layout for your database. This can be found at the following web address:

```
http://www.oracle.com/technetwork/database/bi-datawarehousing/twp-dw-
best-practies-11g11-2008-09-132076.pdf.
```

Defining your database layout

Oracle information is stored within a schema. The schema is the objects (tables, views, sequences, and so on) owned within the database. In a business intelligence and data warehouse solution, there are normally multiple schemas that encompass the solution.

Getting ready

Understand the proposed technology for the project and pre-read the installation requirements to get an understanding of the schema requirements.

How to do it...

Creating schemas within the database allows you to segregate and separate objects. This makes it easier to manage the objects with greater flexibility.

Separate your schemas into two categories:

1. **Application Owners**: These are the required schemas to house the information for the solution:

    a. **EDW_APP**: The Enterprise Data Warehouse schema is for custom applications, to capture or enhance information or common lookups. This becomes a source for the data warehouse.

b. **EDW_STAGE**: The Enterprise Data Warehouse stage schema will store all the objects required within the staging process.

c. **EDW**: The Enterprise Data Warehouse publish schema will store all the objects required for the data warehouse and the presentation area.

d. **EDW_DM_<SA>**: This is the Enterprise Data Warehouse data mart schema, where <SA> is replaced with the name of the subject area. The schema does not normally contain any specific objects, but refers back to the objects within the EDW schema.

2. **Technology/Tool/Repository/Pre-Packaged applications required schemas**: These are the required schemas that enable the technology to build/run the solution. Typical schemas include:

   a. **OWBSYS**: This is the Oracle Warehouse Builder system owner schema; its name cannot be changed.

   b. **OWB_<NAME>**: This is the Oracle Warehouse Builder repository owner schema. It is recommended that you prefix with OWB, and then add an additional descriptive name.

   c. **ODI_<NAME>**: This is the Oracle Data Integrator master/work repository owner schema. It is recommended that you prefix with ODI, and then add an additional descriptive name.

   d. **APEX_PUBLIC_USER**: This is the Oracle Application Express Public User schema; its name cannot be changed.

   e. **APEX_04000**: This is the Oracle Application Express schema; its name cannot be changed, but may differ from version to version.

   f. **FLOW_FILES**: This is the Oracle Application Express schema; its name cannot be changed.

   g. **MDS** and **BIPLATFORM**: These are the Oracle Business Intelligence Enterprise Edition schemas. It is recommended that you prefix the schema names with the environment they are being created in. For example, DEV_MDS, DEV_BIPLATFORM. These are created using the repository creation utility or RCU, during installation.

How it works...

Separating and segregating schemas within your application gives you greater flexibility. It allows you to manage and configure each schema appropriately for its function. The following figure outlines the different schemas. In the EDW_STAGE schema, it should store an image of the source and target objects:

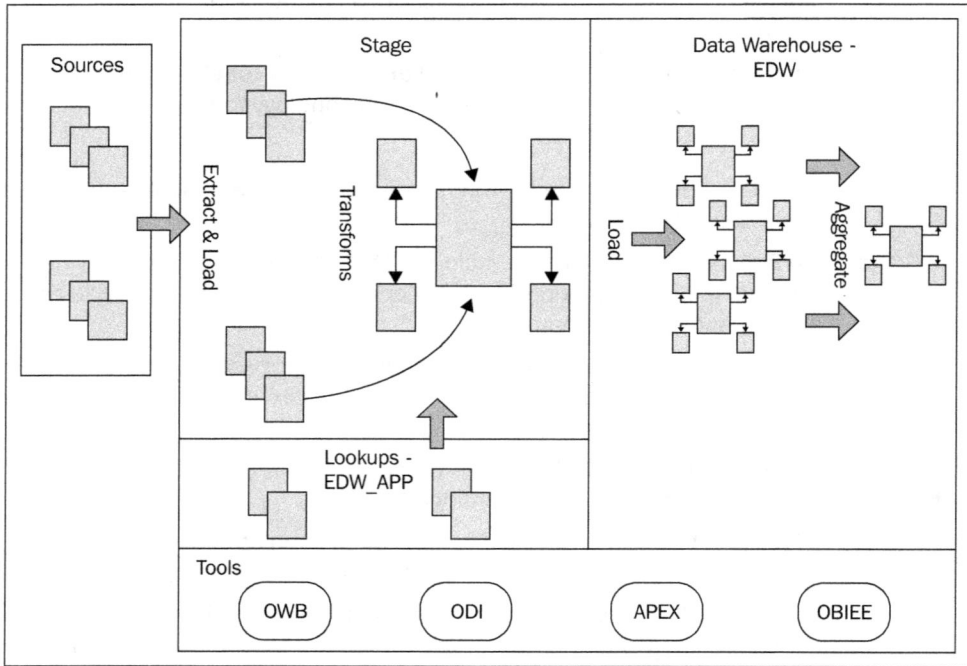

If you have multiple source systems, you may break this into different schemas—a schema for each source environment and a separate schema for the transformed, staged data:'

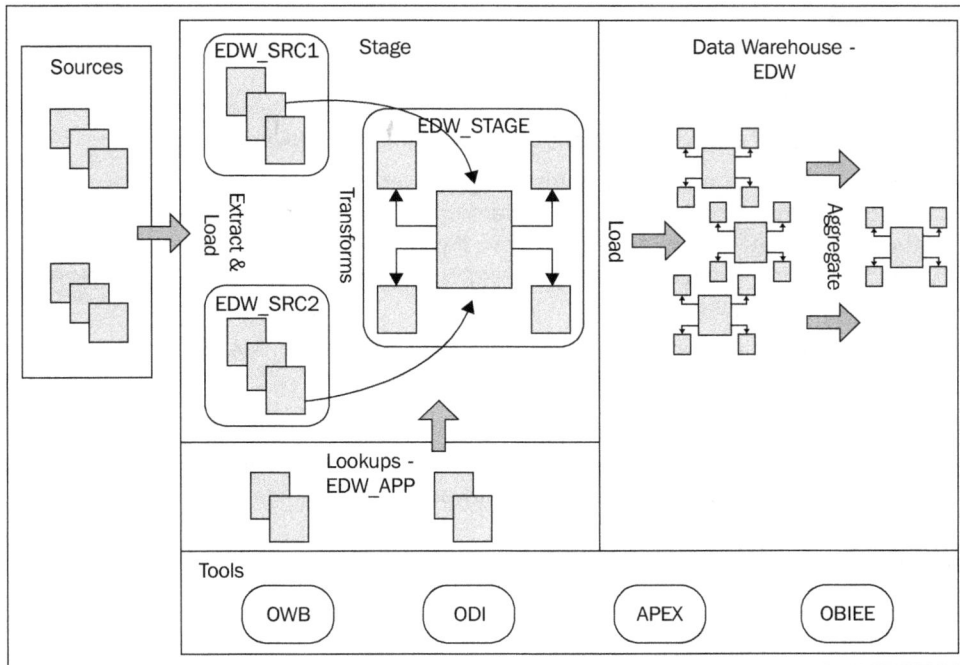

The staging area should have a before picture and an after picture of the information. The before picture should be a representation of the source information within minimal data transformations. The after picture should look like the information that will be loaded into the data warehouse. This allows you to audit information before you load it into the data warehouse, and minimizes the amount of interruption to the users, while manipulating information.

The schemas for each of the tools within the solution should be autonomous to the database. This means that all components for the tool should be contained within a single database. For example, ODI has the concept of a Master and Work Repository. The configuration allows for a single master and multiple work repositories collocated on a single server or across multiple servers, with one or more than one schema. It is recommended that you use a single master with a single work repository within a single schema. Having autonomous environments and objects being exported from one environment to another has several advantages and disadvantages.

Advantages

The advantages of autonomous environments and exporting objects from one environment to another are:

► Redundancy of environments allows you to tolerate hardware faults.

► Ability to upgrade software and test progressively. Having a single master and multiple work repository places software upgrades and downtime requirements on the architecture. This is a great concern if you have to upgrade all your environments first before you can test the latest patch, due to a single master and multiple-work repository configuration.

► Reduced dependency; errors which may cascade between Master and Work repositories will be isolated to a single environment.

► Security; ability to secure environments.

► Segregation and standard development practices; ability to isolate environments and use release management processes between environments.

Disadvantages

The disadvantages are:

► Migration of code is cumbersome

► Potential software version inconsistencies may arise should environments not be patched to the same levels

Oracle has released a white paper—*Oracle Data Integrator: Best Practices for a Data Warehouse*, which can be found at the following web address:

```
http://www.oracle.com/technetwork/middleware/data-integrator/
learnmore/odi-best-practice-data-warehouse-168255.pdf.
```

Based on the previous recipe, you may have several databases, one for your stage area and another for a publish area. The relevant schemas should be placed within the relevant databases.

Within the data warehouse, you will normally have a layer of tables that will hold your atomic-level information. This is the level of information that is extracted from the source environment. Also, in this area, you may have additional objects that will aggregate the information into a model, which is optimized for your reporting tool. This is the presentation layer of information. This layer may change over a period of time, and you should ensure that you can regenerate the information from the atomic level, if required.

There's more...

Oracle has published a white paper—*Best Practices for a Data Warehouse on Oracle Database 11g, An Oracle White Paper,* November 2010. This has a lot of very valuable information with regards to staging, foundation, and presentation layers. This can be found at the following web address:

```
http://www.oracle.com/technetwork/database/bi-datawarehousing/twp-dw-
best-practies-11g11-2008-09-132076.pdf.
```

Selecting the Third Normal Form or a Dimensional model

Using the Third Normal Form or a Dimensional model to support your data warehouse solution is an important and highly debated decision within the industry. Primary reasons for choosing one over the other include:

- ▶ Skills and capabilities within the organizations
- ▶ Preferences
- ▶ The approach to building your warehouse solution

Getting ready

Understand the differences and limitations of a Third Normal Form and or a Dimensional-modeling approach to building your warehouse. Research the technology you plan to implement, to understand which model it works more optimally with.

How to do it...

Third Normal Form modeling is normally used within **Online Transaction Processing Applications (OLTP)**. Dimensional modeling has been refined over the years and is generally accepted for data warehouses:

1. Determine the modeling approach for the initial stage area, which houses a copy of the source. Typically, here you will mirror the source system. Note, you will only bring the relevant information that you require. This schema will therefore use the modeling applied in the source system.

2. Determine the modeling approach for the presentation information used by the application. If you are using OBIEE, then it works more optimally using a dimensional model.

3. Decide on the modeling approach for the atomic-level data model. If you are going to use OBIEE and drill down to detail from the presentation layer, then it is easier to use a dimensional model.

4. The stage area therefore should be built using a model that mirrors your atomic-level data warehouse model.

How it works...

Matching the data model with different areas in your solution increases the amount of transparency within the data model, and makes it easier to troubleshoot. Optimizing your data model for different tool sets allows you to take full advantage of using the capabilities of the tools.

It is recommended that the information in the data warehouse always be at the atomic level (lowest level necessary to recreate any summary information). Therefore, should you change tools over a period of time, you will have the ability to recreate the presentation layer optimized for the new tool.

Other features such as denormalized or snowflake dimensions—type I, II, or III, slowly changing dimensions, and different types of fact tables are other capabilities, which can be embedded within your solution, based on your preferences and standards. There is a lot of information available about these topics. A good place to start is *The 10 Essential Rules of Data Modeling*, from Kimball University (`http://www.informationweek.com/news/software/bi/217700810?pgno=1`).

Additional topics are also available from the Kimball group at:
`http://www.kimballgroup.com/html/articles.html`.

There's more...

Oracle has published a white paper—*Best Practices for a Data Warehouse on Oracle Database 11g, An Oracle White Paper*, November 2010. This has a lot of information with regards to Dimensional (Star) modeling and Third Normal Form.

The white paper can be found at the following web address:

`http://www.oracle.com/technetwork/database/bi-datawarehousing/twp-dw-best-practies-11g11-2008-09-132076.pdf`.

8
Analyzing the Sources

Identifying the right information from the correct source is the key to the success and reputation of the business intelligence and data warehouse project. There can potentially be many different sources for the same information within the organization. If an incorrect source for information is chosen, the level of trust and acceptance for the project will be decreased greatly. This chapter outlines how to analyze data sources to gain a deeper understanding of the information, and how it maps to the requirements and the data model. The recipes help to define the road map of information and how it is used with the project:

- ▶ Validating and enhancing a conceptual data model
- ▶ Creating a business process matrix
- ▶ Creating a report requirements matrix
- ▶ Creating a source matrix
- ▶ Developing the data lineage
- ▶ Defining the detailed transformations

Introduction

Analyzing the data sources and identifying the correct information is essential. In the previous chapters, we looked at a top-down approach for defining our data model. This chapter deals with a bottom-up approach for identifying and mapping information to the requirements. This step is essential as it validates that requirements are achievable, and identifies any potential gaps in information.

Validating and enhancing a conceptual data model

The conceptual data model is a working model for the project and is continually enhanced until it morphs into a physical model. This ensures that the model is continually reviewed and validated throughout the process, and mapped back to the business requirements. This constant morphing caters for iterative development.

Getting ready

Gather the blueprint document from *Chapter 5, The Blueprint*. Identify all the source systems and set up sessions with the process (person or people responsible for a business process), system (person or people responsible for a business system, for example, Enterprise Resource Planning or Customer Relationship Management system) or entity owners (person or people responsible for business information, for example, customer master or product master). The agenda for these sessions is to review the key business information identified in each of the business processes for the specific source systems.

How to do it...

The key to analyzing sources is to gradually gather more information to uncover the source of record for each of the identified entities:

1. Review your blueprint and identify all the sources of information for the business entities. The numbers are merely to assign a unique number to the process and step for identification purposes:

Process #	1	Step #	1
Definition	Orders		
Objectives	Collect information in batches for switches		
Inputs	Customer places an order		
Outputs	Order record		
Business Rules			
Flow Narrative	Customer or Sales person places an order either via the online website or internal order management application		
Actors/Stakeholders	Customer Sales people		

Process #	1	Step #	1
Metrics	Number of orders per period		
	Value of orders per period		
Analysis	Orders by geographical region within a time period		
	Orders by sales people within a time period		
	Orders by product within a time period		
	Backlog orders		
Reports	Order Receipt		
Info Source	Oracle E-Business Suite		
	Web Store Application		
Notes			
Entities	Sales Person		
	Product		
	Customer		
	Orders		
Questions			

2. Create a new workbook named Data lineage. Create a new worksheet named **Source Analysis**. Additional information should be added to the project contacts outlining the process, system, and entity owners:

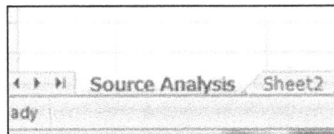

3. Generate a list of sources and the entities which relate to each source as follows:

B	C
Source System	Business Entity
Oracle E Business Suite	Sales Person
	Product

4. For each entity, identify the physical object which relates to the entity:

B	C	D
Source System	Business Entity	Physical Object Name
Oracle E Business Suite	Sales Person	GML.OP_SLSR_MST
	Product	INV.MTL_SYSTEM_ITEMS_B

5. For each physical object identified, outline **Grain** or level of detail stored in the object as indicated by a single record:

Source System	Business Entity	Physical Object Name	Grain
Oracle E Business Suite	Sales Person	GML.OP_SLSR_MST	Each row within the table represents a single sales rep
	Product	INV.MTL_SYSTEM_ITEMS_B	This table holds the definition for inventory items, engineering items and purchasing items.

How it works...

Identifying the major tables and sources of information within source systems allows you to map information back to the requirements. This high-level mapping allows one to identify gaps within information needed to support requirements, and validates if the requirements can be met. By including the grain of the information, you can reconcile the actual grain with the required grain from the definition in *Chapter 6, Analyzing the Requirements*.

During this process, the source analysis should be constantly reviewed by the process, system, and entity owners to ensure that the project is accurately identifying the correct sources for information. Upon completion, this documentation should be approved and agreed upon.

Creating a business process matrix

A **business process matrix** outlines the journey of information through an organization. It is the intersection of which entities are encompassed and used through a business process.

Getting ready

Gather the information collected in the preceding step.

How to do it...

The business process matrix is vital information for the data warehouse, as it aids in the definition and maintenance of the information:

1. Open your data lineage spreadsheet and create an additional tab named **Business Process Matrix**, as shown in the following screenshot:

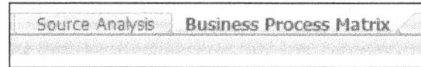

Source Analysis	Business Process Matrix

2. Copy the business entities from your conceptual model in *Chapter 5, The Blueprint*:

Sales Person	Products	Billing Address	Orders	Shipment	Invoices	Payments	Customers	Shipping Address

3. Create a column to insert your **Business Process** as follows:

	A	B	C	D	E	F	G	H	I	J
		Sales Person	Products	Billing Address	Orders	Shipment	Invoices	Payments	Customers	Shipping Address
Business Process										
Order to Payments										

4. Identify for each entity the action performed by **Business Process**. A simple `Create`, `Read`, `Update`, and `Delete` (**CRUD**) annotation identifies how a step within a process uses the information:

	Sales Person	Products	Billing Address	Orders	Shipment	Invoices	Payments	Customers	Shipping Address
Business Process									
Order to Payments									
Order	R	R	CRUD	CRUD				RU	CRUD
Shipping	R	R	R	RU	RU			RU	RU
Invoicing	R	R	RUD	RU	R	CRUD		RU	R
Payment	R	R	R	RU	R	RU	CRUD	RU	R

How it works...

By identifying which business process creates and maintains which information, it is easy to identify where to go if you identify data gaps, or data quality or data governance issues. These business processes are responsible for the quality and integrity of the information within the organization. It is not uncommon for multiple business processes to utilize and maintain the same information. In these cases, it is important to understand how and what each business process interacts with the information so that potential issues can be rectified or avoided.

By identifying how information progresses through the business process, you will understand when your information becomes stable (no more changes) or is in a final state. Each of the steps in the business process which updates information is another point for potentially monitoring the information as it flows though the business process.

Creating a report requirements matrix

A **report requirements matrix** is the intersection of the requested reports and the entities which are used by these reports.

Getting ready

Gather the blueprint information from *Chapter 5*, *The Blueprint*, and report mock-ups.

How to do it...

The **report requirements matrix** is an effective tool for identifying reports and potentially consolidating similar or duplicate reports:

1. Open you data lineage spreadsheet and create an additional tab called **Report Requirements Matrix**:

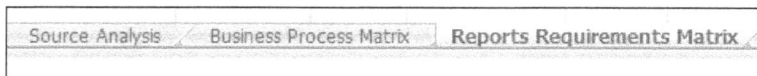

Source Analysis	Business Process Matrix	Reports Requirements Matrix

2. Add your business entities to the top of the worksheet and your report names to the left-hand side of the worksheet:

	Sales Person	Products	Billing Address	Orders	Shipments	Invoices	Payments	Customers	Shipping Address	Calendar
Report Name										
Open Order Report										

3. Map your business entities to your reports by using the semantic model developed in *Chapter 5, The Blueprint*, and the decomposed requirements from *Chapter 6, Analyzing the Requirements*:

	A	B	C	D	E	F	G	H	I	J	K
		Sales Person	Products	Billing Address	Orders	Shipments	Invoices	Payments	Customers	Shipping Address	Calendar
Report Name											
Open Order Report		x			x				x		x

4. Notice when reviewing this information, that we have identified two gaps which we had missed. The region which is part of the **Sales Person** business entity and a new business entity named **Calendar**. These were picked up from the decomposed business requirements.

How it works...

Mapping the reports to the semantic data model facilitates an understanding of how information will be consumed within the business intelligence and data warehouse solution. This allows for users to understand which reports used the specific information. In the event of a change, the matrix can be used to assess the scope of the impact.

By cross referencing the reports with the semantic data model and decomposed requirements, data gaps and missed attributes can be highlighted. Often, reports are requested by multiple people. By listing these reports, it is possible to visually identify which reports are delivering similar content. These similar reports can be combined if appropriate.

Creating a source matrix

Identifying the source of record for information within the conceptual model enables the project team to understand where the key information is sourced.

Getting ready

Gather the blueprint information and information obtained during the first recipe of this chapter.

How to do it...

The **source matrix** identifies the business source of record for each of the business entities:

1. Open your data lineage spreadsheet and create an additional tab called **Source Matrix**:

| Source Analysis | Business Process Matrix | Reports Requirements Matrix | Source Matrix |

2. Place your business entities across the top of the worksheet:

C	D	E	F	G	H	I	J	K	L
Sales Person	Products	Billing Address	Orders	Shipments	Invoices	Payments	Customers	Shipping Address	Calendar

3. From the source analysis worksheet, identify all the sources for the different business entities:

A	B	C	D	E	F	G	H	I	J	K	L
		Sales Person	Products	Billing Address	Orders	Shipments	Invoices	Payments	Customers	Shipping Address	Calendar
	Sources										
Oracle E Business Suite	GML.OP_SLSR_MST	x									
	INV.MTL_SYSTEM_ITEMS_B		x								
Webstore	CUSTOMER								x		
	SLS_REP	x									
	ORD_HDR				x						
	ORD_DTL				x						
	PROD		x								

How it works...

By identifying the source of record for the entities in the conceptual model, it is easy to see where there could be master data management issues, data integrity or quality issues, and areas which require additional logic to combine and/or standardise information from multiple sources.

As systems change over time, the source matrix is also a key to identify the impact of such changes and become the key source of information when trying to determine where information is within the organization. At this stage, do not remove sources for business entities as you need to first determine the correct source of information for the business entity.

Developing the data lineage

Data lineages are diagrams or information which trace information through the system. This gives you the big picture of the information flow within the business intelligence and data warehouse project.

Getting ready

Gather the blueprint information and information obtained during the development of different matrices' recipes for this chapter.

How to do it...

Creating a data lineage creates a visual flow of the information as it is understood by the project team. This provides the basis for the development of mappings to extract and load the data warehouse as follows:

1. Open your data lineage spreadsheet and create an additional tab called **Data Lineage**, as shown in the following screenshot:

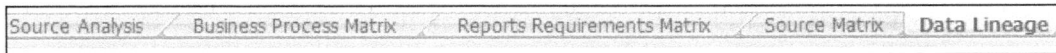

Source Analysis	Business Process Matrix	Reports Requirements Matrix	Source Matrix	**Data Lineage**

2. On the left-hand side, enter your **Business Entities**:

Business Entities
Sales Person
Products
Billing Address
Orders

3. Outline the different stages the data will travel through in the business intelligence and data warehouse project before it gets published to the business users:

	Source				Staging				Presentation		
Business Entities	Source System	Source Object	Link Type	Link Name	Mapping Name	Staging Object	Mapping	Pre Publish Object	Mapping	Presentation Object	

4. Complete the information for each **Source** as it flows through the solution:

B	C	D	E	F	G	H	
	Source				Staging		
Business Entities	Source System	Source Object	Link Type	Link Name	Mapping Name	Staging Object	N
Sales Person		GML.OP_SLSR_MST	Database Link	EBUS	SRC_STG1_SALES_REP_TI	OP_SLSR_MST	S
		SLS_REP	Flat File	f:\Data\sls_rep_<date>.txt	SRC_STG1_SLS_REP_TI	SLS_REP	

How it works...

Identifying the source, staging, and target objects gives you a complete overview of how information flows and is transformed within the solution. This is the initial draft of the data lineage. As the project progresses with data profiling and development, this document should get updated to reflect the most recent information.

There's more...

Enforcing standards

When completing the data lineage, it is important to adhere to standards. This can be enforced within the data lineage spreadsheet by using formulas to automatically populate the mapping names, and so on.

Data lineage diagrams are an alternative or enhancement to building the spreadsheet. The diagram is easier to read and gives a flow of information, but you have the disadvantage of the diagram potentially becoming overcrowded.

Open a diagram tool. Create a new diagram to outline your data lineage:

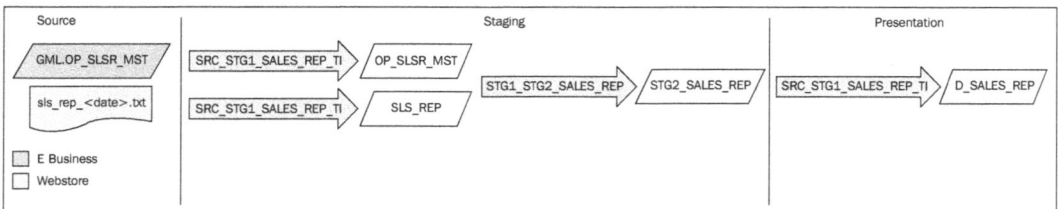

Defining the detailed transformations

Identifying and reusing business rules and transformations enables the standardization of these rules across business processes and subject areas.

Getting ready

Gather the business rules from the requirements gathering.

How to do it...

Data Rules differ from report calculations. These rules are the way information is transformed and manipulated. These rules can potentially change or modify the source information.

1. Open your data lineage spreadsheet and create an additional tab named **Data Rules**, as shown in the following screenshot:

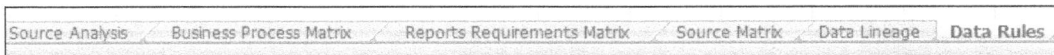

| Source Analysis | Business Process Matrix | Reports Requirements Matrix | Source Matrix | Data Lineage | **Data Rules** |

2. Add columns to the spreadsheet for **Rule #**, **Rule Type**, and **Logic**, as follows:

A	B	C	D
	Rule #	Rule Type	Logic

3. Define the different rule types; examples are as follows:

   - Calculation
   - Data Cleansing
   - Data Standardization

It is a good practice to include the source for the data rule, that is, who provided the information to you for the rule and when.

How it works...

Business rules which can be determined and calculated during the information flow are then standardized within the data model for all to use. This is the most efficient way to reuse these business rules. Business rules which will be included into the processing of the information should be included here.

This chapter has focussed on the high-level definition of the data warehouse. At this stage, the information has been identified to start detailed analysis and design. By starting at the highest level, you are producing a road map for further exploration. In subsequent chapters, you will get into the detailed analysis. When issues are uncovered, the matrices you have created in this chapter will be valuable as they will provide the means to identify the impact and magnitude of issues, for example, if a source system does not contain the correct sales information. From the physical table, you can trace the entities, the reports, and the requirements giving you the complete picture of the impact to an issue or change.

9
Analyzing the Data

Data discovery enables the identification of data discrepancies and business rules which are required to be implemented to enhance data quality. This chapter covers developing data discovery scripts to uncover data issues and gaps. The recipes for data discovery include the following:

- ▶ Building high and low data profiling scripts
- ▶ Building domain/distinct values profiling
- ▶ Building record count profiling scripts
- ▶ Building density data profiling scripts
- ▶ Building hierarchy data profiling scripts
- ▶ Building significant columns data profiling scripts
- ▶ Building data lengths data profiling scripts
- ▶ Building changing information data profiling scripts
- ▶ Building automated data profiling with Oracle Warehouse Builder

Introduction

Data profiling is an effective tool within a business intelligence and warehousing solution to gain a deeper understanding of the information. This process is undertaken to refine and validate assumptions about the information. Business rules are often defined as a result of data discovery and profiling.

Building high and low data profiling scripts

High and low data profiling scripts define the range of values within an attribute. These scripts form the basis of allowable values within the solution. Typical candidates for this type of profiling include the following:

- Date attributes
- Numeric attributes

Getting ready

Review your semantic data model, and identify all attributes which are required to be validated to fall within a range of acceptable values. Once you have identified the entities in your semantic data model, you need to determine the actual source of the information. This information can be found in *Identifying your source of record for your business entities* recipe of *Chapter 5, The Blueprint*, and *Creating a source matrix* recipe of *Chapter 8, Analyzing the Sources*. Once you have the necessary information to connect to the system, you need to identify the source tables for the entities.

How to do it...

Basic profiling scripts can give you great insight into the information you are planning to incorporate into the solution.

1. Identify the source tables for the identified entities:

a. Oracle E Business Suite
i. Sales person - GML.OP_SLSR_MST
ii. Products - INV.MTL_SYSTEM_ITEMS_B

2. Connect to the source environments using a suitable tool, for example, SQL Developer for an Oracle Database. Click on the **New Connection** icon to create a connection:

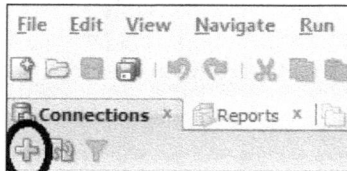

3. Enter the connection details for the source environment:

4. Identify the necessary columns for high and low data profiling.

5. Build the SQL Statement to determine the high and the low values for the information.

Sample SQL Statement:

```
select min(<attribute_name>), max(<attribute_name>)
from <schema.table_name>;
```

Example SQL Statement:

```
select min(start_active_date), max(start_active_date)
frominv.mtl_system_items_b;
```

How it works...

Identifying the high and the low values for different tables allows you to determine acceptable ranges of information. This gives you insight into how information progresses over time. The SQL Statement is a very basic statement which finds the lowest and highest value for an attribute from a specific table.

In the preceding example, the SQL looks for the earliest date by which an item became active and the latest date by which an item became active. This identifies the date range information that should be available for items within the system. If there is information for items earlier than the earliest date, it will signify an issue with data quality.

High and low data profiling scripts are only valid on attributes which contain business information. The attributes which are numeric may be links to a domain value; however, high and low value analysis on these attributes would not be very meaningful.

There's more...

The information gained from performing high and low values data profiling normally becomes data rules embedded within your Extract and Loading process, thus ensuring data quality.

For example:

1. Checks to validate no future dates transactions are included.
2. Checks to validate that specific numbers fall within certain ranges.

These should be added back into the requirements document as shown in *Defining the Business Rules* recipe in *Chapter 6, Analyzing the Requirements*.This way business rules determined by data profiling can be validated and verified by stakeholders.

Building domain/distinct values profiling

Domain values or **distinct values profiling** are really used to determine which values are populated and allowable for an attribute. Domain data profiling gives you an understanding of the information which will be available for the attributes and presented to the users.

Getting ready

Review your report mock ups and requirements from *Decomposing the reports and requirements* recipe of *Chapter 6, Analyzing the Requirements*, and identify all attributes which will be used in filters, drill paths, and page items to start with. Determine the source of record for this information using the *Creating a source matrix* recipe of *Chapter 7, Analyzing the Source*.

How to do it...

Domain values are normally good candidates for standardizing the information which will be presented to the users:

1. Identify the necessary attributes from the semantic data model which relate to the requirements from the report mock ups.
2. Use the data lineage to determine the source systems and tables the attributes belong to.
3. Use SQL Developer to connect to the source environment.

4. Build the SQL statement to determine the distinct values for the information.

Sample SQL statement:

```
select <attribute_name>, count(*)
from<schema.table_name>
group by <attribute_name>;
```

Example SQL statement:

```
select planner_code, count(*)
frominv.mtl_system_items_b;inv.mtl_system_items_b
group by planner_code;
```

How it works...

Domain values are lists of acceptable values for certain attributes. These are normally enforced by the source system or ways to categorize information. By analyzing the attributes which should have domain values, you are verifying whether the information contained within these lists is accurate and valid for performing reporting and data analysis. Domain values are also key areas within the business intelligence and data warehouse solution which may need to be standardized to a common set of values. The same semantic attribute which is sourced from columns in different source systems may have different domain values. These are candidates to be standardized.

Domain values should be captured as business rules within the requirements document. If the information needs to be standardized, a separate business rule for each source system mapping the values from the source system to the standardized values should be documented.

Building record count profiling scripts

Record count profiling scripts are important to understand how much data is available for the solution.

Getting ready

Identify all the tables which will be used in the solution by gathering the information from the *Creating a source matrix* recipe in *Chapter 8, Analyzing the Sources*.

How to do it...

Record counts give you a good indication of data volumes, and potentially change data volumes. They will allow you to determine how much information is relevant to the solution.

1. Use SQL Developer to connect to the source environment.

2. Build the SQL statement to determine the record counts for each table identified in the source matrix.

   Sample SQL statement:
   ```
   select count(*) from<schema.table_name>;
   ```

   Example SQL Statement:
   ```
   select count(*) frominv.mtl_system_items_b;
   ```

3. Review the table and determine if there are any audit columns (create date, modified date, update date, and so on) which can be used to track changes. Should there be such a column, determine the breakdown of the records by these audit columns. Remember that the `date` and `timestamp` columns include the time component in the data. To remove this in order to group data by day, you will need to use the `trunc` function in your SQL statement.

   Sample SQL statement:
   ```
   select <audit_attribute>,count(*)from<schema.table_name>
   group by <audit_attribute>;
   ```

   Example SQL statement:
   ```
   select last_update_date,count(*)
   frominv.mtl_system_items_b
   group by trunc(last_update_date);
   ```
   ```
   select creation_date,count(*)
   frominv.mtl_system_items_b
   group by trunc(creation_date);
   ```

How it works...

By identifying the number or records within the table, you will get an understanding of the volume of information which will be present in the solution. Further identifying how information is created and updated will give you an understanding of the frequency of change.

Building density data profiling scripts

Density profiling scripts are used to determine which values are used the most within a dataset. These scripts are also very informative to determine the percentage of information which has no values. They can be used in place of the domain values scripts if it is important to understand the distribution of information.

Getting ready

Identify all the attributes which require no null values, are used in filters not previously profiled, or require to be standardized from the semantic data model. In addition to these values, you should identify any flag in the system or attributes used to signify status of information.

How to do it...

Data density scripts can be resource-intensive, so be aware of when these are executed so as not to affect the performance of source systems:

1. Identify the necessary attributes from the semantic data model which relate to the requirements from the report mock ups.

2. Use the data lineage to determine the source systems and tables the attributes belong to.

3. Use SQL Developer to connect to the source environment.

4. Build the SQL Statement to determine the distinct values for the information as follows:

   Sample SQL statement:
   ```
   select * from(
   select <attribute_name>,
   count(<attribute_name>),
   count(<attribute_name>)/(select count(<attribute_name>)
   from <schema.table_name>)*100 as contr
   from <schema.table_name>
   group by <attribute_name>)
   order by contr desc;
   ```

   Example SQL statement:
   ```
   select * from(
   select planner_code,
   count(planner_code),
   count(planner_code)/(select count(planner_code)from inv.mtl_
   system_items_b)*100 as contr
   from inv.mtl_system_items_b
   group by planner_code)
   order by contr desc;
   ```

How it works...

The results for the profiling outline the distinct values stored within an attribute. These scripts will also show the distribution of the values as compared to the total records.

This information will aid later in determining the strategy for Extraction and Loading as well as identifying which attributes require data cleansing.

Data distribution values should be captured as informational requirements within the requirements document. If the information needs to be standardized, a separate business rule for each source system, mapping the values from the source system to the standardized values should be documented.

Building hierarchy data profiling scripts

Understanding data in hierarchies is essential to allowing users the capability to drill into the information. Profiling enables you to determine what type of hierarchies are available within the source systems. Hierarchies are generally of the following two types:

▶ **Balanced** – The depth of the hierarchy is consistent across all the parents. Each child value has a single parent.

▶ **Ragged** – The depth of the hierarchy varies depending on the parent.

Getting ready

Review your report mock ups and requirements from the *Decomposing the reports and requirements* recipe in *Chapter 6, Analyzing the Requirements,* and identify all the attributes which will be used in drill paths. Determine the source of record for this information using the *Creating a source matrix* recipe in *Chapter 8, Analyzing the Sources.*

For this recipe, there is a sample script which needs to be executed on a database. These scripts will outline the examples of a balanced and ragged hierarchy. Create a temporary user within a database, and create tables with the following data:

```
create table hier_balanced
(col1 varchar2(10),
col2 varchar2(10),
col3 varchar2(10));
insert into hier_balanced (col1, col2, col3)
values
('Root', 'Parent1', 'Child1');
insert into hier_balanced (col1, col2, col3)
values
('Root', 'Parent1', 'Child2');
insert into hier_balanced (col1, col2, col3)
values
('Root', 'Parent2', 'Child3');
insert into hier_balanced (col1, col2, col3)
values
('Root', 'Parent2', 'Child4');
commit;
create table hier_ragged
(col1 varchar2(10),
col2 varchar2(10));
insert into hier_ragged (col1, col2)
values
('Root', 'Parent1');
```

```
insert into hier_ragged (col1, col2)
values
('Root', 'Parent2');
insert into hier_ragged (col1, col2)
values
('Root', 'Parent3');
insert into hier_ragged (col1, col2)
values
('Parent1', 'Child1');
insert into hier_ragged (col1, col2)
values
('Parent1', 'Child2');
insert into hier_ragged (col1, col2)
values
('Parent2', 'Child3');
insert into hier_ragged (col1, col2)
values
('Parent2', 'Child4');
commit;
```

How to do it...

Understanding the types and composition of hierarchies will help greatly within the project. It is not uncommon to have unbalanced hierarchies with incorrect or multiple parents within the source systems:

1. Connect to the database using the temporary user created in the preceding section.

2. The table `hier_balanced` is a balanced hierarchy and the table `hier_ragged` is a ragged hierarchy. Examine the data.

3. Check whether the children only have a single parent which is not null:

   ❑ **Balanced** – For each level in the hierarchy, check for the child values having only a single parent:

   ```
   select col3, count(*) from (
   select distinct col3, col2
   from hier_balanced
   )
   group by col3, col2
   having count(*) > 1;
   select col2, col1, count(*) from (
   select distinct col2, col1
   from hier_balanced
   )
   group by col2
   having count(*) > 1;
   ```

- ☐ **Ragged** – To check a ragged hierarchy, you can start at a specific position (col1='Root'):

```
select hier, count(*) from (
SELECT LPAD('', level*2, '') || col2 as hier
FROM hier_ragged
START WITH col1 = 'Root'
CONNECT BY PRIOR col2 = col1)
group by hier
having count(*) > 1;
```

How it works...

Hierarchies need to be validated and checked to ensure they have a parent which is not null and only have a single parent. Should there be issues with this, then the data will need to be cleansed before it can be implemented within the solution as a drill path. If the data is not corrected, this can cause incorrect information to be returned as the duplicate relationships in the hierarchies can either cause double counting or circular references. Ensuring child values have one and only one parent and each child has a parent is a key to validating the integrity of the hierarchy. By understanding the type of hierarchy, you can appropriately plan for the inclusion of the information into your design.

Building data lengths data profiling scripts

Understanding the scale, precision, and length of common columns is important to be able to construct your data model.

Getting ready

Gather the source user name and passwords for the source system.

How to do it...

Understanding the scale and precision will allow you to appropriately plan for the correct data structures within the data warehouse:

1. Connect to the source system using Oracle SQL Developer as the schema owner of the objects you are profiling.

2. Determine the datatypes you may be working with.

   Sample SQL statement:
   ```
   select distinct data_type
   from user_tab_columns
   where data_type not like '%$%';
   ```

3. Check the lengths of character datatypes.

   Sample SQL statement:

   ```
   select distinct data_type, data_length from user_tab_columns
   where data_type  like '%CHAR%' and data_length > 1
   order by data_length;
   ```

4. Check the scale and precision of numeric datatypes.

   Sample SQL statement:

   ```
   select distinct data_type, nvl(to_char(data_
   precision),'Default'), nvl(to_char(data_scale),'Default')
   from user_tab_columns
   where data_type  like '%NUMBER%' and data_length > 1;
   ```

How it works...

Review the outputs of the preceding queries to understand what types of data you are dealing with within the solution. Scale and precision allow you to standardize the data model to support the most common values which are found within your source system,for example, two decimal places for currency columns. If you have a higher level of access within your source system, you could use ALL_TAB_COLUMNS or DBA_TAB_COLUMNS in place of USER_TAB_COLUMNS.

Building significant columns data profiling scripts

Significant columns are the proposed natural columns you will be using in your dimensions to uniquely identify an individual record for the dimension. These keys determine the grain of the dimension.

Getting ready

Identify all the dimension entities within your semantic data model and determine the source tables for these dimensions.

How to do it...

Significant columns may differ from the natural key of the table:

1. Connect to the source system using Oracle SQL Developer.
2. Build a SQL statement to validate the grain of the dimension.

Sample SQL statement:
```
select <attribute_name>, <attribute_name>,
<attribute_name> , count(*)
from <schema.table_name>
group by <attribute_name>, <attribute_name>,
<attribute_name>;
```

Sample SQL statement:
```
select planner_code, segment1 , count(*)
from inv.mtl_system_items
group by planner_code, segment1;
```

3. Validate the result set.

How it works...

The results which you get from the query will give you an understanding of all the unique records within your dimension. The count of the information will give you an indication of how many records will be merged into the single record. It is important to correctly define your significant columns because if incorrect, you may merge too many records together or have too many non-unique records within your solution.

If your solution requires you to track changes on a specific column, then these columns become the significant columns. By identifying the significant columns, you are identifying how changes will be tracked in the dimensions. The significant columns will be at least the natural keys for the dimension, and then include any additional columns or no additional columns depending on how you would like to track changes.

Building changing information data profiling scripts

To understand information, it is important to identify how information changes within the system. In order to do this, you will need to track the changes over a period of time. This can sometimes be days or months depending on your source systems, and how frequently information is modified and updated.

Getting ready

Identify all the entities and the relevant source tables. Review the definition of the tables, and group them into two buckets:

▶ **Tables with audit columns** – identify any table with columns which can identify when a record was created or updated. These are normally the event or fact entities.

▶ **Tables without audit columns** – identify any table which does not have any way of easily identifying a change. These are normally the dimension entities.

How to do it...

From this recipe, identifying the rate of change is the goal. This allows you to identify how you can track changes for each table:

1. Connect to the source system using Oracle SQL Developer:

   ❑ For tables with audit columns, build an SQL statement which uses the date to detect updated or new records.

   Sample SQL statement:

   ```
   select trunc(<attribute_name>),count(*)from
   <schema>.<table_name>
   group by trunc(<attribute_name>);
   ```

   Example SQL statement:

   ```
   select trunc(last_update_date),count(*)from inv.mtl_
   system_items_b
   group by trunc(last_update_date);
   ```

   ❑ For tables without audit columns, build an SQL statement that counts the number of rows.

   Sample SQL statement:

   ```
   select count(*)from <schema>.<table_name>;
   ```

   Example SQL statement:

   ```
   select count(*)from inv.mtl_system_items_b;
   ```

2. Record the results of the SQL Statements in a spreadsheet.
3. Wait for a period of time (day, week, and so on), and then re-run the SQL statements.

How it works...

Understanding the amount of change and frequency is important to be able to effectively build an extraction routine for your solution. This information is key in order to determine the following:

▶ The size of environment

▶ Determining the best method to extract information from the source environment

▶ Understanding the types of changes and how information flows

There's more...

To identify what changes, a temporary table is required. In order to accomplish this, the following steps can be performed:

1. Use SQL Developer to connect an environment where you have the necessary privileges to do the following:

    ❑ Create a database link

    ❑ Create tables

2. Create a database link. You may need your Database Administrator (DBA) to create this link for you, and set up a user. The user to which you connect will be the username and password for the source system.

    Sample SQL statement:
    ```
    CREATE [PUBLIC] DATABASE LINK <link_name>
    CONNECT TO <user_name>
    IDENTIFIED BY <password>
    USING '<service_name>';
    ```

3. Create a temporary table from the source system as `table_name`, and then append the date onto the end of the table. Repeat this process for a few days to get a couple of snapshots of the source information.

    Sample SQL statement:
    ```
    CREATE TABLE <TABLE_NAME_DATE> AS SELECT * FROM TABLE_
    NAME@<link_name>;
    ```

4. Once you have at least two tables, you can compare them. The following statement will compare the rows from the first `SELECT` statement, and remove any duplicates from the second `SELECT` statement:

    ```
    SELECT * FROM <TABLE_NAME_DATE>
    MINUS
    SELECT * FROM <TABLE_NAME_DATE>;
    ```

If you do not have any information on how frequently the data changes, you will need to experiment with the frequency of the extract. Initially, extract the data daily and keep approximately three snapshots. If you do not detect any change, then increase the time.

Building automated data profiling with Oracle Warehouse Builder

Oracle Warehouse Builder has a data profiling module which can help with the profiling of information.

Getting ready

Ensure you have Oracle Warehouse Builder installed and configured as per the installation guide. Identify all the source tables required for data profiling.

How to do it...

Oracle Warehouse Builder provides the capability to automate many data profiling scripts. Be aware that the process uses many resources on the source server, so be diligent when they are executed:

1. Create a new Oracle Module for each source system. Expand the project, expand **Databases**, and right-click on **Oracle** to select **New Oracle Module**, as shown in the following screenshot:

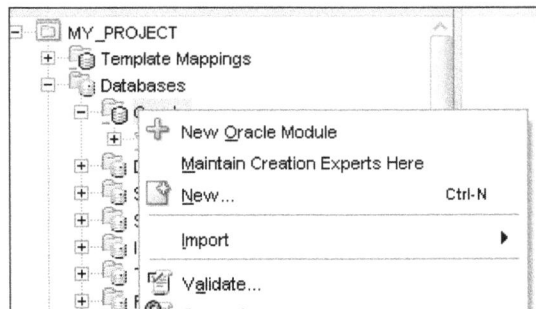

2. The **Create Module Wizard** will appear; click on **Next**:

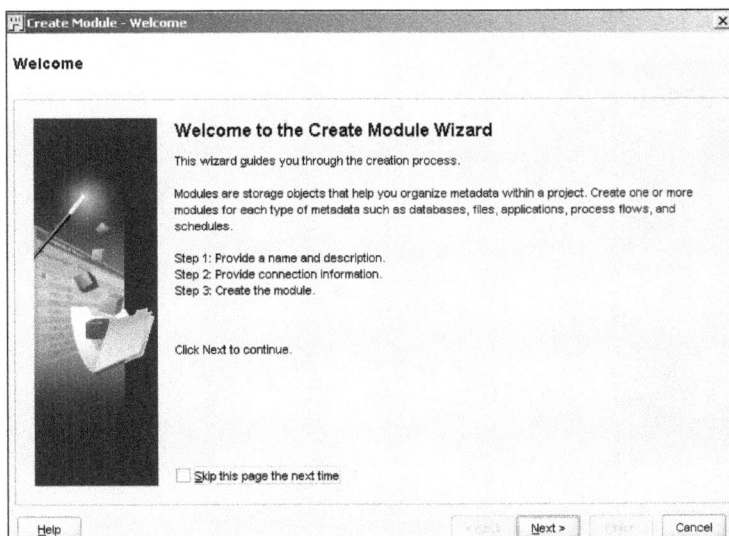

3. Give the module a Name. For the example, we will be using the default Oracle schema name, that is, **SRC_SCOTT**. Click on **Next**:

4. View **Connection Information**, and click on **Edit** to update it:

5. Rename the location **Name** field, enter the source details, and click on **Test Connection**. If successful, click on **OK**:

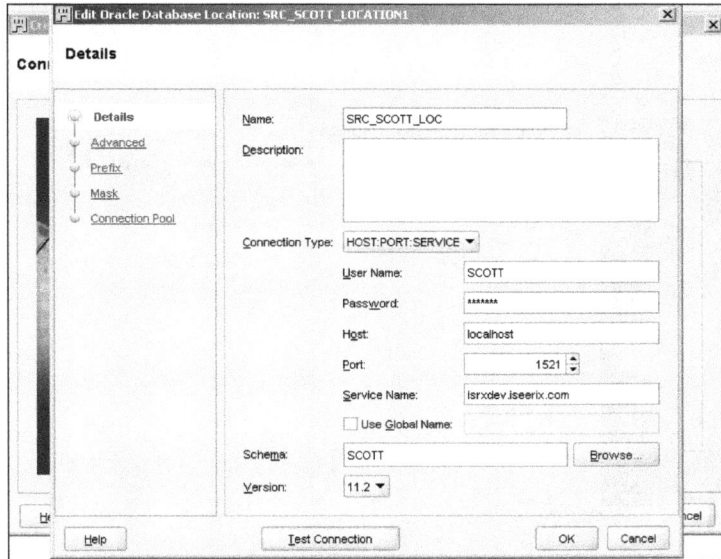

6. Verify the connection details, and check the **Import after finish** box in the lower-left corner. Then, click on **Next**:

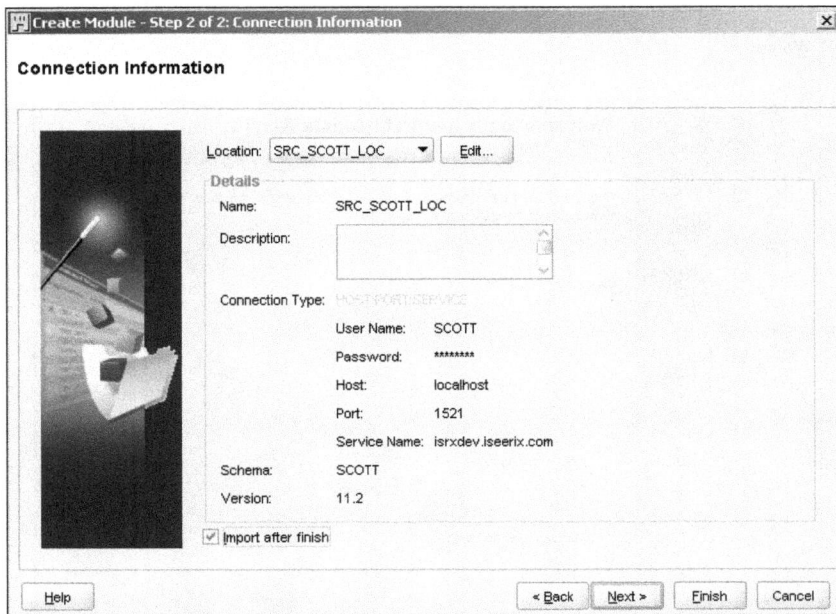

7. The wizard ends with the verification that the module has been completed. Click on **Next**:

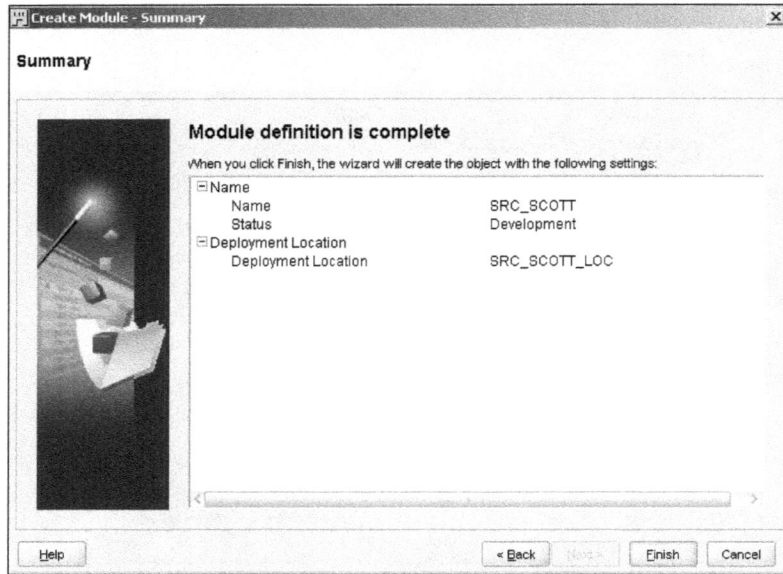

8. Immediately, the **Import Metadata Wizard** will start. Click on **Next**:

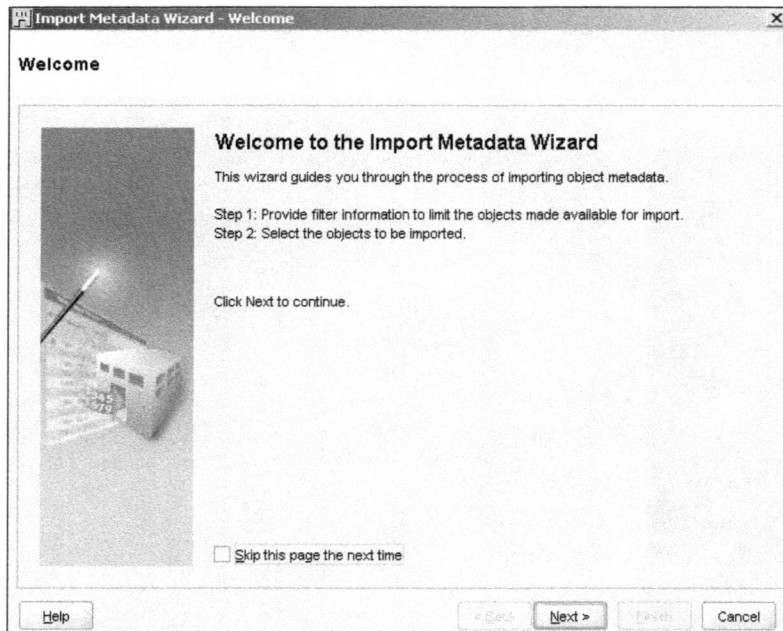

9. Check **Table** for the objects to import. Click on **Next**:

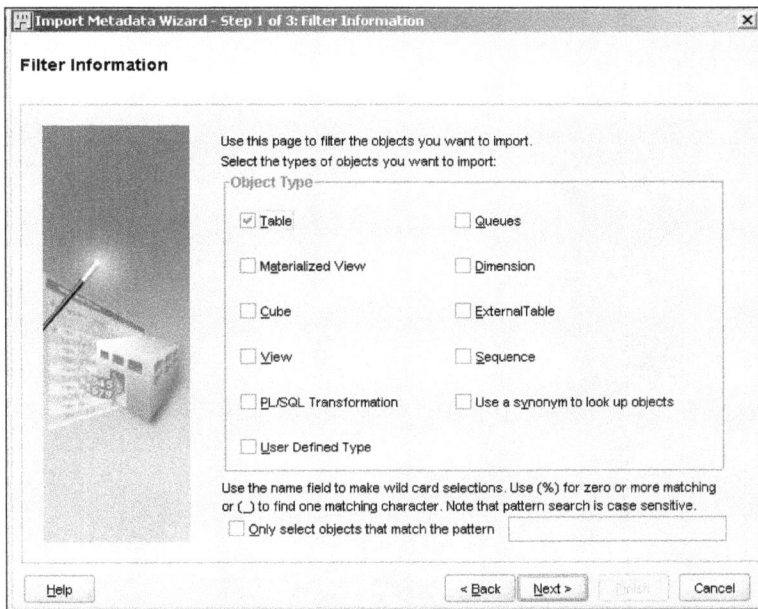

10. From the list of **Tables** on the right-hand side, select all the necessary tables. Once all the tables have been selected, click on **Next**:

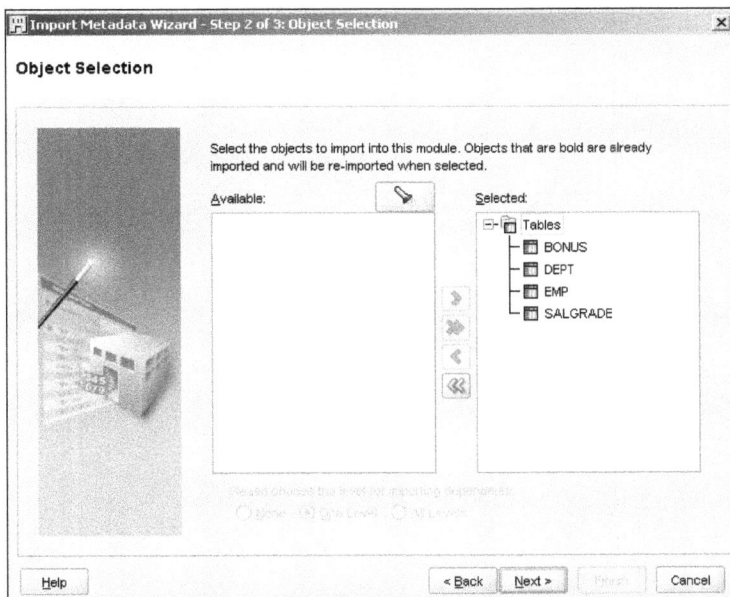

11. Verify all the tables to be imported. Click on **Finish**:

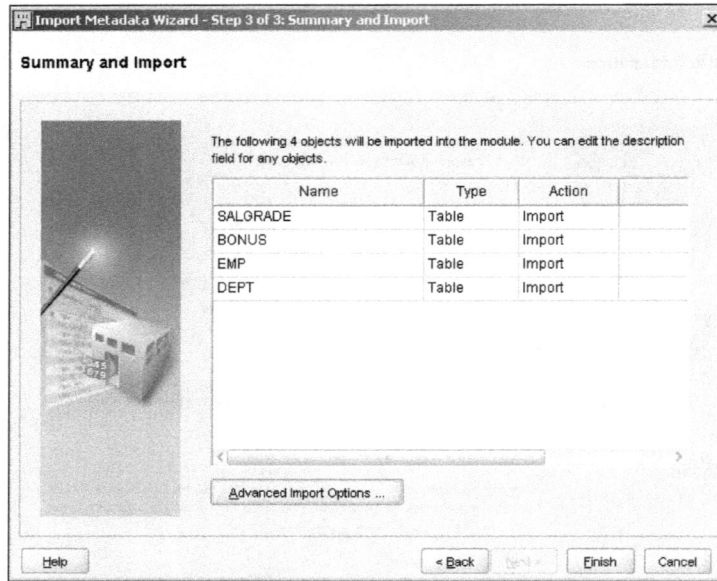

12. The importing could take a few minutes. Validate there are no errors:

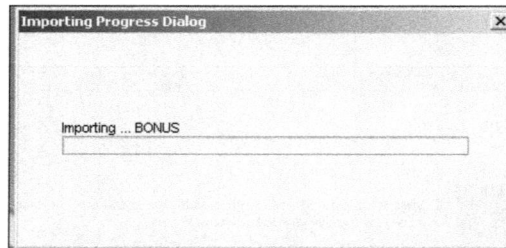

13. Verify whether the tables have been imported, and click on **OK**. The details can be obtained by expanding table names:

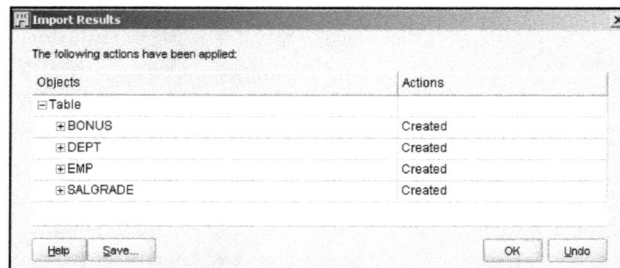

14. Right-click on the **Data Profiles** node within the same project after importing, and select **New Data Profile**, as shown in the following screenshot:

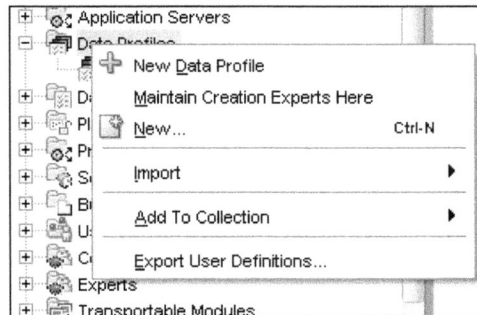

15. The **Data Profile Wizard** will start. Click on **Next**:

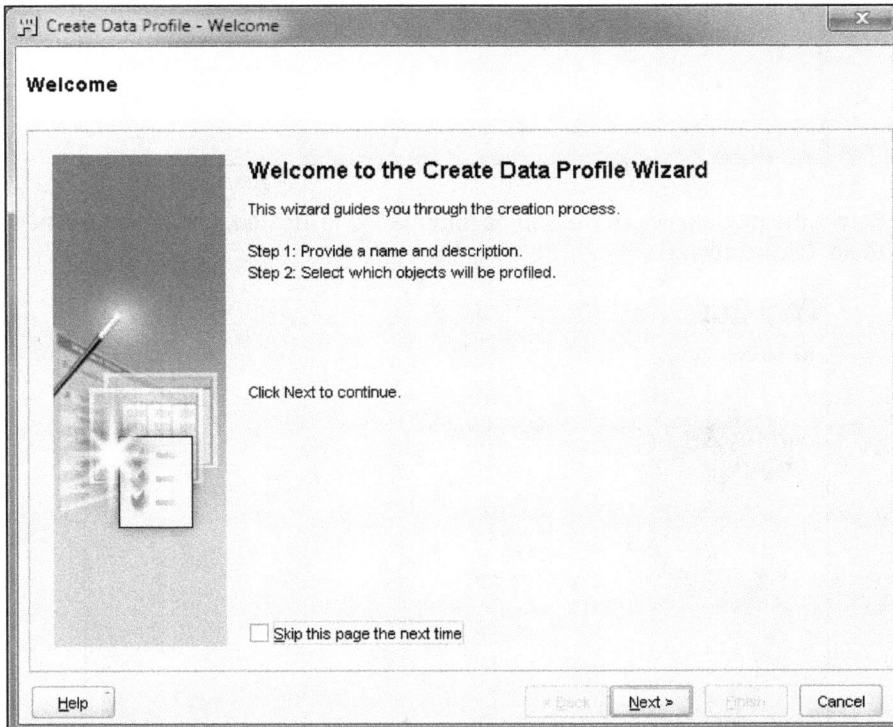

16. Enter **Name:** for the profile. Click on **Next:**

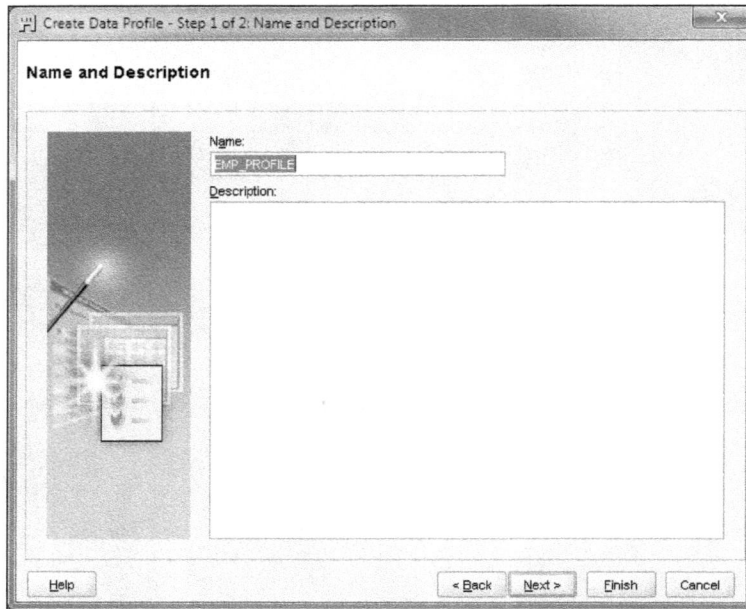

17. Select the module where the source information is located, and select the necessary table. Click on **Next:**

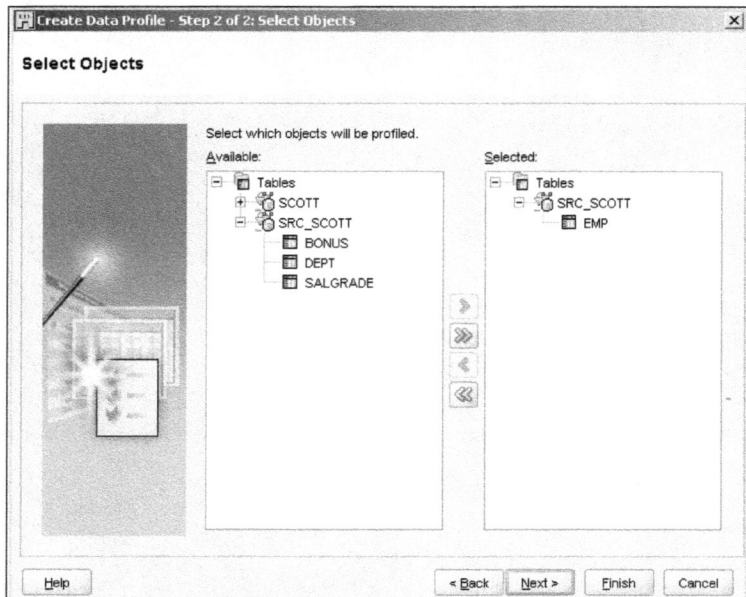

18. Review the source module and the table. Click on **Next**:

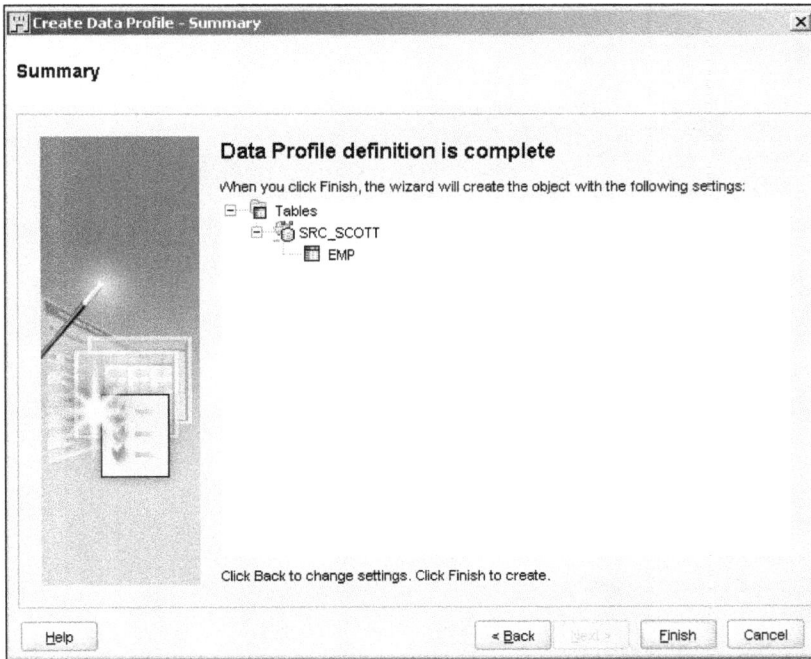

19. A **Warehouse Builder Note** is presented. Click on **OK**:

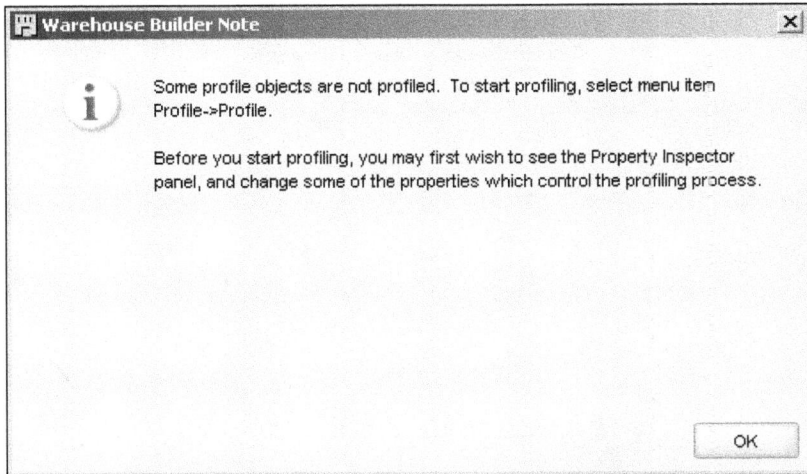

20. On the left-hand side, notice the data profiling options. We will use the defaults as follows:

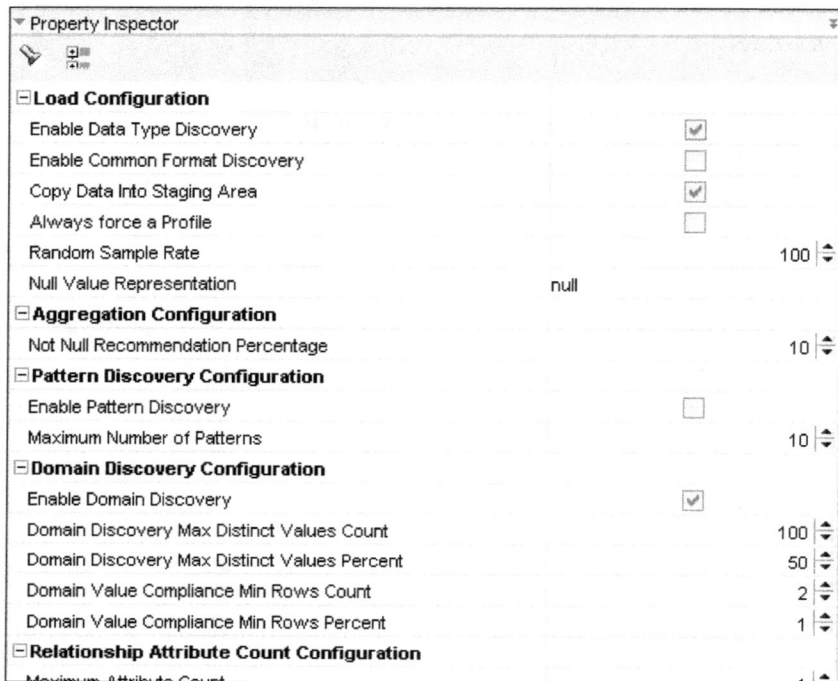

21. Click on the **Profile** menu, and select **Profile**, as shown in the following screenshot:

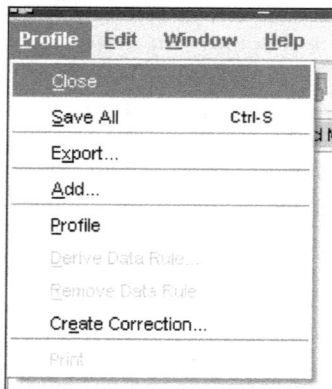

22. The first time you execute a data profile, you will be prompted to enter a username and password. This creates the necessary objects (tables) to support and store data profiling results. The installation requires a system username and password. Enter the **system name** and **password**. Click on **OK**:

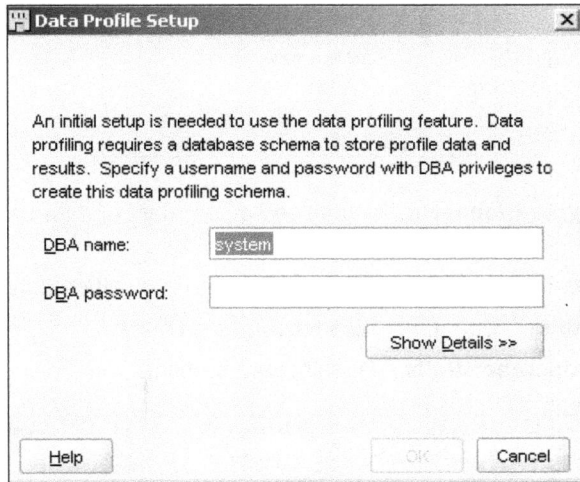

23. Supporting objects will be installed and the profile validated:

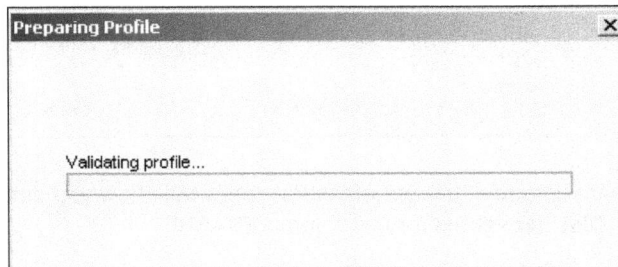

24. Once the profile has been validated, it will be submitted to run. The profiling can take some time, and uses many resources on the source environment. It is recommended that it is performed during off-peak hours. Click on **OK** to view the details:

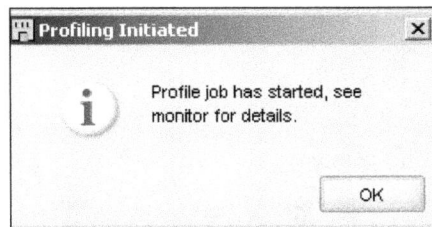

25. Once completed, a pop up will be presented alerting you that it is completed. Click on **Yes** to retrieve the results and view the profile:

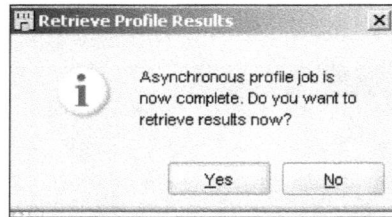

26. Under the **Aggregation** table, you can see a summary of information. It will present the following:

   ❑ **Minimum and Maximum**– The high and low values data profiling

   ❑ **#Distinct** – Domain or distinct values profiling

   ❑ **%Distinctand%Nulls** – Density data profiling

Here are the aggregation analysis results for EMP, which has 8 columns and 14 rows.

Columns	Minimum	Maximum	# Distinct	% Distinct	NOT NULL	Recommen...	# Nulls	% Nulls	Six-Sigma	Average	Median	Std Dev
COMM	0	1400	4	28.6%	No	No	10	71.4%	2.07	550	400	603
DEPTNO	10	30	3	21.4%	No	Yes	0	0%	7.00	22	20	8
EMPNO	7369	7934	14	100%	Yes	Yes	0	0%	7.00	7727	7785	178
ENAME	ADAMS	WARD	14	100%	No	Yes	0	0%	7.00			
HIREDATE	17-DEC-...	23-MAY-87	13	92.9%	No	Yes	0	0%	7.00			
JOB	ANALYST	SALESM...	5	35.7%	No	Yes	0	0%	7.00			
MGR	7566	7902	6	42.9%	No	Yes	1	7.1%	2.97	7739	7698	104

27. As you highlight columns, the panels below them will show you detailed information, for example, **Distinct values** for the column **ENAME**:

28. Click on the **Data Type** tab. This will show information regarding the structure and size of the attributes:

Profile Results Canvas

| Data Profile | Profile Object | Aggregation | Data Type | Pattern | Domain | Unique Key | Functional Dependency | Referential | Data Rule |

Here are the data type analysis results for EMP, which has 8 columns and 14 rows.

Columns	Documented Datatype	Dominant Datatype	% Dominant Datatype	Documented Length	Minimum Length	Maximum Length	Dominant Length	% Dominant Length	Documented Precision	Minimum Precision	Maximum Precision	Dominant Precision	% Dominant Precision	Documented Scale
COMM	NUMBER	NUMBER	28.6%	0	0	0	0	0%	7	1	4	3	14.3%	2
DEPTNO	NUMBER	NUMBER	100%	0	0	0	0	0%	2	2	2	2	100%	0
EMPNO	NUMBER	NUMBER	100%	0	0	0	0	0%	4	4	4	4	100%	0
ENAME	VARCHAR2	VARCHAR2	100%	10	4	6	5	57.1%	0	0	0	0	0%	0
HIREDATE	DATE	DATE	100%	0	0	0	0	0%	0	9	9	9	100%	0
JOB	VARCHAR2	VARCHAR2	100%	9	5	9	7	35.7%	0	0	0	0	0%	0
MGR	NUMBER	NUMBER	92.9%	0	0	0	0	0%	4	4	4	4	92.9%	0
SAL	NUMBER	NUMBER	100%	0	0	0	0	0%	7	3	4	4	85.7%	2

29. Click on the **Domain** tab, and it will show you the domain values for each column and the percentage of records which relate to the values shown.

Profile Results Canvas

| Data Profile | Profile Object | Aggregation | Data Type | Pattern | Domain | Unique Key | Functional |

Here are the domain analysis results for EMP, which has 8 columns and 14 rows.

Columns	Found Domain	% Compliant	Six-Sigma
COMM		0%	-6.25
DEPTNO	30 | 20 | 10	100%	7.00
EMPNO		0%	-6.25
ENAME		0%	-6.25
HIREDATE		0%	-6.25
JOB	SALESMAN | ANALYST | MANAGER | CLERK	92.9%	2.97
MGR	7698 | 7839 | 7566	71.4%	2.07
SAL		0%	-6.25

30. Click on the **Unique Key** tab. This will give you valuable information for the significant columns' profile:

Profile Results Canvas

| Data Profile | Profile Object | Aggregation | Data Type | Pattern | Domain | Unique Key | Functi |

Here are the unique key analysis results for EMP, which has 8 columns and 14 rows.

Unique Key	Documented	Discovered	Local Attribute(s)	# Unique	% Uniq...	Six-Sigma
PK_EMP	Yes	Yes	EMPNO	14	100%	7.00
UK_1	No	Yes	COMM	14	100%	7.00
UK_2	No	Yes	ENAME	14	100%	7.00
UK_3	No	Yes	HIREDATE	13	92.9%	2.97
UK_4	No	Yes	SAL	12	85.7%	2.57

31. There are options to enter and save **Notes** for the profile:

32. By clicking on the **Profile** menu, you can export information by clicking on **Export**, as shown in the following screenshot:

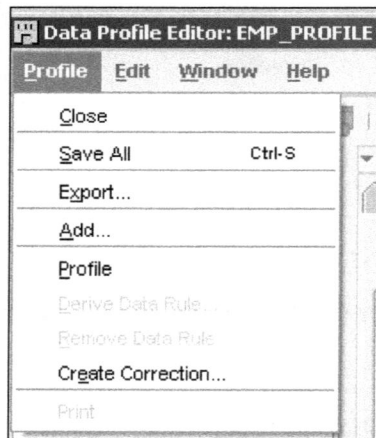

33. A window is presented to select where you would like to save the information and to which format (CSV or HTML). Enter **Filename** and click on **Save**, as shown in the following screenshot:

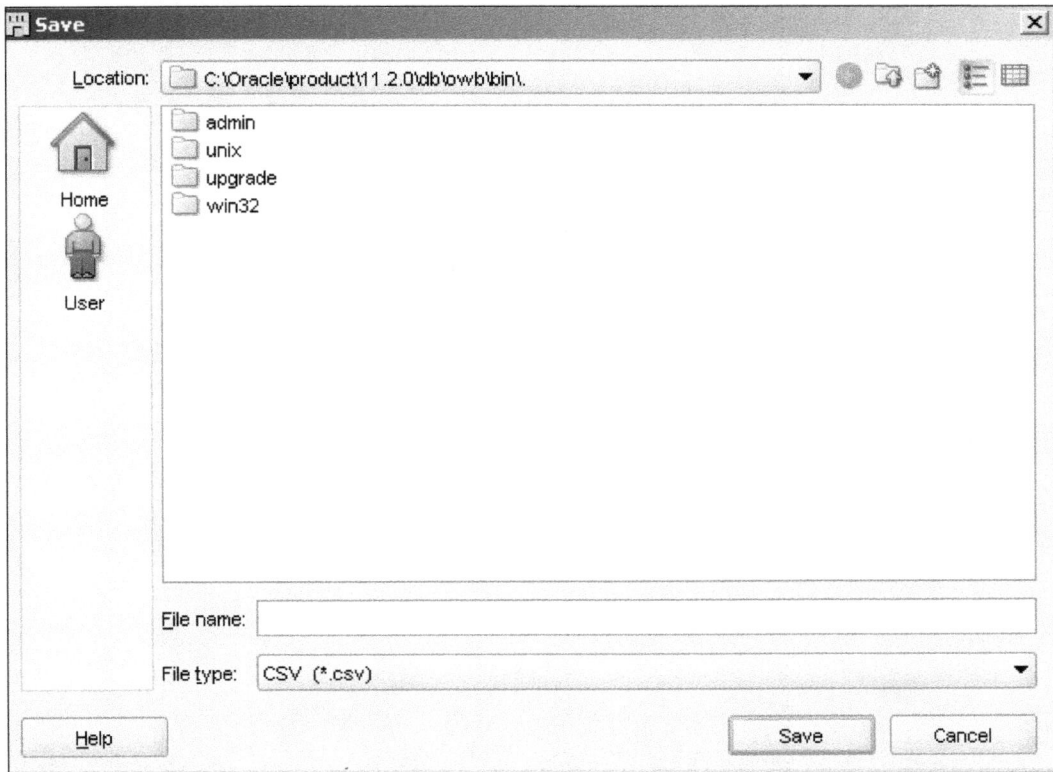

How it works...

Oracle Warehouse Builder data profiling automates most of the manual steps required. It also stores the information for retrieval at a later stage. This information can be used to design and develop your data model as well as build business rules to correct data inconsistencies.

Oracle Warehouse Builder, however, does not provide the capability to analyze hierarchies.

10
Constructing the Data Model

This chapter outlines how to construct the data model with **Oracle SQL Data Modeler** (a free standalone product or embedded within Oracle SQL Developer from Oracle) using a top-down and bottom-up approach. Oracle SQL Data Modeler will be used to build your database logical and physical models. This can be used by Oracle Warehouse Builder and Oracle Data Integrator. **Oracle Business Intelligence Enterprise Edition** (**OBIEE**) will be used to map the physical database model to the the presentation data model used for reporting. The following recipes focus on the database logical and physical data models:

- ▶ Connecting Oracle SQL Data Modeler to Subversion
- ▶ Importing data models into Subversion
- ▶ Checkout data models from Subversion
- ▶ Synchronizing data model changes with Subversion
- ▶ How to import data models
- ▶ How to reverse engineer your relational data model to a logical data model
- ▶ Creating your domains
- ▶ Creating your glossary
- ▶ Adding standard columns to your data model
- ▶ How to forward engineer your logical data model to a relational data model
- ▶ Creating your enterprise models

Introduction

The data model is the most important asset within the entire business intelligence and data warehouse solution as for any administrative information system. This is often overlooked, or not realized. The information which will be stored within the data model is a valuable asset of any organization.

Connecting Oracle SQL Data Modeler to Subversion

Version control systems are good environments to facilitate collaboration and record different versions of information. **Subversion** is the version control tool which is currently integrated with Oracle SQL Data Modeler, and can be primarily used for collaboration. Subversion enables multiple people to use and share the same information.

Data models can be developed from a top-down approach (reports and requirements), or a bottom-up approach (source systems). Up until now, we have focused on the top-down aspect. In this chapter, we will start using a bottom-up approach to validate and verify the assumptions made from the top-down approach.

Getting ready

Ensure the version control server you installed and Oracle SQL Data Modeler are available and functioning.

How to do it...

Information in Subversion is contained within repositories. Before you can check code in or out of Subversion, these repositories need to be created.

1. Connect to the **VisualSVN Server** Manager as follows:

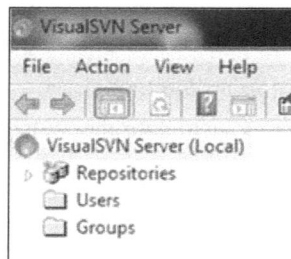

2. Right-click on **Repositories**, and select **Create New Repository**. Enter **Repository Name**, and click on **OK**:

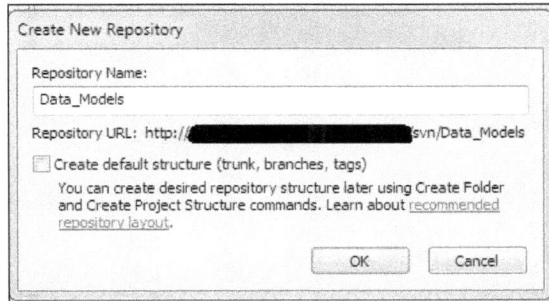

3. Right-click on **Repository Name**, and select **New | Folder**. Create a folder for each subject area within the project:

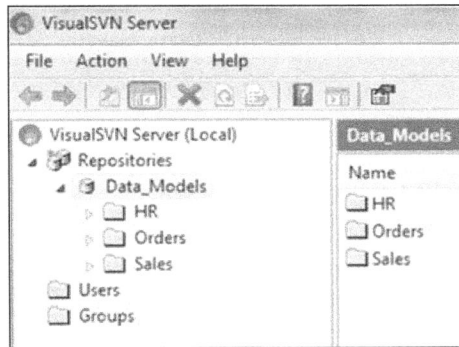

4. Create an additional folder as a consolidation folder, for example, **Enterprise**, as shown in the following screenshot:

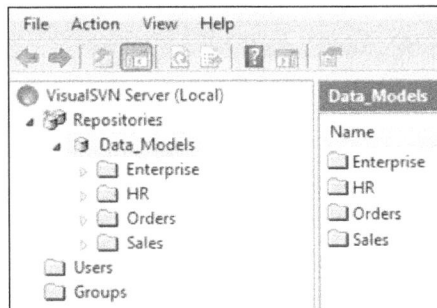

5.   Open Oracle SQL Data Modeler.

6.   Open **Versioning Navigator**. Click on **View**, and select **Team | Versioning Navigator**:

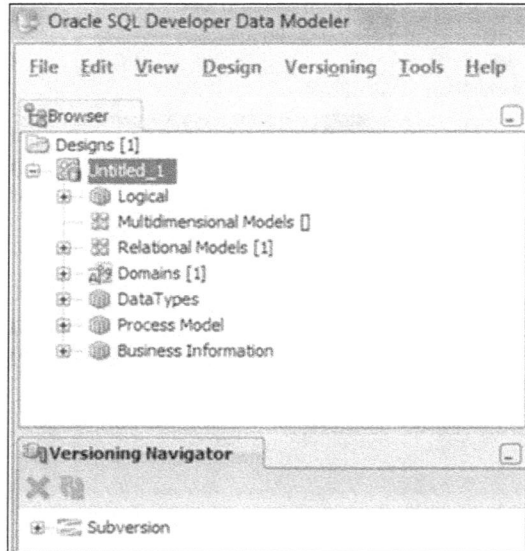

7.   In **Versioning Navigator**, right-click on the top-level node (Subversion), and select **New Repository Connection**:

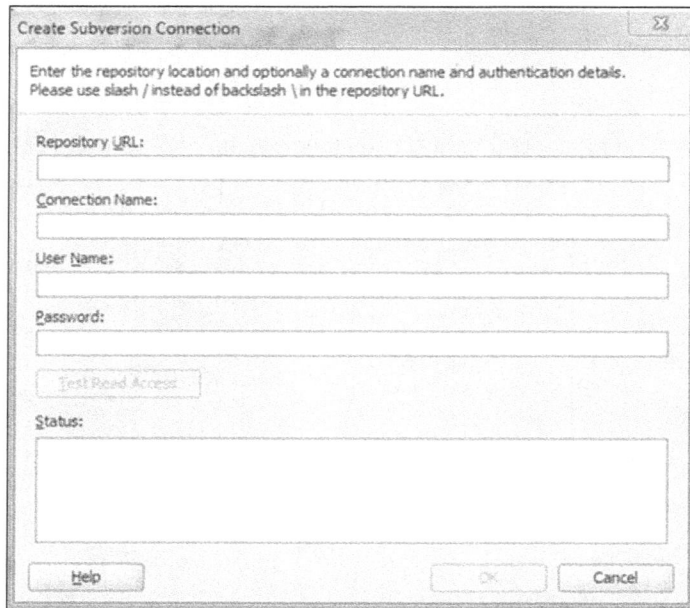

8. Within Subversion, in the **Create Subversion Connection** dialog box, complete the information as follows:

- ❑ **Repository URL**: This can be obtained by right-clicking on **Repository Name** in VisualSVN Server Manager, and selecting **Copy to Clipboard**

- ❑ **Connection Name**: BI Data Models

- ❑ **User Name**: Windows Domain or SVN username

- ❑ **Password**: Enter the password for the preceding specified username

9. Click on **Test Read Access**. If successful, click on **OK**, or else correct the issue and then retry:

10. Validate whether a connection exists; the connection should appear in **Versioning Navigator**:

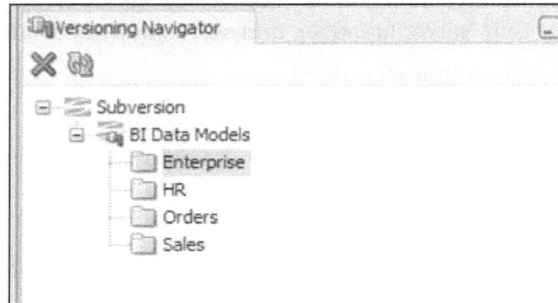

How it works...

Integrating Subversion into Oracle SQL Data Modeler allows you to set up a central location where your data models will be saved. This enables collaboration during the modeling process, and allows multiple people to contribute to the data model.

Importing data models into Subversion

Data models which have previously been created as in *Chapter 5*, *The Blueprint*, and *Chapter 6*, *Analyzing the Requirements*, can be imported into Subversion. Subversion acts as a storage mechanism for the data models.

Getting ready

In *Chapter 5*, *The Blueprint*, and *Chapter 6*, *Analyzing the Requirements*, you created some data models. Find the folder location of these data models on your hard drive.

How to do it...

Information can be imported into Subversion. This process makes a copy of your information on your hard drive, and places it within the repository of Subversion.

1. In Oracle SQL Data Modeler, click on the **Versioning** menu and select **Import Files**:

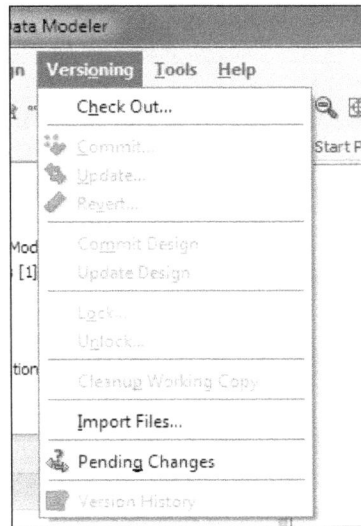

2. The **Import to Subversion Wizard** will appear. Click on **Next**:

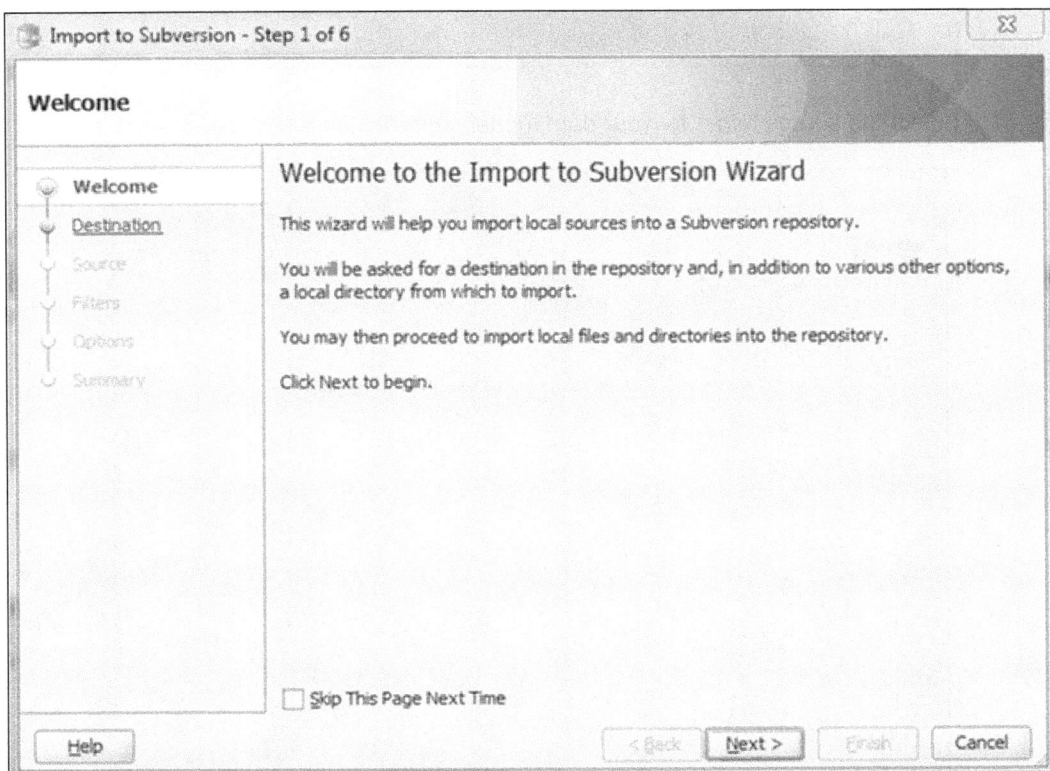

3. Select the destination folder for your data model, and click on **Next**:

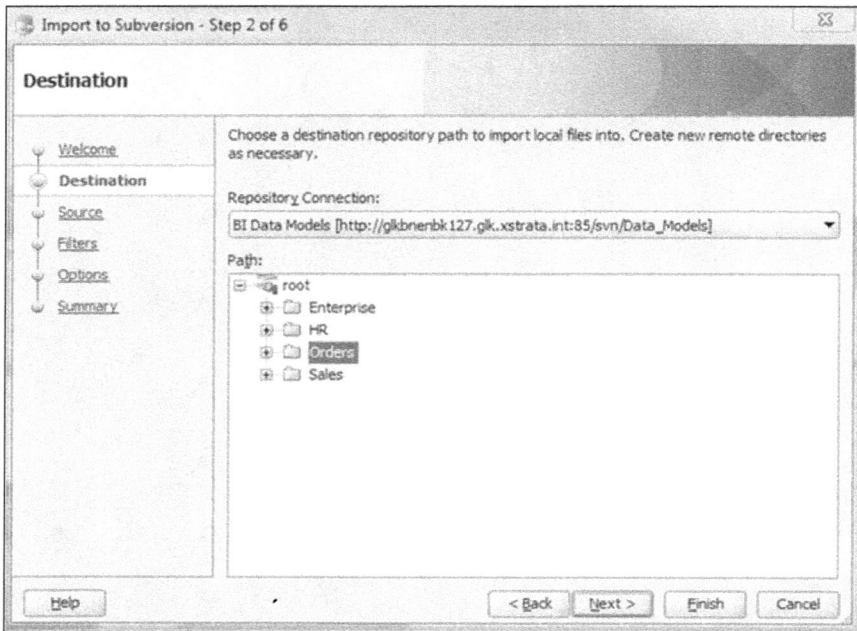

4. Select the source folder for your data model, and click on **Next**:

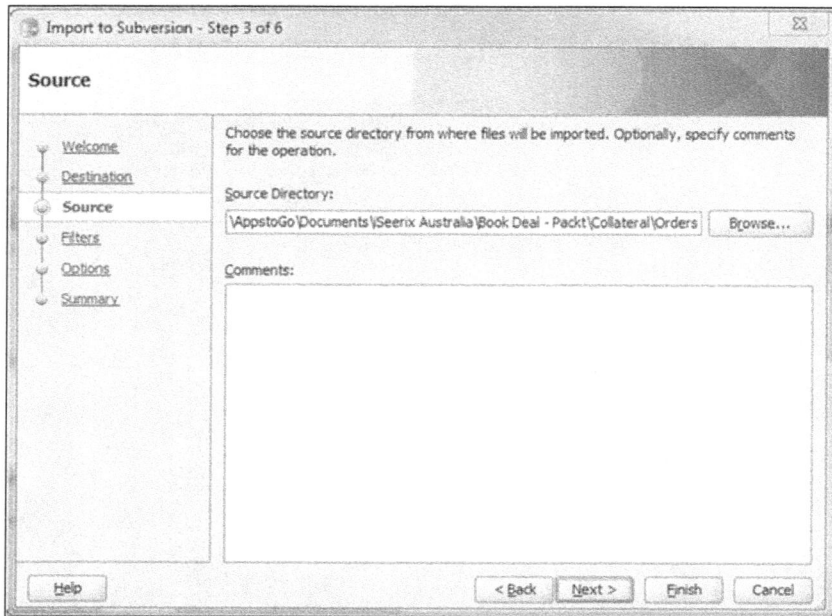

5. Select any filter, and click on **Next**:

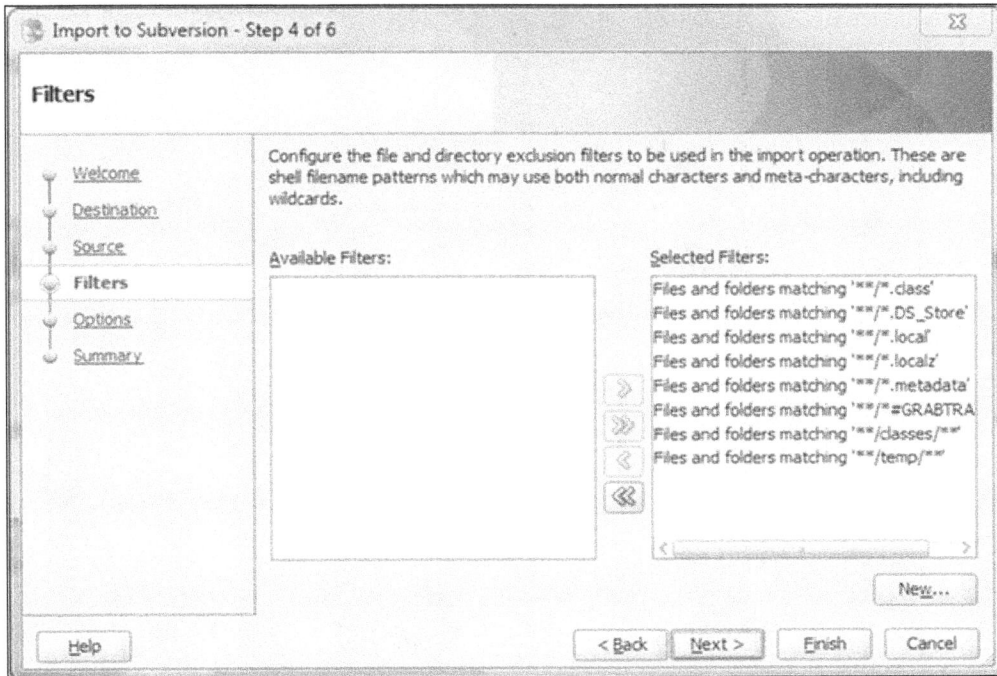

Filters

Welcome

Destination

Source

Filters

Options

Summary

Configure the file and directory exclusion filters to be used in the import operation. These are shell filename patterns which may use both normal characters and meta-characters, including wildcards.

Available Filters:

Selected Filters:

Files and folders matching '**/*.class'
Files and folders matching '**/*.DS_Store'
Files and folders matching '**/*.local'
Files and folders matching '**/*.localz'
Files and folders matching '**/*.metadata'
Files and folders matching '**/*#GRABTRA
Files and folders matching '**/classes/**'
Files and folders matching '**/temp/**'

New...

Help   < Back   Next >   Finish   Cancel

6. Deselect **Perform Checkout**, and click on **Next**:

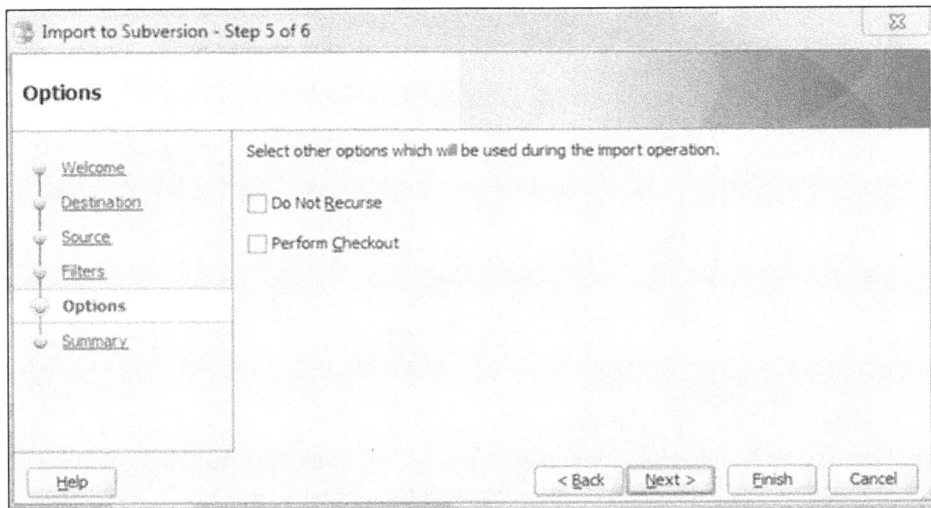

Options

Welcome

Destination

Source

Filters

Options

Summary

Select other options which will be used during the import operation.

☐ Do Not Recurse

☐ Perform Checkout

Help   < Back   Next >   Finish   Cancel

7. Review the import, and click on **Next**:

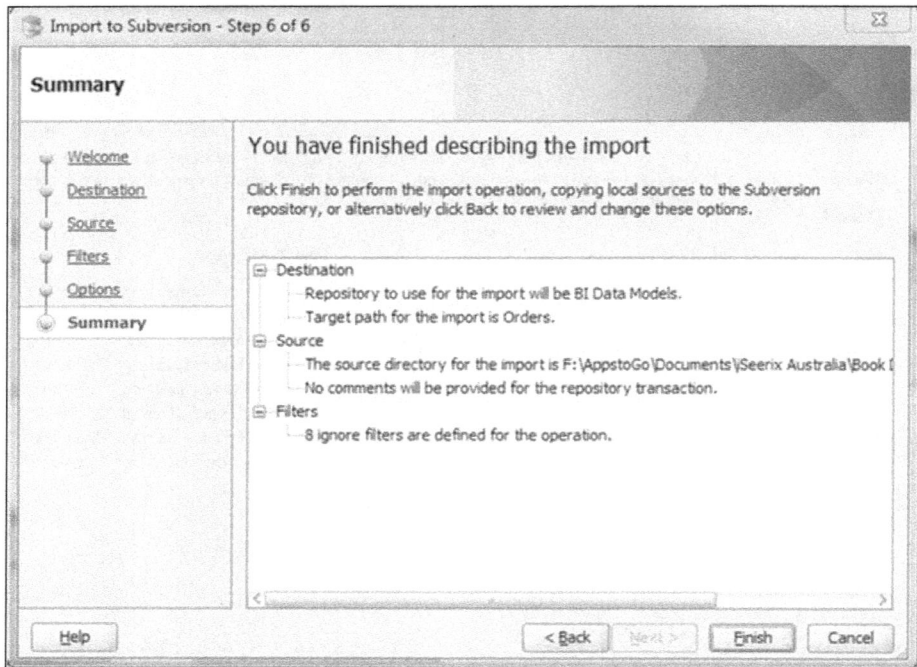

8. Click on the refresh icon in **Versioning Navigator**, and validate whether the information has successfully been imported from your folder to the Subversion repository. Click on **Next**:

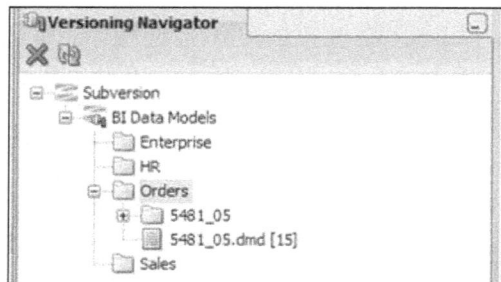

How it works...

Once the data has been imported, the data model is then stored on the Subversion server and under version control. You cannot open or work with the data model directly in Subversion. In the next chapter, you will learn how to check out the data model to a local copy to enable you to open and work with it.

Checkout data models from Subversion

Data models stored within Subversion require a working copy in order to use them within Oracle SQL Data Modeler.

Getting ready

Ensure you have sufficient space on your local hard drive to create a local copy from Subversion.

How to do it...

Checking out will copy the information from the Subversion repository to a location on your computer:

1. Right-click on the **BI Data Models** connection in **Versioning Navigator**. Select **Check Out...**:

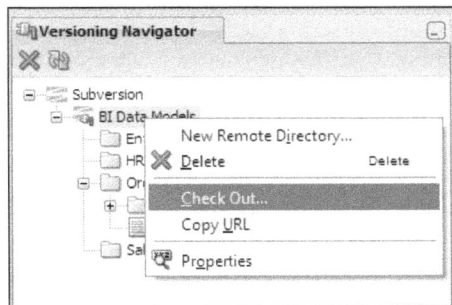

2. A warning will appear as you are checking out from the root. Click on **Yes** to continue:

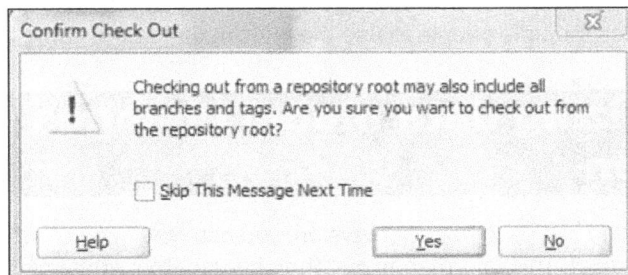

3. Create a directory on your local hard drive for your SVNRepositories, and then a subfolder to store your data models. If the directories do not exist, this process will create them. Then, click on **OK**:

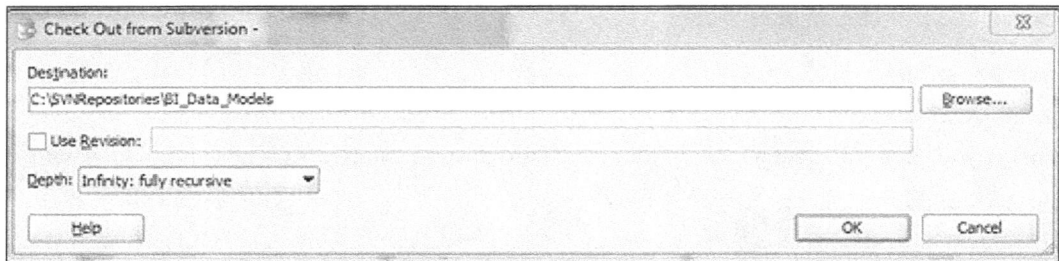

4. Validate in the **SVN Console - Log** window whether the information was successfully checked out:

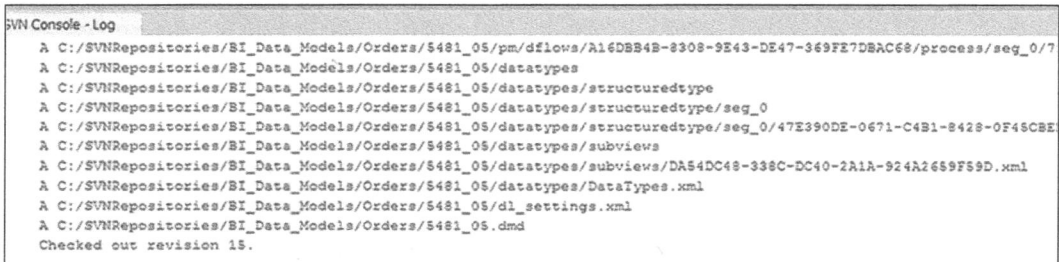

How it works...

By completing the checkout from Subversion, you have created a copy of the information on your computer under the specified folder. This is now available for you to update and enhance. Checking the code out does not lock it for other users, and they can also check out a copy of the code. This enables multiple people to use the information at the same time.

Synchronizing data model changes with Subversion

Once you have checked out code from Subversion, you can now open the local copy within Oracle SQL Data Modeler. This information can then be updated, enhanced, and synchronized with Subversion.

Getting ready

Close any copies of your data models before opening the checked out version.

How to do it...

Oracle SQL Data Modeler works with code stored on your local computer, and makes any changes to the code. Subversion then tracks these changes, and synchronizes the information for you as follows:

1. Open the data model by selecting **File | Data Modeler | Open**. Navigate to the local directory where you used Subversion to create a local copy through the checkout process, and select the file with the .dmd extension:

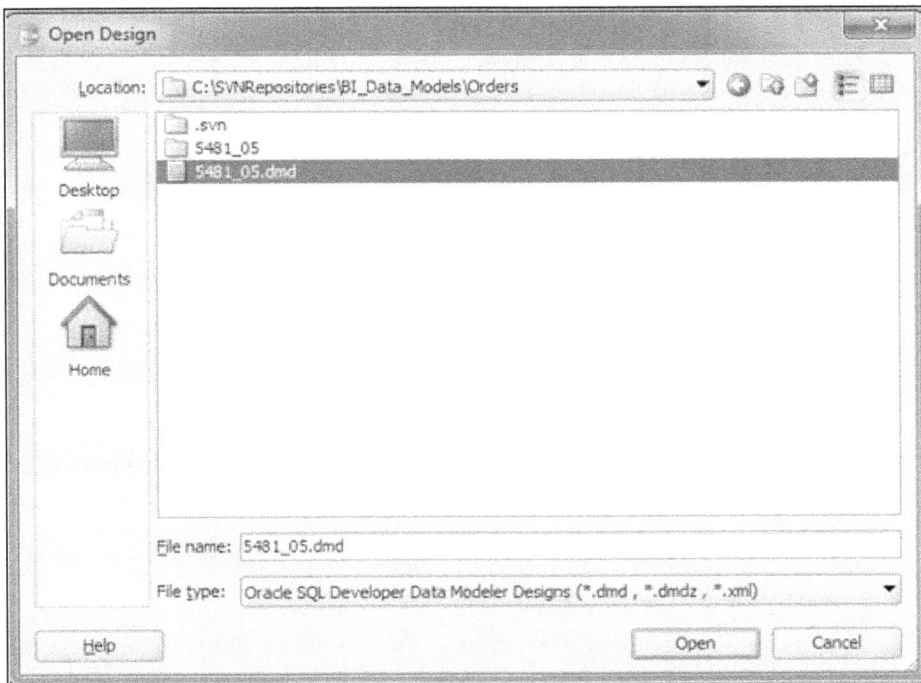

2. Click on **OK** to open the **Relational_1** model. Upon opening it, you may receive a notice to send the integrity setting to the repository. Click on **OK**:

3. The data model opens and is ready to work as follows:

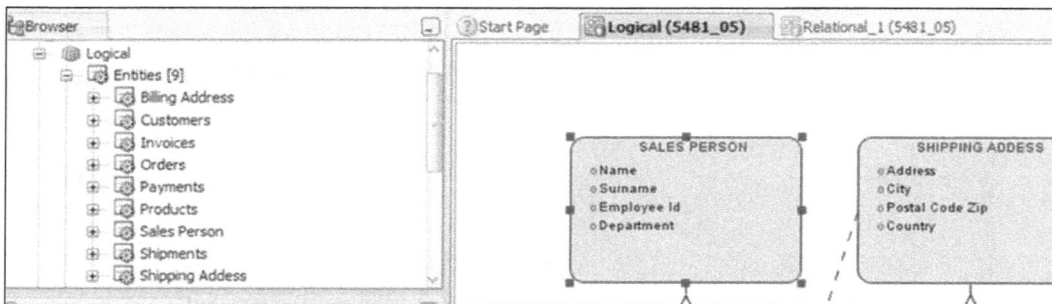

4. Make a change to the data model, for example, double-click on **Sales Person** and update **Short Name** to **SLS_PER**. Click on **Apply**, and then on **OK**:

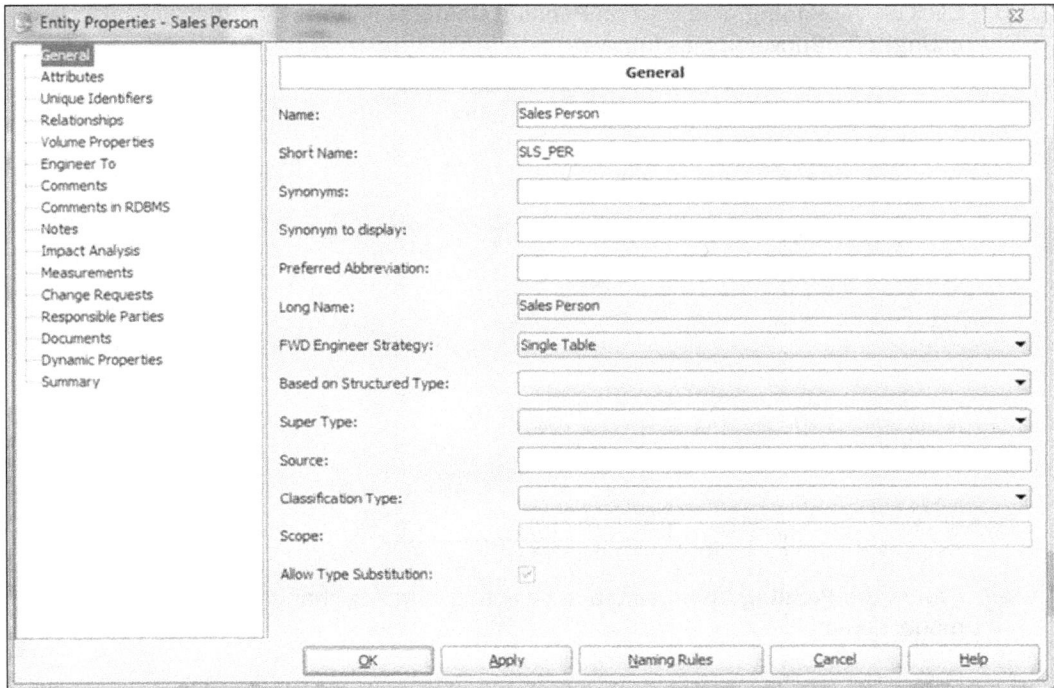

5. Click on **File** and then on **Save** to save the changes, as shown in the following screenshot:

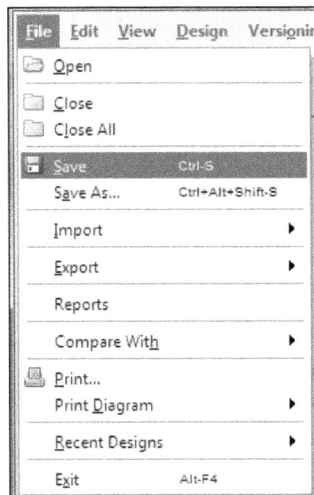

6. Click on **Versioning**, and then on **Pending Changes** to open the tab to view pending changes for Subversion as follows:

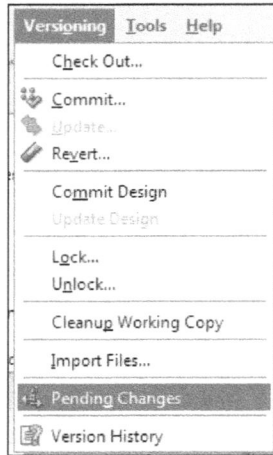

7. Review the **Pending Changes** tab by selecting outgoing changes and expanding the model name:

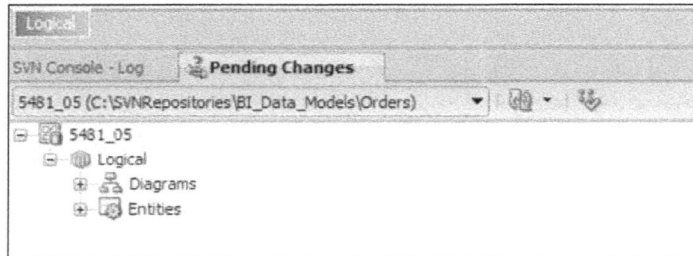

8. Click on the **Commit** icon circled in the following screenshot to upload the changes to Subversion:

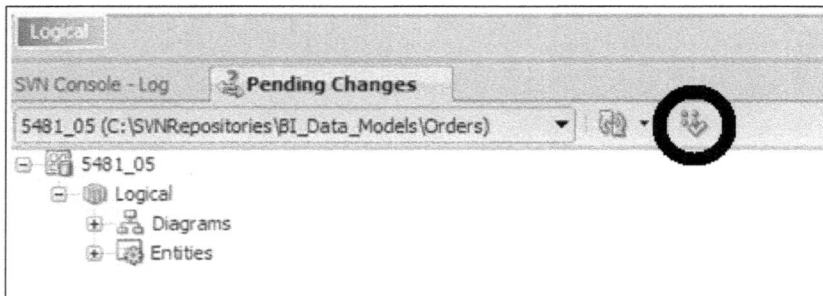

9. Review the changes and click on **OK**:

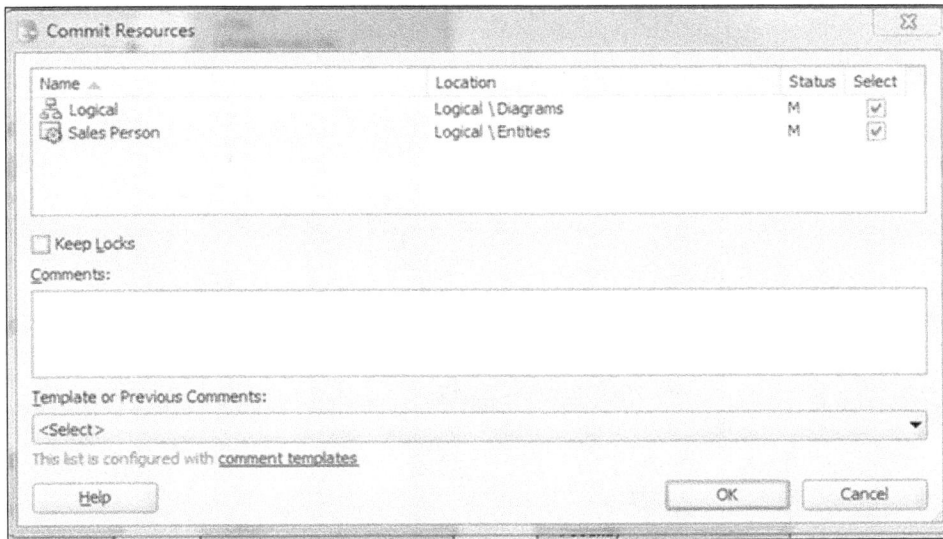

10. Changes will be committed to the server. Check whether no additional changes are required by clicking on the refresh arrow and selecting **Refresh All**, as shown in the following screenshot:

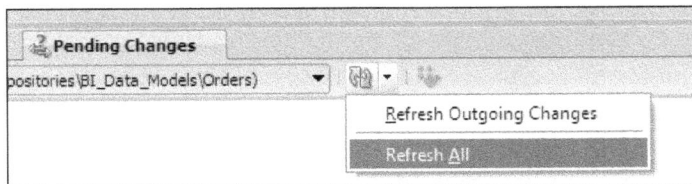

How it works...

Information from Subversion can be synchronized bi-directionally. Before you start working with a model, you should synchronize to incorporate any change which may have been applied by other users since the last time you used the tool. After making changes, save the local copy and then apply your changes to the Subversion copy on a regular basis.

There's more...

Oracle SQL Data Modeler allows you to lock and unlock the model to protect components from being updated:

1. Right-click on the object or container you wish to lock or unlock and select **Versioning**, then **Lock** or **Unlock**:

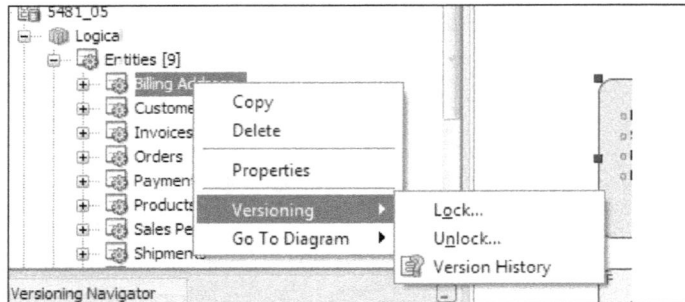

2. Click on **OK** to confirm the lock and apply it to the repository:

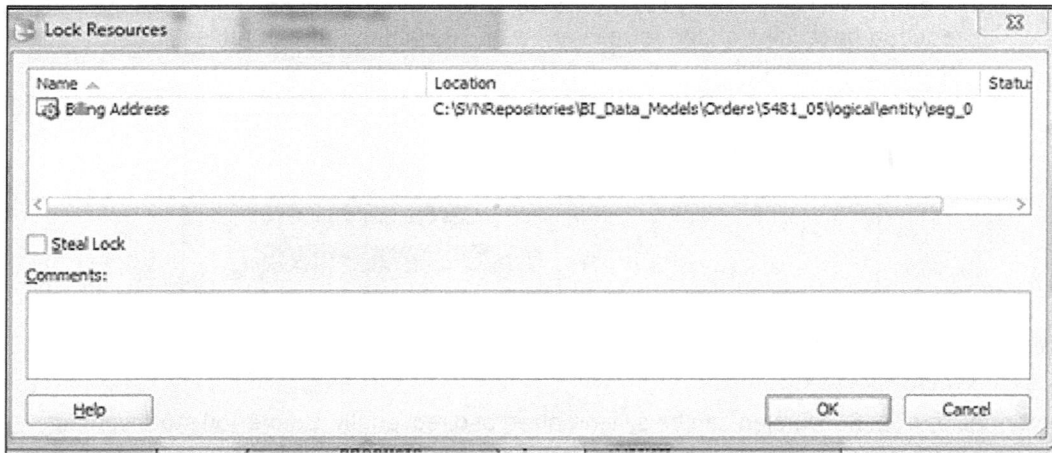

3. Review the messages in the **SVN Console – Log** window to ensure that the lock was applied:

```
SVN Console - Log      Pending Changes
       Committed revision 16.
2012-01-10 17:31:58 - Saving Design and Physical Models
2012-01-10 17:31:58 - Save Design: (0}5481_05
2012-01-10 17:31:58 - Design 5481_05 saved.
commit -m "" -N C:/SVNRepositories/BI Data Models/Orders/5481_05/logical/entity/seg_0/72D6372C-8EE9-9C3D-1001-EA4472ED506D
     Sending C:/SVNRepositories/BI Data Models/Orders/5481_05/logical/entity/seg_0/72D6372C-8EE9-9C3D-1001-EA4472ED506D.xml
     Sending C:/SVNRepositories/BI Data Models/Orders/5481_05/logical/subviews/ECD0B01F-9F21-9419-A7B9-173BB4C0007E.xml
     Transmitting file data ...
     Committed revision 17.
lock -m "" C:/SVNRepositories/BI Data Models/Orders/5481_05/logical/entity/seg_0/361981AB-BC9E-F0AA-D043-44701E342B39.xml
     Orders/5481_05/logical/entity/seg_0/361981AB-BC9E-F0AA-D043-44701E342B39.xml locked by user jgheaton
```

How to import data models

Importing information into Oracle SQL Data Modeler allows you to adopt the definitions of the source tables and attributes. In the previous chapters, we have followed a top-down approach to building the data model; the capability to import tables enables the bottom-up approach to be included into the design of the data model.

Getting ready

Get the necessary connection details for the source environments in order to reverse engineer the necessary information. For this recipe, we will be using the HR sample schema from Oracle. If you wish to use the same example, ensure this is installed in your database.

How to do it...

Importing data models from the database saves vast amounts of time and errors. It can be done as follows:

1. Open Oracle SQL Data Modeler with the data model from *Chapter 5, The Blueprint*:

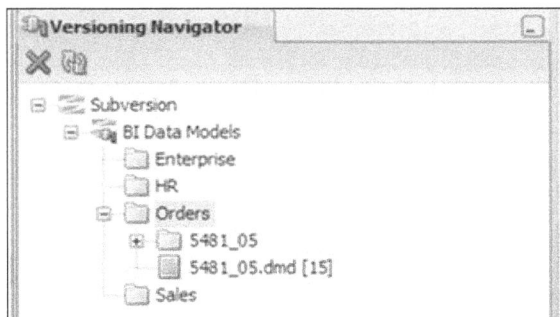

2. Click on **File | Import** to show the capabilities of Oracle SQL Data Modeler, and select **Data Dictionary**:

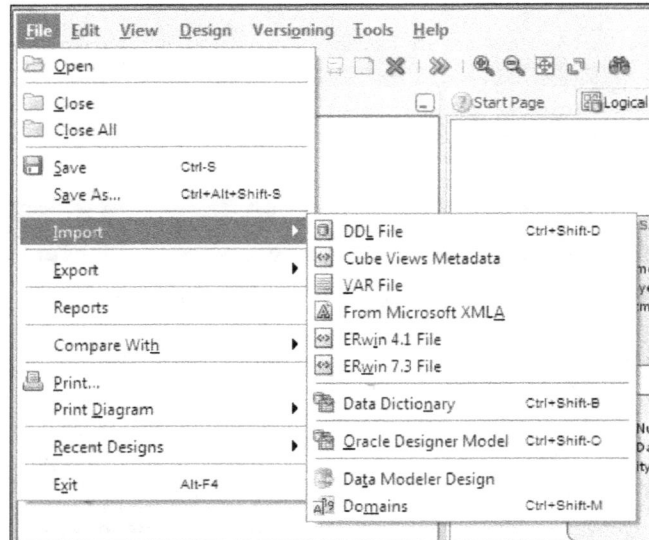

3. A **Data Dictionary Import Wizard** screen will pop up. Click on **Add**:

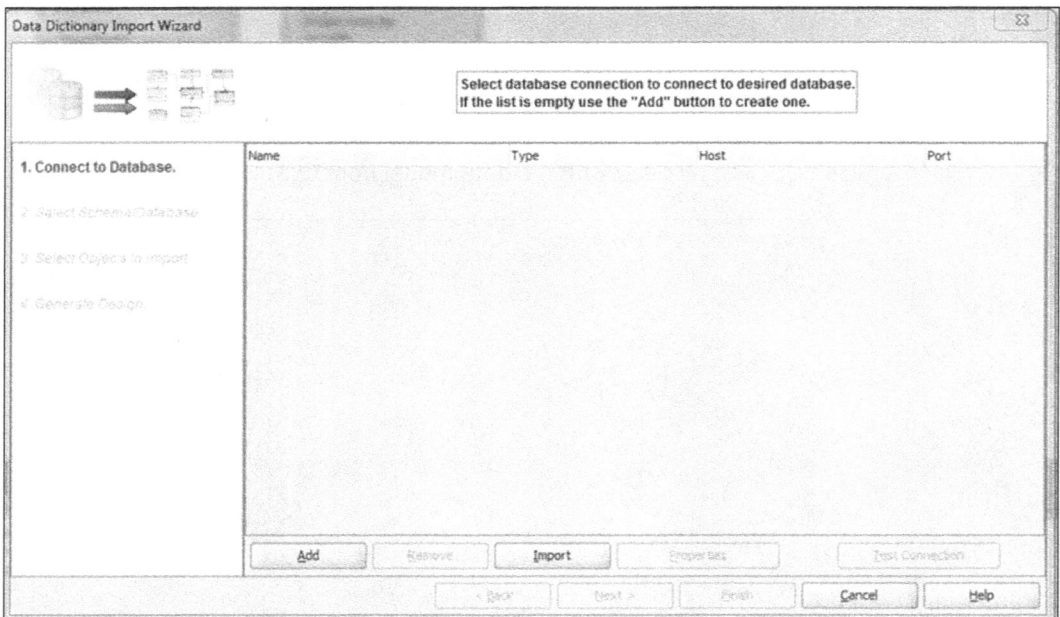

4. Enter the connection details, and select **Test Connection** to validate credentials. Click on **OK** in the **Message** window, and then click on **OK** again in the **Connection** window:

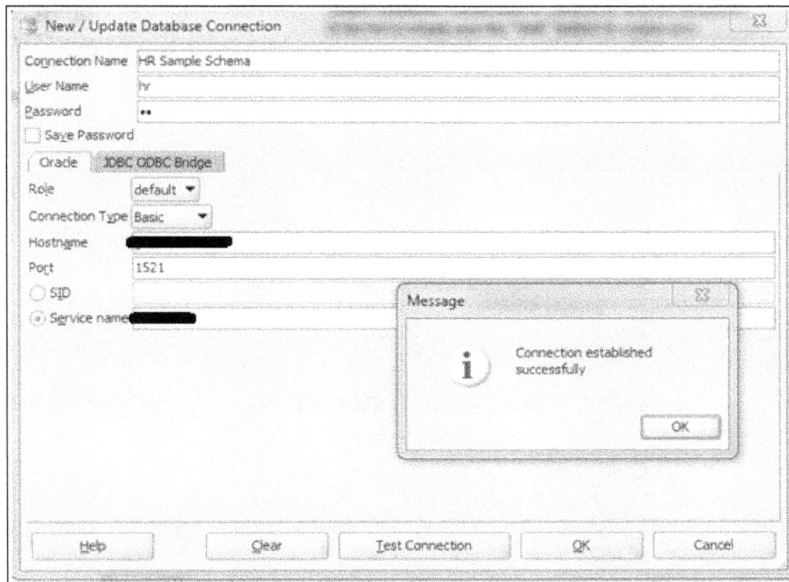

5. Highlight the connection information and click on **Next**. You may be prompted for the password. Enter the password and click on **OK**:

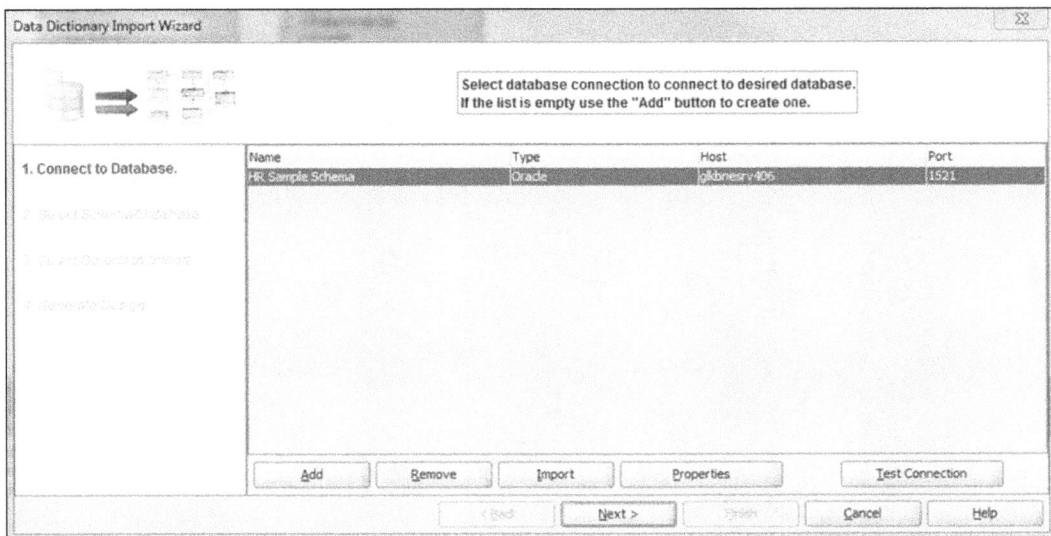

6. Select the **HR** schema, and change the **Import to:** from the drop-down to **New Relational Model**. Click on **Next:**

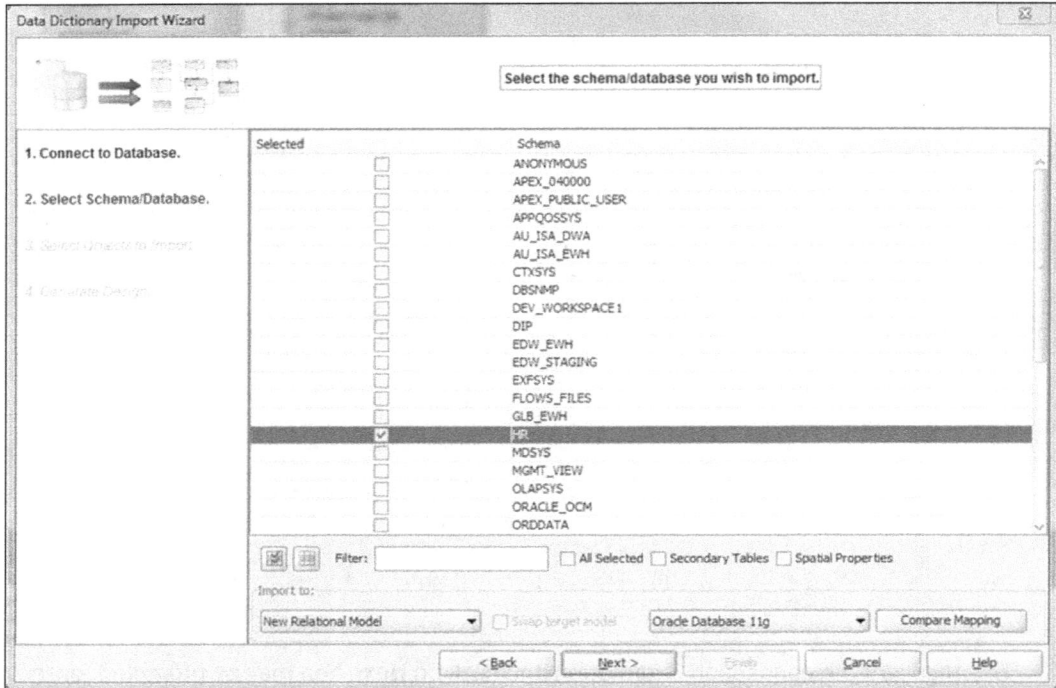

7. Click on the checkboxes to the left of the object name as depicted in the following screenshot to select which objects are to be imported. By changing the tabs at the bottom, you can select different objects. Select all the tables and views. Click on **Next:**

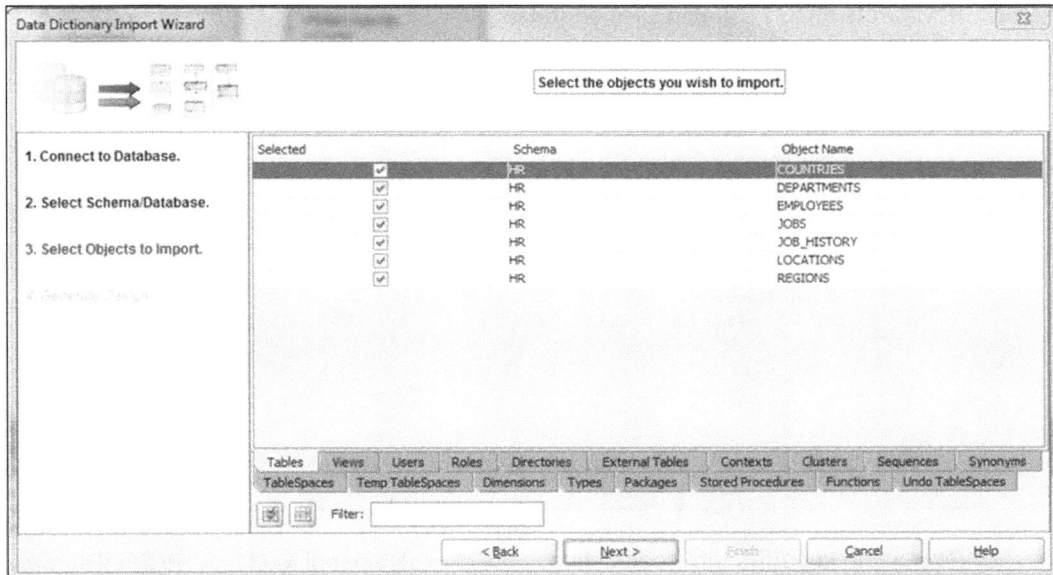

8. Review the selected objects. Click on **Finish**. If prompted, enter the password again and click on **OK**:

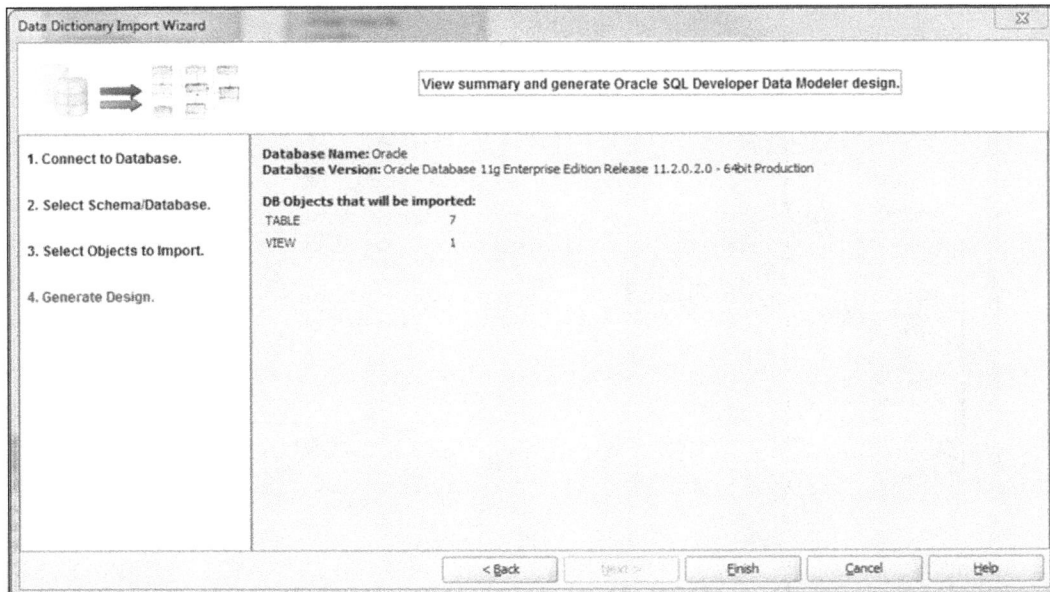

9. Review the import log, and click on **Close**:

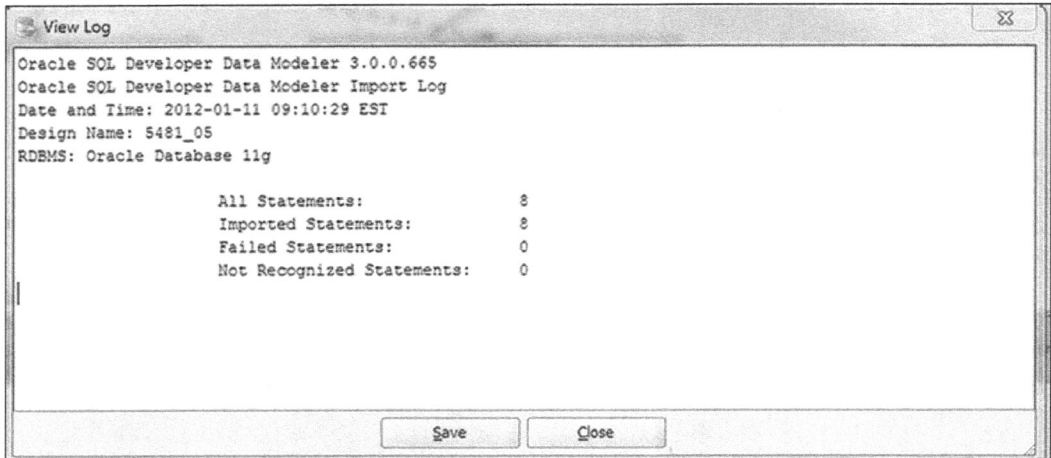

```
View Log                                                          ⊠

Oracle SQL Developer Data Modeler 3.0.0.665
Oracle SQL Developer Data Modeler Import Log
Date and Time: 2012-01-11 09:10:29 EST
Design Name: 5481_05
RDBMS: Oracle Database 11g

              All Statements:                  8
              Imported Statements:             8
              Failed Statements:               0
              Not Recognized Statements:       0

                        Save          Close
```

10. Review the imported table definitions in the New Relational Model. Save the diagram, and commit the changes to Subversion:

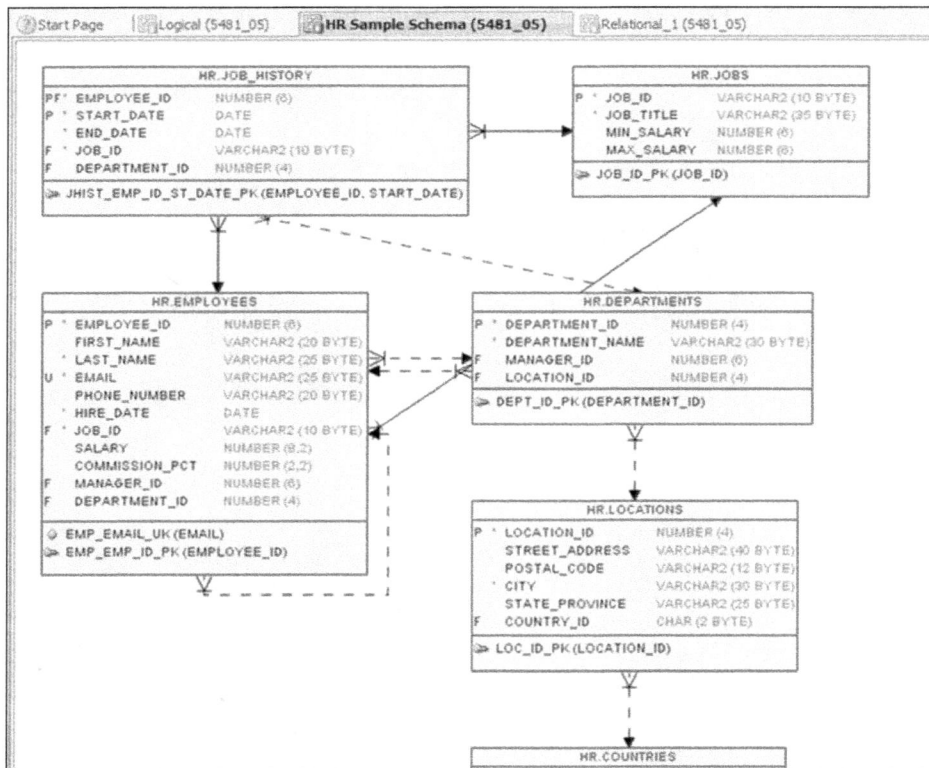

How it works...

Importing information into Oracle SQL Developer allows you to follow a bottom-up approach to modeling information models from data sources. This allows you to visualize and utilize the information from the source systems.

How to reverse engineer your relational data model to a logical data model

Reverse engineering tables to entities supports the bottom-up approach to data modeling.

Getting ready

Import all your source data models as in the previous recipe. Ensure you have saved your model and synchronized with Subversion.

How to do it...

1. Open the relational model, and click on the **Engineer to Logical Model** icon or select **Design | Engineer to Logical Model**:

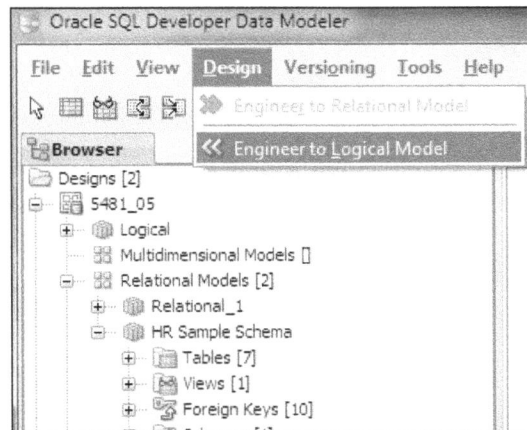

2. Select the tables you are interested in reverse engineering, and click on **Engineer**:

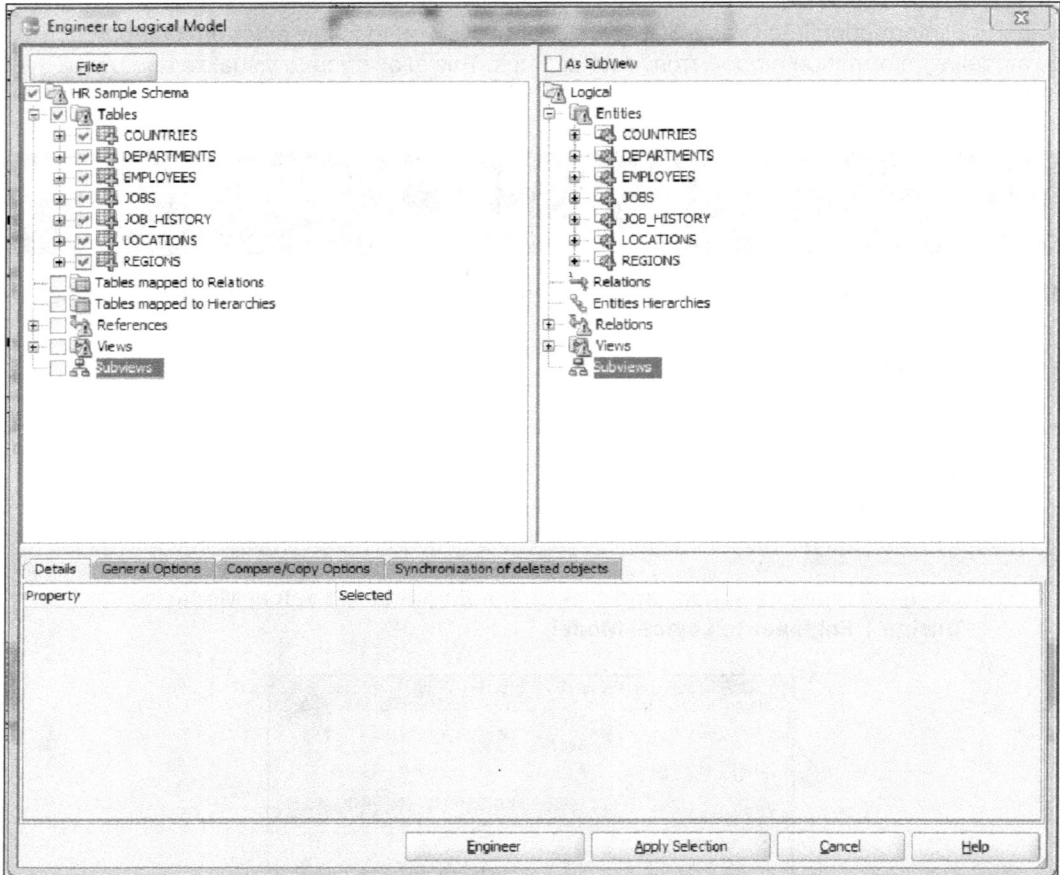

3. Validate whether the tables have been reverse engineered:

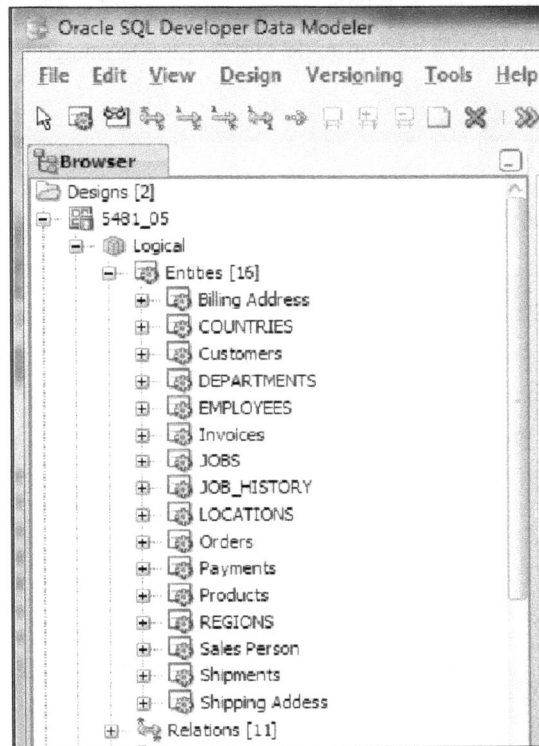

How it works...

Reverse engineering your tables converts them into entities. These can be used within your data model to build your semantic definition, and support a bottom-up approach to modeling. These new entities should be renamed to conform to your naming standards for entities. Once imported, you will need to classify the entities as facts or dimensions. Review the attributes, keep the required attributes, and remove attributes not needed to support your data model. Rename columns to be more business-friendly, and enter descriptions to complete your logical data model.

Creating your domains

Domains are ways to standardize the datatype and lengths to assign to attributes.

Getting ready

Review your results of data profiling from the *Building data lengths data profiling scripts* recipe of *Chapter 9, Analyzing the Data*.

How to do it...

Identifying standard lengths and datatypes for columns by creating domains simplifies the maintenance and management of the data model as follows:

1. Click on **Tools | Domains Administration**:

2. Click on **Add** to include a new domain, as shown in the following screenshot:

3. Enter details for the domain such as **Name**, **Logical Type**, **Units**, **Size** or **Precision**, and **Scale**. Click on **Modify**:

4. Click on **Save**, and then on **Close** to save the domain.

5. Double-click on an entity to apply the domain, and select **Attributes**.

6. Click on an attribute to assign the domain to it, as shown in the following screenshot:

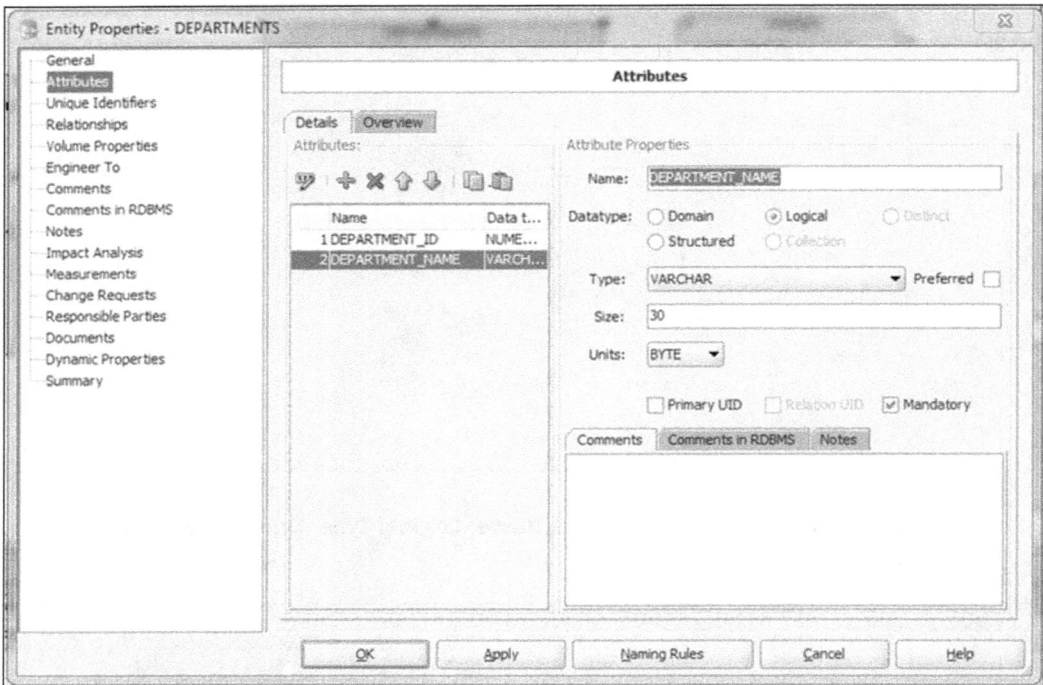

7. Select the **Domain** radio button, and then select **TEXT_SHORT20** as the domain. Click on **Apply**, and then on **OK** to close the entity:

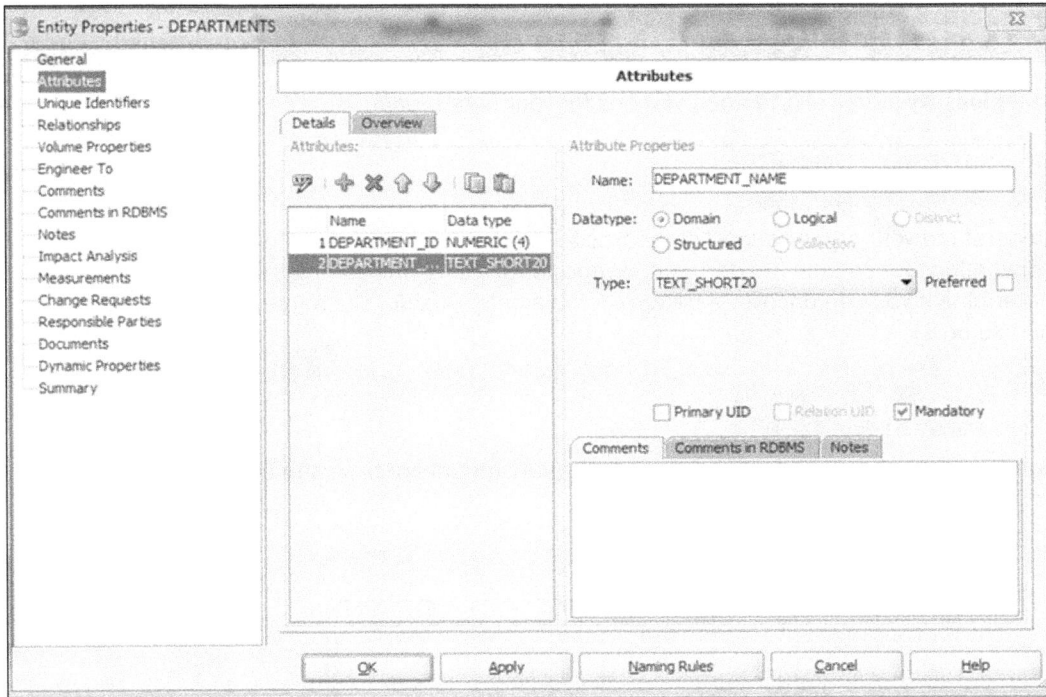

How it works...

Creating domains allow you to define standard datatypes and lengths. These can be determined by ranging the results from the *Building data lengths data profiling scripts* recipe in *Chapter 9, Analyzing the Data*. The goal is to reduce the number of different variations of the datatype. In the domains, create standard domains which will cater for all the different datatypes' variations, for example, TEXT_SHORT20 for codes, TEXT_MEDIUM150 for descriptions, TEXT_LONG4000 for comments, NUMBER_PERCENTAGE for percentages, NUMBER_CURRENCY for currency values, NUMBER_ZIP for zip code, and so on. Once you have the list of domains, you can assign them to the columns in your logical data model. Any changes to datatypes can therefore be achieved by modifying the domain, thus cascading to all the attributes which have been assigned the domain. This saves updating each and every attribute affected individually.

Creating your glossary

The **glossary** stores all the abbreviations for your data model.

Getting ready

Understand your organizations' standards to shorten names and standard naming conventions for column headers within reports. Gather some samples if they do not exist to determine if you can uncover a pattern, for example, Cust for Customer, Sup for Suppliers, and so on.

How to do it...

By creating a glossary, you can save substantial amounts of time and apply standards consistently as follows:

1. Click on **Tools | Glossary Editor**:

2. Navigate to your **BI_Data_Models** directory, and enter a name for the file. Then, click on **Open**:

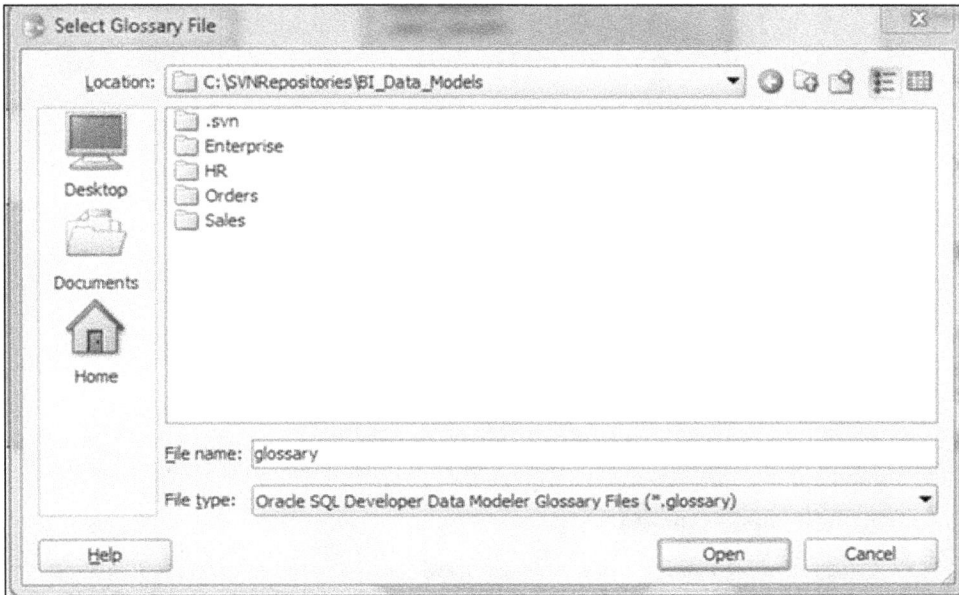

3. Enter **Name**, **Description**, and begin adding your words by using the **+** (plus) icon:

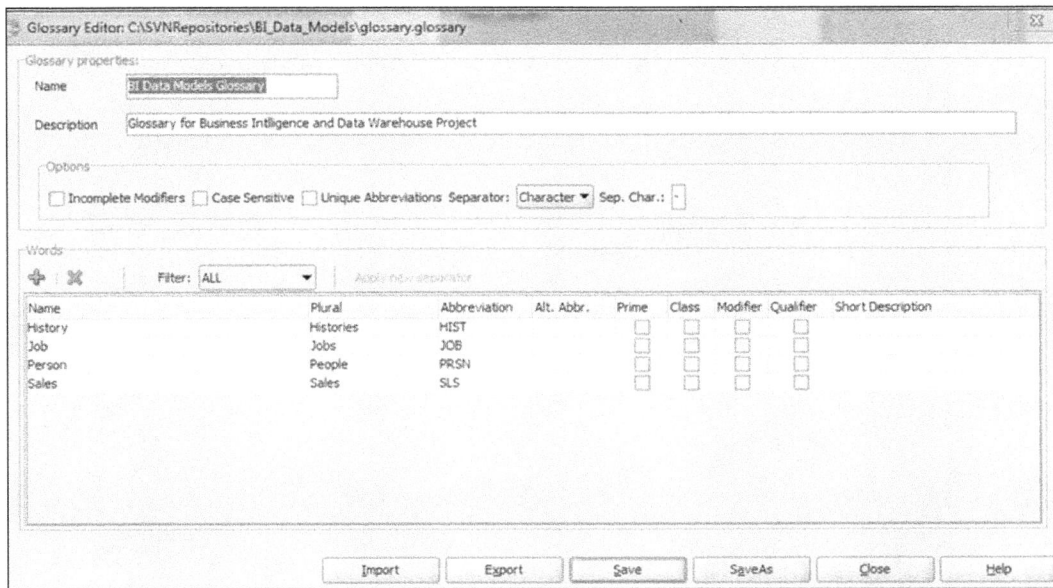

4. Apply the glossary to the environment. Click on **Tools | Preferences**:

5. Click on **Naming Standard**:

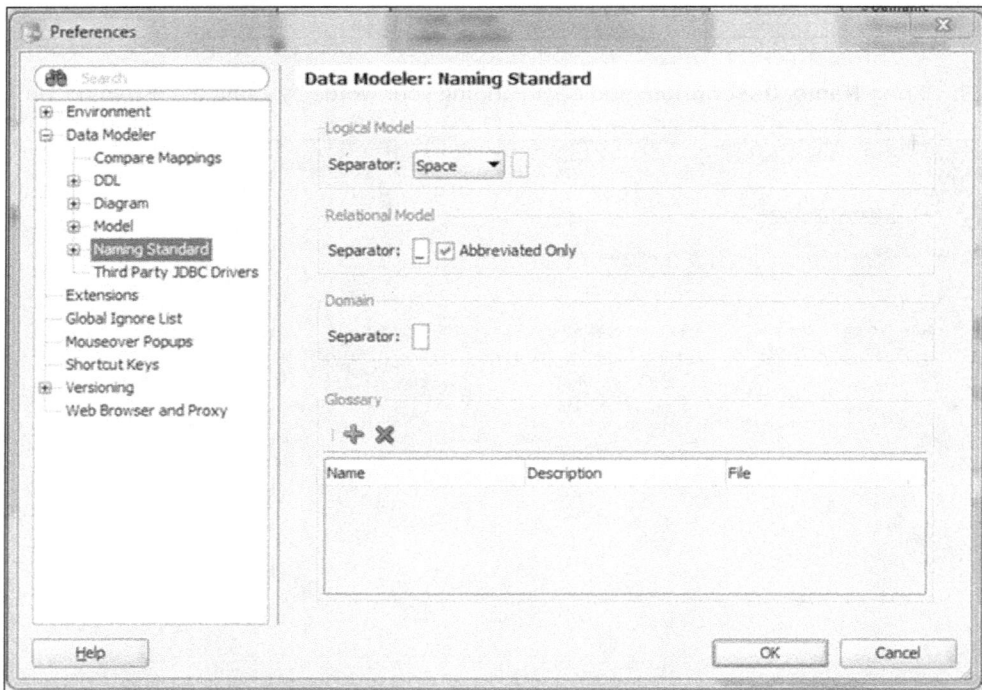

6. Check the **Abbreviated Only** checkbox for **Relational Model**, and click on the **+** (plus) icon to specify the glossary file. Navigate to your directory, and select the **glossary. glossary** file. Click on **Open**, and then on **OK**:

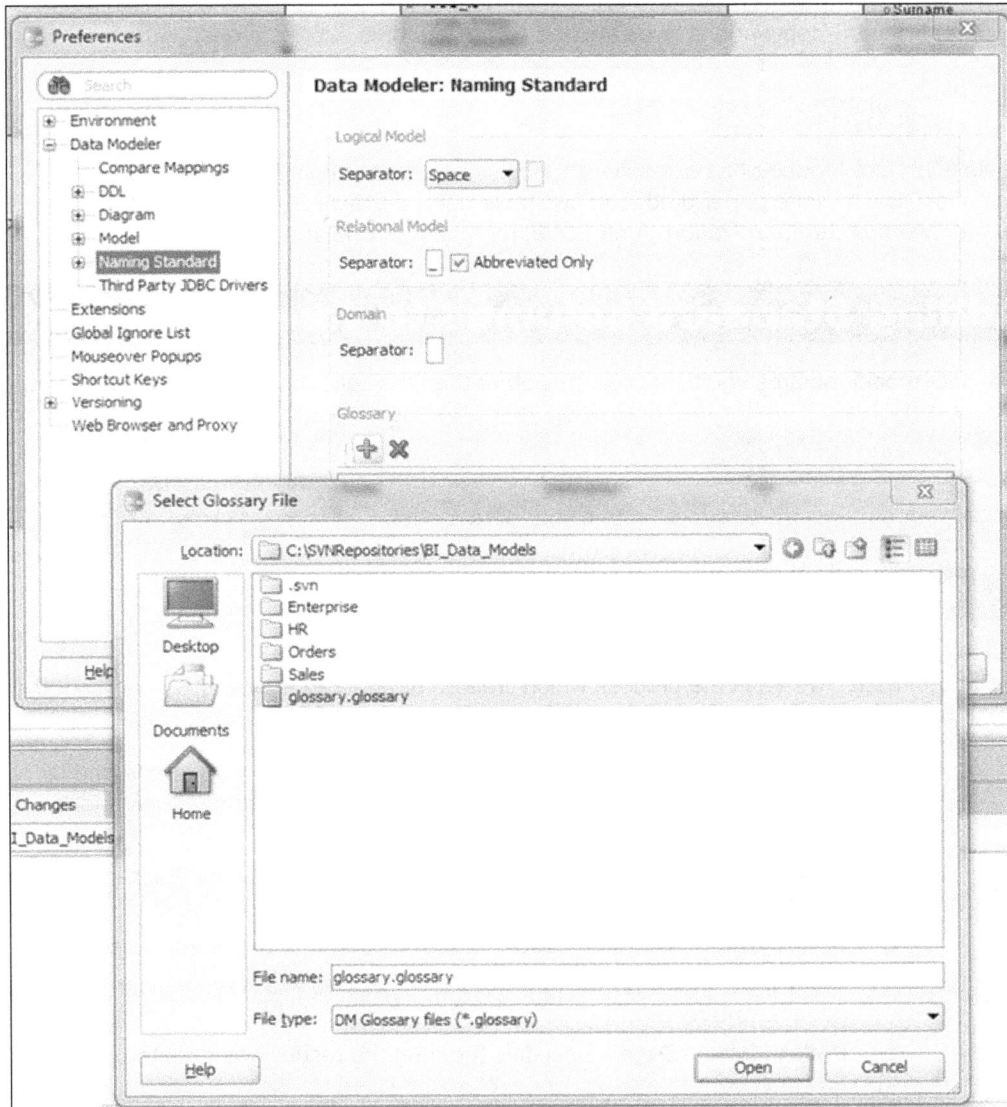

How it works...

The glossary will be used by Oracle SQL Data Modeler when converting your logical model into a physical model. It will enforce your naming standards for your table names. This allows for consistent naming conventions to be applied across multiple subject areas.

There's more...

Oracle SQL Data Modeler has extensive capabilities to apply naming standards. Please consult an Oracle white paper produced by Oracle named *Oracle SQL Developer Data Modeler Naming Standardization*, June 2009, for more options and capabilities.

Adding Standard columns to your data model

Each data model requires additional columns other than the columns requested by the solution.

Getting ready

Identify your dimensions and facts within your data model.

How to do it...

Tracking changes in a BI data model is a little different to a standard database application. In the BI data model, we track the process which created or updated the database and not the actual user:

1. For facts and dimensions, we will want to track when changes were made and by whom. For this, we need to add the standard audit columns. Double-click on the entity, select **Attributes**, and add the following columns:

   - **Create By – Domain – Varchar 32 Characters** – specifies which process or mapping created the record.
   - **Create Date – Domain – Date** – specifies the date the record was created.
   - **Update By – Varchar 32 Characters** – specifies which process or mapping updated the record.
   - **Update Date – Date** – specifies the date the record was updated.

2. Additional attributes to track changes may include the following:

i.	Batch number – identifies the last batch which updated the record.
ii.	Record Source System – identifies which source system created or updated the record last.

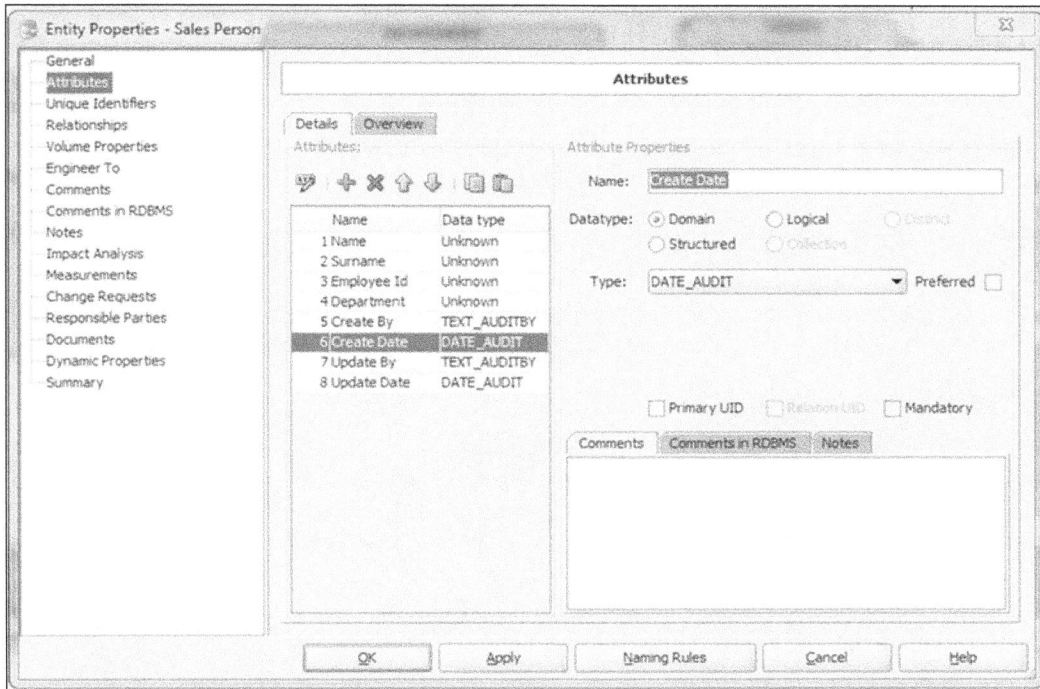

How it works...

Adding standard columns to your data model enhances the information for users. The preceding example adds audit columns. Other examples for adding standard columns include the following:

- ▶ **Varying descriptions** – Add columns for codes, short descriptions, and long descriptions for attributes in dimensions. This allows you to use codes as column values, short descriptions as filters, and long descriptions (code plus short descriptions) as row values. For example, if you have Country Code and Country Description, you could create a long description by combining the two attributes.

- ▶ **Flags** – When applying rules to information, add a flag to the record to specify the outcome. For example, determining whether a customer is a national or regional customer. Add a specific column to the dimension to contain the national or regional flag.

These standard columns are not found in the source data, but will enhance the data model and make it easier to use. Adding information to the data model and storing the values often provides performance gains for the reports.

How to forward engineer your logical data model to a relational data model

Forward engineering converts logical entities into physical tables which can be installed onto the database.

Getting ready

Ensure all your entities and attributes have been named correctly, domains assigned, and all the additional columns have been added before you forward engineer your logical model.

How to do it...

Forward engineering is a top-down approach to developing your physical data model. Using a data modeling tool to develop the data model is more efficient and easier to maintain than using the limited capabilities of your Extraction, Transformation, and Loading tool, such as OWB:

1. Click on **Design | Engineer to Relational Model**:

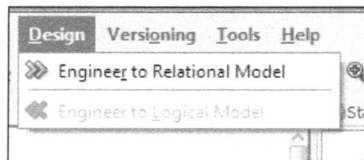

2. Deselect all objects by clicking on the checkbox located to the left-hand side of the **Logical** node in the tree. Select the relational model from the drop-down list in the top-right panel. Select the necessary **Entities** by clicking on the checkbox next to the entity name. Then, click on **Engineer**:

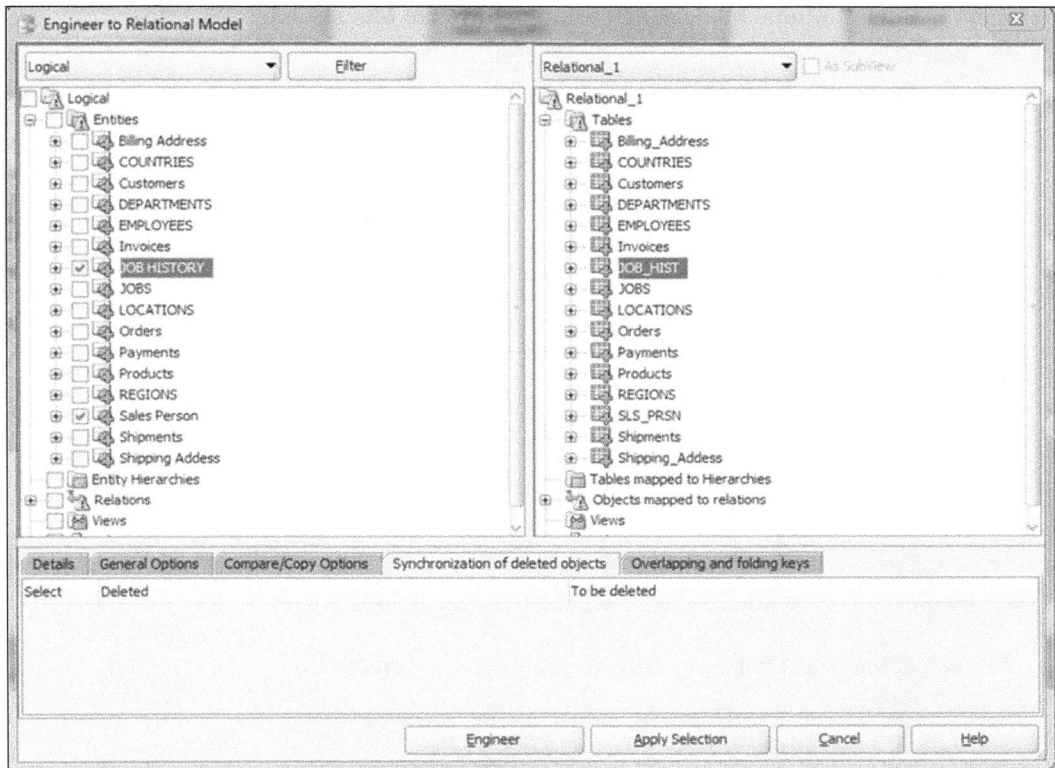

3. Review the tables. Notice that the names have changed to the values from the glossary previously defined:

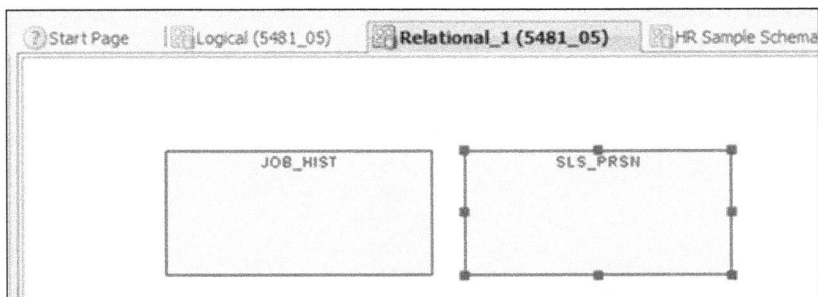

4. Expand **Relational Models**, right-click on **Physical Models**, and select **New**:

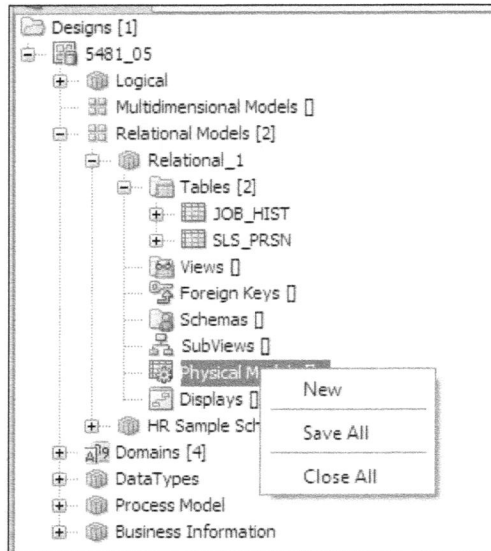

5. Select the target database type and version. Click on **OK**:

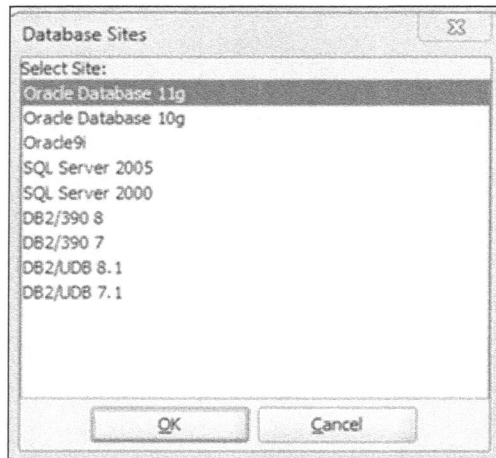

6. Review the physical objects you can add to your model:

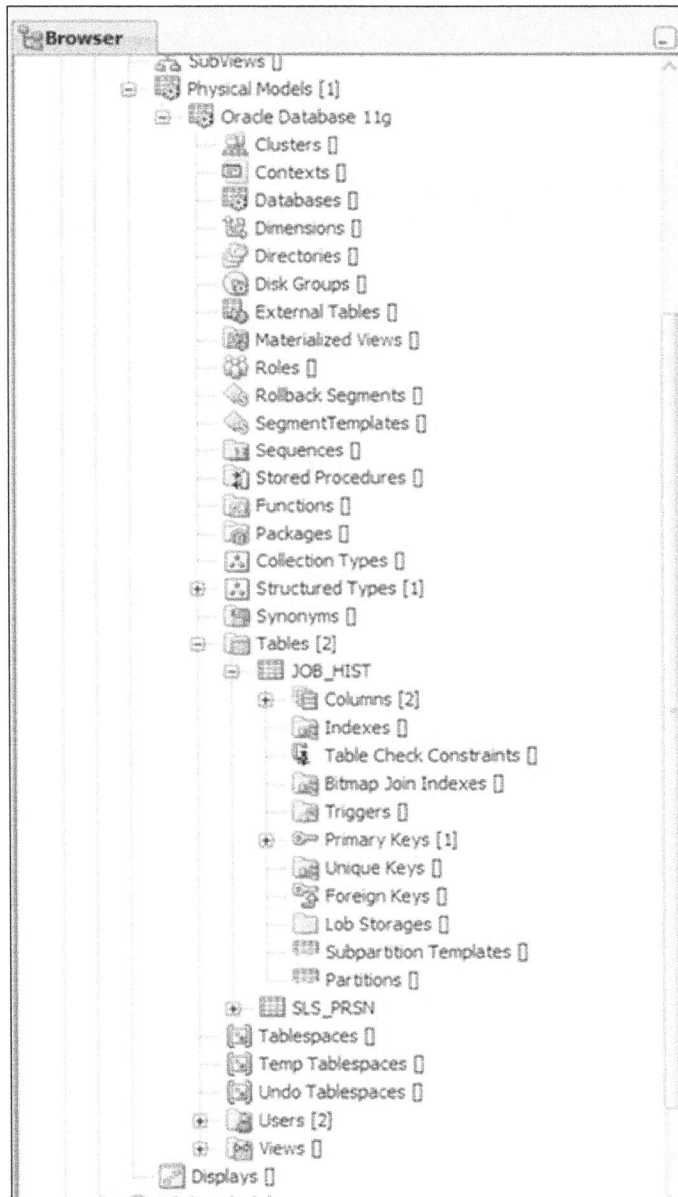

How it works...

Forward engineering converts the entities to tables by applying the glossary and naming standards defined previously. By adding the physical model, you can now add specific features based on the database and version. Oracle SQL Data Modeler can store a lot of physical definitions required to design your database.

Creating your enterprise data models

The **import** feature allows you to integrate or consolidate multiple data models in Oracle SQL Developer into a single data model or enterprise data model.

Getting ready

Ensure all the data models are saved, synchronized with Subversion, and closed.

How to do it...

Enterprise Design Models Enterprise Design Models are normally a culmination of all the different individual models for the different subject areas.

1. Right-click on **Design**, and select **New Design** to create a new enterprise design as follows:

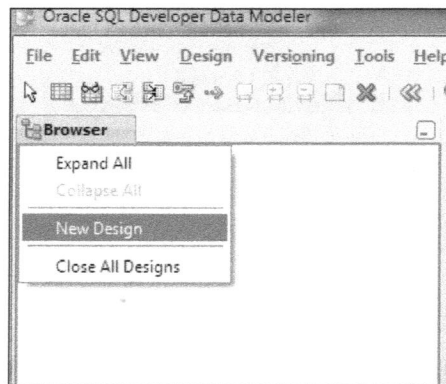

2. Click on **File | Import** to show the capabilities of Oracle SQL Data Modeler, and select **Data Modeler Design**:

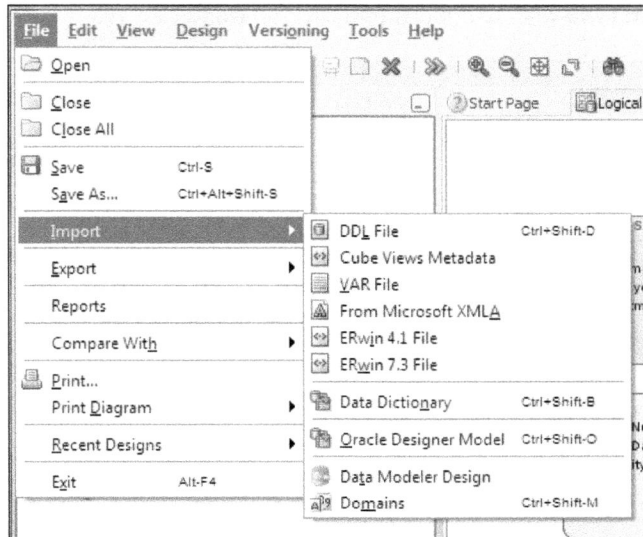

3. Navigate to your data model design under the working copy. Highlight the `.dmd` file, and click on **Open**:

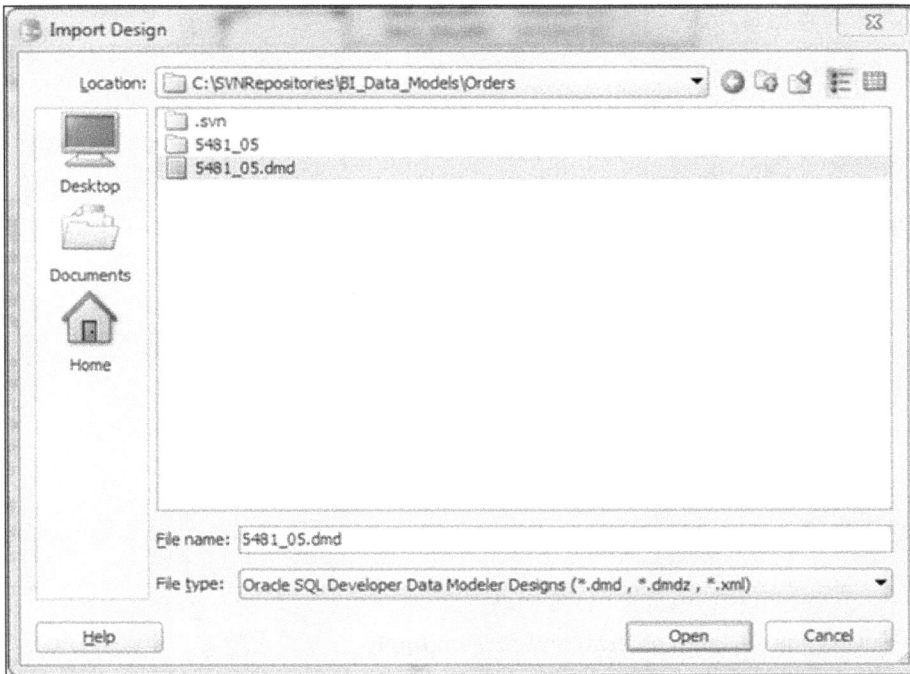

4. Select **Model** you wish to import, and click on **Next**:

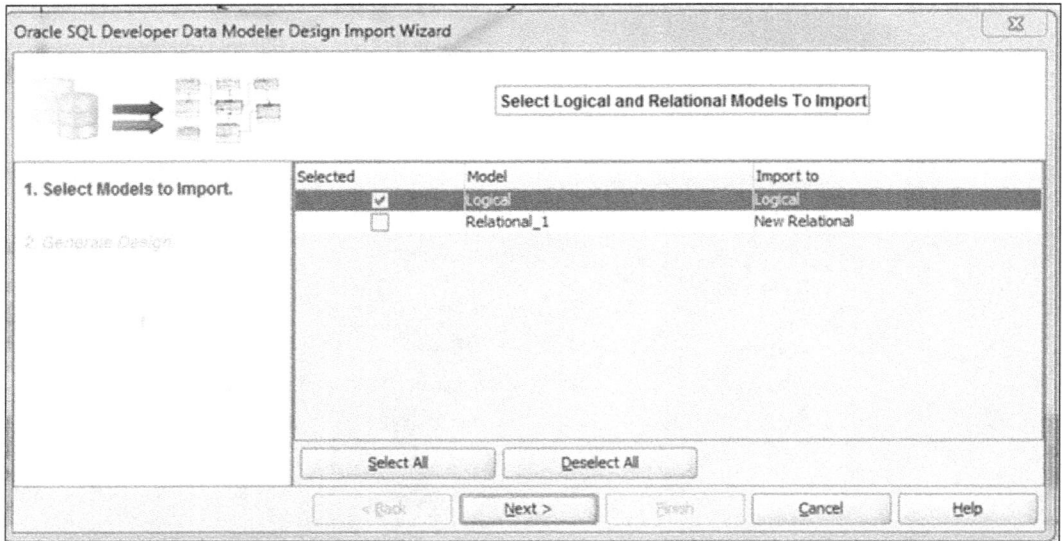

5. Review the selection, and click on **Finish**:

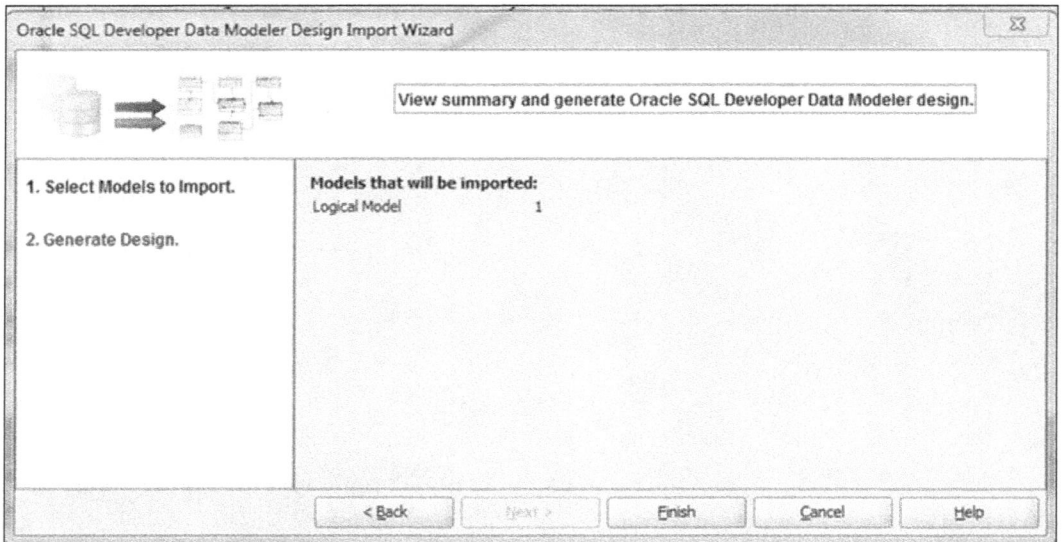

6. Review the selected objects, and click on **Apply**:

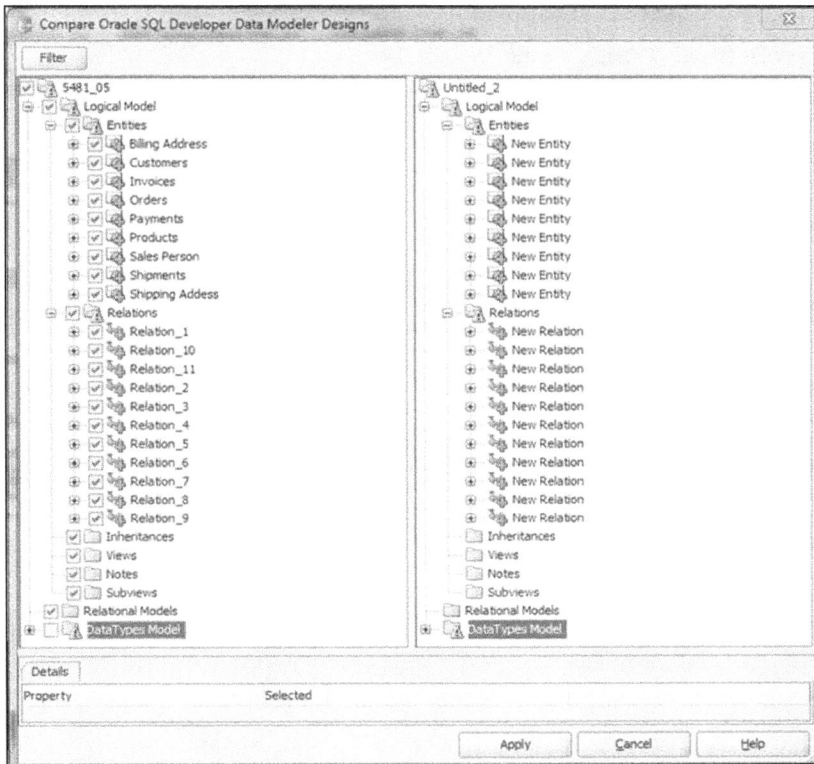

7. Validate the objects which have been imported into the new data model:

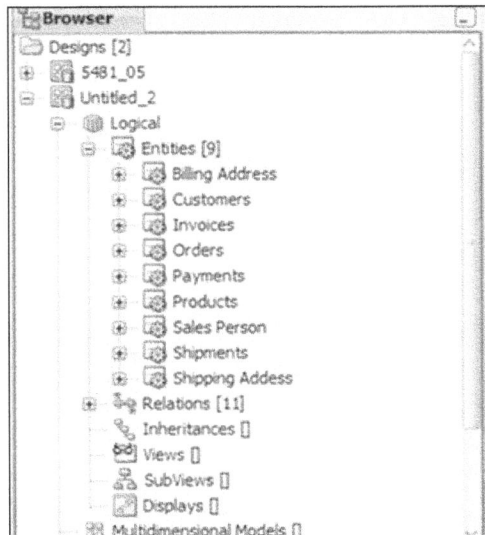

8. Click on **File | Save** to save your new enterprise model.

9. Select **Untitled_2 Design**, and click on **OK**:

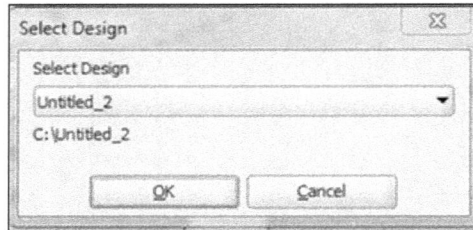

10. Navigate to the SVNRepositories directory under Enterprise, and enter a filename. Click on **Save**:

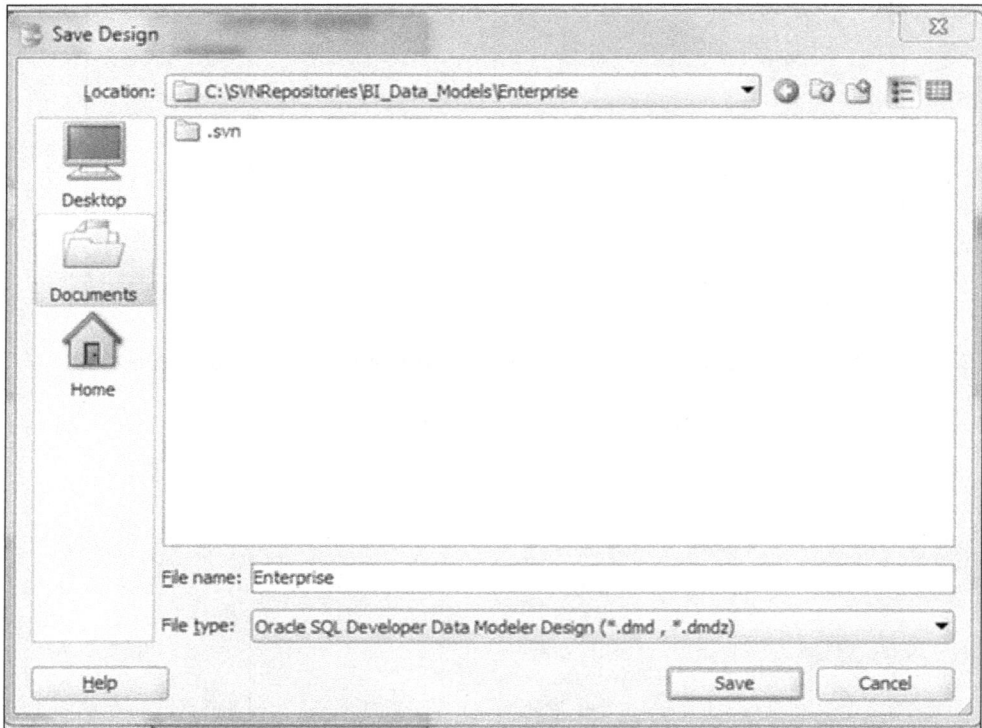

11. Click on **Yes** to add the data model to version control. It may ask you to select a folder to store system types. Navigate to the same folder, and click on **OK**:

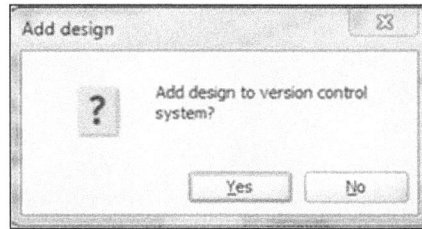

How it works...

Individual subject areas can be modeled and then integrated into an enterprise model. Individual subject areas can also import common definitions from the enterprise model. This offers a lot of flexibility and allows one to have working copies for subject areas in development but an enterprise model for the environment. Enterprise models are best kept at the logical level so as to not to include all the physical definitions of all the different models. A BI solution is built over time, as will be your enterprise model.

11
Defining the ETL/ELT

Extraction, Transformation, and Loading or Extraction, Loading, and Transformation tools are very common on the market. Implementing a business intelligence and data warehouse project without using one of these tools is highly unlikely as they offer so many benefits. However, just because you implement one of these tools does not mean that there are some areas which are overlooked and not included in the framework. This chapter outlines some of those areas that are often overlooked but are essential within your ETL/ELT framework. The following recipes focus on building the key framework components to be included in each ETL/ELT mapping or process:

- ▶ Abstracting your source system
- ▶ Separating your extraction from your loading and transforming routines
- ▶ Adding additional columns to facilitate error trapping and correction
- ▶ Designing ETL error trapping, detection, and correction routines
- ▶ Designing ETL data reconciliation routines
- ▶ Designing a notification routine

Introduction

ETL and ELT development within the business intelligence and data warehouse project is a significant part of the effort to implement the solution. Most ETL tools today have some form of statistics and error correction capabilities. These, however, are not normally sufficient as one needs to build a certain amount of intelligence and project-specific rules into the processes. These components are key pieces of technology that are required to be built, and then can be reused throughout different mappings and processes.

Abstracting your source system

For a business intelligence and data warehouse project, there are normally numerous source systems. All these source systems will have their individual data models and standards. Whether you are connecting to packaged or custom applications, at some time during the lifecycle of the project, these systems will undergo application upgrades. It is important to be able to abstract the business intelligence and data warehouse project from these upgrades so as to minimize the impact, and create a single point of failure.

Getting ready

Identify all your source tables from the Developing the data lineage recipe in *Chapter 8*, *Analyzing the Sources*. Obtain usernames and passwords for all the source systems with the necessary privileges. Determine the privileges you have within the source system.

How to do it...

Abstracting your data in the source system gives you a level of flexibility, should the source system or definition for the data change.

1. Open your **Data lineage** spreadsheet, and navigate to the **Data Lineage** tab.

2. Add an additional column into the spreadsheet after the **Source Object** column to capture abstraction views for source systems where you have privileges to create objects:

C	D	E
Source		
Source System	Source Object	Abstraction View
	GML.OP_SLSR_MST	
	SLS_REP	

3. Add an additional column into the spreadsheet after the **Staging Object** column to capture abstraction views for source systems where you have privileges to create objects:

H	I	J
Staging		
Mapping Name	Staging Object	Abstraction View
SRC_STG1_SALES_REP_TI	OP_SLSR_MST	
SRC_STG1_SLS_REP_TI	SLS_REP	

4. Name the views as per the semantic definition of the information they contain. A naming standard is recommended, such as SOURCE SYSTEM with SEMANTIC NAME:

C	D	E	F	G	H	I	J
Source Source System	Source Object	Abstraction View	Link Type	Link Name	Staging Mapping Name	Staging Object	Abstraction View
EBUS	GML.OP_SLSR_MST	EBUS_SLS_REP	Database Link	EBUS	SRC_STG1_SALES_REP_TI	OP_SLSR_MST	
WEB	SLS_REP		Flat File	f:\Data\sls_rep_<date>.txt	SRC_STG1_SLS_REP_TI	SLS_REP	WEB_SLS_REP

5. Create Data Definition Language (DDL) for the views:

```
Create or replace view ebus_sls_rep as
select * from gml.op_slsr_mst;
```

How it works...

By abstracting the source objects from the business intelligence and data warehouse project, you have minimized the impact and point of failure within the project. This single point can provide an easier solution to manage and maintain any change within the organization. Basic transformations (change date formats, trim whitespace, uppercase codes, and descriptions) can be performed in this layer. Do not include complex transformations within this layer as this is not the goal or the purpose of the abstraction layer. The data should remain as close to the source format as possible in order to simplify auditing and traceability of information.

These abstraction views can also standardize the view for the information being presented. For example, if you have multiple source systems for a single entity, you could create the abstraction views with the same definition by just mapping to different source attributes. This simplifies the ETL or ELT routines necessary.

When creating these abstraction views, it is important to consider where they will be created. Should they reside in the source system or in the staging area of the project? The answer to this will largely depend on the application you are connecting to and the privileges you are able to obtain. Never create views which cause a local and a remote table join (one table in the source is filtered or joined with one table in the target) as these will have a severe impact on resources and performance. Abstraction views, if used correctly, can greatly simplify and support your ETL/ELT framework. If you are creating abstraction views within a source application, ensure you get your own schema to create the views. This then ensures that the views are not part of the packaged application, and should not be tampered with during upgrades or patches.

Separating your extraction from your loading and transforming routines

Extracting data from the source system can be very repetitive and time-consuming. The mappings to extract data from the source system are normally very basic with minimal transformations. Building these in an ELT or ETL tool can often take a large amount of time for very little benefit. As an alternative, a generic extraction routine which can be scheduled and executed is normally more flexible and quicker to integrate into the framework.

Getting ready

Identify all the abstraction views created in the previous recipe. Ensure you have a schema created in your staging database for staging objects.

How to do it...

1. Determine which objects can be loaded incrementally and which objects require full extracts.

2. Design a controlling table to register the objects that require extracting:

```
CREATE TABLE "JHEATON"."DW_EXTRACT_CNTRL"
   (
      "XTR_CHANNEL"         NUMBER,
      "XTR_SEQ"             NUMBER,
      "XTR_ID"              NUMBER,
      "SRC_SYSTEM"          VARCHAR2(50),
      "SRC_DB_LINK"         VARCHAR2(32),
      "SRC_OBJECT_NAME"     VARCHAR2(128),
      "TRG_OBJECT_NAME"     VARCHAR2(128),
      "INCR_COLUMN_NAME"    VARCHAR2(32),
      "INCR_COLUMN_VALUE"   VARCHAR2(200),
      "INCR_COLUMN_FRMT"    VARCHAR2(200),
      "TRG_OBJECT_COLUMNS"  VARCHAR2(4000));
```

3. Change your target tables to utilize Oracle Interval Partitioning. Create the table definitions in the same way as the abstraction view definitions, and add a LOAD_DATE column. This will then automatically partition the data into daily partitions for all your extracts:

```
CREATE TABLE <TABLE_NAME>
(LOAD_DATE DATE DEFAULT SYSDATE,
<SRC_COLUMNS> )
)
PARTITION BY RANGE (LOAD_DATE)
INTERVAL (NUMTODSINTERVAL(1,'day'))
(PARTITION p_first VALUES LESS THAN ('01-JAN-2011'));
```

4. Design a status table to track the status of the objects being extracted:

```
CREATE TABLE "JHEATON"."DW_EXTRACT_STS"
   (
     "XTR_ID" NUMBER,
     "LOAD_DATE" DATE,
     "XTR_STATUS" VARCHAR2(50),
     "XTR_ROWS"   NUMBER(38,0));
```

5. Create your generic extract package. This package extracts data from the source and loads it into the target, based on the information contained in the tables created in the preceding step. The following code has comments in it to explain the logic of the code:

```
create or replace
PACKAGE BODY DW_GENERIC_LOAD AS
----------------------------------------------------
--- Generic Extract Package
--- 27th Jan 2012
--- John Heaton
--- Execute information below
--- begin
---     DW_GENERIC_LOAD.XTR_LOAD_DATE(1);
--- end;
----------------------------------------------------
PROCEDURE XTR_LOAD_DATA (XTR_CHANNEL_NO NUMBER, XTR_LOAD_DATE
NUMBER
   ) IS
--ERROR TRAPPING VARIABLES
V_ERR_CODE NUMBER(38);
V_ERR_MESG VARCHAR2(300);
V_PROC_NAME CONSTANT VARCHAR2(32) := 'DW_GENERIC_LOAD.XTR_LOAD_
DATE';
-- VARIABLES
V_SQL_STATEMENT VARCHAR2(32767) := NULL;
V_TABLE_NAME DW_EXTRACT_CNTRL.TRG_OBJECT_NAME%TYPE;
V_XTR_ID DW_EXTRACT_CNTRL.XTR_ID%TYPE;
V_INCR_COLUMN_NAME DW_EXTRACT_CNTRL.INCR_COLUMN_NAME%TYPE;
-- CURSOR TO GET ALL THE REGISTERED TABLES AND THE SPECIFIC
DETAILS
TO EXTRACT INFORMATION
CURSOR c_GET_TABLES
IS
  SELECT
    XTR_ID,
    SRC_SYSTEM ,
```

```
            SRC_DB_LINK,
            SRC_OBJECT_NAME,
            TRG_OBJECT_NAME,
      TRG_OBJECT_COLUMNS,
      INCR_COLUMN_NAME,
      INCR_COLUMN_VALUE,
            INCR_COLUMN_FRMT
        FROM DW_EXTRACT_CNTRL
        WHERE XTR_CHANNEL = xtr_channel_no
        ORDER BY XTR_SEQ;
V_XTR_ROW_REC C_GET_TABLES%ROWTYPE;
V_STATUS VARCHAR2(30);
V_CNT NUMBER;
-- MERGE STATEMENT TO UPDATE STATUS TABLE
V_MERGE_STATEMENT VARCHAR2(32767)
                            := 'MERGE INTO DW_EXTRACT_STS USING DUAL '
                            || ' ON (XTR_ID =  NVL(:1,-99) '
                            || ' AND TO_NUMBER(to_char(LOAD_
DATE,''YYYYMMDD'')) = :2'
                            || ' )'
                            || ' WHEN MATCHED THEN UPDATE '
                            || ' SET   XTR_STATUS = :3'
                            || ', XTR_ROWS = :4'
                            || ' WHEN NOT MATCHED THEN INSERT (XTR_
ID,LOAD_DATE,XTR_STATUS)'
                            || ' VALUES (:5,'
                            || ' TO_DATE(:6,''YYYYMMDD''),:7)' ;
V_UPDATE_STATEMENT VARCHAR2(32767) := NULL;
  BEGIN
  DBMS_OUTPUT.ENABLE(100000);
-- LOOP TO LOAD DATA
FOR  V_XTR_ROW_rec IN c_GET_TABLES
  LOOP
     V_TABLE_NAME := V_XTR_ROW_REC.TRG_OBJECT_NAME;
     V_XTR_ID := V_XTR_ROW_REC.XTR_ID;
     V_INCR_COLUMN_NAME  := V_XTR_ROW_REC.INCR_COLUMN_NAME;
         V_SQL_STATEMENT :=
                            'INSERT INTO '
                            ||V_XTR_ROW_REC.TRG_OBJECT_NAME
                            ||' ('|| V_XTR_ROW_REC.TRG_OBJECT_
COLUMNS||',LOAD_DATE)'
                            ||' SELECT '|| V_XTR_ROW_REC.TRG_
OBJECT_COLUMNS
                            ||' ,'
```

```
                                    || 'TO_DATE('|| xtr_load_
date||','''YYYYMMDD''')'
                                    ||' FROM '
                                    ||V_XTR_ROW_REC.SRC_OBJECT_NAME
                                    ||( CASE WHEN V_XTR_ROW_REC.SRC_DB_
LINK IS NOT NULL
                                        THEN V_XTR_ROW_REC.SRC_DB_LINK
ELSE NULL
                                    END)
                                    || (CASE WHEN V_XTR_ROW_REC.INCR_
COLUMN_NAME IS NOT NULL
                                        THEN ' WHERE '|| V_XTR_ROW_
REC.INCR_COLUMN_NAME ||' > '
                                            || REPLACE(V_XTR_ROW_REC.
INCR_COLUMN_FRMT,'<COLUMN_VALUE>',V_XTR_ROW_REC.INCR_COLUMN_VALUE)
                                    END)
                                        ;
            DBMS_OUTPUT.PUT_LINE(V_SQL_STATEMENT);
-- SETTING EXTRACT STATUS
            V_STATUS := 'Extracting';
            V_CNT := 0;
-- UPDATED EXTRACT STATUS FOR CURRENT TABLE
            EXECUTE IMMEDIATE V_MERGE_STATEMENT
            using V_XTR_ID ,XTR_LOAD_DATE, V_STATUS, v_cnt, V_XTR_ID
,XTR_LOAD_DATE ,V_STATUS;
-- EXTRACTING DATA FOR CURRENT TABLE
            EXECUTE IMMEDIATE(V_SQL_STATEMENT );
            DBMS_OUTPUT.PUT_LINE((CASE WHEN V_XTR_ROW_REC.INCR_
COLUMN_NAME IS NULL
                            THEN 'Full Extract - ' ||
SQL%ROWCOUNT || ' Rows extracted - '||V_XTR_ROW_REC.SRC_OBJECT_
NAME
                            ELSE 'Incremental Extract - ' ||
SQL%ROWCOUNT || ' Rows extracted - '|| V_XTR_ROW_REC.SRC_OBJECT_
NAME||' - '|| V_XTR_ROW_REC.INCR_COLUMN_NAME ||' > '
                                    || REPLACE(V_XTR_ROW_REC.
INCR_COLUMN_FRMT,'<COLUMN_VALUE>',V_XTR_ROW_REC.INCR_COLUMN_VALUE)
END)
            || ' - ' ||V_SQL_STATEMENT );
-- SETTING EXTRACT STATUS
            V_STATUS := 'Completed';
            V_CNT := SQL%ROWCOUNT;
-- UPDATED EXTRACT STATUS FOR CURRENT TABLE
            DBMS_OUTPUT.PUT_LINE(V_MERGE_STATEMENT );
            EXECUTE IMMEDIATE V_MERGE_STATEMENT
```

```
            USING V_XTR_ID ,XTR_LOAD_DATE, V_STATUS, V_CNT, V_XTR_
ID, XTR_LOAD_DATE ,V_STATUS;
-- UPDATE FOR CONTROL TABLE FOR MAX VALUE IN THE INCREMENTAL
COLUMN
            V_UPDATE_STATEMENT := 'UPDATE DW_EXTRACT_CNTRL '
                        || ' SET INCR_COLUMN_VALUE = '
                        || ' (SELECT MAX('||v_incr_column_name
                        ||' ) FROM ' || V_TABLE_NAME
|| ' WHERE TRUNC(LOAD_DATE) = TO_DATE('|| xtr_load_date ||','
                        || '''YYYYMMDD'')'
                        || ' )'
  || ' WHERE UPPER(TRG_OBJECT_NAME) = UPPER('''
                        || V_TABLE_NAME
                        || ''') ';
            DBMS_OUTPUT.PUT_LINE(V_UPDATE_STATEMENT );
            EXECUTE IMMEDIATE V_UPDATE_STATEMENT ;
    END LOOP;
EXCEPTION
-- GENERIC ERROR TRAPPING
  WHEN OTHERS THEN
    V_ERR_CODE := SQLCODE;
    V_ERR_MESG  := SUBSTR(SQLERRM,1,256);
    DBMS_OUTPUT.PUT_LINE(v_PROC_NAME || ' - ' || v_ERR_CODE||' -
'||
      v_ERR_MESG);
END;
END DW_GENERIC_LOAD;DW_GENERIC_LOAD;
```

6. Load data into your control table for all the source views.

How it works...

By creating a generic extract routine which is largely data-driven and placing information into partitions by load date, you have the ability to audit information from the source system as well as reload data when needed. By storing the extracted information in load partitions, it gives you the capability to reload source information without having to re-extract information from the source system. The abstraction layer created in the preceding recipe does not store history, therefore your extraction layer is the layer in which the history is stored.

There's more...

As an enhancement to this package, you can add additional features such as the following:

▶ Rolling partitions to store several periods of data. Once the limit is reached, the partitions are reused.

- Ability to lock partitions and retain them indefinitely.

- Ability to archive partitions to a file for potential future usage or to utilize data within another environment.

- Capability to combine incremental extract partitions into a single consolidated partition.

Adding additional columns to facilitate error trapping and correction

Error detection, trapping, and correction are complex operations within the business intelligence and data warehouse solution. Adding them into ETL/ELT slows down the performance of the mappings and process flows. For this reason, it is recommended to add columns to the tables and mappings in order to detect, trap, and correct errors post mapping or process flow.

Getting ready

Identify all the fact tables within the data model, and understand their natural or business keys.

How to do it...

In a business intelligence or data warehouse solution, fact tables normally use surrogate keys (system generated columns to replace business or natural keys) to link dimensional information. Once information in the fact tables is processed, it is hard to relate records with errors back to the dimensional information:

1. Identify all the dimensions which relate to the fact tables and determine the business or natural keys.

2. Include these keys on the fact tables as columns within your data model.

How it works...

By adding the business or natural key columns for error trapping and correction, you can take advantage of Oracle's bulk processing statements to gain better performance while maintaining data transparency. During your ETL/ELT process, if a match to a dimension is not found, you can replace this with an error surrogate key, for example, -1. This indicates that ETL/ELT could not find a match in the dimension for the values stored in the business or natural keys for the record.

This allows you to process data more efficiently while still maintaining the necessary columns to trap and correct errors at a later stage. Adding the business or natural keys allows you to identify the original source of information, and correct the information if necessary. Error surrogate keys can be standardized within ETL/ELT to provide consistent meaning. Thus a -1 surrogate key could mean no data found and a -99 surrogate key could mean not applicable. Error surrogate keys are recommended to have negative values as normally surrogate keys are generated using Oracle sequence numbers, which are positive values.

Designing ETL error trapping and detection routines

There are many ways in which you can detect and trap errors. Tools such as **Oracle Warehouse Builder** and **Oracle Data Integrator** provide some capabilities to detect data quality errors and provide mechanisms to correct the issues. The Oracle database allows you to add constraints to your data model (primary, foreign, unique, and check constraints) to enforce data integrity. They are useful and help to trap some errors; the problem with them is in detecting an error. For example, if you get a duplicate key error and are using a primary key constraint with bulk transformation within Oracle, a few things will happen. The first is the bulk transformation will encounter an error and potentially stop. If you have a failover to row processing, the process will start again, processing a single row at a time. The first duplicate record will be inserted into the target table, and the rest will return an error and can be configured to be placed into an overflow table. This sounds acceptable; however, which duplicate record is indeed correct? There are a few scenarios where you need additional control over the information to trap, detect, and correct the errors within the environment.

Getting ready

Identify all the tables you wish to track errors. Not all the tables will require error trapping. The typical candidates for tables to track errors are the fact tables.

How to do it...

Some errors in the data warehouse may be acceptable and others may not. For example, if one row in 1,000,000 is incorrect, this may not have a statistical impact on the result of the information and therefore can be tolerated. However, if you are generating financial statements to support business processes and decisions, your error may be statistically important and therefore needs to be corrected.

1. Create the error trapping, detection, and correction control table:

```
CREATE TABLE "DW_ERR_TRAP"
(
   "ERR_ID"                    NUMBER NOT NULL,
    "ERR_TYPE"          VARCHAR2(100),
```

```
    "STG_SRC_TABLE"    VARCHAR2(50),
      "STG_COR_TABLE"    VARCHAR2(50),
        "ERR_DETECT"                  VARCHAR2(4000),
          "ERR_REMOVE"            VARCHAR2(4000),
            "ERR_CORRECT"              VARCHAR2(4000),
              "ERR_CLEANUP"            VARCHAR2(4000),
                CONSTRAINT ERR_TRAP_PK PRIMARY_KEY (ERR_ID)
);
```

2. Create the error trapping, detection, and correction status table:

```
CREATE TABLE "DW_ERR_TRAP_STATUS"
(
   "ERR_ID"                          NUMBER NOT NULL,
     "ERR_DATE"             DATE NOT NULL,
       "ERR_DETECT_CNT"   NUMBER,
         "ERR_REMOVE_CNT"   NUMBER,
           "ERR_CORRECT_CNT" NUMBER,
             "ERR_CLEANUP_CNT" NUMBER
);
ALTER TABLE "DW_ERR_TRAP_STATUS"
ADD CONSTRAINT ERR_TRAP_STATUS_UK
UNIQUE KEY (ERR_ID, ERR_DATE) ;
ALTER TABLE "DW_ERR_TRAP_STATUS"
ADD CONSTRAINT ERR_TRAP_FK
FOREIGN KEY (ERR_ID)
REFERENCES "DW_ERR_TRAP" (ERR_ID);
Create error tables for the fact tables:
CREATE TABLE "<TABLE_NAME>_ERR"
  SELECT * FROM <TABLE_NAME> WHERE 1=2;
Add additional error columns:
ALTER TABLE "<TABLE_NAME>_ERR"
ADD (
  "ERR_TYPE" VARCHAR2 (100),
  "ERR_DATE" DATE
);
```

3. Create correction tables for the fact tables:

```
CREATE TABLE "<TABLE_NAME>_COR"
 SELECT * FROM <TABLE_NAME>_ERR WHERE 1=2;
```

4. Add a generic function to your DW_UTILS package to process the error:

```
create or replace
PACKAGE "DW_UTILS" IS
-------------------------------------------------------
--- Generic Utilities Package
--- 27th Jan 2012
--- John Heaton
```

```
----------------------------------------------------
FUNCTION ERR_TRAP (SRC_TABLE VARCHAR2)
RETURN NUMBER;
end DW_UTILS;
create or replace
PACKAGE BODY DW_UTILS
AS
/*
   DW_UTILS         Package Body
   Version       : Initial Version
   Date:         : 10/11/2011
*/
FUNCTION err_trap(src_table varchar2
  ) return number
IS
-- CURSOR TO SELECT ERROR TRAP INFORMATION
  CURSOR C_GET_ERR_TRAPS
  IS
    SELECT
    ERR_ID,
    ERR_TYPE,
    SRC_TABLE,
    ERR_DETECT,
    ERR_REMOVE,
    ERR_CORRECT,
    ERR_CLEANUP
    FROM DW_ERR_TRAP
    WHERE STG_SRC_TABLE = SRC_TABLE;
-- ERROR TRAP RECORD TYPE TO STORE INFORMATION
  V_ERR_TRAP_REC C_GET_ERR_TRAPS%ROWTYPE;
  V_SQL VARCHAR2(4000);
  V_ERR_ID NUMBER;
  V_DETECT_CNT NUMBER;
  V_REMOVE_CNT NUMBER;
  V_CORRECT_CNT NUMBER;
  V_CLEANUP_CNT NUMBER;
-- MERGE STATEMENT TO INSERT INFORMATION INTO STATUS TABLE
  V_MERGE_STATEMENT VARCHAR2(32767)
:= 'MERGE INTO DW_ERR_TRAP_STATUS USING
DUAL '
|| ' ON (ERR_ID =  NVL(:1,-99) AND (TRUNC(ERR_DATE) =
TRUNC(SYSDATE)
'
                        || ' )'
```

```
                          || ' WHEN MATCHED THEN UPDATE '
                          || ' SET   ERR_DETECT_CNT = :2'
                          || ', ERR_REMOVE_CNT  = :3'
                          || ', ERR_CORRECT_CNT  = :4'
                          || ', ERR_CLEANUP_CNT  = :5'
                          || ' WHEN NOT MATCHED THEN INSERT '
                          || ' (ERR_ID ERR_DATE, ERR_DETECT_CNT,
ERR_REMOVE_CNT,ERR_CORRECT_CNT, ERR_CLEANUP_CNT)'
                          || ' VALUES (:6,SYSDATE, :7,:8,:9,10)';
BEGIN
-- LOOP TO CYCLE THROUGH INFORMATION IN THE ERROR TRAP RECORD
FOR  V_ERR_TRAP_REC IN C_GET_ERR_TRAPS
  LOOP
-- DYNAMIC SQL STATEMENT TO DETECT ERROR
      V_SQL := V_ERR_TRAP_REC.ERR_DETECT;
      DBMS_OUTPUT.PUT_LINE(V_SQL);
      EXECUTE IMMEDIATE(V_SQL);
      V_DETECT_CNT := SQL%ROWCOUNT;
-- DYNAMIC SQL STATEMENT TO REMOVE ERROR
      V_SQL := V_ERR_TRAP_REC.ERR_REMOVE;
      DBMS_OUTPUT.PUT_LINE(V_SQL);
      EXECUTE IMMEDIATE(V_SQL);
      V_REMOVE_CNT := SQL%ROWCOUNT;
-- DYNAMIC SQL STATEMENT TO CORRECT ERROR
      V_SQL := V_ERR_TRAP_REC.ERR_CORRECT;
      DBMS_OUTPUT.PUT_LINE(V_SQL);
      EXECUTE IMMEDIATE(V_SQL);
      V_CORRECT_CNT := SQL%ROWCOUNT;
-- DYNAMIC SQL STATEMENT TO CLEANUP ERROR
      V_SQL := V_ERR_TRAP_REC.ERR_CLEANUP;
      DBMS_OUTPUT.PUT_LINE(V_SQL);
      EXECUTE IMMEDIATE(V_SQL);
      V_CORRECT_CNT := SQL%ROWCOUNT;
-- DYNAMIC SQL STATEMENT TO UPDATE ERROR TRAP STATUS TABLE
      EXECUTE IMMEDIATE(V_SQL)
      USING
        V_ERR_ID ,
        V_DETECT_CNT ,      .
        V_REMOVE_CNT ,
        V_CORRECT_CNT ,
        V_CLEANUP_CNT ,
        V_ERR_ID ,
        V_DETECT_CNT ,
        V_REMOVE_CNT ,
```

```
                V_CORRECT_CNT ,
                V_CLEANUP_CNT ;
           END LOOP;
     return 0;
     -- EXCEPTION HANDLING
     EXCEPTION
        WHEN OTHERS THEN
             dbms_output.put_line('Error! '||SUBSTR(SQLERRM, 1, 200));
             RETURN 1;
     END err_trap;
     END DW_UTILS;
```

How it works...

By determining the scenarios you wish to design error traps for, you can build a generic error trap, detection, and correction routine. This routine runs and identifies the data that is suspect, and moves the information into an error table. Once in the error table, you can run the automatic correction routines to try and correct any incorrect data. Data corrected can be re-inserted into the staging table, and deleted from the error tables. The remaining data in the error tables can be corrected manually or reprocessed when the next ETL/ELT is executed.

Types of error trapping include:

▶ Duplicate rows. In this check, you will use all the columns in the table to detect any duplicate records within the staging table. From there, you will move the data into the err table. The example is as follows:

- ❑ ERR_ID – 1
- ❑ ERR_TYPE – Duplicate
- ❑ SRC_TABLE – FACT1
- ❑ ERR_DETECT –

```
INSERT INTO FACT1_ERR (KEY1, KEY2, COL1, COL2, ERR_TYPE, ERR_DATE)
SELECT F.KEY1, F.KEY2, F.COL1, F.COL2, 'DUPLICATES', SYSDATE
FROM FACT1 F,
(SELECT KEY1, KEY2, COL1, COL2 , COUNT(*)
FROM FACT1
GROUP BY KEY1, KEY2, COL1, COL2
HAVING COUNT(*) > 1 ) DUP_RECS
WHERE F.KEY1 = DUP_RECS.KEY1
AND F.KEY2 = DUP_RECS.KEY2
AND F.COL1 = DUP_RECS.COL1
AND F.COL2 = DUP_RECS.COL2
```

❏ ERR_REMOVE –

```
DELETE FROM FACT1 WHERE EXISTS (SELECT 1
FROM FACT1_ERR
WHERE FACT1_ERR.KEY1 = FACT1.KEY1
AND FACT1_ERR.KEY2 = FACT1.KEY2
AND FACT1_ERR.COL1 = FACT1.COL1
AND FACT1_ERR.COL2 = FACT1.COL2)
```

❏ ERR_CORRECT –

```
INSERT INTO FACT1_CORR (KEY1, KEY2, COL1, COL2, ERR_TYPE, ERR_
DATE)
SELECT KEY1, KEY2, COL1, COL2, ERR_TYPE, SYSDATE
FROM FACT1_ERR
WHERE ERR_TYPE = 'DUPLICATES'
GROUP BY KEY1, KEY2, COL1, COL2, ERR_TYPE
HAVING COUNT(*) > 1)
```

❏ ERR_CLEANUP –

```
DELETE FROM FACT1_ERR WHERE EXISTS (SELECT 1
FROM FACT1_CORR
WHERE FACT1_CORR.ERR_TYPE = 'DUPLICATES'
AND FACT1_CORR.ERR_TYPE = FACT1_ERR.ERR_TYPE
AND FACT1_CORR.KEY1 = FACT1_ERR.KEY1
AND FACT1_CORR.KEY2 = FACT1_ERR.KEY2
AND FACT1_CORR.COL1 = FACT1_ERR.COL1
AND FACT1_CORR.COL2 = FACT1_ERR.COL2)
```

▶ Invalid surrogate key.
▶ Missing business or natural keys.

Error trapping, detection, and correction routines need to be placed into the ETL/ELT process flow to be executed automatically. To be effective, they need to be placed in the correct places before information is published to the end user.

By implementing the error trap, detection, and correction routines at the end of mappings within the staging area, erroneous data can be caught before being published to end users. This maintains the integrity of the information, while potentially limiting the number of reloads or restatements of information.

Designing ETL data reconciliation routines

Reconciliation routines are automated ways to check the data integrity using predefined business rules. These routines look at the content of the information and record the results. Information is then compared to determine if it matches.

Getting ready

Identify the business rules to compare and validate information as it flows through the business intelligence and data warehouse solution from the source environment to the target environment. Review your data lineage from *Chapter 8, Analyzing the Sources*, specifically for fact table loads. Along the stream for fact loads are excellent places for data reconciliation scripts.

How to do it...

Proving data integrity to the business users is key. Automating this allows one to include it into the process flow and have it generated upon load automatically:

1. Create the reconciliation control table:

```
CREATE TABLE "DW_RECONCILE"
(
    "SCRIPT_ID"              NUMBER,
    "SCRIPT_NAME"            VARCHAR2(50),
    "SCRIPT_PHASE"           VARCHAR2(50),
    "SCRIPT_SEQ"             NUMBER,
    "SCRIPT_SQL"             VARCHAR2(4000)
    );
```

2. Create the reconciliation status table:

```
CREATE TABLE "DW_RECONCILE_STATUS"
(
    "SCRIPT_ID"              NUMBER,
    "SCRIPT_DATE"        DATE,
    "RESULT1"                    VARCHAR2(200),
    "RESULT2"                    VARCHAR2(200),
    "RESULT3"                    VARCHAR2(200),
    "RESULT4"                    VARCHAR2(200),
    "RESULT5"                    VARCHAR2(200)
);
```

3. Add a generic function to your DW_UTILS package to execute the reconciliation scripts and to compare the results:

```
create or replace
PACKAGE BODY DW_UTILS
AS
/*
    DW_UTILS        Package Body
    Version     : Initial Version
    Date:       : 10/11/2011
```

```
*/
FUNCTION err_trap(src_table varchar2
  ) return number
IS
-- Code removed to abbreviate example. Refer to the
-- previous recipe.
EXCEPTION
  WHEN OTHERS THEN
    dbms_output.put_line('Error! '||SUBSTR(SQLERRM, 1, 200));
    RETURN 1;
END err_trap;
FUNCTION RECON_EXECUTE (SCRPT_NAME VARCHAR2, SCRPT_PHASE VARCHAR2,
  SCRPT_DATE DATE)
RETURN NUMBER
IS
-- CURSOR TO RETRIEVE RECONCILLIATION SCRIPTS
CURSOR C_GET_RECON_SCRIPTS
  IS
    SELECT
    SCRIPT_ID,
    SCRIPT_PHASE,
    SCRIPT_SEQ,
    SCRIPT_SQL
    FROM DW_RECONCILE
    WHERE SCRIPT_NAME = SCRPT_NAME AND
    SCRIPT_PHASE = SCRPT_PHASE
    ORDER BY SCRIPT_SEQ;
-- VARIABLE SETUP AND CREATION
V_RECON_REC C_GET_RECON_SCRIPTS%ROWTYPE;
V_SCRIPT_ID DW_RECONCILE.SCRIPT_ID%TYPE;
V_SQL DW_RECONCILE.SCRIPT_SQL%TYPE;
BEGIN
-- LOOP TO CYCLE THROUGH RECONILLIATION SCRIPTS
FOR  V_RECON_REC  IN C_GET_RECON_SCRIPTS
  LOOP
    V_SCRIPT_ID := V_RECON_REC.SCRIPT_ID;
    V_SQL := V_RECON_REC.SCRIPT_SQL;
-- DYNAMIC SQL STATEMENT TO RUN RECONCILLIATION SCRIPT
    EXECUTE IMMEDIATE(V_SQL)
    USING
    V_SCRIPT_ID,
    SCRPT_DATE;
    END LOOP;
    RETURN 0 ;
```

```
EXCEPTION
  WHEN OTHERS THEN
    dbms_output.put_line('Error! '||SUBSTR(SQLERRM, 1, 200));
    RETURN 1;
    END RECON_EXECUTE ;
    FUNCTION RECON_COMPARE(SCRPT_NAME VARCHAR2, SCRPT_DATE DATE)
    RETURN NUMBER
   IS
-- CURSOR TO COMPARE RECONILLIATION SCRIPTS
CURSOR GET_RECON_RESULTS
   IS
    SELECT R.SCRIPT_ID, R.SCRIPT_NAME ,
    S.SCRIPT_DATE, S.RESULT1, S.RESULT2, S.RESULT3, S.RESULT4,
      S.RESULT5
    FROM DW_RECONCILE R,
    DW_RECONCILE_STATUS S
    WHERE R.SCRIPT_NAME = SCRPT_NAME
    AND R.SCRIPT_ID = S.SCRIPT_ID
    AND TRUNC(S.SCRIPT_DATE) = TRUNC(SCRPT_DATE)
    ORDER BY R.SCRIPT_SEQ;
-- VARIABLE SETUP
V_RETURN NUMBER :=0;
V_ROWCNT NUMBER :=1;
V_RECON_REC GET_RECON_RESULTS%ROWTYPE;
V_RESULT1 DW_RECONCILE_STATUS.RESULT1%TYPE ;
V_RESULT2 DW_RECONCILE_STATUS.RESULT2%TYPE ;
V_RESULT3 DW_RECONCILE_STATUS.RESULT3%TYPE ;
V_RESULT4 DW_RECONCILE_STATUS.RESULT4%TYPE ;
V_RESULT5 DW_RECONCILE_STATUS.RESULT5%TYPE ;
BEGIN
-- LOOP TO CYCLE AND COMPARE RESULTS
FOR  V_RECON_REC  IN GET_RECON_RESULTS
   LOOP
     IF V_ROWCNT = 1 THEN
       V_RESULT1 := V_RECON_REC.RESULT1 ;
       V_RESULT2 := V_RECON_REC.RESULT2 ;
       V_RESULT3 := V_RECON_REC.RESULT3 ;
       V_RESULT4 := V_RECON_REC.RESULT4 ;
       V_RESULT5 := V_RECON_REC.RESULT5 ;
     ELSE
       IF    (NVL(V_RESULT1,-99) <> NVL(V_RECON_REC.RESULT1,-99) OR
         NVL(V_RESULT2,-99) <> NVL(V_RECON_REC.RESULT2,-99) OR
         NVL(V_RESULT3,-99) <> NVL(V_RECON_REC.RESULT3,-99) OR
         NVL(V_RESULT4,-99) <> NVL(V_RECON_REC.RESULT4,-99) OR
```

```
        NVL(V_RESULT5,-99) <> NVL(V_RECON_REC.RESULT5,-99))
      THEN V_RETURN :=1;
      END IF;
    END IF;
    V_ROWCNT := V_ROWCNT + 1;
  END LOOP;
  RETURN V_RETURN;
EXCEPTION
  WHEN OTHERS THEN
    dbms_output.put_line('Error! '||SUBSTR(SQLERRM, 1, 200));
    RETURN 1;
  END RECON_COMPARE ;
END DW_UTILS;
```

How it works...

By identifying reconciliation scripts at different points within the process, you can proactively determine if the information is correct within the warehouse before it is published to the end user. These automated reconciliation scripts increase the integrity levels of information stored within the solution. Typical points include extracting from source, processing into staging, and then loading into the warehouse. The business keys are the preferred ways to compare information as they are easier to use and have not been modified along the way.

Data reconciliation scripts need to be inserted into the process at different points to gather statistics and information. Once the information has been collected, it can be compared to determine if there is a data integrity issue.

Before these scripts can be automated and embedded into the solution, it is important that they are tested and verified. To reduce this effort, build these reconciliation scripts as part of unit testing so that they can be used and verified manually during the development phase of the project.

Designing a notification routine

Most ETL/ELT tools have a notification mechanism embedded within the product. However, in the solution, you may require notifications at many different places across different products (Shell Scripts, Scheduled Jobs, APEX, OWB, ODI, and so on). For this reason, it may be more beneficial to utilize a custom notification mechanism which can be embedded into multiple processes.

Getting ready

Review the types of notifications which are required within your projects and also from which products. Determine if a standard mechanism exists before building a custom notification routine. If more than one exists, consider building your own custom notification routine.

How to do it...

Notifications can be an easy way to send results. Ensure that the information sent is meaningful and actionable. Refrain from spamming every status:

1. Create Access Contol Lists (ACLs) and privileges. In Oracle 11g, you are required to create an ACL as SYS. Log in as SYS. Create an ACL for a specific user with the connect privilege:

```
begin
  DBMS_NETWORK_ACL_ADMIN.CREATE_ACL (
    ACL              => 'emailsrv.xml',
    description      => 'Access to Email Server',
    principal        => '<ROLE_NAME>/<USER_NAME>',
    is_grant         => TRUE,
    privilege        => 'connect',
    start_date       => null,
    end_date         => null
  );
end;
```

2. Validate whether the ACL has been created:

```
SELECT any_path FROM resource_view WHERE any_path like
  '/sys/acls/%.xml';
Add additional privileges.
begin
  dbms_network_acl_admin.add_privilege (
    acl              => 'emailsrv.xml',
    principal        => '<ROLE_NAME>/<USER_NAME>',
    is_grant         => TRUE,
    privilege        => 'resolve',
    start_date       => null,
    end_date         => null);
end;
```

3. Assign the ACL to a specific resource:

```
begin
  dbms_network_acl_admin.assign_acl (
  acl => 'emailsrv.xml',
```

```
    HOST => '<hostname>',
    LOWER_PORT => <port>,
    upper_port => <port>);
end;
```

4. Create a message table to store messages and a sequence for unique message numbers:

```
CREATE TABLE "JHEATON"."DW_MSG"
   (
     "MSG_ID"      NUMBER,
     "MSG_APP"     VARCHAR2(200),
     "MSG_FROM"    VARCHAR2(200),
     "MSG_TO"      VARCHAR2(200),
     "MSG_SUBJECT" VARCHAR2(200),
     "MSG_TEXT"    VARCHAR2(4000),
     "MSG_DATE" DATE,
     "MSG_TYPE" VARCHAR2(200 BYTE)
   );
CREATE SEQUENCE  "MSG_SEQ"  MINVALUE 1 INCREMENT BY 1 START WITH 1
   NOCACHE   NOORDER   NOCYCLE ;
```

5. Create a function to send e-mail:

```
CREATE OR REPLACE
PACKAGE BODY DW_UTILS
AS
   /*
   DW_UTILS         Package Body
   Version        : Initial Version
   Date:          : 10/11/2011
   */
FUNCTION SEND_MSG(
     MSG_APP      VARCHAR2,
     MSG_TYPE     VARCHAR2,
     MSG_TO       VARCHAR2,
     MSG_SUBJECT VARCHAR2,
     MSG_TEXT     VARCHAR2 )
   RETURN NUMBER
IS
   C UTL_SMTP.CONNECTION;
   RC        INTEGER;
   MSG_FROM VARCHAR2(50)  := '<FROM_EMAL>';
   MAILHOST VARCHAR2(30)  := '<MAILHOST>'; -- Mail Host
BEGIN
   INSERT
   INTO DW_MSG
     (
```

```
                         MSG_ID,
                         MSG_APP,
                         MSG_TYPE,
                         MSG_FROM,
                         MSG_TO,
                         MSG_SUBJECT,
                         MSG_TEXT,
                         MSG_DATE
                       )
                    VALUES
                       (
                         MSG_SEQ.NEXTVAL,
                         MSG_APP,
                         MSG_TYPE,
                         MSG_FROM,
                         MSG_TO,
                         MSG_SUBJECT,
                         MSG_TEXT,
                         SYSDATE
                       );
                 C := UTL_SMTP.OPEN_CONNECTION(MAILHOST, 25); -- SMTP on port 25
                 UTL_SMTP.HELO(C, MAILHOST);
                 UTL_SMTP.MAIL(C, MSG_FROM);
                 UTL_SMTP.RCPT(C, MSG_TO);
                 UTL_SMTP.DATA(C,'From: Oracle Database' || UTL_TCP.CRLF || 'To:
'
                    || MSG_TO || UTL_TCP.CRLF || 'Subject: ' || MSG_SUBJECT ||
                       UTL_TCP.CRLF || MSG_TEXT);
                 UTL_SMTP.QUIT(C);
                 RETURN 0;
              EXCEPTION
              WHEN UTL_SMTP.INVALID_OPERATION THEN
                DBMS_OUTPUT.PUT_LINE(' Invalid Operation in Mail attempt using
                   UTL_SMTP.');
                RETURN 1;
              WHEN UTL_SMTP.TRANSIENT_ERROR THEN
                DBMS_OUTPUT.PUT_LINE(' Temporary e-mail issue - try again');
                RETURN 1;
              WHEN UTL_SMTP.PERMANENT_ERROR THEN
                DBMS_OUTPUT.PUT_LINE(' Permanent Error Encountered.');
                RETURN 1;
              WHEN OTHERS THEN
                DBMS_OUTPUT.PUT_LINE('Error! '||SUBSTR(SQLERRM, 1, 200));
                RETURN 1;
              END SEND_MSG;
              END DW_UTILS;
```

How it works...

By developing a custom notification routine and table, you can capture and store notifications from multiple places. The solution also allows for a historical journal of all the notifications that have been sent out. This can be a valuable source of information as you may see trends developing for reoccurring breakages.

The notification routine will need to be included in the different processes which require information to be communicated to different people.

Capturing notifications along the data load process gives an insight into the issues which arise normally. Capturing the information within a table first and then emailing the information to the specific people minimizes the potential for loss. As a secondary notification mechanism, these notifications can be reported in other formats in a centralized location (reports on a dashboard for system status). If you have a defect management system which can support automatic logging of tickets from e-mail, the notification routine can send the information to the ticketing system where it can be assigned and corrected.

12
Enhancing the Data

When building data warehouse/business intelligence solutions, it is normal for data gaps to be present. These are typically key pieces of information required to match information or perform some analysis, or could be as simple as updating descriptive information. Enhancing the source application is often not an option due to cost, and/or limitations in the application.

The data gaps are normally fixed through manual processes that involve submitting requests for data modifications within the data warehouse/business intelligence environment, or building an application to enable users to manage their own data gaps. The following recipes will help you automate the process of enhancing the data within the data warehouse:

  ► Creating your application schema
  ► Creating your application tables
  ► Developing the journal tables to track changes
  ► Defining the audit triggers
  ► Defining the APEX Upload application
  ► Creating the Upload interface

Introduction

In a business intelligence and data warehousing solution, there is nearly always a need to enhance or add information to the solution. For this reason, a simple but functional user interface is always needed to support the requirements.

Oracle Application Express (**APEX**) is a robust, web-enabled design, development, and run environment, used to build custom applications within an Oracle database. APEX is shipped as part of an Oracle database, and is currently free. The tight integration with the Oracle database, ease of use, and cost make APEX ideal to build an automated solution to fill the data gaps.

Creating your application schema

The APEX application will connect to a database schema. It is recommended that all database objects be placed into their own separate schema. By separating these objects, you ensure that the data cannot be compromised in other areas within the data warehouse.

Getting ready

With a separate schema for the APEX application, it segregates the objects from the source table information stored within the staging schemas. This segregation makes for easier maintenance and security of the tables.

How to do it...

When building an APEX application, you first need to select the schema to which you want to connect. If there are additional tables in this schema, it would be possible for a screen to be built directly on the data warehouse tables.

1. Firstly, we will create a database user, app, to be the schema owner:

    ```
    create user app identified by app
    default tablespace users
    temporary tablespace temp;
    ```

2. Assign roles and privileges to the schema owner:

    ```
    -- Default roles for demo
    grant connect, resource to app;

    -- Included to enable the use of autotrace
    GRANT select_catalog_role TO app;

    -- Included to enable the use of autotrace
    GRANT SELECT ANY dictionary TO app;
    ```

How it works..

Creating a separate schema for your application allows you to segregate the information from your business intelligence and data warehousing solution. This allows you to manage and maintain the applications separately and independently from the solution.

Creating your application tables

Application tables will contain the information that is required for the data warehouse solution, but cannot be obtained from any existing source system. The APEX application will provide a means to capture this information and store it within the application tables.

Getting ready

Log in to your database schema created in the previous recipe.

How to do it...

The following steps will create some sample tables which will be used by the APEX application for the upload screen:

1. The table we will use is a simple customer table, defined as follows:

```
CREATE TABLE "APP_CUSTOMER"
  (
  "CUST_SEQ"        NUMBER NOT NULL ENABLE,
  "CUST_NUM"        VARCHAR2(50 BYTE) NOT NULL ENABLE,
  "CUST_NAME"       VARCHAR2(50 BYTE),
  "CUST_ADDRESS1"   VARCHAR2(50 BYTE),
  "CUST_ADDRESS2"   VARCHAR2(50 BYTE),
  "CUST_CITY"       VARCHAR2(50 BYTE),
  "CUST_PCODE_ZIP"  VARCHAR2(20 BYTE),
  "CUST_STATE"      VARCHAR2(50 BYTE),
  "CUST_COUNTRY"    VARCHAR2(50 BYTE),
  "REGION"          VARCHAR2(50 BYTE),
  "CREATE_DATE"     DATE,
  "CREATE_BY"       VARCHAR2(50 BYTE),
  "UPDATE_DATE"     DATE,
  "UPDATE_BY"       VARCHAR2(50 BYTE),

  "APPROVED_DATE"   DATE,
  "APPROVED_BY"     VARCHAR2(50 BYTE),

  CONSTRAINT "CUSTOMER_PK"
  PRIMARY KEY ("CUST_SEQ") USING INDEX
  );
```

2. Create a sequence to support an automated primary key:

```
CREATE SEQUENCE CUSTOMER_SEQ
START WITH 1
INCREMENT BY 1
NOCACHE
NOCYCLE;
```

How it works...

By adding application tables, you are creating a source for the business intelligence and data warehousing solution. These tables will support the application, which will enhance your data.

Developing the journal tables to track changes

The application tables are becoming a source of information for the data warehouse solution. Changes against these tables should be recorded so that a complete audit log can be constructed.

Getting ready

In order to track changes, a journal table is needed. This table is identical to the definition of the original table, but has a few additional columns to record information on actions, the date, and the user who made the change.

How to do it...

Journal tables are useful for auditing the changes that are made to information, and can be used to roll back information, should it be required.

The journal table we will use is a track change in the customer table, as shown in the following code snippet:

```
CREATE TABLE "APP_CUSTOMER_JRNL"
  (
  "CUST_SEQ"        NUMBER NOT NULL ENABLE,
  "CUST_NUM"        VARCHAR2(50 BYTE) NOT NULL ENABLE,
  "CUST_NAME"       VARCHAR2(50 BYTE),
  "CUST_ADDRESS1"   VARCHAR2(50 BYTE),
  "CUST_ADDRESS2"   VARCHAR2(50 BYTE),
  "CUST_CITY"       VARCHAR2(50 BYTE),
  "CUST_PCODE_ZIP"  VARCHAR2(20 BYTE),
```

```
    "CUST_STATE"       VARCHAR2(50 BYTE),
    "CUST_COUNTRY"     VARCHAR2(50 BYTE),
    "REGION"           VARCHAR2(50 BYTE),
    "CREATE_DATE"      DATE,
    "CREATE_BY"        VARCHAR2(50 BYTE),
    "UPDATE_DATE"      DATE,
    "UPDATE_BY"        VARCHAR2(50 BYTE),
    "JRNL_DATE"        DATE,
    "JRNL_ACTION"      VARCHAR2(50 BYTE),
    "JRNL_BY"          VARCHAR2(50 BYTE),
    "APPROVED_DATE"    DATE,
    "APPROVED_BY"      VARCHAR2(50 BYTE)
    PRIMARY KEY ("CUST_SEQ","JRNL_DATE") USING INDEX
);
```

How it works..

Journal tables allow you to track changes within the application. These journals are required to identify who made changes when. This allows for full auditing of all changes, and the capability to roll back the changes.

Defining the audit triggers

Changes to the application tables should be recorded in real time, in an automated manner. Oracle database triggers will be used to accomplish this.

Getting ready

Before creating the triggers to track the changes, first ensure that you have created the application table.

How to do it..

The triggers will track any changes to the data in the APP_CUSTOMER table and transfer the information to the journal table:

1. **Delete Trigger**: This trigger will track all deletes and place the deleted record into the journal table:

```
CREATE OR REPLACE TRIGGER "TRI_APP_CUSTOMER_DEL"
BEFORE DELETE
ON APP_CUSTOMER REFERENCING NEW AS New OLD AS Old
FOR EACH ROW
BEGIN
```

```
INSERT INTO APP_CUSTOMER_JRNL
  (APPROVED_BY,
  APPROVED_DATE,
  JRNL_ACTION,
  JRNL_DATE,
  JRNL_BY,
  CUST_SEQ,
  CUST_NUM,
  CUST_NAME,
  CUST_ADDRESS1,
  CUST_ADDRESS2 ,
  CUST_CITY,
  CUST_PCODE_ZIP,
  CUST_STATE,
  CUST_COUNTRY,
  REGION,
  CREATE_DATE,
  CREATE_BY,
  UPDATE_DATE,
  UPDATE_BY
)
VALUES
(:old.APPROVED_BY,
  :old.APPROVED_DATE,
  'Delete',
  SYSDATE,
  upper(nvl(apex_custom_auth.get_username,user)),
  :old.CUST_SEQ,
  :old.CUST_NUM,
  :old.CUST_NAME,
  :old.CUST_ADDRESS1,
  :old.CUST_ADDRESS2 ,
  :old.CUST_CITY,
  :old.CUST_PCODE_ZIP,
  :old.CUST_STATE,
  :old.CUST_COUNTRY,
  :old.REGION,
  :old.CREATE_DATE,
  :old.CREATE_BY,
  :old.UPDATE_DATE,
  :old.UPDATE_BY);

EXCEPTION
WHEN OTHERS THEN

  dbms_output.put_line('Error code:' ||sqlcode);
  dbms_output.put_line('Error msg:' ||sqlerrm);
END;


ALTER TRIGGER "TRI_APP_CUSTOMER_DEL" ENABLE;
```

2. **Update Trigger**: This trigger will track all changes and place the old record into the journal table. It will also check to see if the current user can approve the information; if not, it will set the approved attributes to null:

```
CREATE OR REPLACE TRIGGER "TRI_APP_CUSTOMER_UPD"
BEFORE UPDATE
ON APP_CUSTOMER REFERENCING NEW AS New OLD AS Old
FOR EACH ROW
BEGIN
DECLARE
  v_APPROVER APP_VAL_APPR.USERNAME%TYPE;

CURSOR c_Get_Approver IS
  SELECT DISTINCT USERNAME
  FROM APP_VAL_APPR
  WHERE TABLE_NAME = 'APP_CUSTOMER'
  AND USERNAME = upper(nvl(apex_custom_auth.get_username,user))
  AND APPROVE_FLAG = 'Y';

BEGIN
  INSERT INTO APP_CUSTOMER_JRNL
  (APPROVED_BY,
  APPROVED_DATE,
  JRNL_ACTION,
  JRNL_DATE,
  JRNL_BY,
  CUST_SEQ,
  CUST_NUM,
  CUST_NAME,
  CUST_ADDRESS1,
  CUST_ADDRESS2 ,
  CUST_CITY,
  CUST_PCODE_ZIP,
  CUST_STATE,
  CUST_COUNTRY,
  REGION,
  CREATE_DATE,
  CREATE_BY,
  UPDATE_DATE,
  UPDATE_BY
  )
VALUES
  (:old.APPROVED_BY,
  :old.APPROVED_DATE,
  'Update',
  SYSDATE,
  upper(nvl(apex_custom_auth.get_username,user)),
  :old.CUST_SEQ,
```

```
            :old.CUST_NUM,
            :old.CUST_NAME,
            :old.CUST_ADDRESS1,
            :old.CUST_ADDRESS2 ,
            :old.CUST_CITY,
            :old.CUST_PCODE_ZIP,
            :old.CUST_STATE,
            :old.CUST_COUNTRY,
            :old.REGION,
            :old.CREATE_DATE,
            :old.CREATE_BY,
            :old.UPDATE_DATE,
            :old.UPDATE_BY
            );

    OPEN c_Get_Approver ;

    FETCH c_Get_Approver INTO v_APPROVER;

    IF v_APPROVER =
      upper(nvl(apex_custom_auth.get_username,user))
      AND (NVL(:old.approved_by,'*') =
      '*' AND NVL(:old.approved_date,SYSDATE) =
      SYSDATE) THEN
      :new.update_by :=
      upper(nvl(apex_custom_auth.get_username,user));
      :new.update_date := sysdate;
    ELSE
      :new.approved_by := NULL;
      :new.approved_date := NULL;
      :new.update_by :=
      upper(nvl(apex_custom_auth.get_username,user));
      :new.update_date := sysdate;
    END IF;
    CLOSE c_Get_Approver;
    EXCEPTION
    WHEN OTHERS THEN
      dbms_output.put_line('Error code:' ||sqlcode);
      dbms_output.put_line('Error msg:' ||sqlerrm);

      :new.approved_by := NULL;
      :new.approved_date := NULL;
      :new.update_by :=
      upper(nvl(apex_custom_auth.get_username,user));
      :new.update_date := sysdate;
    END;
    END;

    ALTER TRIGGER "TRI_APP_CUSTOMER_UPD" ENABLE;
```

3. **Insert Trigger**: This trigger is for all inserts; it sets all the values within the audit columns:

```
CREATE OR REPLACE TRIGGER "TRI_APP_CUSTOMER_INS"
BEFORE INSERT
ON APP_CUSTOMER REFERENCING NEW AS New OLD AS Old
FOR EACH ROW
BEGIN
        :new.approved_by := NULL;
        :new.approved_date := NULL;
        :new.create_by := upper(nvl(apex_custom_auth.get_
username,user));
        :new.create_date := sysdate;
EXCEPTION
WHEN OTHERS THEN
        dbms_output.put_line('Error code:' ||sqlcode);
        dbms_output.put_line('Error msg:' ||sqlerrm);
        :new.approved_by := NULL;
        :new.approved_date := NULL;
        :new.create_by := upper(nvl(apex_custom_auth.get_
username,user));
        :new.create_date := sysdate;
END;


        ALTER TRIGGER "TRI_APP_CUSTOMER_INS" ENABLE;
```

With all the triggers in place, any data changes to the application tables will be audited. Insert the default data into APP_CUSTOMER, as shown in the following code:

```
Insert into APP_CUSTOMER (CUST_SEQ,CUST_NUM,CUST_NAME,CUST_
ADDRESS1,CUST_ADDRESS2,CUST_CITY,CUST_PCODE_ZIP,CUST_STATE,CUST_
COUNTRY,REGION) values (1,'1','Starbucks','680 Monroe Avenue',null,'Ro
chester','14607','NY','USA','EAST');

Insert into APP_CUSTOMER (CUST_SEQ,CUST_NUM,CUST_NAME,CUST_
ADDRESS1,CUST_ADDRESS2,CUST_CITY,CUST_PCODE_ZIP,CUST_STATE,CUST_
COUNTRY,REGION) values (2,'2','Walmart','1902 Empire Boulevard',null,'
Webster','14580','NY','USA','EAST');

Insert into APP_CUSTOMER (CUST_SEQ,CUST_NUM,CUST_NAME,CUST_
ADDRESS1,CUST_ADDRESS2,CUST_CITY,CUST_PCODE_ZIP,CUST_STATE,CUST_
COUNTRY,REGION) values (3,'3','Walmart','3838 South Semoran Boulevard'
,null,'Orlando','32822','FL','USA','SOUTH');

Insert into APP_CUSTOMER (CUST_SEQ,CUST_NUM,CUST_NAME,CUST_
ADDRESS1,CUST_ADDRESS2,CUST_CITY,CUST_PCODE_ZIP,CUST_STATE,CUST_
COUNTRY,REGION) values (4,'4','Starbucks','110 W. Main Street',null,'V
isalia','93291','CA','USA','WEST');
```

Notice that the values of the audit column are corrected after the insert operation.

How it works...

The trigger tracks any `update`, `insert`, or `delete` commands. As APEX connects to the database as a single user, the procedure call to determine who is making the update is accomplished by using the `apex_custom_auth.get_username` procedure call in the code at the database level.

These triggers are created on the application table. They place all the changes made through `Update` or `Delete` into the journal table.

Defining the APEX Upload application

APEX is installed within an Oracle database. The development environment and runtime environment are accessible through a web browser.

Getting ready

When APEX was installed, you should have had an APEX workspace created. Also, your administrator would have created a username with a password for you. You will need these before you begin. In addition to the username and password, your application schema will need to be associated with your workspace. If you do not have access to an environment, you can use an Oracle-hosted environment, and request for a workspace at `http://apex.oracle.com`. Note that this should not be used for a production environment, but can be used as a training or limited development environment.

How to do it...

Before starting, ensure you have the correct URLs for your web browser to connect to the APEX development environment. Open a compatible web browser and navigate to the URL for Oracle Application Express. For example, `http://machine_name:port/apex`.

1. Log in to **Oracle Application Express**:

ORACLE® Application Express

Enter Application Express workspace and credentials.

Workspace |SEERIX DEVELOPMENT

Username JOHN.HEATON@ISEERIX.COM

Password

(Login)

Click here to learn how to get started

Oracle Application Express is a rapid Web application development tool that lets you share data and create custom applications.
Using only a Web browser and limited programming experience, you can develop and deploy powerful applications that are both fast
and secure.

Language: Deutsch, **English**, Español, Français, Italiano, Português (Brasil), 中文 (繁體), 中文 (简体), 日本語, 한국어

2. On the **Workspace** home page, click the **Application Builder** icon:

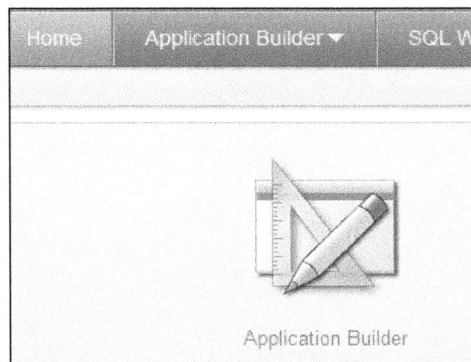

3. Click **Create**:

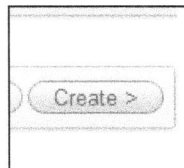

4. For **Method**, select **Database** and click **Next**:

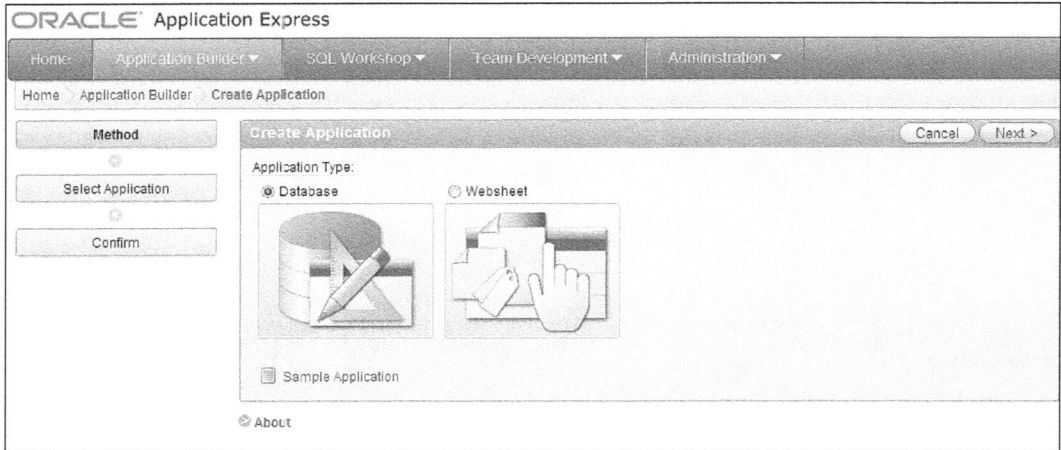

5. Select **From Scratch** and click **Next**:

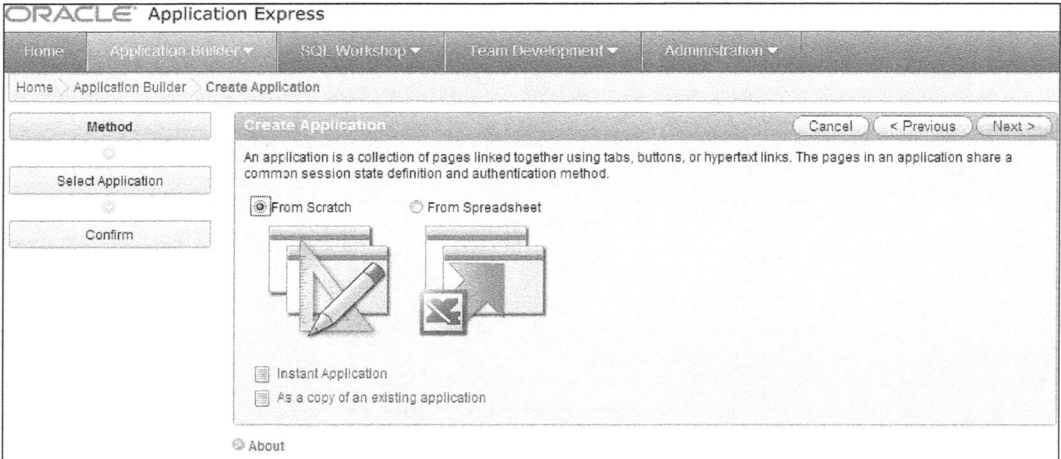

6. Specify the following:

   ❑ For **Name**, enter **CSV Uploader**.

   ❑ Accept the remaining defaults and click **Next**:

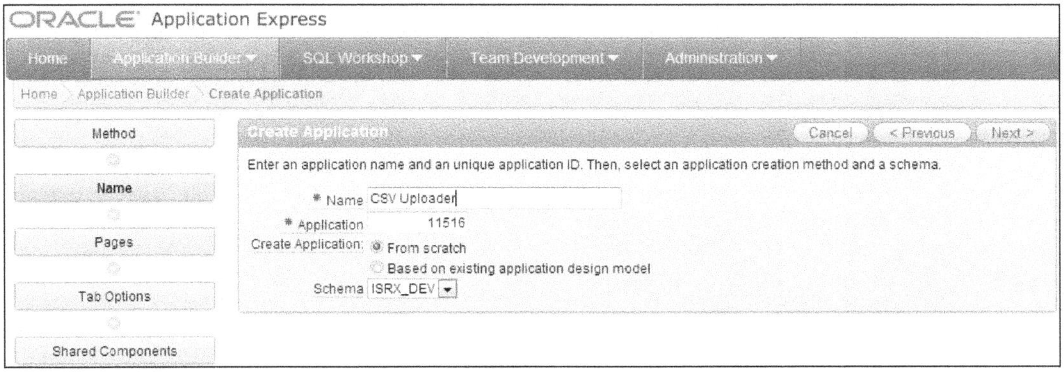

7. Add a blank page:

   Under **Select Page Type**, select **Blank**. At the bottom, type **Interface** for the **Page Name** and click **Add Page**. Click **Create** on the top panel to create the application:

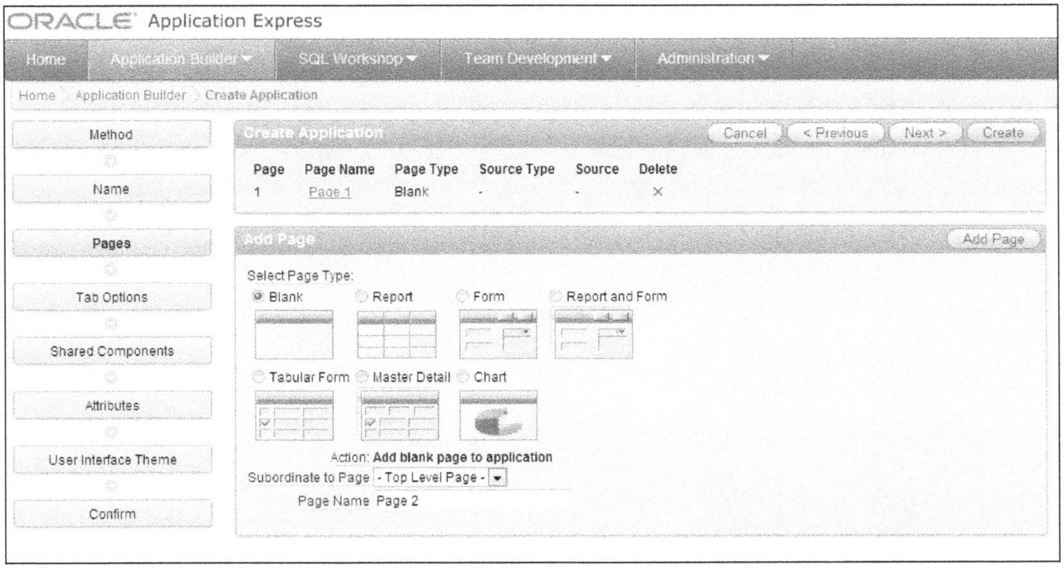

8. Continue through the wizard, selecting the defaults for the values:

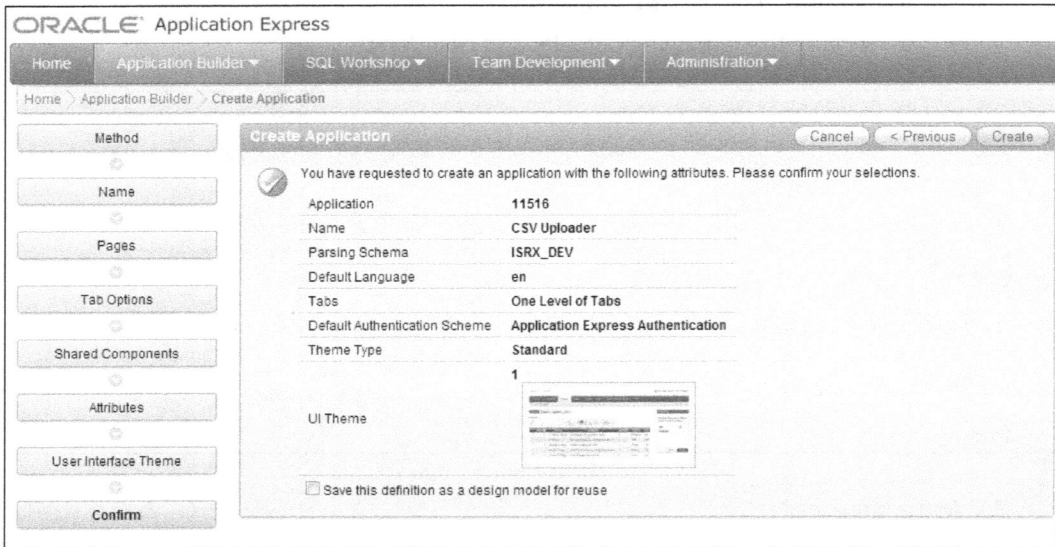

How it works...

The Upload application is initially created with a blank page. This page will be completed at a later stage.

Creating the Upload interface

Before APEX 4.1, uploading CSV files into an Oracle database using APEX was very manual. With the latest release, APEX has built-in functionality to cater for the uploading and parsing of CSV files into an Oracle database.

Getting ready

Log on to APEX and open the application.

How to do it...

Creating the upload interface in APEX 4.1 is significantly easier than in previous versions. One of the most common requests in a data warehouse is the ability for end users to upload data from a CSV file. In APEX 4.1, this is the default functionality:

1. Click the **Create Page >** button:

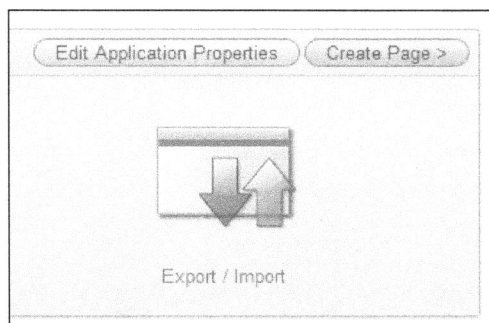

2. Select **Data Loading** and click **Next >**:

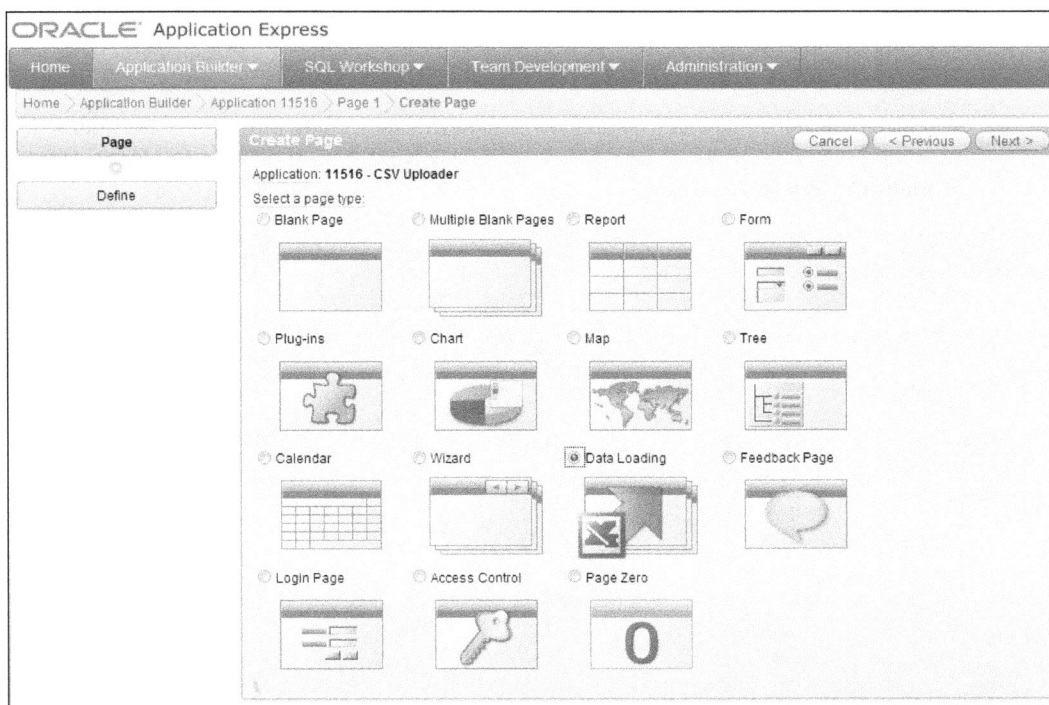

3. Enter the **Data Load Definition Name**; select the **Owner, Table Name**, and the required **Unique Column** fields. Click **Next >**:

4. You have the ability to add lookups and transformation rules if required. For this example, leave the settings as default, and click **Next >** on the **Table Lookups and Transformation Rules** pages:

5. Review the data load steps and click **Next >**:

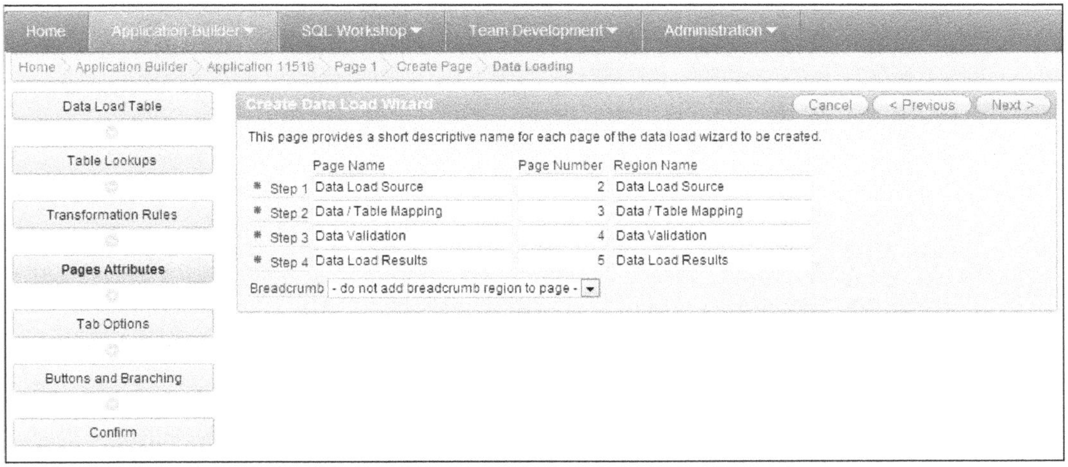

6. Select **Use an existing tab set and create a new tab within the existing tab set**.
    Enter **Customer Upload** for **New Tab Label**. Click **Next >**:

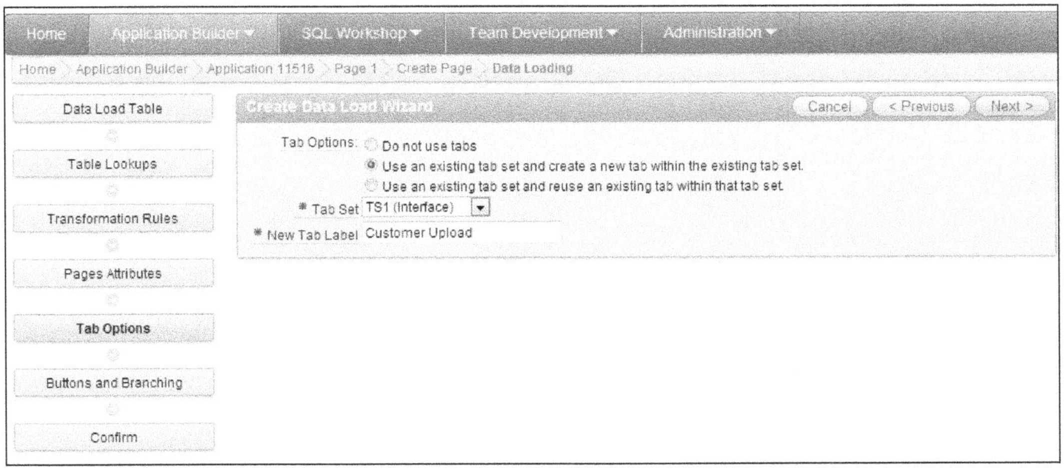

7. Enter **1** for the **Branch to Page** field. Click **Next >**:

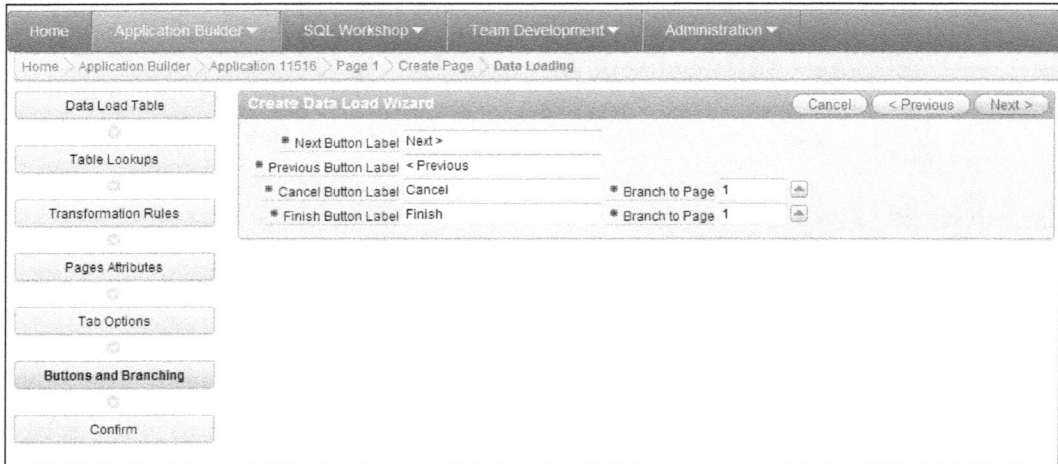

8. Review the page definition and click **Finish**:

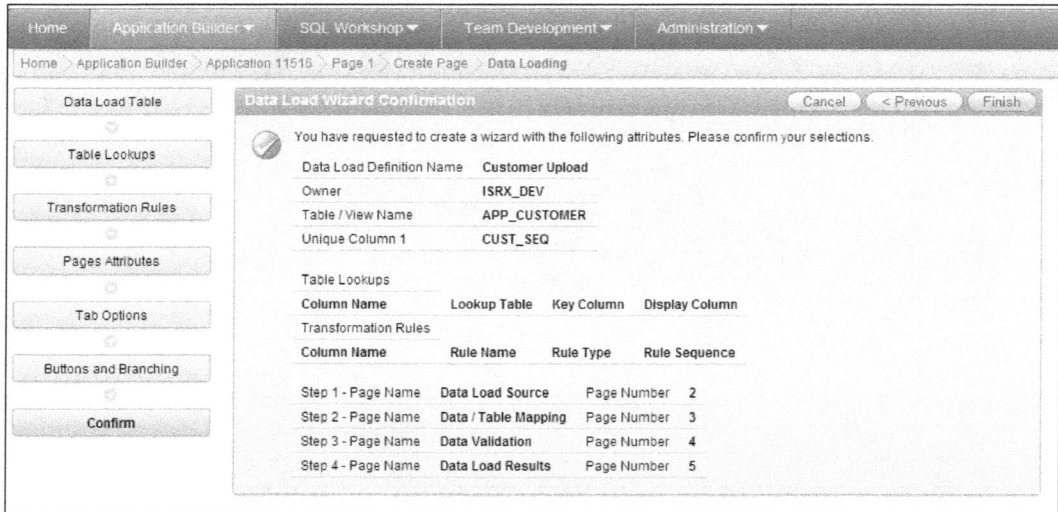

9. Click **Run Page** to run the application and test the upload:

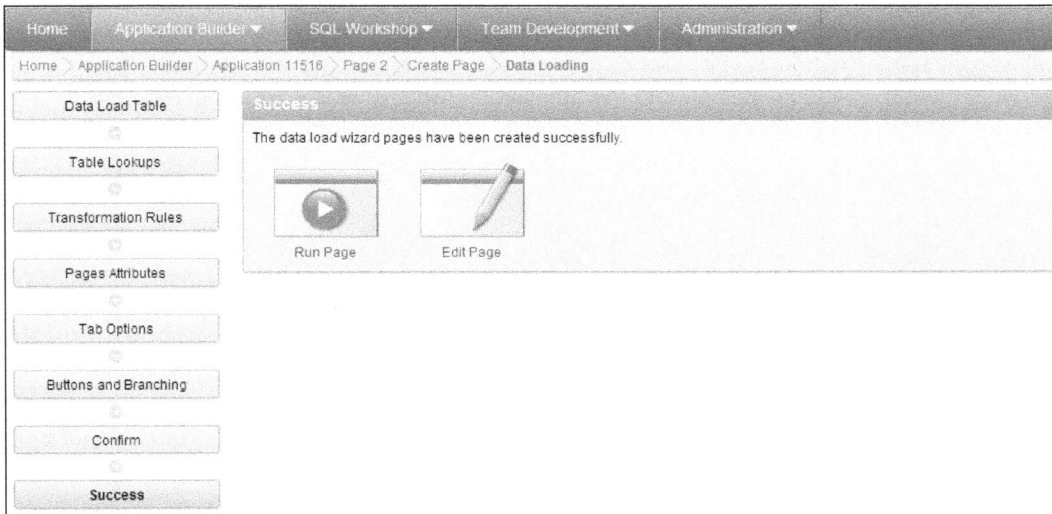

10. Enter username and password, then review the application:

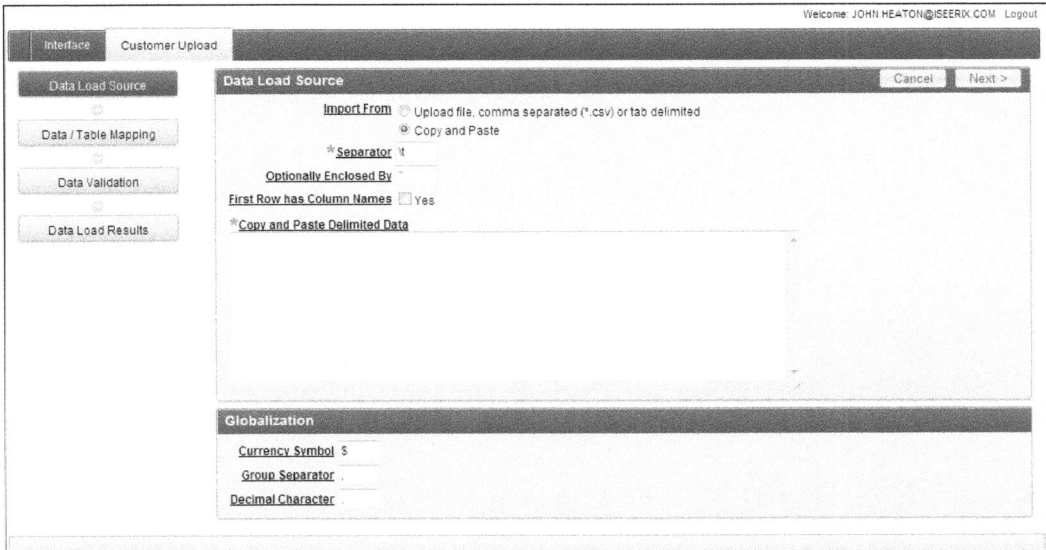

How it works..

This page will allow the user to identify the CSV file and enter the file specification. Once selected, the information will be uploaded into the upload table and then parsed. Upon parsing, the information is placed into the application table. This is a common request in a data warehouse application, and with APEX 4.1, this is a default functionality.

13
Optimizing the Access

The business intelligence and data warehouse solution culminates in the presentation of information to stakeholders. This component of the solution is most visible to stakeholders and represents all the work done within the project. It is the key to presenting information in an accurate, easy to use, and visually correct way which is customized to your audience. The following recipes touch on a few of these subjects:

- ▶ Developing your standards and guidelines
- ▶ Abstracting your tables using aliases
- ▶ Developing level-based hierarchies
- ▶ Creating multi-table hierarchies
- ▶ Consolidating reports using the column selector
- ▶ Enabling dynamic column headings
- ▶ Enabling dynamic descriptions
- ▶ Enabling multi-language for the shared captions
- ▶ Enabling double columns

Introduction

Information access and presentation is the most visible component of the business intelligence and data warehouse project. It is important to understand the limitations of the software and the expectations of the consumers in order to be successful. Prototyping and interaction with key consumers during the project will greatly assist in refining and delivering a high quality product at the end of the project.

Developing your standards and guidelines

User interfaces are regularly judged on how they look before anyone takes notice of the content. If the user interface is intuitive and appropriate for the audience, they are more likely to adopt and use the solution.

Getting ready

Developing visualisation standards and guidelines is important to the business intelligence and data warehouse project. These standards will affect the way information is presented to the consumer, and ultimately the acceptance and usage of the information. Spending time defining and prototyping standards before any development work is started will save rework. Socializing the interface to key consumers before the project is completed will also reduce rework and set realistic expectations. The key reference material for this would include:

1. Research good visualization techniques. There are a number of visualization experts such as *Stephen Few* (http://www.perceptualedge.com/blog/), *Julie Steele* (http://radar.oreilly.com/julies/), *Edward Tufte* (http://www.edwardtufte.com/tufte/), and *Nathan Yau* (http://flowingdata.com/).

2. Educate yourself on the capabilities of the tool you will utilize to present the information, in this case, Oracle Business Intelligence Enterprise Edition(OBIEE).

How to do it...

Standards and guidelines are key to developing a quality functional application which delivers information in a meaningful way. It is not about using the latest and greatest widget to present information, but rather finding an effective means of presenting information to your audience:

1. Install the Oracle Business Intelligence Sample Application. It is available from Oracle Technology Network at http://www.oracle.com/technetwork/middleware/bi-foundation/obiee-samples-167534.html.

2. Identify the different dashboards for the application—See *Chapter 6, Analyzing the Requirements*, for your requirements.

3. Determine the basic outline of each of the different pages you will create within dashboards. An example is as follows:
   - Overview Page
   - Analysis page
   - Detail Page

4. Identify the standard screen resolution within your organization.

5. Determine a color palette for your application.

6. Gather images and graphics to customize the application.

7. Identify the positioning of prompts on a page.

8. Understand default behaviours of drilling.

9. Identify default fonts.

10. Identify different presentation formats for different datatypes.

11. Decide on the graph types to portray information in a clear and meaningful manner.

12. Identify additional sections to be included.

How it works...

By identifying the standards near the beginning of the project, you can segregate these standards into design and development standards and considerations. Most of these may be discretionary and therefore become design considerations when initially designing the system. Non-discretionary standards become development standards and should be created as a checklist for a developer to complete while building dashboards, pages, and reports. Standards are important but it is also key to understand the cost of adding the standards. Wherever possible, try and stay as close to the default functionality of the application. Most of the components in OBIEE can be modified by overriding different settings. This will add to the development time and effort. Understand this trade-off to find a balance between effective standards and non-essential standards.

Abstracting your tables using aliases

Aliases are a standard way to abstract a physical table within OBIEE. Therefore a single table can be referenced multiple times by using an alias.

Getting ready

Open the BI Administration tool. Import all the tables which are required.

How to do it...

Abstraction allows you to reference an object using a different name. This is effective if you wish to reference the same object multiple times for different reasons (roles).

1. Expand your connection under the physical model.

2. Select your table, right-click on it, and select **New Object | Alias**:

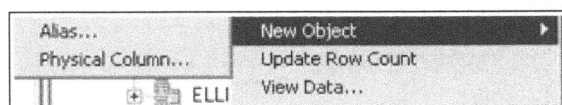

How it works...

In OBIEE, it is best practice to use an alias with all your tables. Aliases are useful for the following purposes:

- Self joins to a table. Thus, you can create multiple aliases on the same table.
- Tables can be reused multiple times; for example, a `time` dimension may connect to the fact table on multiple dates (open date, closed date, order date, and so on). You would not want multiple tables with the same information. In this case, you can use an alias to create another dimension named `Open Dates`, which refers to the `time` dimension. This is referred to as a role. Therefore the `time` dimension will have multiple roles (aliases) for the fact table.
- If a table is used in multiple business models, then it is advised that a unique alias is used for each business model.
- Modeling multiple hierarchies within a single dimension would require an alias to be created per hierarchy.

Developing level-based hierarchies

Hierarchies allow a person to start analyzing information from a summary level with the capability to expand nodes to gain additional details. They are an efficient way to give the user a lot of flexibility and control to view and understand the information.

Getting ready

Open the BI Administration tool.

How to do it...

Hierarchies comprise two main types within OBIEE, namely, Level-Based and Parent-Child. A level-based hierarchy has predefined levels and depth within the hierarchy, which are consistent. Parent-Child is a recursive hierarchy with no set levels or depth.

1. Identify all your tables and join them correctly, based on the key columns within the business model and mapping layer. If this is not done correctly, then the option to create a Dimension object will not exist.

2. Create your dimensions by right-clicking on the tables, and selecting **New Object | Dimension with Level-Based Hierarchy**:

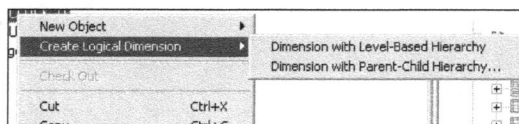

3. Map your columns as normal.

4. In the properties of the dimension, you can specify whether it is a **Ragged** hierarchy or a **Skipped Levels** hierarchy:

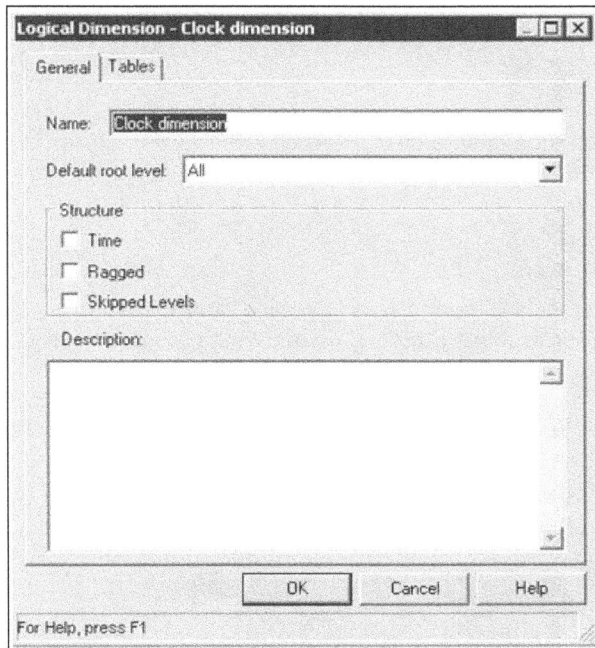

How it works...

The new OBIEE capability of Ragged a Ragged hierarchy contains at least one member with a different base level, creating a "ragged" base level for the hierarchy. Organization dimensions are frequently ragged. A Skipped Level hierarchy contains at least one member whose parents are more than one level above it, creating a hole in the hierarchy. For example, in a geographical dimension with levels for City, State, and Country, Washington D.C. is a city that does not have a State value; it's parent is United States at the Country level. OBIEE now detects for NULL in the levels of the hierarchy and presents the data accordingly. This in conjunction with the *Enabling dynamic column headings* recipe, allows you to model some very flexible and generic hierarchies which can be configured and mapped at the time of access. These should be used with caution and tested to determine the impact on performance.

Creating multi-table hierarchies

Hierarchies are not always restricted to a single table and may span across multiple tables. For this reason, OBIEE supports the ability to create hierarchies across multiple tables.

Getting ready

In the BI Administration tool, ensure all the source tables are imported and are joined together correctly.

How to do it...

In many cases, hierarchies may span across multiple tables. OBIEE has the capability to create hierarchies across multiple tables, thus reducing the need to create additional physical objects:

1. Ensure there are joins between the tables you wish to create a hierarchy upon. These should be inner joins.

2. In the Business Model and Mapping layer, create a new logical table and base it on a single table:

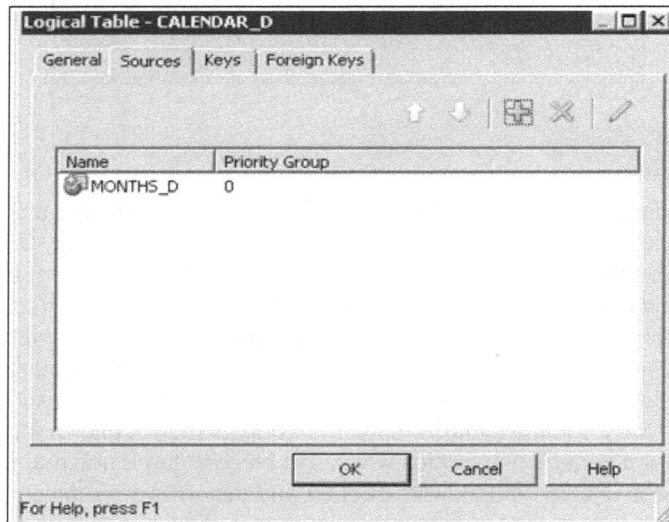

3. Select the **Sources** table and edit the source by clicking on the pencil icon. Click on the plus icon, and select the additional sources for the logical table. Only sources with **Joins** will be visible:

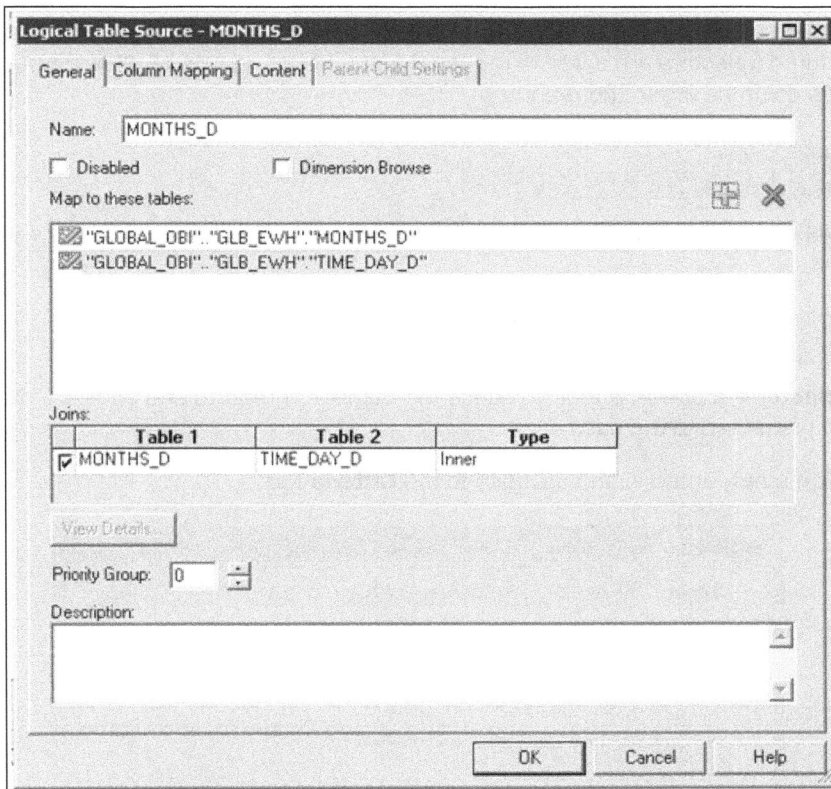

How it works...

Once the multiple sources have been added to the table, the logical table can now be joined into Business Model and Mapping. This logical table needs to be joined to a fact table. Once joined, you will be able to create a dimension on the logical table and select either **Dimension with Level-Based Hierarchy** or **Dimension with Parent-Child Hierarchy**:

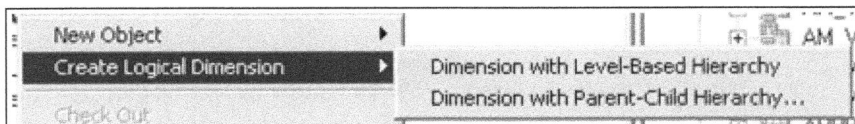

Consolidating reports using the column selector

When using a powerful reporting tool, it is easy to design and potentially develop many reports. Column Selectors are a way to reduce the number of reports by allowing the user to swap columns within the report.

Getting ready

Upon logging into OBIEE, you may need to create a new analysis in answers, based on a subject area.

How to do it...

Column Selector is a powerful tool to reduce the number of reports and enhance the information presented to the user:

1. Open a new analysis and navigate to the **Criteria** tab:

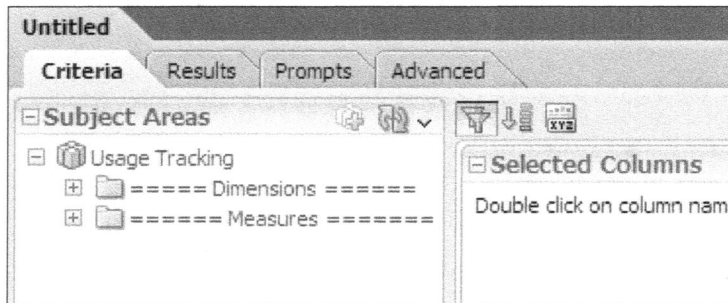

2. Select the columns you require in the analysis. Do not add all the columns you want to include in Column Selector, just add the columns needed:

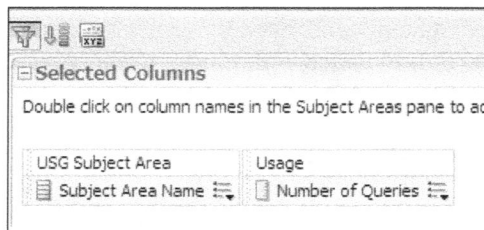

3. Click on the **Results** tab.

4. Select the New View icon and add **Column Selector from Other Views**, as shown in the following screenshot:

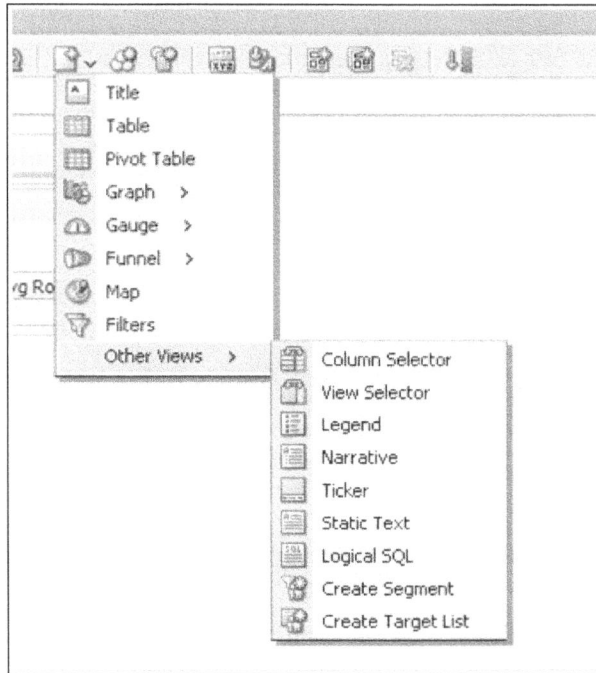

5. Select the columns that you wish to replace. In the following example we are selecting two column selectors, one for the dimensional information and one for the metric:

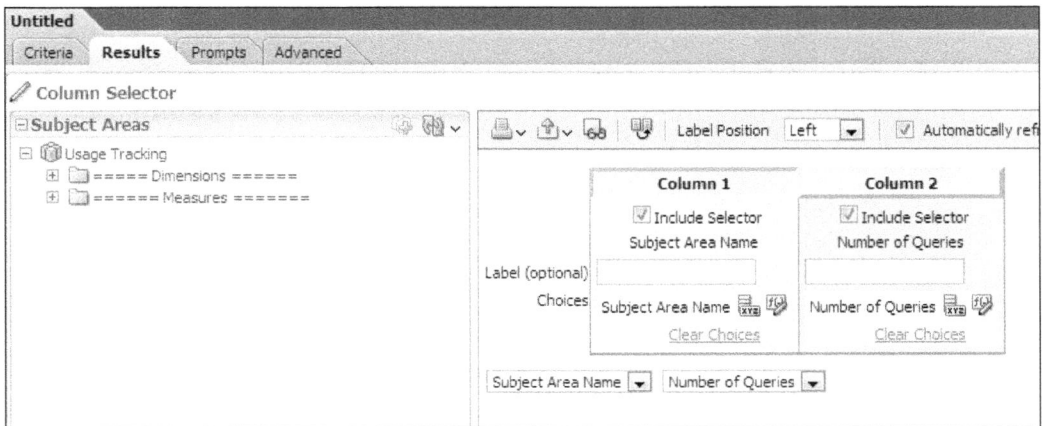

6. Click on the **Column 1** heading to select the Column Selector. Expand the folders on the left and highlight the column you want to add to Column Selector. Once highlighted, double-click on the column name and it should appear under **Column 1** as an option in Column Selector. Repeat the same for **Column 2**:

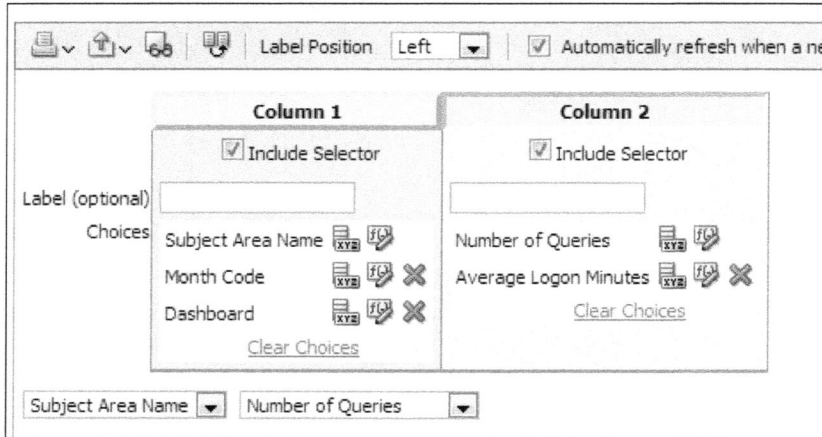

7. Should you wish to order Column Selectors, return to the **Criteria** tab and drag the columns in the correct displayed order:

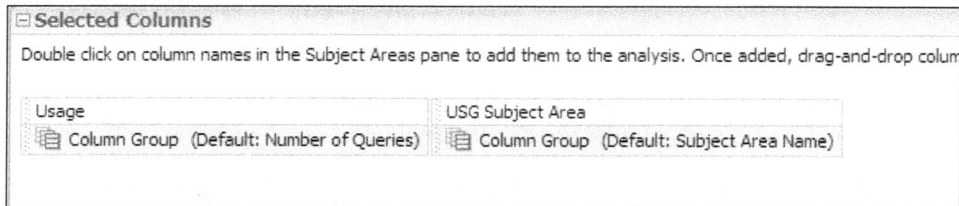

8. Drag your Column Selector section to the top of your table. Click on the pencil icon to edit the Column Selector:

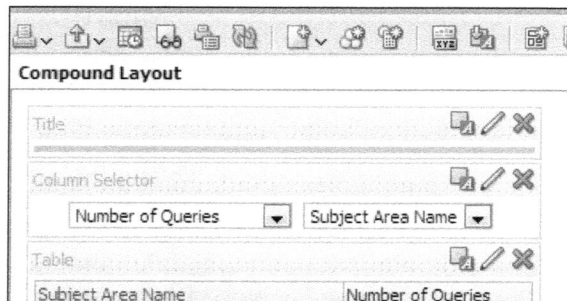

9. Label your Column Selectors for easier use:

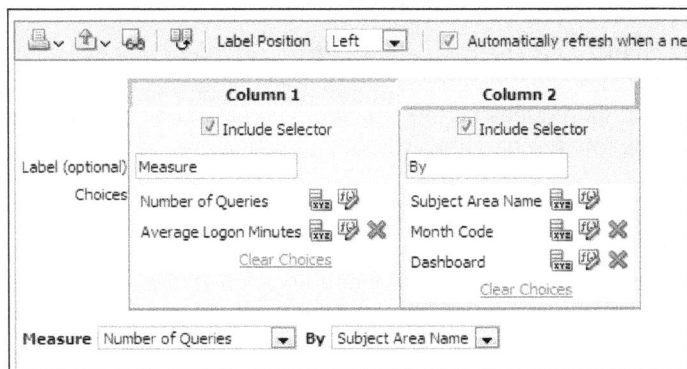

10. Click on **Done** and you will see the results of Column Selector:

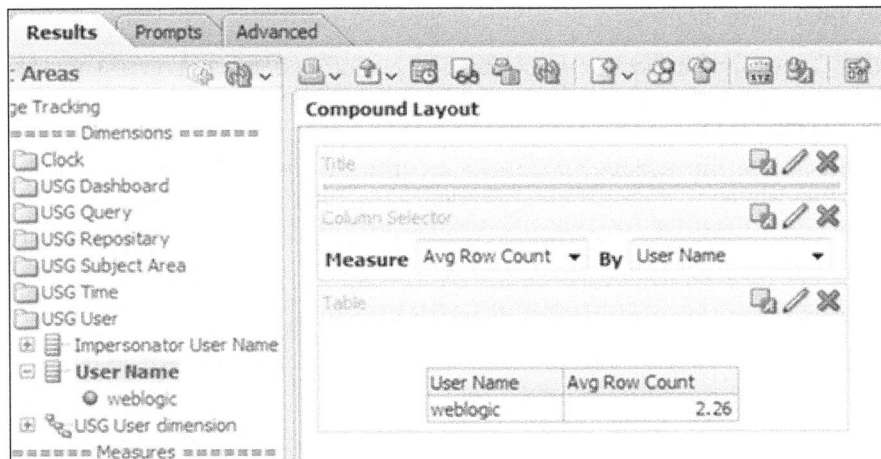

How it works...

Column Selectors allow you to switch different columns out on the report, thus enabling a report to view information from different perspectives with different measures.

Enabling dynamic column headings

Reporting heading changes can be frequent within a solution during development, and in ongoing processes through the life of the solution. Each time, this normally entails changing the actual reports, and then releasing the changes to production. Externalized strings give one the capabilities to maintain the headings without changing the report code.

Getting ready

OBIEE has the framework for creating custom headings which are externalized strings. To enable this, open the BI Administration Tool and open the repository file (RPD).

How to do it...

The **repository file** stores all the definitions of the subject areas and data model. This is located on the middle-tier server:

1. Select the presentation layer objects to be customized. It is not necessary to select all the objects or a whole subject area; the technique can be used for a reduced set of objects.

2. Right-click on the subject area. Select **Externalize Display Names | Generate Custom Name**, as shown in the following screenshot:

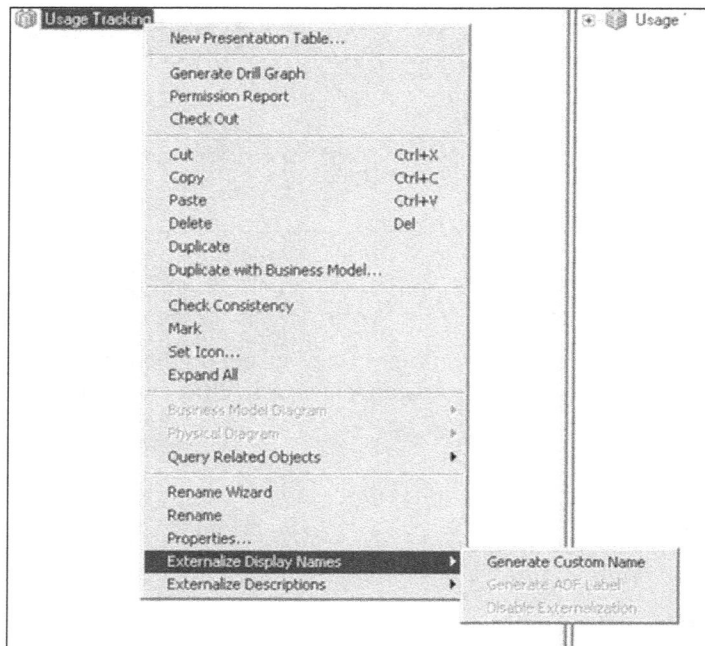

3. Click on **Tools**. Select **Utilities | Externalize Strings**, and click on **Execute...**:

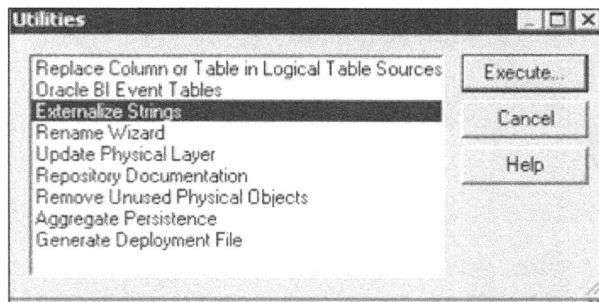

4. In the **Externalize Strings** window, select the subject area that contains the objects to customize:

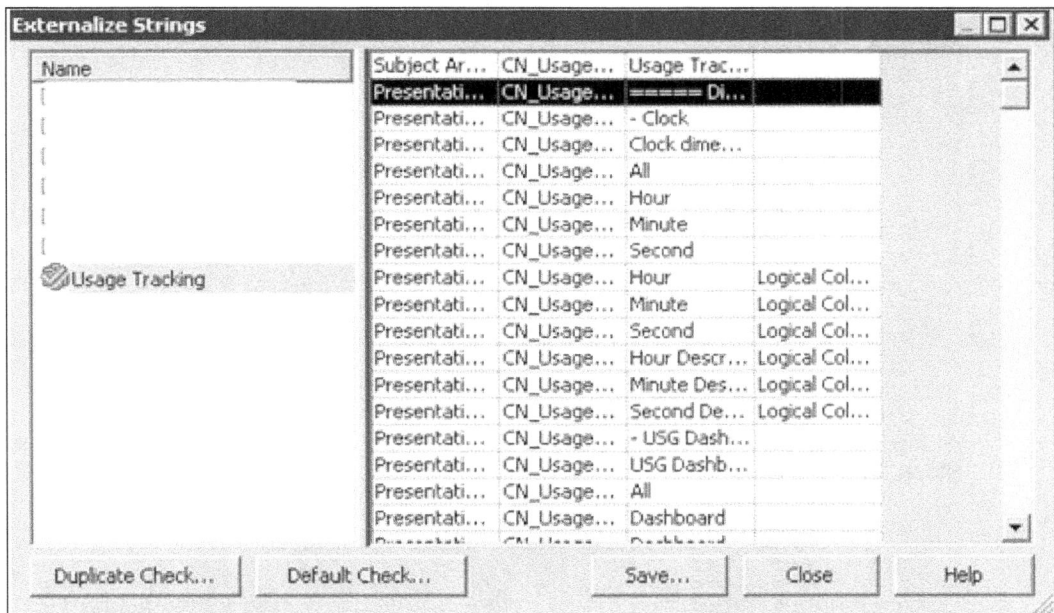

5. Click on **Save...** to save the results to a CSV file.

6. Create a table in the database named `REF_DATA_HEADINGS`:

```
CREATE TABLE "REF_DATA_HEADINGS"
("OBJECT_NAME" VARCHAR2(500) NOT NULL ENABLE,
"LANGUAGE" VARCHAR2(2) NOT NULL ENABLE,
"SESSION_VARIABLE" VARCHAR2(500) NOT NULL ENABLE,
"HEADING" VARCHAR2(50) NOT NULL ENABLE
     );
```

7. Load the CSV file into the `REF_DATA_HEADINGS` table and map the following columns:

   ▸ Csv column 1 -> `OBJECT_NAME`

   ▸ Csv column 2 -> `SESSION_VARIABLE`

   ▸ Csv column 3 -> `HEADING`

   ▸ 'en' / 'es' / 'fr' -> `LANGUAGE`

The language should be loaded as a constant.

1. In the OBIEE Administration tool, import the `REF_DATA_HEADINGS` table to the physical layer. Right-click on your connection and select **Import Metadata**. Step through the wizard and select the table to import.

2. Create an alias for the table. Right-click on the table once imported and select **New Object | Alias**.

3. Open the BI Administration tool and create a new Initialization Block. Select **Manage | Variables**:

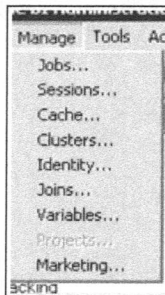

4. Within **Session | Initialization Blocks** , right-click and select **New Initialization Block...**:

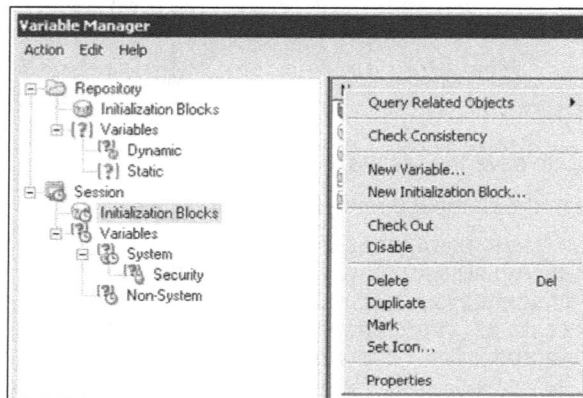

5. Create a session variable named **LOC_LANGUAGE**, as shown in the following screenshot:

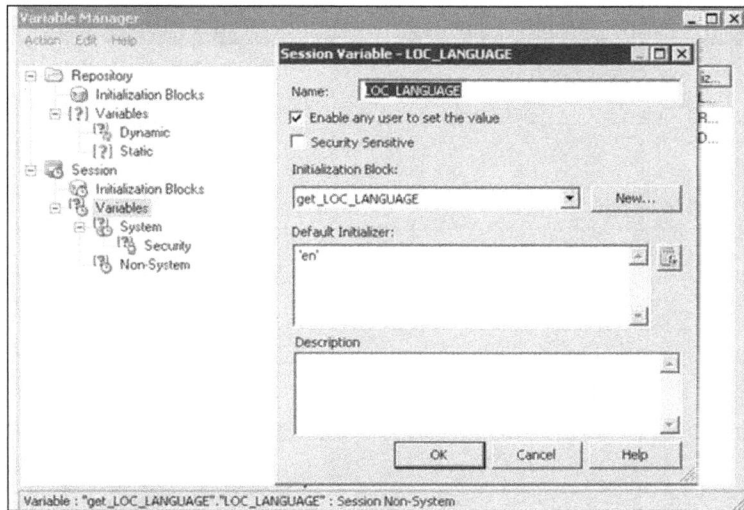

6. Create an initialization block named **get_LOC_LANGUAGE** in order to load the variable with the following SQL:

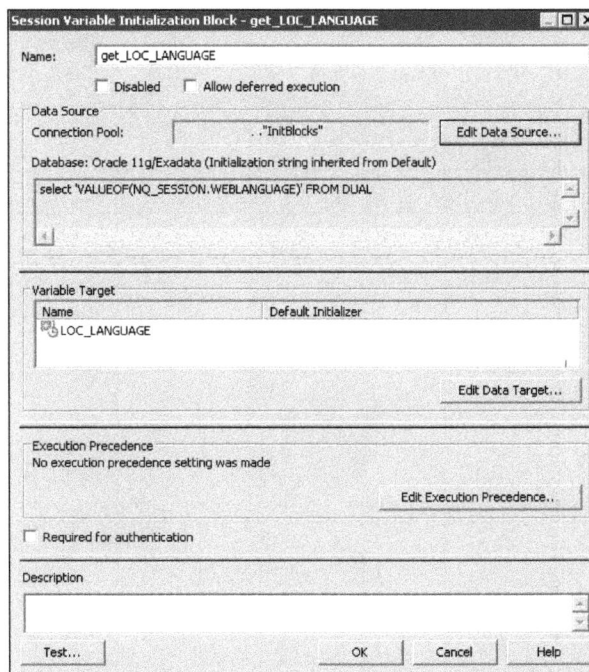

7. Create an initialization block named **get_CUSTOM_HEADINGS**, as shown in the following screenshot:

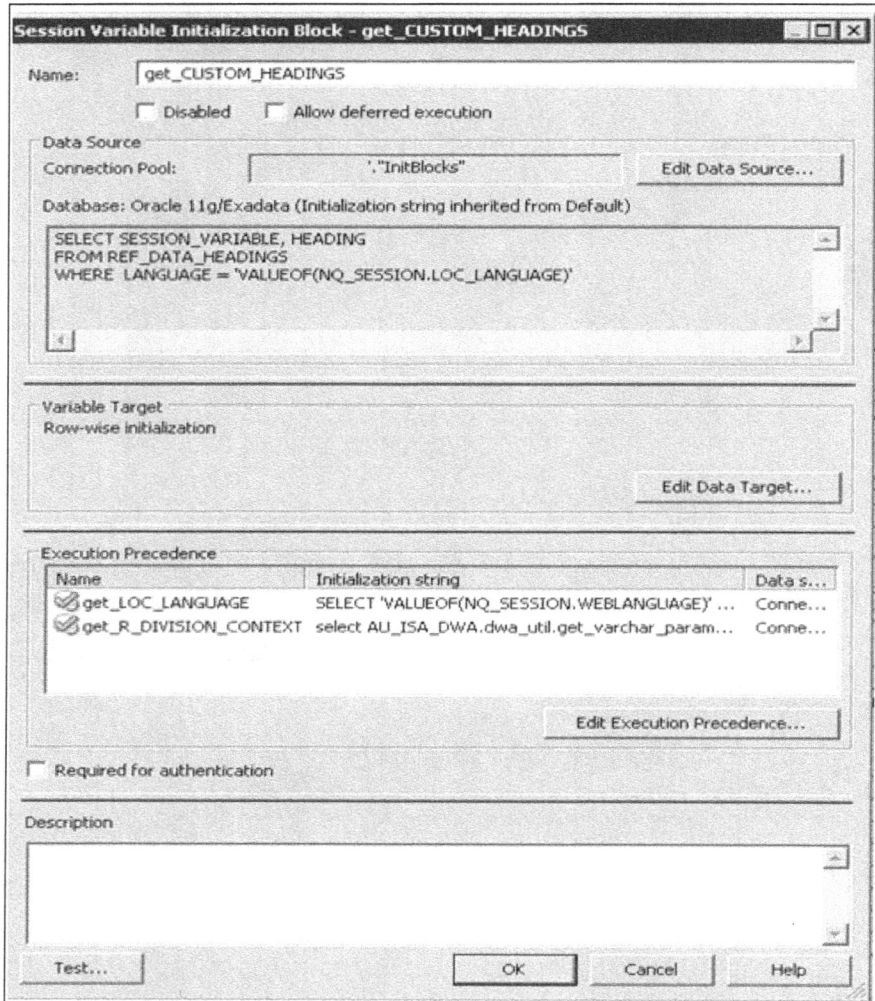

How it works...

By externalizing the strings and loading them into a table, the custom headings are loaded into the repository at runtime. All the objects chosen are updated to include the reference to the session variables to display the custom headings. This can be checked by right-clicking on a column name from the subject area and viewing the properties:

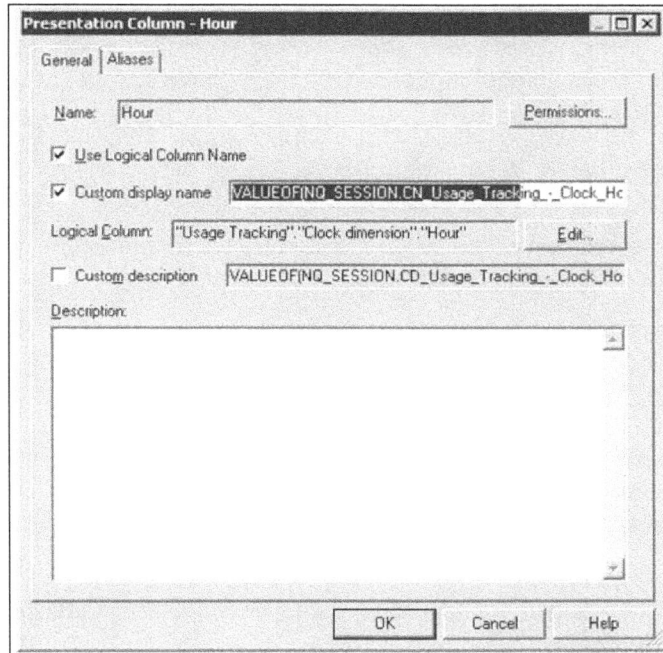

Notice that the **Custom display name** has been checked and a formula is entered. The formula loads the custom heading from the session variable. This variable was loaded by the initialization block and the language variable. Each heading has a unique session variable. You can now add additional rows into the table for the same session variable for a different language. The heading can now be translated into the new language. The translated heading will appear in OBIEE when the associated language is selected.

Enabling dynamic descriptions

Descriptions for codes can potentially mean different things for different people, for example, different languages. To enable this, one can store this information in a table and the tool can retrieve the information at runtime.

Getting ready

Identify all the code values and descriptions which may require customizations within the semantic model.

How to do it..

Enabling **dynamic description** allows you to standardize information within your data model by placing it within a table in the database:

1. Create a lookup table in the database to store the dynamic description translations for each potential language:

```
CREATE TABLE "REF_DATA_DESCRIPTIONS"
    ("LANGUAGE" VARCHAR2(2) NOT NULL ENABLE,
"CODE_TYPE" VARCHAR2(10) NOT NULL ENABLE,
"CODE_VALUE" VARCHAR2(50) NOT NULL ENABLE,
"DESCRIPTION" VARCHAR2(250) NOT NULL ENABLE
    );
```

2. Open the BI Administration tool and create a new Initialization Block. Select **Manage | Variables**:

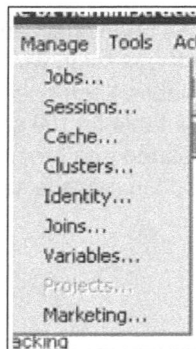

3. Within **Session | Initialization Blocks**, right-click and select **New Initialization Block...**:

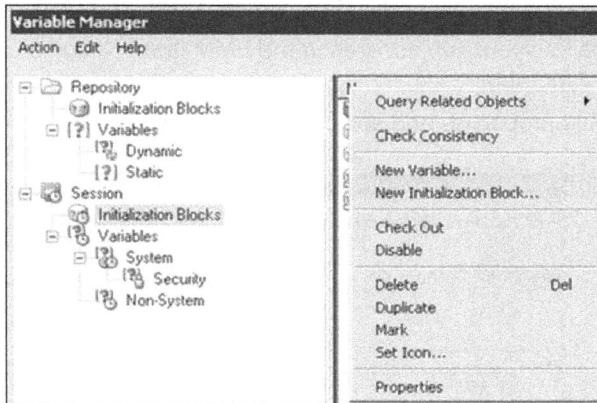

4. Give the Initialization Block a name, select **Data Source** and enter the SQL statement to get the information from the REF_DATA_LOOKUP table. Select **Row-wise initialization** for **Variable Target**, and click on **OK**:

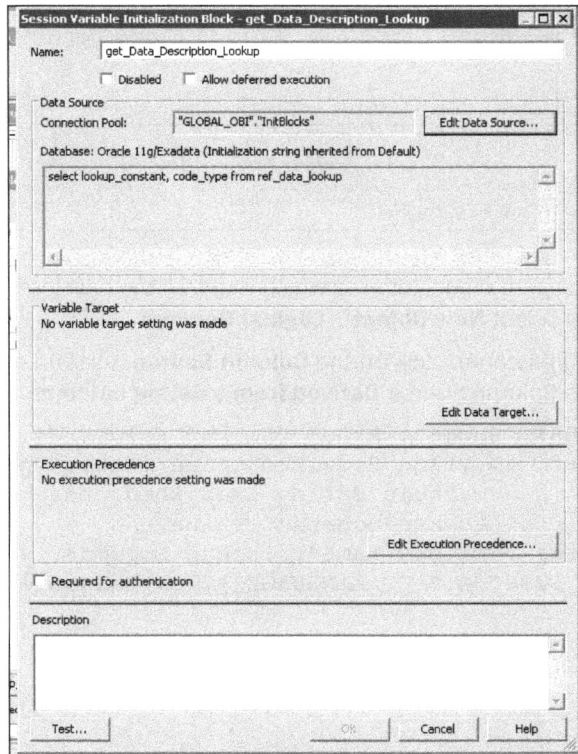

5. Import the `REF_DATA_DESCRIPTIONS` table into your Physical Model, and create an Alias on the table.

6. Specify the key columns as **LANGUAGE**, **CODE_TYPE**, and **CODE_VALUE**.

7. Drag the table into your subject area in the BMM layer. Notice that the table will be created as a Fact table.

8. Select the table properties and select **Lookup Table**:

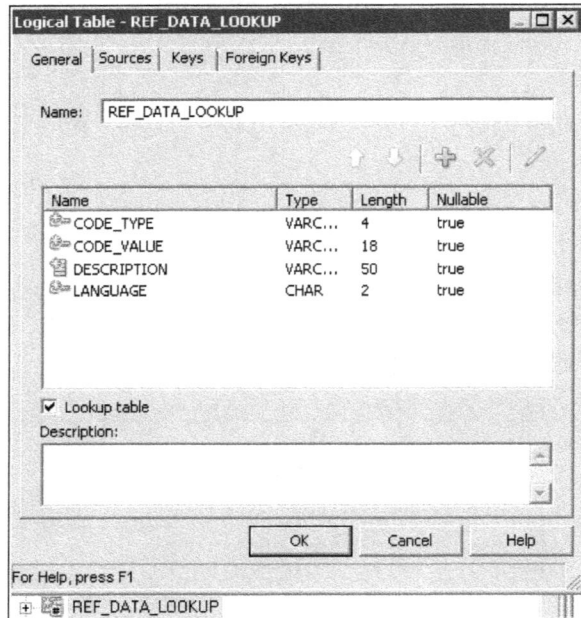

9. Locate the table in the subject area which requires the new lookup description. Right-click and select **New Object | Logical Column**:

10. Give the column a name, click on the **Column Source** tab, and enter the following formula for the Column Source **Derived from existing columns using an expression**:

```
Lookup(SPARSE "Subject Area"."Lookup Folder Name"."Lookup
Column Name", -> Value Required to be looked up
'Not Found', -> Default String used when code not found
'CODE TYPE', -> Lookup constant value
"Subject Area"."Folder Name"."Lookup Column", -> Lookup column
VALUEOF(NQ_SESSION."LOC_LANGUAGE"), -> Language Variable)
```

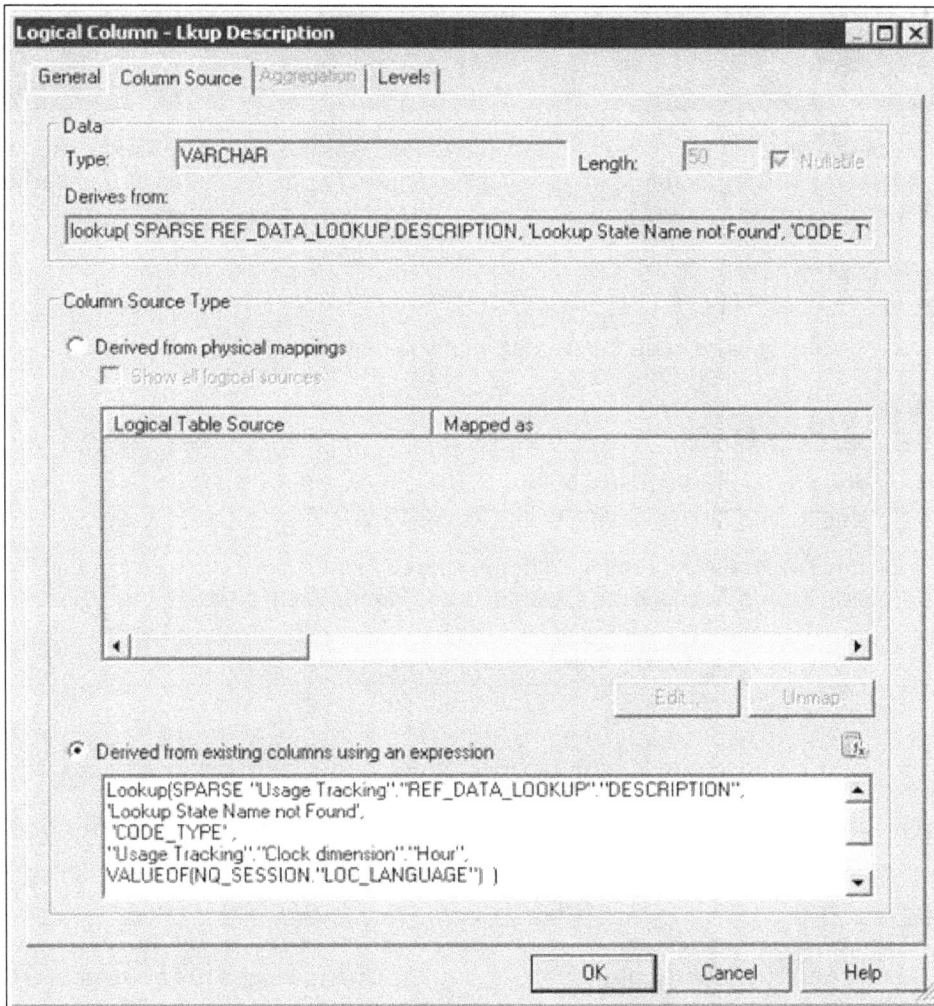

11. Repeat this for all the customized description columns you require.

How it works...

By creating a table for column descriptions, you can change the values based on user preferences and language. This allows flexibility within the application to cater for multi-language.

Enabling multi-language for the shared captions

Shared captions encompass all the text and information which is stored within the definition of the report. These are stored within an XML file on the server to be loaded at the startup of the software.

Getting ready

Open Catalog Manager and open the catalog in offline mode.

How to do it...

Shared captions are text that are presented on the screen within OBIEE, which is stored within the catalog. This cannot be placed in a database to be translated:

1. Expand the **Tree** view and highlight the **shared** folder. Select the menu option **Tools | Export Captions**, as shown in the following screenshot:

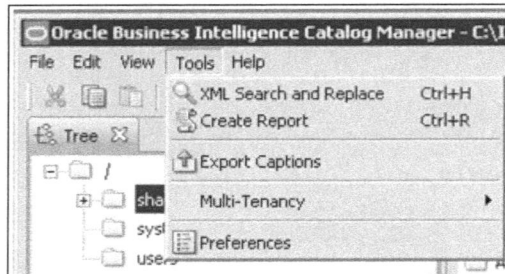

2. Ensure no check boxes are set. Make sure the **Create unique IDs even for identical strings** radio button is selected. Enter the folder name and click on **OK**:

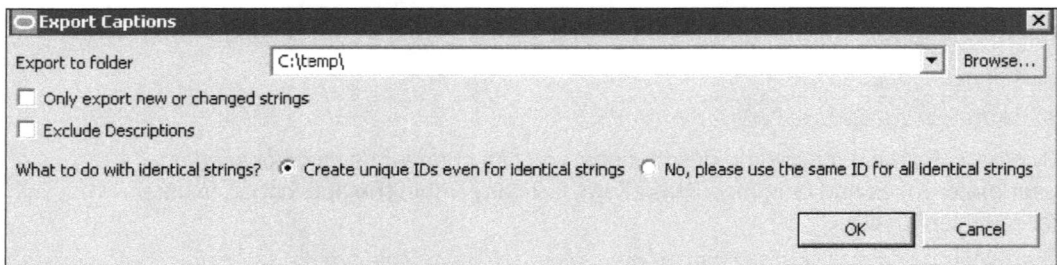

3. This will create a file in `C:\Temp` named `sharedcaptions.xml`.

4. Open the file in Notepad. Look at the values stored within the tags `<TEXT>Text</TEXT>`. These are all the captions in the frontend.

5. Copy this file to a duplicate file for different languages; for example, copy the file `sharedcaptions.xml` to a new file named `sharedcaptions-<lang>.xml`.

6. Open your new file in an editor.

7. Search and replace the `<TEXT>Text Description</TEXT>` strings with the relevant translated values.

8. Navigate to your language directories typically found in the following location for Windows and Linux:

    ```
    <ORACLE_HOME>\instances\<instance>\bifoundation\coreapplication_
    obips1\msgdb\l_<lang>\captions
    ```

9. Create the directory for the language if it does not exist. Remove any old files if present. Copy your new `sharedcaptions-<lang>.xml` into the directory.

10. Repeat the translation for all the different languages you wish to support.

11. Restart your BI Presentation Services.

How it works...

When the `sharedcaptions.xml` file exists for a language, upon login and the selection of the language, it will use the translated values in the file to present the information in the chosen language. All captions should be translated through this file except for action links at the moment.

As you build new content for your application (additional pages and dashboards), you need to follow the same procedure and generate another `sharedcaptions.xml` file. This new file will only contain the information related to the new content. Repeat the procedure to translate the strings in the file. This additional file must be placed in the same folder as the previous file.

14
Security

Security is a very broad and complex topic. Within a business intelligence and data warehousing project there are many facets to the topic. The recipes within this chapter will cover the following:

- ► Creating an APEX custom authentication procedure
- ► Creating a row-level Virtual Private Database (VPD)
- ► Creating a column-level Virtual Private Database
- ► Creating Virtual Private application context
- ► Configuring OBIEE for multiple security providers
- ► Integrating Microsoft Active Directory into OBIEE
- ► Creating and configuring OBIEE roles
- ► Configuring OBIEE privileges
- ► Configuring OBIEE catalog security
- ► Enabling Virtual Private Database in OBIEE

Introduction

Security is divided into three broad categories:

- ► **Authentication**: Validates the identity of a person trying to access restricted resources (network, machines, applications, and others)
- ► **Authorization**: Grants or denies access to specific content, for a given resource once an individual has been authenticated (roles, privileges, screens, tables, and so on)
- ► **Data**: Grants or denies access to row- or column-level information based on security rules (rows and columns)

Creating an APEX custom authentication procedure

APEX provides default authentication schemes. If these do not suit your needs, or are not flexible enough, then you can build your own.

Getting ready

In order to create an APEX custom authentication, you will need to create some tables. In order to do this, you will require a schema that is registered with APEX. For this example, we are integrating into different LDAP servers depending on the domain for the user. Open SQL Developer and log in as the owner of the schema where the tables will be created.

How to do it...

Using a single authentication provider (LDAP, Microsoft Active Directory) across the entire solution reduces the amount of work and maintenance. For this, the user interface created in *Chapter 12, Enhancing the Data*, will need to be integrated into LDAP to utilize the same security provider that OBIEE will, as outlined later in this chapter:

1. Open SQL Developer and log on as your application user created in *Chapter 12, Enhancing the Data*.

2. Run the CREATE TABLE script for the registration table, which will contain the LDAP server details and the associated domain:

```
CREATE TABLE "REF_LDAP_DETAILS"
  (
    "LDAP_DOMAIN" VARCHAR2(32 BYTE),
    "LDAP_HOST"   VARCHAR2(500 BYTE),
    "LDAP_PORT"   NUMBER
  );
```

3. Run the CREATE TABLE script for the APEX users table, which will contain the users and their associated domains:

```
CREATE TABLE "APEX_USERS"
  (
    "ID"         NUMBER NOT NULL ENABLE,
    "LOGIN_NAME" VARCHAR2(1020 CHAR) NOT NULL ENABLE,
    "FIRST_NAME" VARCHAR2(1020 CHAR) NOT NULL ENABLE,
    "LAST_NAME"  VARCHAR2(200 CHAR) NOT NULL ENABLE,
    "EMAIL"      VARCHAR2(1020 CHAR),
    "WORK_PHONE" VARCHAR2(80 CHAR),
    "IS_ACTIVE"  VARCHAR2(4 CHAR) DEFAULT 'Y' NOT NULL ENABLE,
```

```
    "CREATED_ON" DATE NOT NULL ENABLE,
    "CREATED_BY" NUMBER,
    "UPDATED_ON" DATE,
    "UPDATED_BY" NUMBER,
    "DOMAIN"      VARCHAR2(10),
    CONSTRAINT "APEX_USERS_APX_PK"
    PRIMARY KEY ("ID")
    USING INDEX PCTFREE 10 INITRANS 2 MAXTRANS 255
  )
```

4. Run the `create` function script for the authentication process that will connect to the LDAP server, and authenticate the users:

```
create or replace
  FUNCTION "LDAP_AUTHENTICATE"
    (p_username in varchar2, p_password in varchar2)
return BOOLEAN is
  b_result boolean;
L_LDAP_HOST varchar2(256) ;
L_LDAP_PORT varchar2(256) ;
L_LDAP_USER    APEX_USERS.LOGIN_NAME%TYPE;
L_LDAP_PASSWD  varchar2(256) := P_PASSWORD;
L_LDAP_DOMAIN  APEX_USERS_APX.DOMAIN%TYPE;


L_RETVAL       PLS_INTEGER;
L_SESSION      DBMS_LDAP.session;


begin  -- Choose to raise exceptions.  --

select LDAP.LDAP_HOST, LDAP.LDAP_PORT, USR.DOMAIN
  into L_LDAP_HOST,L_LDAP_PORT, L_LDAP_DOMAIN
  from REF_LDAP_DETAILS LDAP, APEX_USERS USR
where LDAP.LDAP_DOMAIN = USR.DOMAIN
  and USR.LOGIN_NAME = P_USERNAME;
--
  L_LDAP_USER := L_LDAP_DOMAIN ||'\'||P_USERNAME;

DBMS_LDAP.USE_EXCEPTION := true;
--     DBMS_OUTPUT.PUT_LINE('Connecting');
  -- Connect to the LDAP server.
L_SESSION :=
  DBMS_LDAP.INIT(L_LDAP_HOST,L_LDAP_PORT);
--     DBMS_OUTPUT.PUT_LINE
        ('Init done ..Session is ' || L_SESSION);
L_RETVAL := DBMS_LDAP.SIMPLE_BIND_S(
```

```
         LD => L_SESSION,
         DN =>  L_LDAP_USER,
         PASSWD => L_LDAP_PASSWD);
--       DBMS_OUTPUT.PUT_LINE('Connected');
         -- Disconnect from the LDAP server.
     L_RETVAL := DBMS_LDAP.UNBIND_S(L_SESSION);
--       DBMS_OUTPUT.PUT_LINE
             ('L_RETVAL: ' || L_RETVAL);
--       DBMS_OUTPUT.PUT_LINE('All Done!!');
     case
       when L_RETVAL > 0 then
         return (false);
       else
         RETURN(true);
     end case;


--          return(true);


     EXCEPTION
       when OTHERS then
         RAISE_APPLICATION_ERROR
           (-20001,'Error - '||SQLCODE||' '||SQLERRM);
         RETURN (FALSE);
     END;
```

5. Log on to the APEX application builder:

6. Navigate to **Application Builder** and open your application:

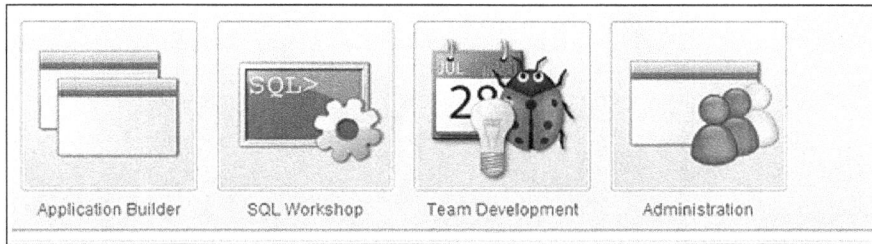

7. Click on **Shared Components**:

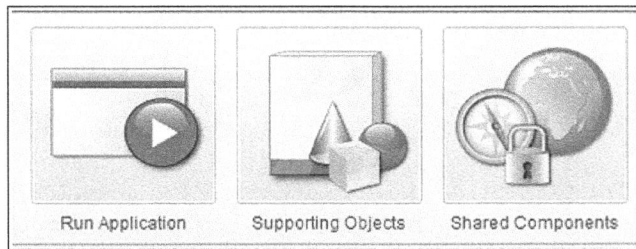

8. Click on **Authentication Schemes**:

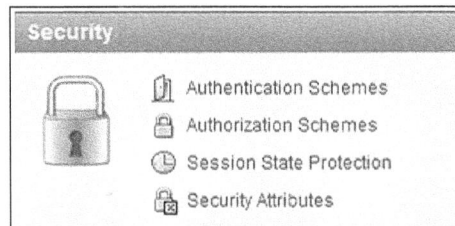

9. Click on **Create >**:

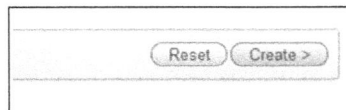

10. Select **Based on a pre-configured scheme from the gallery**:

11. Enter **Name**, and select **Custom** for **Schema Type**. Enter a name for **Authentication Function Name** and then click **Create**:

12. You will be directed back to the Application Builder. Click
CustomAuthenticationScheme, then click **Make Current
Scheme**, and finally, click **OK** for the pop-up box:

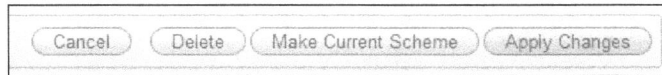

(Cancel) (Delete) (Make Current Scheme) (Apply Changes)

How it works...

Your custom function needs to accept a few parameters, namely username and password,
and return a Boolean indicating `true` or `false` for a connection result. When the function is
integrated into APEX, the standard login screen will pass the username and password into the
function. At this stage, the function will look up the user within the table to determine which
LDAP server to authenticate against and make the relevant connection. If the user connects
successfully, the function will return the value `true`, and allow APEX to continue. Should the
value `false` be returned, APEX will not allow the user to gain access to the application.

Creating a row-level Virtual Private Database (VPD)

Oracle provides the framework to provide custom row-level security. This needs to be defined
and built using PL/SQL and some of the default Oracle packages.

Getting ready

In order to create the VPD functions, we will need to have a sample schema. This sample
schema will be used throughout the recipes. Open SQL Developer and log in to the database
using an administrator user (SYS, system, and others) and create a schema owner for the
sample objects. Ensure you grant the following permissions to the schema owner; replace
`<Schema>` with your schema owner name:

```
GRANT CONNECT, RESOURCE TO <Schema>;
GRANT select_catalog_role TO <Schema>; -- Included to enable the use
of autotrace
GRANT SELECT ANY dictionary TO <Schema>; -- Included to enable the use
of autotrace
GRANT execute on DBMS_RLS to <Schema>; -- Included to enable the
creation of policies
GRANT CREATE ANY CONTEXT to <Schema>; -- Included to enable the
creation of application contexts
```

How to do it...

VPD, which is a part of the Oracle Enterprise edition, is a functionality that enables the database to secure information at the row-level, enabling a different set of data to be visible or returned based on user security:

1. Using SQL Developer log on to your schema owner.

2. Create the following tables:

```
CREATE TABLE LDAP_USER_GROUP
  (
    USER_CODE    VARCHAR2(200 CHAR),
    GROUP_CODE   VARCHAR2(200 CHAR),
    DOMAIN_NAME  VARCHAR2(200 CHAR)
  );

CREATE TABLE USAGE_STATS
  (
    SUBJECT_AREA              VARCHAR2(512 CHAR),
    DASHBOARD                 VARCHAR2(600 CHAR),
    PAGE                      VARCHAR2(600 CHAR),
    USER_CODE                 VARCHAR2(512 CHAR),
    ACCESS_MONTH              VARCHAR2(20),
    ACCESS_DAY                VARCHAR2(20),
    FIRST_LOGON_TIME          VARCHAR2(8),
    LAST_LOGON_TIME           VARCHAR2(8),
    QUERY_EXECUTION_MINUTES   NUMBER,
    ACCESS_COUNT              NUMBER,
    DISTINCT_USER_COUNT       NUMBER,
    SITE                      VARCHAR2(10),
    ELAPSED_MINUTES           NUMBER
  );
```

3. Insert some data into the tables:

```
INSERT INTO LDAP_USER_GROUP
VALUES ('weblogic','VPD_ROLE','GLB');

INSERT INTO LDAP_USER_GROUP
VALUES ('scott','NONVPD_ROLE','GLB');

COMMIT;

INSERT INTO USAGE_STATS
VALUES
```

```
('VPD','VPD','Dashboard','weblogic','FEB-2012','01-Feb-
2012','08:00','16:00',15,1,1,'GLB',480);

INSERT INTO USAGE_STATS
VALUES
('VPD','VPD','Dashboard','weblogic','FEB-2012','02-Feb-
2012','08:30','13:30',30,1,1,'GLB',300);

INSERT INTO USAGE_STATS
VALUES
('VPD','VPD','Dashboard','weblogic','FEB-2012','03-Feb-
2012','08:30','14:30',10,1,1,'GLB',360);

INSERT INTO USAGE_STATS
VALUES
('VPD','VPD','Dashboard','scott','FEB-2012','11-Feb-
2012','08:00','16:00',15,1,1,'GLB',480);

INSERT INTO USAGE_STATS
VALUES
('VPD','VPD','Dashboard','scott','FEB-2012','12-Feb-
2012','08:30','13:30',30,1,1,'GLB',300);

INSERT INTO USAGE_STATS
VALUES
('VPD','VPD','Dashboard','scott','FEB-2012','13-Feb-
2012','08:30','14:30',10,1,1,'GLB',360);

COMMIT;
```

4. Create a function to restrict access:

```
CREATE OR REPLACE
FUNCTION USAGE_SEC
( p_schema IN VARCHAR2 DEFAULT NULL, P_object IN VARCHAR2 DEFAULT
NULL)
RETURN VARCHAR2
IS
BEGIN
RETURN ' UPPER(USER_CODE) = upper(user)';
EXCEPTION
WHEN OTHERS
THEN RETURN ('1=2');
END;
```

5. Add the VPD policy:

```
BEGIN
  DBMS_RLS.ADD_POLICY
    (OBJECT_SCHEMA => '<Schema>',
      OBJECT_NAME => 'USAGE_STATS',
      policy_name =>
    'USAGE_SEC_POL', function_schema =>
    '<Schema>', policy_function => 'USAGE_SEC');
END;
```

6. Select data from the table:

```
SELECT * FROM USAGE_STATS;
```

Note that now as the policy has been enabled, there will be no rows returned due to the row-level security.

7. Insert additional data (replace <Schema> with your schema name):

```
INSERT INTO USAGE_STATS
VALUES
('VPD','VPD','Dashboard','<Schema>','FEB-2012','11-Feb-
2012','08:00','16:00',15,1,1,'GLB',480);

INSERT INTO USAGE_STATS
VALUES
('VPD','VPD','Dashboard','<Schema>','FEB-2012','12-Feb-
2012','08:30','13:30',30,1,1,'GLB',300);

INSERT INTO USAGE_STATS
VALUES
('VPD','VPD','Dashboard','<Schema>','FEB-2012','13-Feb-
2012','08:30','14:30',10,1,1,'GLB',360);

COMMIT;
```

8. In SQL Developer, enter the following command to select data from the table, right-click on the statement, and select **Autotrace**:

```
SELECT * FROM USAGE_STATS;
```

Script Output ×	Explain Plan ×	Query Result ×	Autotrace ×	
SQL | 0.475 seconds				
OPERATION	OBJECT_NAME	COST		LAST_CR_BUFFER_GETS
SELECT STATEMENT		3		
TABLE ACCESS (FULL)	USAGE_STATS	3		7
Filter Predicates				
UPPER(USER_CODE)=UPPER(USER @!)				

How it works...

The USAGE_SEC function adds an additional WHERE clause as can be seen in step 8. This WHERE clause (predicate) is not applied unless the policy is added in step 5. The only data that will be retrieved from the table will be the specific user information as per the business rule in the function. The function is executed and applied for each row within the table. For this reason, it is important to write the functions efficiently, or else there will be a significant impact on performance.

There's more...

VPD is a great technology to enforce security. However, for some schemas within the data warehouse, it is important not to have VPD enabled. There is a global grant that can be executed as an administrator user:

```
grant exempt access policy to <user>;
```

This is an extremely dangerous grant to give to a user. It would be more advisable to code within your functions with these exceptions.

Creating a column-level Virtual Private Database

In addition to row-level security, the same Oracle packages also provide the ability to create column-level security.

Getting ready

Oracle also supports column masking as an option with VPD. This allows the database to apply a security function to determine whether a column within a row being returned should be masked or not. Log into SQL Developer as the schema owner from the previous recipe.

How to do it...

Column masking or column-level VPD is very useful to mask and hide sensitive information within a row. For example, Social Security numbers, and so on. The rules that enforce column masking are enforced the same way as row-level security with the business rules in a function and a policy to enforce the function:

1. Create a function which will secure the columns:

```
CREATE OR REPLACE FUNCTION USAGE_COL_SEC
( p_schema IN VARCHAR2 DEFAULT NULL, P_object IN VARCHAR2 DEFAULT
NULL)
```

```
RETURN VARCHAR2
IS
  CURSOR GET_GROUP IS
      SELECT GROUP_CODE FROM LDAP_USER_GROUP
      WHERE USER_CODE = USER;

  V_GROUP_CODE     LDAP_USER_GROUP.GROUP_CODE%TYPE;

BEGIN
  OPEN GET_GROUP;
  FETCH GET_GROUP INTO V_GROUP_CODE;
  CLOSE GET_GROUP;
  IF V_GROUP_CODE = 'VPD_ROLE' THEN
      RETURN ('1=1');
  ELSE
      RETURN ('1=2');
  END IF;
EXCEPTION
WHEN OTHERS
THEN RETURN ('1=2');
END;
```

2. Create a policy to apply the function:

```
BEGIN
DBMS_RLS.ADD_POLICY (OBJECT_SCHEMA => '<Schema>',
OBJECT_NAME =>'USAGE_STATS',
POLICY_NAME => 'USAGE_STATS_COL',
FUNCTION_SCHEMA=> '<Schema>',
POLICY_FUNCTION => 'USAGE_COL_SEC',
SEC_RELEVANT_COLS =>
' ACCESS_DAY, FIRST_LOGON_TIME, LAST_LOGON_TIME',
SEC_RELEVANT_COLS_OPT => DBMS_RLS.ALL_ROWS);
END;
```

3. In SQL Developer, enter the following command to select data from the table, right-click on the statement, and select **Autotrace**:

```
SELECT * FROM USAGE_STATS;
```

Script Output ×	Explain Plan ×	Query Result ×	Autotrace ×		
SQL	0.475 seconds				
OPERATION		OBJECT_NAME	COST		LAST_CR_BUFFER_GETS
SELECT STATEMENT			3		
TABLE ACCESS (FULL)		USAGE_STATS	3		7
Filter Predicates					
UPPER(USER_CODE)=UPPER(USER@!)					

How it works...

Adding the function to the table allows one to secure columns. The parameter `SEC_RELEVANT_COLS_OPT` needs to be set to `DBMS_RLS.ALL_ROWS`. If not, it will cause the rows to be filtered (row-level security) when the column security is enforced. Column masking nulls out the contents of the column where the business rules fail. From the **Autotrace** tab, it cannot be seen that there is column security added.

Creating Virtual Private application context

An application context is a name-value pair, which Oracle stores in memory. These name-value pairs exist within a namespace. The application context is a global variable, which can be accessed within a database session. Application contexts can support database sessions (user database sessions) and global application contexts (for sessionless models—for example, web applications using session pooling or multi-tiered applications).

Getting ready

Log on to SQL Developer under the schema owner to create the packages for the application context.

How to do it...

Application context is a way to create variables that can be reused within the Oracle database:

1. Create a package to set application contexts:

```
create package context_package as
procedure name_value(n varchar2, v varchar2);
end;
create package body context_package as
procedure name_value(n varchar2, v varchar2) as
begin
-- can only be called within the package to which it belongs
-- If you try to execute DBMS_SESSION.SET_CONTEXT you'll get an
error, as
shown here:
-- ORA-01031: insufficient privileges
-- APP_SECURITY is the namespace for the context
-- n is the name of the variable
-- v is the value of the variable
dbms_session.set_context('DW',n,v);
end;
end;
```

2. Create a context, with the same name as the namespace, in the context package as VPD:

```
create context DW using context_package;
```

3. Recreate the row-level security function to include the application context:

```
CREATE OR REPLACE
FUNCTION USAGE_SEC
( p_schema IN VARCHAR2 DEFAULT NULL, P_object IN VARCHAR2 DEFAULT
NULL)
RETURN VARCHAR2
IS
BEGIN
RETURN 'UPPER(USER_CODE) = UPPER(SYS_CONTEXT(''DW'',''APP_
USER''))';
EXCEPTION
WHEN OTHERS
THEN RETURN ('1=2');
END;
```

4. Recreate the column-level security function to include the application context:

```
CREATE OR REPLACE FUNCTION USAGE_COL_SEC
( p_schema IN VARCHAR2 DEFAULT NULL, P_object IN VARCHAR2 DEFAULT
NULL)
RETURN VARCHAR2
IS
BEGIN
   IF SYS_CONTEXT('DW','APP_USER_ROLE') = 'VPD_ROLE' THEN
      RETURN ('1=1');
   ELSE
     RETURN ('1=2');
   END IF;
EXCEPTION
WHEN OTHERS
THEN RETURN ('1=2');
END;
```

5. Select the data from USAGE_STATS:

```
select * from USAGE_STATS;
```

6. Set the context as the user WEBLOGIC, and query the data:

```
BEGIN
  CONTEXT_PACKAGE.NAME_VALUE('APP_USER','WEBLOGIC');
  CONTEXT_PACKAGE.NAME_VALUE('APP_USER_ROLE','VPD_ROLE');
END;


SELECT * FROM USAGE_STATS;
```

Note that the information returned includes only data for the user WEBLOGIC, and does not mask the last three columns (**ACCESS_DAY**, **FIRST_LOGON_TIME**, and **LAST_LOGON_TIME**). This is due to the row-level security limiting the access to rows, and the column-level security allowing access to the columns, for VPD_ROLE.

7. Set the context as the user SCOTT, and query the data:

```
BEGIN
    CONTEXT_PACKAGE.NAME_VALUE('APP_USER','SCOTT');
    CONTEXT_PACKAGE.NAME_VALUE('APP_USER_ROLE','NONVPD_ROLE');
END;

SELECT * FROM USAGE_STATS;
```

Note that the information returned only includes data for the user SCOTT, and masks the last three columns (**ACCESS_DAY**, **FIRST_LOGON_TIME**, and **LAST_LOGON_TIME**). This is due to the row-level security limiting the row- and column-level security, not allowing access to the columns for NONVPD_ROLE.

How it works...

Using the application context, variables can be set at the database level. These variables can be set and then used within the security functions to apply the security business rules.

Including VPD in an application design enables a designer/developer to place the security within the database. VPD allows the security to become transparent to the application, making application code simpler. Security is applied globally to all users of the information, making the data more secure.

VPD comes standard with the Oracle Enterprise Edition, and should be considered in every database application that requires security. As VPD enforces the security at the database level, all applications can take advantage of the security as it is a single location to maintain. The last three recipes have focused on configuring the database to utilize VPD. In the *Enabling Virtual Private Database in OBIEE* recipe later in the chapter, you will see how to incorporate VPD into OBIEE.

Configuring OBIEE for multiple security providers

OBIEE has the capability to utilize multiple security providers to authenticate users. This is useful in organizations that may have multiple LDAP directories, or different ways to authenticate users.

Getting ready

Before starting this recipe, log into the BI Administration tool and create a new subject area based on LDAP_USER_GROUP and USAGE_STATS. Create some basic reports using this information and create a Dashboard called VPD.

OBIEE has the capability to support multiple security providers. Each of these security providers can be used to authenticate individuals. In order to enable this, there are a few settings that have to be changed. Contact your LDAP support personnel and understand how the LDAP has been implemented, and which attributes in the directory contain the username. To start, you will need to log on to the OBIEE Enterprise Manager website.

How to do it...

In OBIEE you have the option to integrate multiple security providers to provide authentication to the application. This is useful should you have multiple LDAP directories or different authentication means within your organization:

1. Open a web browser and navigate to OBIEE Enterprise Manager.
2. Log in to Enterprise Manager using the administrator account (default is weblogic):

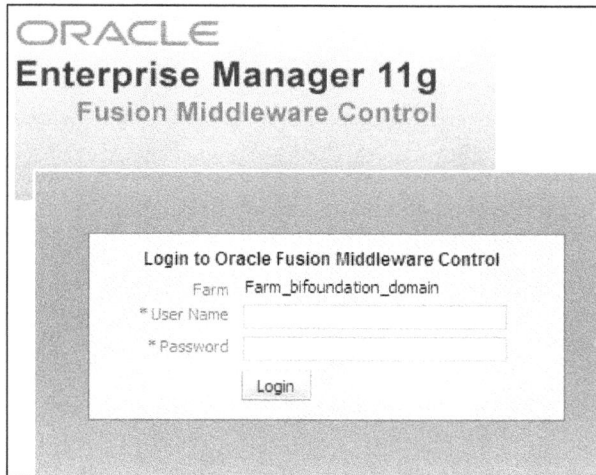

3. Expand the **WebLogic Domain** domain, right-click on the node below the folder, and select **Security | Security Provider Configuration**:

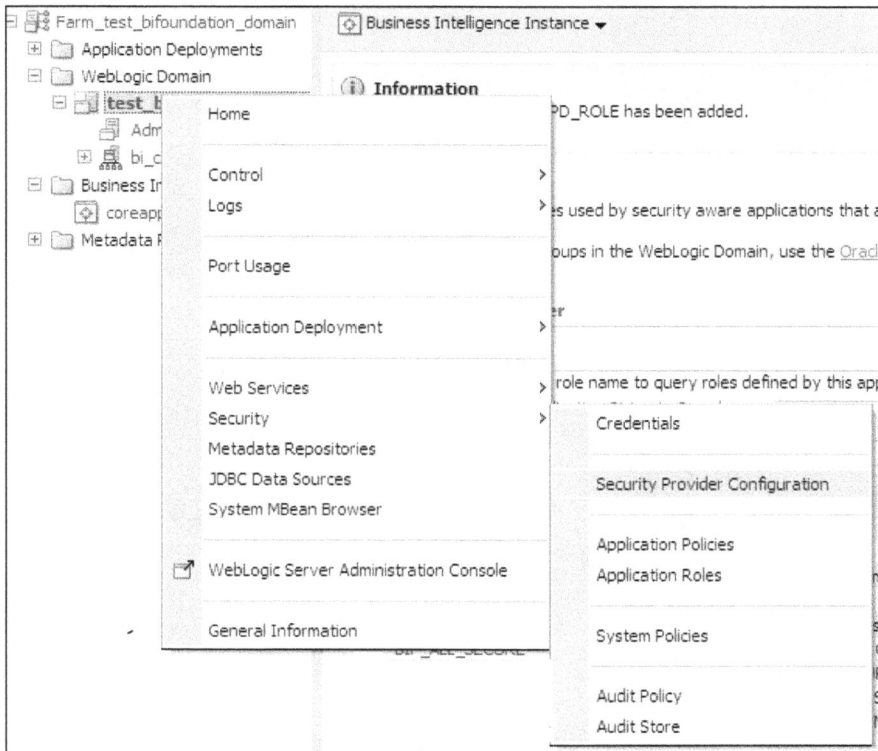

4. Expand **Identity Store Provider**, and click **Configure...**:

5. Click **+Add** to include additional properties:

6. Enter **virtualize** as the property name, with **Value** as **true**. Click **OK**:

7. If you are integrating Microsoft Active Directory, it is best to understand which attribute is used in the directory to store the username. Follow the aforementioned steps and register the `user.login.attr` and `username.attr` properties with OBIEE, using the correct directory attribute. In this example, Microsoft Active Directory stores the username in the **sAMAccountName** attribute:

How it works...

The **virtualize** property configures OBIEE to take the directory information from multiple security providers and create a virtual, consolidated LDAP within OBIEE. This then has all the usernames and information in a centralized place. The additional properties fine tune OBIEE with its integration into Microsoft Active Directory.

Integrating Microsoft Active Directory into OBIEE

Microsoft Active Directory is a common LDAP directory within the industry. OBIEE integrates out of the box with Microsoft Active Directory, enabling it to be used for user authentication.

Getting ready

Before integrating any LDAP server into OBIEE, it is important to have an understanding of the information contained within LDAP. It is recommended that you get a tool which will allow you to interrogate the LDAP structure and view information. Without this, it could be difficult to troubleshoot and obtain the correct information. ADExplorer from Microsoft is available from their website.

How to do it...

To integrate Microsoft Active Directory with OBIEE you need to provide all the connection details and where in Microsoft Active Directory the information is located. OBIEE has a predefined security provider which will request all the necessary information:

1. Log on to OBIEE Administration Console:

2. Click the **Lock & Edit** button:

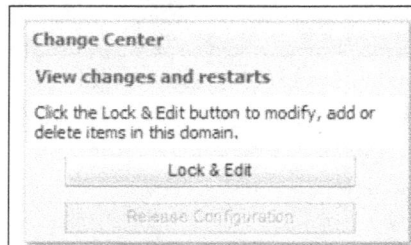

3. Navigate to **Security Realms**:

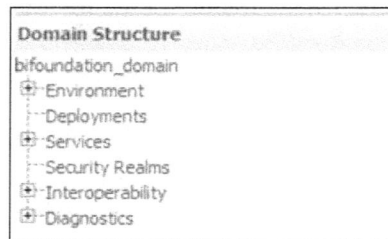

4. Select the default realm, **myrealm**:

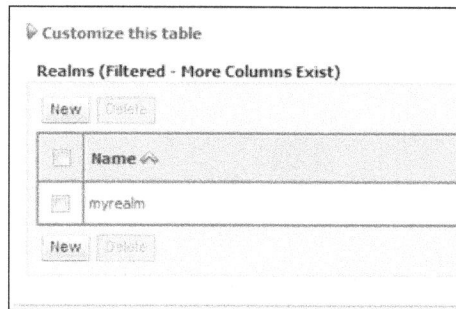

5. Select the **Providers** tab and click **New**:

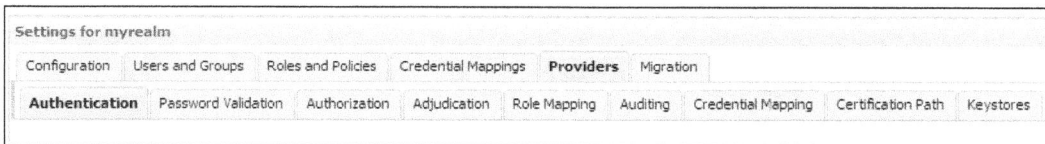

6. Enter a name for the provider and select **ActiveDirectoryAuthenticator** for the type of authenticator provider. Click **OK**:

7. Click on the newly created security provider. You can also reorder the providers:

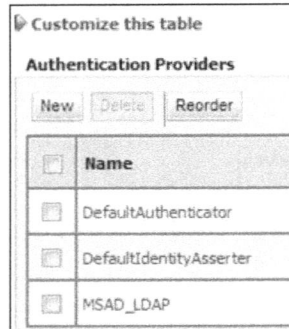

8. Click on the **Common** tab and set **Control Flag** to **SUFFICIENT**. Click **Save**, and repeat the same for the **DefaultAuthenticator** security provider:

9. Click on the **Provider Specific** tab to start the integration with Microsoft Active Directory. Enter the following information; once completed, click **Save**:

   ☐ **Host**: The LDAP server
   ☐ **Port** A standard port to connect to
   ☐ **Principal**: A user to connect to LDAP

- ❏ **Credential**: The password for a user to connect to LDAP
- ❏ **Confirm Credential**: Re-enter password for confirmation
- ❏ **User Base DN**: The starting point in the directory to search for users
- ❏ **All Users Filter**: Filter to search users
- ❏ **User Name Attribute**: The name of the attribute in LDAP that contains the username
- ❏ **Group Base DN**: The starting point in the directory to search for groups

Configuration	Performance	
Common	**Provider Specific**	

Save

Use this page to define the provider specific configuration for this Active Directory Authentication provider.

Connection

Host:		localhost
Port:		389
Principal:		

10. On the main page, click the **Activate Changes** button:

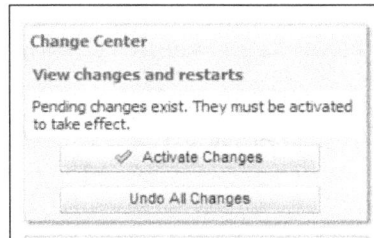

Change Center

View changes and restarts

Pending changes exist. They must be activated to take effect.

✓ Activate Changes

Undo All Changes

11. Restart the services to activate all the changes.

How it works...

Integrating OBIEE into LDAP allows you to make use of the user information stored within LDAP. This minimizes the amount of maintenance. Groups from LDAP can also be used to control content within OBIEE.

In the previous example, we are still using the default security provider from Weblogic for all the admin accounts, and Microsoft Active Directory for all the user accounts.

Creating and configuring OBIEE roles

In OBIEE, 11g roles are created in the Enterprise Management Console and do not need to be created in the Business Intelligence Administration tool.

Getting ready

To control access to content, OBIEE uses roles. Within LDAP you can have one or more groups, and when you integrate OBIEE into LDAP, these groups become visible. To control access to content, these LDAP groups are mapped to OBIEE roles. OBIEE roles can also be assigned multiple privileges.

Open a browser and navigate to the Enterprise Manager web address for OBIEE.

How to do it...

OBIEE roles are mapped to specific content within the application, allowing access to any user mapped to the LDAP group that is mapped to the OBIEE role:

1. Log on to Enterprise Manager as the administrator (`weblogic`):

2. Expand the **Business Intelligence** folder; right-click on the node under the folder, and select **Security | Application Roles**:

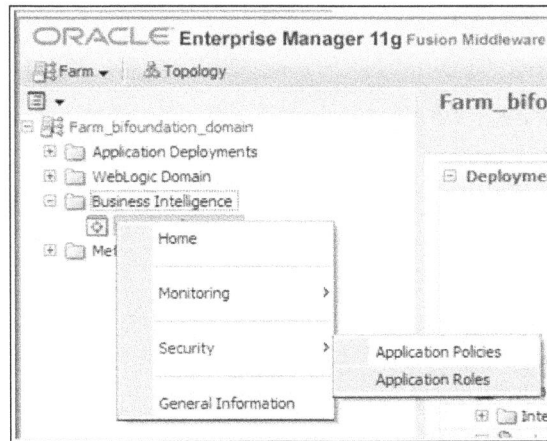

3. Click **Create...** to create a new role:

Application Roles

Application roles are the roles used by security aware applications that are specific to the application. These roles are seeded by applications

☞ To manage users and groups in the WebLogic Domain, use the Oracle WebLogic Server Security Provider.

⊟ **Policy Store Provider**

Scope	WebLogic Domain
Provider	XML
Location	./system-jazn-data.xml

⊟ **Search**

Enter search keyword for role name to query roles defined by this application. Use application stripe to search if application uses a stripe th

Select Application Stripe to Search	☑ obi	▼
Role Name		⊚

| 📄 Create... | 📄 Create Like... | ✏ Edit... | ✖ Delete... |

Role Name	Members
BISystem	BISystemUser, G-GLK-BISystem
BIAdministrator	BIAdministrators, G-GLK-BIAdministrator

4. Enter a name for the role. Click on **+Add Application Role** to add application roles. Similarly, click on **+Add Group** to add groups, or **+Add User** to add users. Click **OK**:

5. Restart the services to ensure the changes have been applied.

How it works...

Creating your own roles will allow you to map groups (from the security providers in the Administration Console) and specific users to the application roles. These roles can then be used within the **Catalog** tab to control access to content. It is important to set up these roles in all environments so that when code is migrated between environments the security is in place.

There's more...

By default, the BI Consumer role has the authenticated role mapped into it. This basically means any user who has been authenticated, will be granted the BI Consumer default role. This role has a few privileges and it is a good idea to remove the authenticated role from the BI Consumer role.

Configuring OBIEE privileges

Privileges control access to certain functionality within the OBIEE. They can be configured and controlled.

Getting ready

OBIEE has a lot of privileges; each privilege performs a specific function. These can be customized to suit your specific needs. Open a web browser and navigate to the main home page for OBIEE.

How to do it...

OBIEE privileges allow the user to perform specific tasks and functions within OBIEE. These privileges grant access to standard content and functionality. For example, Access to Answers:

1. Log in as the administrator (`weblogic`), and click on **Administration**:

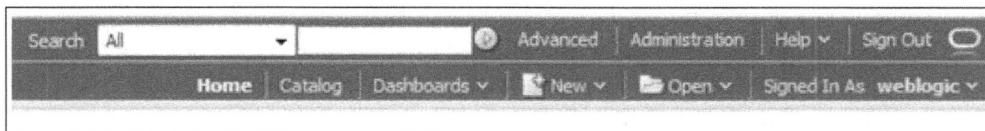

2. Under **Security**, select **Manage Privileges**:

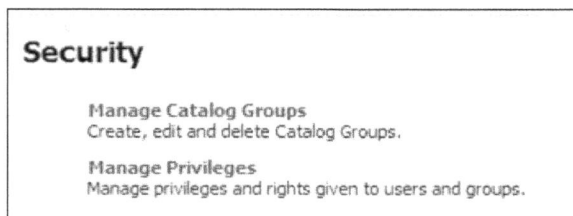

Security

Manage Catalog Groups
Create, edit and delete Catalog Groups.

Manage Privileges
Manage privileges and rights given to users and groups.

3. Navigate to the necessary privileges and add or remove roles by clicking on the highlighted role adjacent to the privilege:

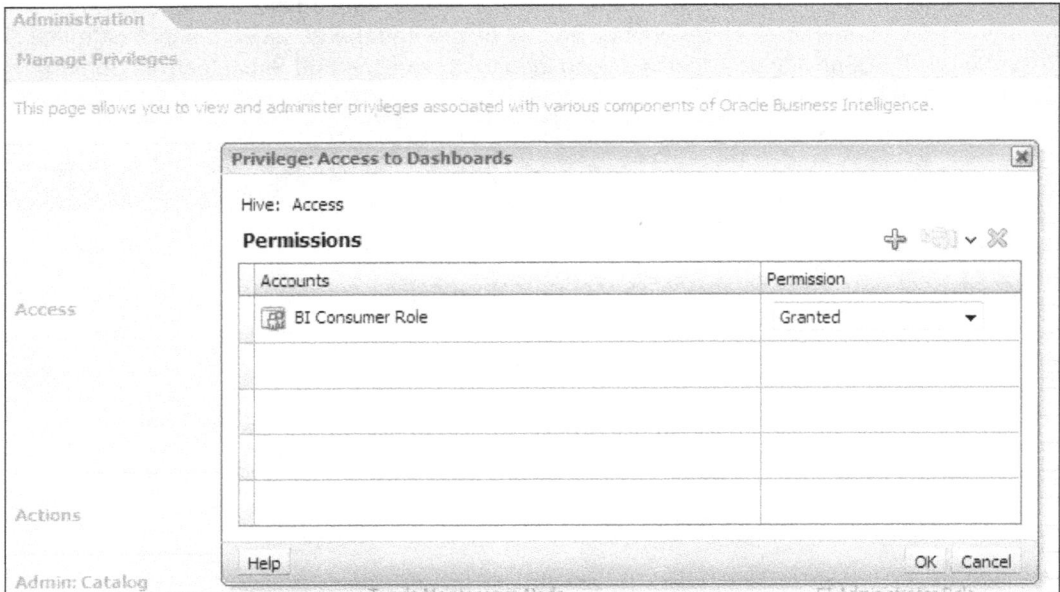

How it works...

By understanding the privileges you can roll out the functionality to some or all users; for example, Access to Answers. By creating specific application roles in the previous recipe, you can now assign certain privileges to the application roles. It is a good practice to review the defaults and either create your own application roles and remove all members from the default application roles, or understand the privileges.

Configuring OBIEE catalog security

Catalog security controls the access to content for a role or user. This access can be configured at an object or object-container level.

Getting ready

Open a web browser and navigate to the main home page for OBIEE.

How to do it...

The catalog contains all the content that you have developed for your application (reports, dashboard pages, analyses, and others). You need to grant access to these contents in order for users to see and interact with your application:

1. Log in as the administrator (weblogic), and click on **Catalog**:

2. Select the folder you need to set the permissions on:

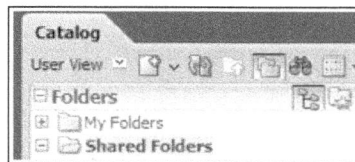

3. After selecting the folder, click on the **Permissions** link at the bottom-left corner of the page:

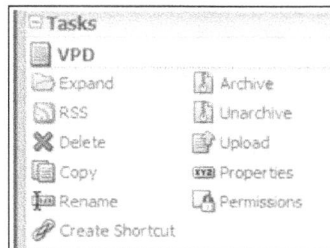

4. Upon clicking the **Permission** link, a window will open allowing you to add users and roles to the folder. Click **+** to add more users and roles:

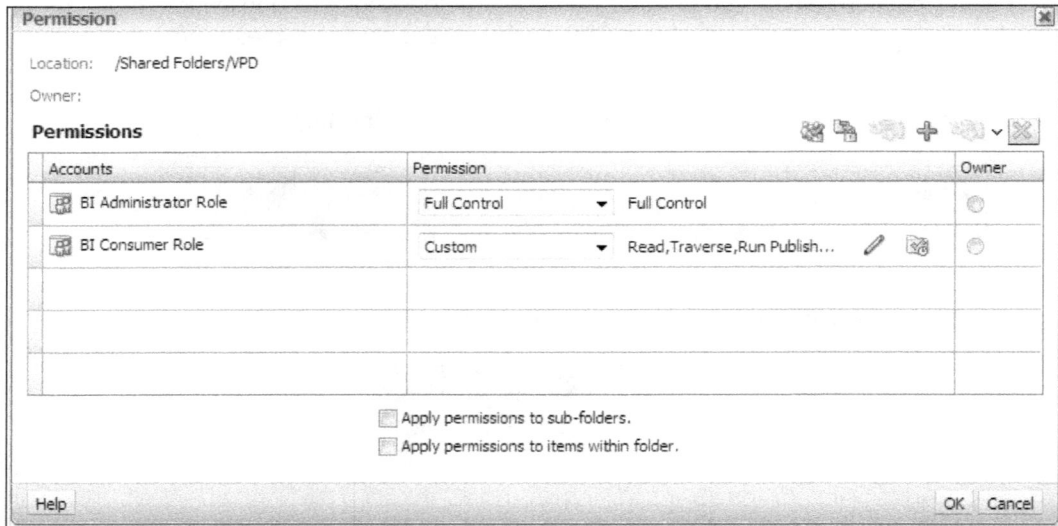

5. You may search for the required roles, and add them by highlighting the application role and using the arrows (**>**, **>>**, **<**, **<<**) to add them to and remove them from the right pane. Select the permission from the drop-down box below the right pane. Click **OK** when completed:

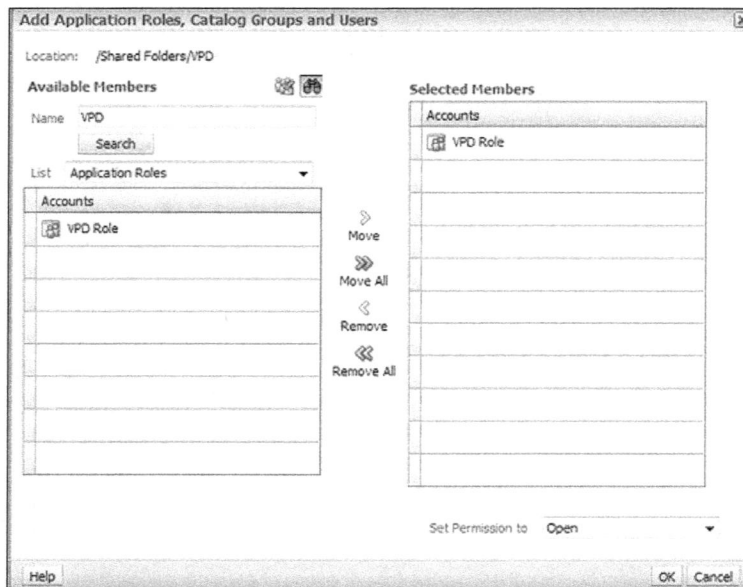

6. Review the permissions. If a folder with a padlock icon appears to the right of a role, it means that the parent folder does not allow this role access. Click the folder icon to correct this. Highlight **BI Consumer Role** and click **X** to remove it:

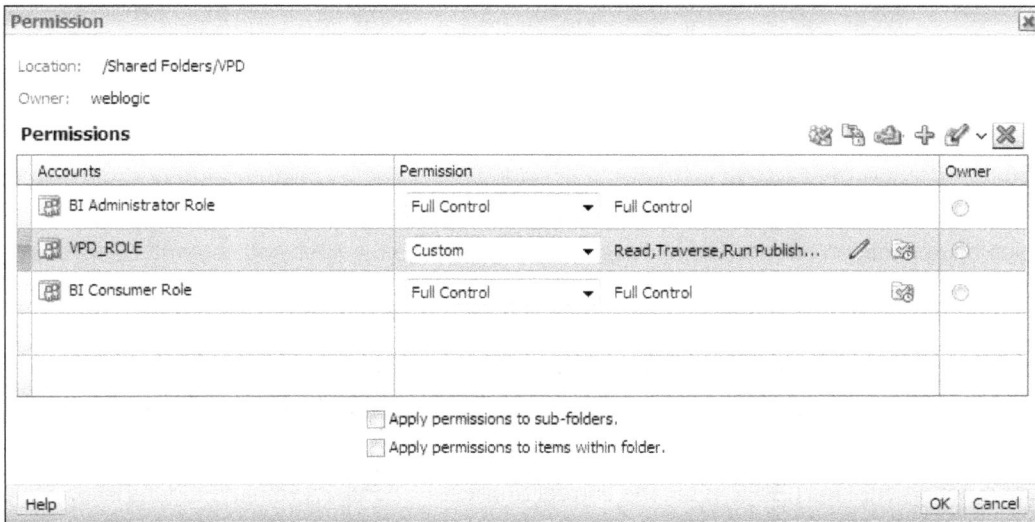

Permission

Location: /Shared Folders/VPD
Owner: weblogic

Permissions

Accounts	Permission			Owner
BI Administrator Role	Full Control	▼	Full Control	○
VPD_ROLE	Custom	▼	Read,Traverse,Run Publish...	○
BI Consumer Role	Full Control	▼	Full Control	○

☐ Apply permissions to sub-folders.
☐ Apply permissions to items within folder.

Help   OK   Cancel

7. Review the permissions. Click **OK**:

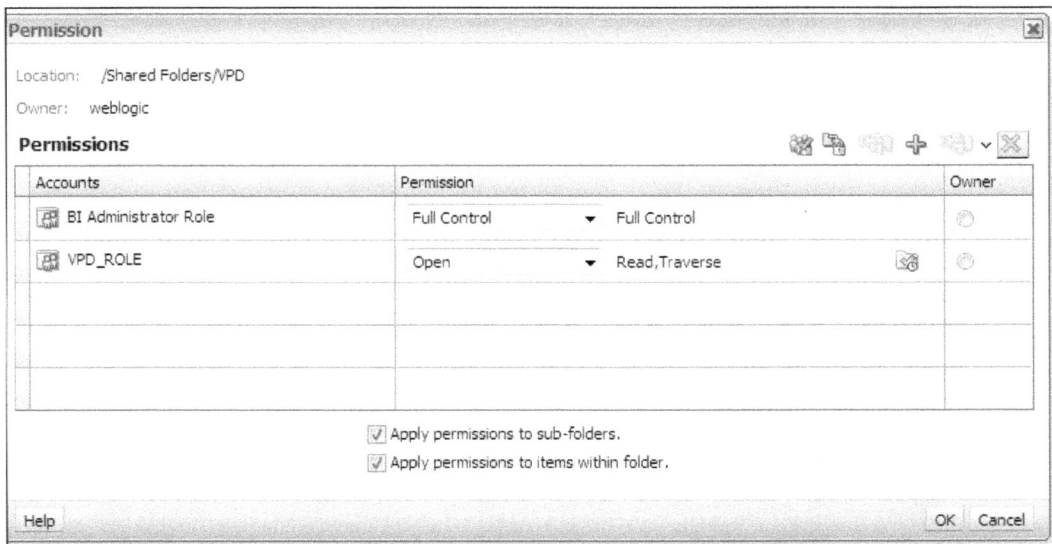

Permission

Location: /Shared Folders/VPD
Owner: weblogic

Permissions

Accounts	Permission			Owner
BI Administrator Role	Full Control	▼	Full Control	○
VPD_ROLE	Open	▼	Read,Traverse	○

☑ Apply permissions to sub-folders.
☑ Apply permissions to items within folder.

Help   OK   Cancel

8. Restart the services. After restarting the services, you can log in. You should see the new dashboard available under **Dashboards**:

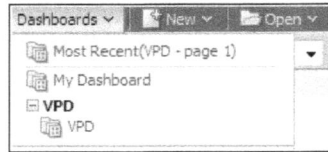

How it works...

Mapping application roles to the catalog enables access to the specified content. Users are mapped to LDAP groups, LDAP groups are mapped to application roles, and application roles are mapped to the catalogue. In this fashion, access can be granted and revoked.

Enabling Virtual Private Database in OBIEE

Once the VPD is set at the database level, it needs to be enabled within OBIEE. The configuration enables OBIEE to set the correct application contexts within the database.

Getting ready

Open the **Oracle BI Administration Tool** window and connect to the repository. Open SQL Developer and log in as the schema owner.

How to do it...

In the previous recipes for VPD, you created an application context package and some function, to restrict row and column data. In this recipe, we will build upon that knowledge to integrate the same concepts into OBIEE to be able to provide row- and column-level security.

1. Update your context package to set all the necessary context values for OBIEE in SQL Developer. This will replace the previous package we had created:

```
create or replace
package context_package as
procedure NAME_VALUE(N varchar2, V varchar2);
PROCEDURE OBIEE_SET_VPD(U VARCHAR2, R VARCHAR2);
function SET_NAME_VALUE (N varchar2, V varchar2) return varchar2;
END;
```

```
create or replace
package body CONTEXT_PACKAGE as
procedure OBIEE_SET_VPD(U varchar2, R varchar2) as
begin
-- can only be called within the package to which it belongs
-- If you try to execute DBMS_SESSION.SET_CONTEXT you'll get an
error, as shown here:
-- ORA-01031: insufficient privileges
-- APP_SECURITY is the namespace for the context
-- n is the name of the variable
-- v is the value of the variable

CONTEXT_PACKAGE.NAME_VALUE('APP_USER',U);
CONTEXT_PACKAGE.NAME_VALUE('APP_USER_ROLE',R);
end;

procedure name_value(n varchar2, v varchar2) as
begin
-- can only be called within the package to which it belongs
-- If you try to execute DBMS_SESSION.SET_CONTEXT you'll get an
error, as shown here:
-- ORA-01031: insufficient privileges
-- APP_SECURITY is the namespace for the context
-- n is the name of the variable
-- v is the value of the variable
DBMS_SESSION.SET_CONTEXT('DW',N,V);
insert into APP_AUDIT values (sysdate, N,V);
COMMIT;
END;

FUNCTION SET_NAME_VALUE (N VARCHAR2, V VARCHAR2)
RETURN VARCHAR2 IS
BEGIN
    DBMS_SESSION.SET_CONTEXT('DW',N,V);
    RETURN SYS_CONTEXT('DW',N);
END;

END;
```

2. Within **BI Administration Tool**, enable **Virtual Private Database** for your database. In order to do this, right-click on your database and select **Properties**. Select **Virtual Private Database**, and click **OK**:

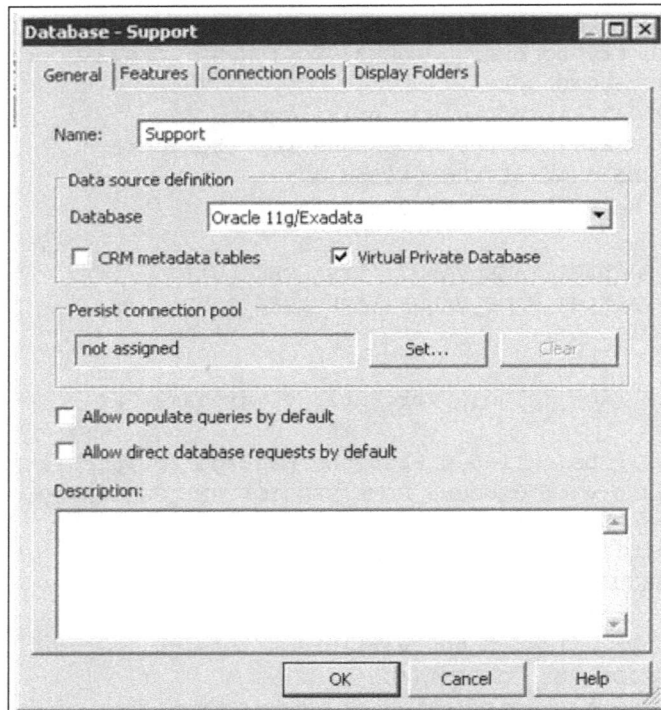

3. Next, right-click on **Connection Pool**, from which information is retrieved. Click on the **Connection Scripts** tab. Expand the **Execute before query** section, and click **New...**. Insert a call to your package to set the application context values as an **Execute Before Query** script:

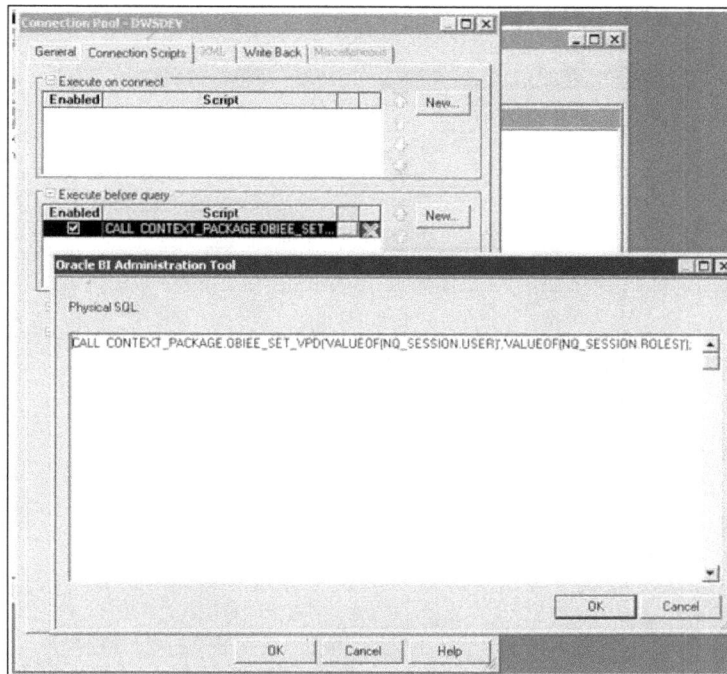

4. Create security sensitive session variables by navigating to **Manage | Variables...**. Click on **Action | New | Session** | **Variable...**:

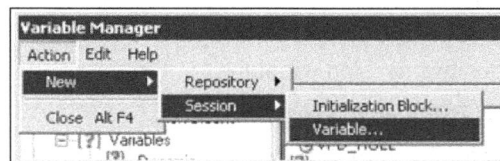

5. Create sensitive session variables for users:

    a. Enter **VPD_USER** as the variable name.

    b. Click **New** for **Session Variable Initialization Block**.

    c. Enter **get_VPD_USER** for the name of the initialization block.

    d. Click the **Edit Data Source...** button, and insert the following code:

       SELECT 'VALUEOF(NQ_SESSION.USER)' FROM DUAL

    e. Select the Initialization Blocks connection pool from your database connection.

    f. Select the **Required for authentication** checkbox, and click **OK**.

Securitysegment>

g. Click **OK** again.

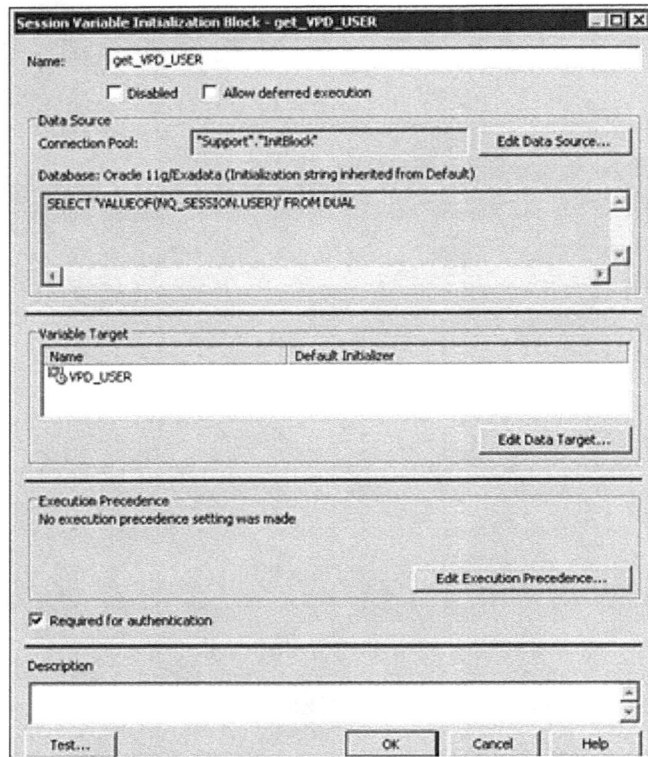

6. Create security sensitive session variables for roles:

    a. Enter **VPD_ROLE** as the variable name.

    b. Click **New** for **Session Variable Initialization Blocks**.

    c. Enter **get_VPD_ROLE** for the name of the initialization block.

    d. Click the **Edit Data Source...** button, and insert the following code:

       SELECT 'VALUEOF(NQ_SESSION.ROLES)' FROM DUAL

    e. Select the **Initialization Blocks** connection pool from your database connection.

    f. Select the **Required for authentication** checkbox, and click **OK**.

    g. Click on **OK** again.

340

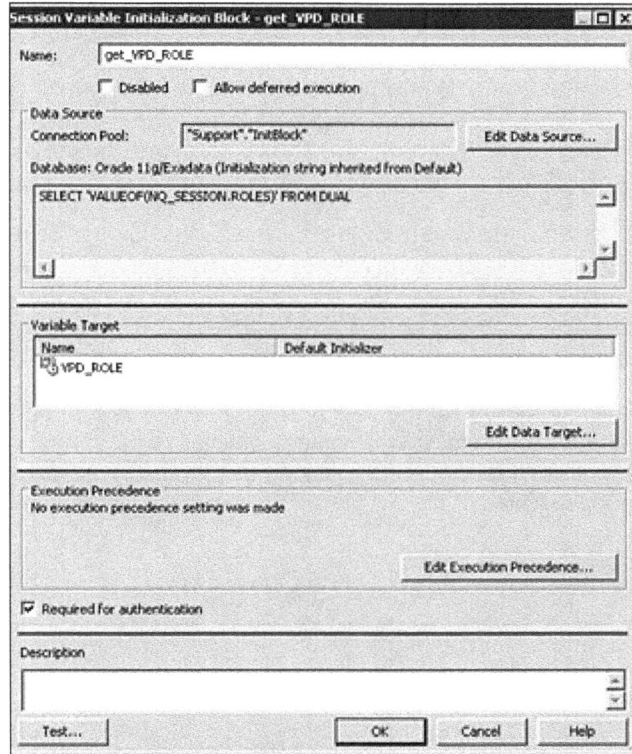

7. Create a basic analysis report using answers from the usage information as generated in the *Creating a row-level Virtual Private Database* (*VPD*) recipe.

8. Add the analysis report to a dashboard, which is available to the two different roles, **VPD_ROLE** and **VPD_NONROLE**. If you log in as a different user, you will notice the different information available, based on the row-level security defined in the *Creating a row-level Virtual Private Database* (*VPD*) recipe.

How it works...

Specifying your database as a Virtual Private Database in step 2 ensures that the information returned is reliant on the user's credentials. Steps 5 and 6 identify which variables are security-sensitive when using row- and column-level security. These variables are used by OBIEE when comparing cache entries.

OBIEE caches all information retrieved from the database. If a user requests information and the OBIEE compares the request to results already in cache, then the cached information is returned without requesting information from the database. By setting the variable in steps 5 and 6, cache hits only occur on cache entries that include and match all the security sensitive variables. If a cache hit is not achieved, the information is requested from the database.

Step 3 sets the application context for the user and the role at the database level. These are then used by the row- and column-level VPD security policies to determine what result set to return. OBIEE restricts row information or masks the columns in this example. This is all performed at the database level.

Index

A

additional columns
adding, for error trapping 245, 246
Aggregation table
#Distinct 184
Minimum and Maximum 184
APEX 261
APEX code artifacts
about 77
creating 77, 78
working 79
APEX custom authentication procedure
creating 306-311
working 311
APEX Upload application
defining 270-274
working 274
Application Builder icon 271
Application Express option 79
application schema
about 262
creating 262
working 262
application tables
about 263
creating 263
working 264
attribute 97
Attributes property 110
audit triggers
about 265
delete trigger 265, 266
insert trigger 269

update trigger 267, 268
working 270
automated data profiling
building, OracleWarehouse Builder used 172-187
working 187

B

BI Initiatives
about 7
as program 8-11
as project 8-11
Blueprint
about 15, 87
building 111
working 112-114
Bugs option 57
bug tracking module 57, 58
business case 121
business culture
acquisition-based organization growth 13
contraction phase 14
growth phase 14
mapping 11, 12
metric driven organizations 14
organic-based organization growth 13
Report managed organizations 14
working 12, 13
business drivers
using, for business requirement categorization 120-122
working 122

business entities
  record sources, identifying 106-108
  record sources, working 108-110
business entities definition
  analysis, decomposing 97-100
  reports, decomposing 97-100
Business Event 100
Business Intelligence 71
Business Intelligence Initiative.
    See **BI Initiatives**
business intelligence solution
  structure 139
business processes
  analysis, categorizing 92-96
  metrics, categorizing 92-96
  outlining 88, 89
  reports, categorizing 92-96
  working 89-92
business process matrix
  about 150
  working 152
business requirements
  about 115
  categorizing, business drivers used 120-122
  prioritizing 122, 123
  working 124
business rules
  about 119
  defining 119
  working 120

C

changing information data profiling scripts
  about 170
  building 171, 172
  table definitions, grouping into 170
C-Level 11
client tools
  installing, for collaborative environment
    65-68
  working 69
code artifacts
  APEX 77
  OBIEE 75
  ODI 79

OWB 72
  script artifacts, creating 80
collaborative environment
  about 60
  client tools, installing 65-68
  client tools, working 69
  setting up 60-64
  working 64
column headings
  enabling 292-296
  working 297
column-level VPD
  about 315
  creating 315, 316
  working 317
column selector
  about 288
  reports, consolidating 288-291
  working 291
Commit icon 204
communications loop
  about 84
  creating 84, 85
  working 85
conceptual data model
  about 148
  enhancing 148-150
  validating 148-150
  working 150
Connection Pool 338
constant feedback
  about 84
  creating 84, 85
  working 85
continuous development capability,
    for enhancement
  building 81-83
  working 83
contraction phase 14
Create Bug button 58
Create Feature button 48
cyclical build
  about 58
  creating 59
  working 59

D

database layout
  advantages 144
  defining 140
  disadvantages 144
  schemas, separating 140, 141
  working 142, 143
database type
  Data Warehouse category 138
  general purpose category 138
  selecting 137, 138
  transaction processing category 137
  working 139, 140
data dictionary
  about 129
  defining 129, 130
  working 131, 132
Data Dictionary Import Wizard screen 208
data discovery
  about 159
  automated data profiling, building 172
  changing information data profiling scripts, building 170
  data lengths data profiling scripts, building 168
  density data profiling scripts, building 164
  domain/distinct values profiling, building 162
  hierarchy data profiling scripts, building 166
  high/low data profiling scripts, building 160
  record counts profiling scripts, building 163
  significant columns data profiling scripts, building 169
data discovery phase 26
Data Discovery work package
  about 26
  creating 26, 27
  working 27
data enhancing
  APEX Upload application, defining 270
  application schema, creating 262
  application tables, creating 263
  audit triggers, defining 265
  journal tables, developing 264
  Upload interface, creating 274
data gaps 261

data lengths data profiling scripts
  building 168
  working 169
data lineages
  about 155
  developing 155, 156
  diagram 156
  standards, adhering to 156
  working 156
data models
  about 190
  changes synchronizing, Subversion used 200-206
  checking, from Subversion 199, 200
  enterprise data models, creating 230
  importing 207-213
  importing to, Subversion 194-198
  Standard columns, adding to 224, 225
Data Modeler Design 230
data retention requirements
  defining 134, 136
  working 136
data sources
  analyzing 147
  business process matrix 150
  conceptual data model 148
  data lineage 155
  report requirements matrix 152
  source matrix 153
DataType tab 185
defects 57
Definition 8, 24
definition phase 24
definition work package
  about 24
  creating 24, 25
  working 25, 26
delete trigger 265
density data profiling scripts
  about 164
  building 165
  working 165
detailed transformations
  about 157
  data rules, defining 157
  working 158

detection routines
  designing 246-251
development phase 28
development work package
  about 28
  creating 28, 29
  Production documentation 30
  Project document 30
  working 29
Dimensional model. *See* **Third Normal Form**
domain/distinct values profiling
  about 162
  building 162, 163
  working 163
domains
  about 216
  creating 216-219
Domain tab 185
drills 124
dynamic descriptions
  enabling 298-301
  working 301

E

effort drivers
  about 38
  identifying 38, 39
  working 40
ELT 237
enhancements 57
enterprise data models
  about 230
  creating 230-235
EnterpriseDesignModels 230
entity 97
estimation tool
  about 40
  algorithms 41
  creating 40
  Standard Deviation 41
  three point estimation 41
  Weighted Average 41
  Weighted Average with Estimate 41
  working 41
ETL 237

ETL data reconciliation routines
  designing 251-254
  working 255
ETL error trapping
  designing 246-251
  tools 246
  types 250, 251
extraction
  separating, from loading 240-245
  separating, from transforming routines
      240-245
  working 244
Extraction, Loading and Transformation. *See*
      ELT
Extraction, Transformation, and Loading. *See*
      ETL

F

File|DataModeler|Open 201
flags 225
flow icon 91
forward engineering
  relational to logical data model 226-229
  working 230

G

glossary
  about 220
  creating 220-223
  working 224
Groupings 124
growth phase 14

H

hierarchies
  adding, to semantic data model 124-126
hierarchy data profiling scripts
  about 166, 167
  balanced type 166
  building 167, 168
  ragged type 166
  working 168

high/low data profiling scripts
building 160, 161
candidates 160
working 161, 162

I

ImportafterFinish box 175
import feature 230
Import to Subversion Wizard 195
insert trigger 269
Integration Testing 32
issue management register
about 53
creating 54
working 55
IT manager 11

J

journal tables
developing to track changes 264, 265
working 265

K

KPIs 128

L

level-based hierarchies
developing 284, 285
working 285
line manager 11
Lock & Edit button 324
Logical node 226

M

metric driven organizations 14
Metric Register 12
metrics
adding, to semantic data model 128, 129
Microsoft Active Directory
integrating, into OBIEE 323-327
working 327

multi-table hierarchies
about 286
creating 286, 287
working 287

N

Negative data sets 32
New Information Structure option 110
notification routine
designing 255-258
working 259

O

OBIEE
about 189
catalog security, configuring 332-336
configuring, for multiple security providers
320-323
Microsoft Active Directory, integrating into
323-327
privileges, configuring 331
roles, configuring 328
roles, creating 328
VPD, enabling 336-342
working 323
OBIEE catalog security
configuring 332-336
OBIEE code artifacts
about 75
creating 75, 76
working 76
OBIEE privileges
about 331
configuring 331, 332
working 332
OBIEE roles
configuring 328-330
creating 328-330
working 330
ODI code artifacts
about 79
creating 80
working 80

OLTP 145
Online Transaction Processing
    Applications. *See* OLTP
Oracle Application Express. *See* APEX
Oracle Business Intelligence Enterprise
    Edition. *See* OBIEE
Oracle Data Integrator 246
Oracle SQL Data Modeler
    connecting, to Subversion 190-194
OracleSQLDataModeler 189
Oracle SQL Developer Data Modeler 131
OracleWarehouse Builder
    about 246
    automated data profiling, building 173-187
OWB code artifacts
    about 72
    creating 72-74
    working 74

P

Pending Changes tab 204
Performance Testing 32
positive data sets 32
Priority 122
Production 34
production phase 34
production work package
    about 34
    creating 34, 35
    working 35
program 9
project
    about 9
    controlling 43
    setting up 23
project charter 121
Project Control Register
    about 55
    defects, recording 55
    enhancements, recording 55
    using 55, 56
    working 57
project delivery methodology
    about 15
    adapting 15, 16
    working 17

Project Readiness Worksheet 7
project team
    about 20
    assessing 17-19
    organizing 20, 21
    working 19
Promote 33
promote phase 32
promote work package
    about 32
    creating 33
    working 34

R

record counts profiling scripts
    about 163
    building 163, 164
    working 164
Release folder 81
Report managed organizations 14
Report Register 12
report requirements matrix
    about 152, 153
    working 153
reports
    consolidating, column selector used 288-291
    decomposing 116-118
repository file 292
requirements
    decomposing 116-118
    working 118
Requirements Traceability Matrix
    about 44
    creating 44-46
    hierarchical number system 44, 45
    Oracle Application Express 47-49
    team members 47
    working 47
reverse engineering 213
    relational to logical data model 213-215
    working 215
Risk Priority Number. *See* RPN
risk register
    about 50
    creating 50-52
    working 53

row-level VPD
about 311
creating 311-314
working 315
RPN 50

S

script artifacts
creating 80, 81
security
authentication 305
authorization 305
data 305
security requirements
authentication 133
authorization 133
data 133
defining 132, 134
working 134
semantic data model
about 100
defining, Oracle SQL Developer Data Model
used 103-106
developing 100-102
hierarchies, adding 124-126
metrics, adding 128, 129
working 103, 127, 128
server 65
shared captions
about 302
multi-language, enabling 302, 303
working 303
significant columns data profiling scripts
about 169
building 169
working 170
source matrix
about 153
creating 154
working 154
source system
data, abstracting 238, 239
working 239
Standard columns
adding, examples 225
adding, to data models 224, 225

standard work breakdown structure
about 36
building 36, 37
working 38
Subversion
about 190
data model changes, synchronizing 200-206
data models, checking 199, 200
data models, importing to 194-198
Oracle SQL Data Modeler, connecting to
190-194
Subversion tips
Add 69
Check out 69
Commit 69
Update 69
SVNConsole-Log window 200
SVNRepositories directory 234

T

table abstraction
aliases, using 283
working 284
task drivers. *See* **effort drivers**
Testing 30
testing phase 30
testing work package
about 30
creating 30, 31
integration testing 32
performance testing 32
unit testing 32
working 31
test process
about 58
creating 59
working 59
Test Read Access 193
Third Normal Form
about 145
selecting 145, 146
working 146
Tools |Domains Administration 216
Tools | Export Captions 302

U

UniqueKey tab 185
update trigger 267, 268
Upload interface
  about 274
  creating 274-279
  working 280

V

Versioning Navigator 198
virtualize property 323
Virtual Private application context
  creating 317-319
  working 319

Virtual Private Database. *See* **VPD**
visualisation standards
  developing 282, 283
  key reference material 282
  working 283
VPD
  about 311
  column-level VPD, creating 315
  enabling, in OBIEE 336-342
  row-level VPD, creating 311

W

white box testing 32
Wiki 84
Work Packages 24

**Thank you for buying
Business Intelligence Cookbook: A Project Lifecycle
Approach Using Oracle Technology**

About Packt Publishing

Packt, pronounced 'packed', published its first book "*Mastering phpMyAdmin for Effective MySQL Management*" in April 2004 and subsequently continued to specialize in publishing highly focused books on specific technologies and solutions.

Our books and publications share the experiences of your fellow IT professionals in adapting and customizing today's systems, applications, and frameworks. Our solution-based books give you the knowledge and power to customize the software and technologies you're using to get the job done. Packt books are more specific and less general than the IT books you have seen in the past. Our unique business model allows us to bring you more focused information, giving you more of what you need to know, and less of what you don't.

Packt is a modern, yet unique publishing company, which focuses on producing quality, cutting-edge books for communities of developers, administrators, and newbies alike. For more information, please visit our website: www.PacktPub.com.

About Packt Enterprise

In 2010, Packt launched two new brands, Packt Enterprise and Packt Open Source, in order to continue its focus on specialization. This book is part of the Packt Enterprise brand, home to books published on enterprise software – software created by major vendors, including (but not limited to) IBM, Microsoft and Oracle, often for use in other corporations. Its titles will offer information relevant to a range of users of this software, including administrators, developers, architects, and end users.

Writing for Packt

We welcome all inquiries from people who are interested in authoring. Book proposals should be sent to author@packtpub.com. If your book idea is still at an early stage and you would like to discuss it first before writing a formal book proposal, contact us; one of our commissioning editors will get in touch with you.

We're not just looking for published authors; if you have strong technical skills but no writing experience, our experienced editors can help you develop a writing career, or simply get some additional reward for your expertise.

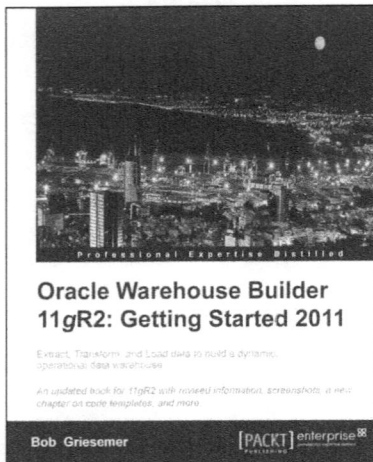

Oracle Warehouse Builder 11*g* R2: Getting Started 2011

ISBN: 978-1-84968-344-9   Paperback: 424 pages

Extract Transform, and Load data to build a dynamic operational data warehouse

1. Build a working data warehouse from scratch with Oracle Warehouse Builder

2. Cover techniques in Extracting, Transforming, and Loading data into your data warehouse

3. Use a multi-dimensional design with an underlying relational star schema

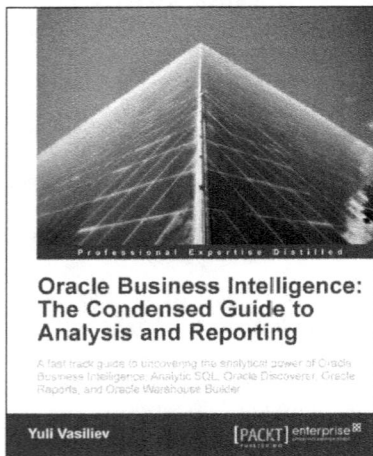

Oracle Warehouse Builder 11*g*R2: Getting Started 2011

Extract, Transform, and Load data to build a dynamic operational data warehouse

An updated book for 11gR2 with revised information, screenshots, a new chapter on code templates, and more.

Bob Griesemer   [PACKT] enterprise ⚙

Oracle Business Intelligence: The Condensed Guide to Analysis and Reporting

ISBN: 978-1-84968-118-6   Paperback: 184 pages

A fast track guide to uncovering the analytical power of Oracle Business Intelligence: Analytic SQL, Oracle Discover, Oracle Reports, and Oracle Warehouse Builder

1. Install, configure, and deploy the components included in Oracle Business Intelligence Suite (SE)

2. Gain a comprehensive overview of components and features of the Oracle Business Intelligence package

3. A fast paced, practical book that provides you with quick steps to answer common business questions and help you make informed business decisions

Oracle Business Intelligence: The Condensed Guide to Analysis and Reporting

A fast track guide to uncovering the analytical power of Oracle Business Intelligence: Analytic SQL, Oracle Discoverer, Oracle Reports, and Oracle Warehouse Builder

Yuli Vasiliev   [PACKT] enterprise ⚙

Please check **www.PacktPub.com** for information on our titles

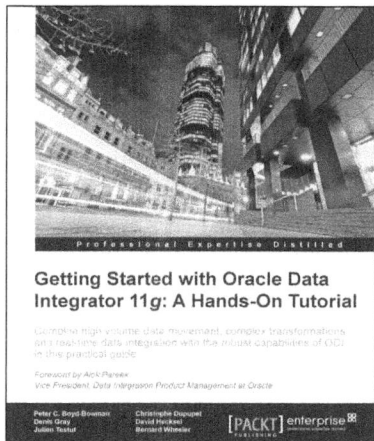

Getting Started with Oracle Data Integrator 11*g*: A Hands-On Tutorial

ISBN: 978-1-84968-068-4   Paperback: 384 pages

Combine high volume data movement, complex transformations and real-time data integration with the robust capabilities of ODI in this practical guide

1. Discover the comprehensive and sophisticated orchestration of data integration tasks made possible with ODI, including monitoring and error-management

2. Get to grips with the product architecture and building data integration processes with technologies including Oracle, Microsoft SQL Server and XML files

3. A comprehensive tutorial packed with tips, images and best practices

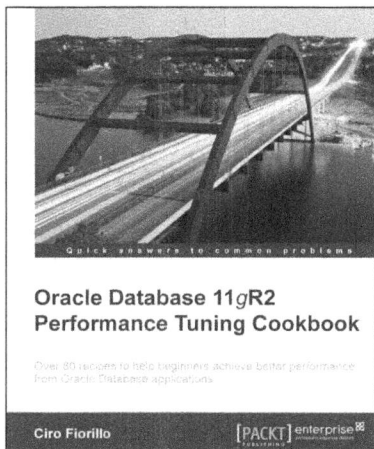

Oracle Database 11*g*R2 Performance Tuning Cookbook

ISBN: 978-1-84968-260-2   Paperback: 542 pages

Over 80 recipes to help beginners achieve better performance from Oracle Database applications

1. Learn the right techniques to achieve best performance from the Oracle Database

2. Avoid common myths and pitfalls that slow down the database

3. Diagnose problems when they arise and employ tricks to prevent them

Please check **www.PacktPub.com** for information on our titles

www.ingramcontent.com/pod-product-compliance
Lightning Source LLC
Chambersburg PA
CBHW080716220326
41598CB00033B/5438